To Save Everything, Click Here

To Save Everything, Click Here

Technology, Solutionism and the Urge to Fix Problems That Don't Exist

Evgeny Morozov

ALLEN LANE
an imprint of
PENGUIN BOOKS

ALLEN LANE

Published by the Penguin Group

Penguin Books Ltd, 80 Strand, London WC2R 0RL, England

Penguin Group (USA) Inc., 375 Hudson Street, New York, New York 10014, USA

Penguin Group (Canada), 90 Eglinton Avenue East, Suite 700, Toronto, Ontario,
Canada M4P 2Y3 (a division of Pearson Penguin Canada Inc.)

Penguin Ireland, 25 St Stephen's Green, Dublin 2, Ireland
(a division of Penguin Books Ltd)

Penguin Group (Australia), 707 Collins Street, Melbourne,
Victoria 3008, Australia (a division of Pearson Australia Group Pty Ltd)

Penguin Books India Pvt Ltd, 11 Community Centre,
Panchsheel Park, New Delhi – 110 017, India

Penguin Group (NZ), 67 Apollo Drive, Rosedale, Auckland 0632, New Zealand
(a division of Pearson New Zealand Ltd)

Penguin Books (South Africa) (Pty) Ltd, Block D, Rosebank Office Park, 181 Jan Smuts Avenue, Parktown North,
Gauteng 2193, South Africa

Penguin Books Ltd, Registered Offices: 80 Strand, London WC2R 0RL, England

www.penguin.com

First published in the United States of America by PublicAffairs™,
a Member of the Perseus Books Group 2013
First published in Great Britain by Allen Lane 2013

001

Copyright © Evgeny Morozov, 2013

The moral right of the author has been asserted

Printed in Great Britain by Clays Ltd, St Ives plc

A CIP catalogue record for this book is available from the British Library

Hardback ISBN: 978-1-846-14548-3
Trade Paperback ISBN: 978-1-846-14549-0

www.greenpenguin.co.uk

Penguin Books is committed to a sustainable
future for our business, our readers and our planet.
This book is made from Forest Stewardship
Council™ certified paper.

ALWAYS LEARNING   PEARSON

To my parents

Contents

Introduction

> *"In an age of advanced technology,*
> *inefficiency is the sin against the Holy Ghost."*
> —ALDOUS HUXLEY

> *"Complexity is a solvable problem in the right hands."*
> —JEFF JARVIS

Silicon Valley is guilty of many sins, but lack of ambition is not one of them. If you listen to its loudest apostles, Silicon Valley is all about solving problems that someone else—perhaps the greedy bankers on Wall Street or the lazy know-nothings in Washington— have created.

"Technology is not really about hardware and software any more. It's really about the mining and use of this enormous data to make the world a better place," Eric Schmidt, Google's executive chairman, told an audience of MIT students in 2011. Facebook's Mark Zuckerberg, who argues that his company's mission is to "make the world more open and connected," concurs. "We don't wake up in the morning with the primary goal of making money," he proclaimed just a few months before his company's rapidly plummeting stock convinced all but its most die-hard fans that Facebook and making money had parted ways long ago. What, then, gets Mr. Zuckerberg out of bed? As he told the audience of the South by Southwest festival in 2008, it's the desire to solve global problems. "There are a lot of really big issues for the world to get solved and, as a company, what we are trying to do is to build an infrastructure on top of which to solve some of these problems," announced Zuckerberg.

In the last few years, Silicon Valley's favorite slogan has quietly changed from "Innovate or Die!" to "Ameliorate or Die!" In the grand scheme of things, what exactly is being improved is not very important; being able to change things, to get humans to behave in more responsible and sustainable ways, to maximize efficiency, is all that matters. Half-baked ideas that might seem too big even for the naïfs at TED Conferences—that Woodstock of the intellectual effete—sit rather comfortably on Silicon Valley's business plans. "Fitter, happier, more productive"—the refreshingly depressive motto of the popular Radiohead song from the mid-1990s—would make for an apt welcome sign in the corporate headquarters of its many digital mavens. Technology can make us better—and technology will make us better. Or, as the geeks would say, given enough apps, all of humanity's bugs are shallow.

California, of course, has never suffered from a deficit of optimism or bluster. And yet, the possibilities opened up by latest innovations make even the most pragmatic and down-to-earth venture capitalists reach for their wallets. After all, when else will they get a chance to get rich by saving the world? What else would give them the thrill of working in a humanitarian agency (minus all the bureaucracy and hectic travel, plus a much better compensation package)?

How will this amelioration orgy end? Will it actually accomplish anything? One way to find out is to push some of these nascent improvement efforts to their ultimate conclusions. If Silicon Valley had a designated futurist, her bright vision of the near future— say, around 2020 or so—would itself be easy to predict. It would go something like this: Humanity, equipped with powerful self-tracking devices, finally conquers obesity, insomnia, and global warming as everyone eats less, sleeps better, and emits more appropriately. The fallibility of human memory is conquered too, as the very same tracking devices record and store everything we do. Car keys, faces, factoids: we will never forget them again. No need to feel nostalgic, Proust-style, about the *petite madeleines* you devoured as a child; since that moment is surely stored somewhere in your smartphone—or, more likely, your smart, all-recording glasses—you can stop fantasizing and simply rewind to it directly. In any event, you can count on Siri, Apple's trusted voice assistant, to tell you the truth you never wanted to face back then: all those *madeleines* dramatically raise your blood glucose levels and ought to be avoided. Sorry, Marcel!

Politics, finally under the constant and far-reaching gaze of the electorate, is freed from all the sleazy corruption, backroom deals, and inefficient horse trading. Parties are disaggregated and replaced by Groupon-like political campaigns, where users come together—once—to weigh in on issues of direct and immediate relevance to their lives, only to disband shortly afterward. Now that every word—nay, sound—ever uttered by politicians is recorded and stored for posterity, hypocrisy has become obsolete as well. Lobbyists of all stripes have gone extinct as the wealth of data about politicians—their schedules, lunch menus, travel expenses— are posted online for everyone to review.

As digital media make participation easier, more and more citizens ditch bowling alone—only to take up blogging together. Even those who've never bothered to vote in the past are finally provided with the right incentives—naturally, as a part of an online game where they collect points for saving humanity—and so they rush to use their smartphones to "check in" at the voting booth. Thankfully, getting there is no longer a chore; self-driving cars have been invented for the purpose of getting people from place to place. Streets are clean and shiny; keeping them that way is also part of an elaborate online game. Appeals to civic duty and responsibility to fellow citizens have all but disappeared—and why wouldn't they, when getting people to do things by leveraging their eagerness to earn points, badges, and virtual currencies is so much more effective?

Crime is a distant memory, while courts are overstaffed and underworked. Both physical and virtual environments—walls, pavements, doors, log-in screens—have become "smart." That is, they have integrated the plethora of data generated by the self-tracking devices and social-networking services so that now they can predict and prevent criminal behavior simply by analyzing their users. And as users don't even have the chance to commit crimes, prisons are no longer needed either. A triumph of humanism, courtesy of Silicon Valley.

And then, there's the flourishing new "marketplace" of "ideas."
Finally, the term "marketplace" no longer feels like a misnomer;
cultural institutions have never been more efficient or responsive
to the laws of supply and demand. Newspapers no longer publish
articles that their readers are not interested in; the proliferation of
self-tracking combined with social-networking data guarantees that
everyone gets to read a highly customized newspaper (down to the
word level!) that yields the highest possible click rate. No story goes
unclicked, no headline untweeted; customized, individual articles
are generated in the few seconds that pass between the click of a
link and the loading of the page in one's browser.

The number of published books has skyrocketed—most of
them are self-published—and they are perfectly efficient as well.
Many even guarantee alternative endings—and in real time!—
based on what the eye-tracking activity of readers suggests about
their mood. Hollywood is alive and kicking; now that everyone
wears smart glasses, a movie can have an infinite number of alternative endings, depending on viewers' mood at a given moment as
they watch. Professional critics are gone, having been replaced first
by "crowds," then by algorithms, and finally by customized algorithmic reviews—the only way to match films with customized alternative endings. The edgiest cultural publications even employ
algorithms to write criticism of songs composed by other algorithms. But not all has changed: just like today, the system still
needs imperfect humans to generate the clicks to suck the cash
from advertisers.

This brief sketch is not an excerpt from the latest Gary Shteyn-
gart novel. Nor is it dystopian science fiction. In fact, there is a
good chance that at this very moment, someone in Silicon Valley
is making a pitch to investors about one of the technologies described above. Some may already have been built. A dystopia it isn't;
many extremely bright people—in Silicon Valley and beyond—
find this frictionless future enticing and inevitable, as their memos
and business plans would attest.

I, for one, find much of this future terrifying, but probably not
for the reasons you would expect. All too often, digital heretics like
me get bogged down in finding faults with the feasibility of the
original utopian schemes. Is perfect efficiency in publishing actually

attainable? Can all environments be smart? Will people show up to vote just because they are playing a game? Such skeptical questions over the efficacy of said schemes are important, and I do entertain many of them in this book. But I also think that we, the heretics, also need to take Silicon Valley innovators at their word and have just a bit more faith in their ingenuity and inventiveness. These, after all, are the same people who are planning to scan all the world's books and mine asteroids. Ten years ago, both ideas would have seemed completely crazy; today, only one of them does.

So perhaps we should seriously entertain the possibility that Silicon Valley will have the means to accomplish some of its craziest plans. Perhaps it won't overthrow the North Korean regime with tweets, but it could still accomplish a lot. This is where the debate ought to shift to a different register: instead of ridiculing the efficacy of their means, we also need to question the adequacy of the innovators' ends. My previous book, *The Net Delusion*, shows the surprising resilience of authoritarian regimes, which have discovered their own ways to profit from digital technologies. While I was—and remain—critical of many Western efforts to promote "Internet freedom" in those regimes, most of my criticisms have to do with the means, not the ends, of the "Internet freedom agenda," presuming that the ends entail a better climate for freedom of expression and more respect for human rights. In this book, I have no such luxury, and I question both the means and the ends of Silicon Valley's latest quest to "solve problems." I contend here that Silicon Valley's promise of eternal amelioration has blunted our ability to do this questioning. Who today is mad enough to challenge the virtues of eliminating hypocrisy from politics? Or of providing more information—the direct result of self-tracking—to facilitate decision making? Or of finding new incentives to get people interested in saving humanity, fighting climate change, or participating in politics? Or of decreasing crime? To question the appropriateness of such interventions, it seems, is to question the Enlightenment itself.

And yet I feel that such questioning is necessary. Hence the premise of this book: Silicon Valley's quest to fit us all into a digital straightjacket by promoting efficiency, transparency, certitude, and perfection—and, by extension, eliminating their evil twins of friction, opacity, ambiguity, and imperfection—will prove to be prohibitively expensive in the long run. For various ideological reasons to be explained later in these pages, this high cost remains hidden from public view and will remain so as long as we, in our mindless pursuit of this silicon Eden, fail to radically question our infatuation with a set of technologies that are often lumped together under the deceptive label of "the Internet." This book, then, attempts to factor in the true costs of this highly awaited paradise and to explain why they have been so hard to account for.

Imperfection, ambiguity, opacity, disorder, and the opportunity to err, to sin, to do the wrong thing: all of these are constitutive of human freedom, and any concentrated attempt to root them out will root out that freedom as well. If we don't find the strength and the courage to escape the silicon mentality that fuels much of the current quest for technological perfection, we risk finding ourselves with a politics devoid of everything that makes politics desirable, with humans who have lost their basic capacity for moral reasoning, with lackluster (if not moribund) cultural institutions that don't take risks and only care about their financial bottom lines, and, most terrifyingly, with a perfectly controlled social environment that would make dissent not just impossible but possibly even unthinkable.

The structure of this book is as follows. The next two chapters provide an outline and a critique of two dominant ideologies—what I call "solutionism" and "Internet-centrism"—that have sanctioned Silicon Valley's great ameliorative experiment. In the seven ensuing chapters, I trace how both ideologies interact in the context of a particular practice or reform effort: promoting transparency, reforming the political system, improving efficiency in the cultural sector, reducing crime through smart environments and data, quantifying the world around us with the help of self-tracking and life-logging, and, finally, introducing game incentives—what's known as gamification—into the civic realm. The last chapter offers a more forward-looking perspective on how we can transcend the limitations of both solutionism and Internet-centrism and design and employ technology to satisfy human and civic needs.

Now, why oppose such striving for perfection? Well, I believe that not everything that could be fixed should be fixed—even if the latest technologies make the fixes easier, cheaper, and harder to resist. Sometimes, imperfect is good enough; sometimes, it's much better than perfect. What worries me most is that, nowadays, the very availability of cheap and diverse digital fixes tells us what needs fixing. It's quite simple: the more fixes we have, the more problems we see. And yet, in our political, personal, and public lives—much like in our computer systems—not all bugs are bugs; some bugs are features. Ignorance can be dangerous, but so can omniscience: there is a reason why some colleges stick to need-blind admissions processes. Ambivalence can be counterproductive, but so can certitude: if all your friends really told you what they thought, you might never talk to them again. Efficiency can be useful, but so can inefficiency: if everything were efficient, why would anyone bother to innovate?

The ultimate goal of this book, then, is to uncover the attitudes, dispositions, and urges that comprise the solutionist mind-set, to show how they manifest themselves in specific projects to ameliorate the human condition, and to hint at how and why some of these attitudes, dispositions, and urges can and should be resisted, circumvented, and unlearned. For only by unlearning solutionism—that is, by transcending the limits it imposes on our imaginations and by rebelling against its value system—will we understand why attaining technological perfection, without attending to the intricacies of the human condition and accounting for the complex world of practices and traditions, might not be worth the price.

CHAPTER ONE

Solutionism and Its Discontents

"In the future, people will spend less time trying to get technology to work . . . because it will just be seamless. It will just be there. The Web will be everything, and it will also be nothing. It will be like electricity. . . . If we get this right, I believe we can fix all the world's problems."
—ERIC SCHMIDT

"'Solutionism' [interprets] issues as puzzles to which there is a solution, rather than problems to which there may be a response."
—GILLES PAQUET

"The overriding question, 'What might we build tomorrow?' blinds us to questions of our ongoing responsibilities for what we built yesterday."
—PAUL DOURISH AND SCOTT D. MAINWARING

Have you ever peeked inside a friend's trash can? I have. And even though I've never found anything worth reporting—not to the KGB anyway—I've always felt guilty about my insatiable curiosity. Trash, like one's sex life or temporary eating disorder, is a private affair par excellence; the less said about it, the better. While Mark Zuckerberg insists that all

1

activities get better when performed socially, it seems that throwing away the garbage would forever remain an exception—one unassailable bastion of individuality to resist Zuckerberg's tyranny of the social.

Well, this exception is no more: BinCam, a new project from researchers in Britain and Germany, seeks to modernize how we deal with trash by making our bins smarter and—you guessed it—more social. Here is how it works: The bin's inside lid is equipped with a tiny smartphone that snaps a photo every time someone closes it—all of this, of course, in order to document what exactly you have just thrown away. A team of badly paid humans, recruited through Amazon's Mechanical Turk system, then evaluates each photo. What is the total number of items in the picture? How many of them are recyclable? How many are food items? After this data is attached to the photo, it's uploaded to the bin owner's Facebook account, where it can also be shared with other users. Once such smart bins are installed in multiple households, BinCam creators hope, Facebook can be used to turn recycling into a game-like exciting competition. A weekly score is calculated for each bin, and as the amounts of food waste and recyclable materials in the bins decrease, households earn gold bars and leaves. Whoever wins the most bars and tree leaves, wins. Mission accomplished; planet saved!

Nowhere in the academic paper that accompanies the BinCam presentation do the researchers raise any doubts about the ethics of their undoubtedly well-meaning project. Should we get one set of citizens to do the right thing by getting another set of citizens to spy on them? Should we introduce game incentives into a process that has previously worked through appeals to one's duties and obligations? Could the "goodness" of one's environmental behavior be accurately quantified with tree leaves and gold bars? Should it be quantified in isolation from other everyday activities? Is it okay not to recycle if one doesn't drive? Will greater public surveillance of one's trash bins lead to an increase in eco-vigilantism? Will participants stop doing the right thing if their Facebook friends are no longer watching?

Questions, questions. The trash bin might seem like the most mundane of artifacts, and yet it's infused with philosophical puzzles and dilemmas. It's embedded in a world of complex human practices, where even tiny adjustments to seemingly inconsequential acts might lead to profound changes in our behavior. It very well may be that, by optimizing our behavior *locally* (i.e., getting people to recycle with the help of games and increased peer surveillance), we'll end up with suboptimal behavior *globally*, that is, once the right incentives are missing in one simple environment, we might no longer want to perform our civic duties elsewhere. One local problem might be solved—but only by triggering several global problems that we can't recognize at the moment.

A project like BinCam would have been all but impossible fifteen years ago. First, trash bins had no sensors that could take photos and upload them to sites like Facebook; now, tiny smartphones can do all of this on the cheap. Amazon didn't have an army of bored freelancers who could do virtually any job as long as they received their few pennies per hour. (And even those human freelancers might become unnecessary once automated image-recognition software gets better.) Most importantly, there was no way for all our friends to see the contents of our trash bins; fifteen years ago, even our personal websites wouldn't get the same level of attention from our acquaintances—our entire "social graph," as the geeks would put it—that our trash bins might receive from our Facebook friends today. Now that we are all using the same platform—Facebook—it becomes possible to steer our behavior with the help of social games and competitions; we no longer have to save the environment at our own pace using our own unique tools. There is power in standardization!

These two innovations—that more and more of our life is now mediated through smart sensor-powered technologies and that our friends and acquaintances can now follow us anywhere, making it possible to create new types of incentives—will profoundly change the work of social engineers, policymakers, and many other do-gooders. All will be tempted to exploit the power of these new techniques, either individually or in combination, to solve a particular problem, be it obesity, climate change, or congestion. Today we already have smart mirrors that, thanks to complex sensors, can track and display our pulse rates based on slight variations in the brightness of our faces; soon, we'll have mirrors that, thanks to their ability to tap into our "social graph," will nudge us to lose weight because we look pudgier than most of our Facebook friends.

Or consider a prototype teapot built by British designer-cum-activist Chris Adams. The teapot comes with a small orb that can either glow green (making tea is okay) or red (perhaps you should wait). What determines the coloring? Well, the orb, with the help of some easily available open-source hardware and software, is connected to a site called Can I Turn It On? (http://www.caniturnit on.com), which, every minute or so, queries Britain's national grid for aggregate power-usage statistics. If the frequency figure returned by the site is higher than the baseline of 50 hertz, the orb glows green; if lower, red. The goal here is to provide additional information for responsible teapot use. But it's easy to imagine how such logic can be extended much, much further, BinCam style. Why, for example, not reward people with virtual, Facebook-compatible points for not using the teapot in the times of high electricity usage? Or why not punish those who disregard the teapot's warnings about high usage by publicizing their irresponsibility among their Facebook friends? Social engineers have never had so many options at their disposal.

Sensors alone, without any connection to social networks or data repositories, can do quite a lot these days. The elderly, for example, might appreciate smart carpets and smart bells that can detect when someone has fallen over and inform others. Even trash bins can be smart in a very different way. Thus, a start-up with the charming name of BigBelly Solar hopes to revolutionize trash collecting by making solar-powered bins that, thanks to built-in sensors, can inform waste managers of their current capacity and predict when they would need to be emptied. This, in turn, can optimize trash-collection routes and save fuel. The city of Philadelphia has been experimenting with such bins since 2009; as a result, it cut its center garbage-collecting sorties from 17 to 2.5 times a week and reduced the number of staff from thirty-three to just seventeen, bringing in $900,000 in savings in just one year.

Likewise, city officials in Boston have been testing Street Bump, an elaborate app that relies on accelerometers, the now ubiquitous motion detectors found in many smartphones, to map out potholes on Boston's roads. The driver only has to turn the app on and start driving; the smartphone will do the rest and communicate with the central server as necessary. Thanks to a series of algorithms, the app knows how to recognize and disregard manhole covers and speed bumps, while diligently recording the potholes. Once at least three drivers have reported bumps in the same spot, the bump is recognized as a pothole. Likewise, Google relies on GPS-enabled Android phones to generate live information about traffic conditions: once you start using its map and disclose your location, Google knows where you are and how fast you are moving. Thus, it can make a good guess as to how bad the road situation is, feeding this information back into Google Maps for everyone to see. These days, it seems, just carrying your phone around might be an act of good citizenship.

The Will to Improve (Just About Everything!)

That smart technology and all of our social connections (not to mention useful statistics like the real-time aggregate consumption of electricity) can now be "inserted" into our every mundane act, from throwing away our trash to making tea, might seem worth celebrating, not scrutinizing. Likewise, that smartphones and social-networking sites allow us to experiment with interventions impossible just a decade ago seems like a genuinely positive development. Not surprisingly, Silicon Valley is already awash with plans for improving just about everything under the sun: politics, citizens, publishing, cooking.

Alas, all too often, this never-ending quest to ameliorate—or what the Canadian anthropologist Tania Murray Li, writing in a very different context, has called "the will to improve"—is short-sighted and only perfunctorily interested in the activity for which improvement is sought. Recasting all complex social situations either as neatly defined problems with definite, computable solutions or as transparent and self-evident processes that can be easily optimized—if only the right algorithms are in place!—this quest is likely to have unexpected consequences that could eventually cause more damage than the problems they seek to address.

I call the ideology that legitimizes and sanctions such aspirations "solutionism." I borrow this unabashedly pejorative term from the world of architecture and urban planning, where it has come to refer to an unhealthy preoccupation with sexy, monumental, and narrow-minded solutions—the kind of stuff that wows audiences at TED Conferences—to problems that are extremely complex, fluid, and contentious. These are the kinds of problems that, on careful examination, do not have to be defined in the singular and all-encompassing ways that "solutionists" have defined them; what's contentious, then, is not their proposed solution but their very definition of the problem itself. Design theorist Michael Dobbins has it right: solutionism presumes rather than investigates the problems that it is trying to solve, reaching "for the answer before the questions have been fully asked." How problems are composed matters every bit as much as how problems are resolved.

Solutionism, thus, is not just a fancy way of saying that for someone with a hammer, everything looks like a nail; it's not just another riff on the inapplicability of "technological fixes" to "wicked problems" (a subject I address at length in *The Net Delusion*). It's not only that many problems are not suited to the quick-and-easy solutionist tool kit. It's also that what many solutionists presume to be "problems" in need of solving are not problems at all; a deeper investigation into the very nature of these "problems" would reveal that the inefficiency, ambiguity, and opacity—whether in politics or everyday life—that the newly empowered geeks and solutionists are rallying against are not in any sense problematic. Quite the opposite: these vices are often virtues in disguise. That, thanks to innovative technologies, the modern-day solutionist has an easy way to eliminate them does not make them any less virtuous.

It may seem that a critique of solutionism would, by its very antireformist bias, be the prerogative of the conservative. In fact, many of the antisolutionist jibes throughout this book fit into the tripartite taxonomy of reactionary responses to social change so skillfully outlined by the social theorist Albert Hirschman. In his influential book *The Rhetoric of Reaction*, Hirschman argued that all progressive reforms usually attract conservative criticisms that build on one of the following three themes: perversity (whereby the proposed intervention only worsens the problem at hand), futility (whereby the intervention yields no results whatsoever), and jeopardy (where the intervention threatens to undermine some previous, hard-earned accomplishment).

Although I resort to all three of these critiques in the pages that follow, my overall project does differ from the conservative resistance studied by Hirschman. I do not advocate inaction or deny that many (though not all) of the problems tackled by solutionists—from climate change to obesity to declining levels of trust in the political system—are important and demand immediate action (how exactly those problems are composed is, of course, a different matter; there is more than one way to describe each). But the urgency of the problems in question does not automatically confer legitimacy upon a panoply of new, clean, and efficient technological solutions so in vogue these days. My preferred solutions—or, rather, responses—are of a very different kind.

It's also not a coincidence that my critique of solutionism bears some resemblance to several critiques of the numerous earlier efforts to put humanity into too tight a straitjacket. Today's straitjacket might be of the digital variety, but it's hardly the first or the tightest. While the word "solutionism" may not have been used, many important thinkers have addressed its shortcomings, even if using different terms and contexts. I'm thinking, in particular, of Ivan Illich's protestations against the highly efficient but dehumanizing systems of professional schooling and medicine, Jane Jacobs's attacks on the arrogance of urban planners, Michael Oakeshott's rebellion against rationalists in all walks of human existence, Hans Jonas's impatience with the cold comfort of cybernetics; and, more recently, James Scott's concern with how states have forced what he calls "legibility" on their subjects. Some might add Friedrich Hayek's opposition to central planners, with their inherent knowledge deficiency, to this list.

These thinkers have been anything but homogenous in their political beliefs; Ivan Illich, Friedrich Hayek, Jane Jacobs, and Michael Oakeshott would make a rather rowdy dinner party. But these highly original thinkers, regardless of political persuasion, have shown that their own least favorite brand of solutionist—be it Jacobs's urban planners or Illich's professional educators—have a very poor grasp not just of human nature but also of the complex practices that this nature begets and thrives on. It's as if the solutionists have never lived a life of their own but learned everything they know from books—and those books weren't novels but manuals for refrigerators, vacuum cleaners, and washing machines.

Thomas Molnar, a conservative philosopher who, for his smart and vehement critique of technological utopianism written in the early 1960s, also deserves a place on the antisolutionist pantheon, put it really well when he complained that "when the utopian writers deal with work, health, leisure, life expectancy, war, crimes, culture, administration, finance, judges and so on, it is as if their words were uttered by an automaton with no conception of real life. The reader has the uncomfortable feeling of walking in a dreamland of abstractions, surrounded by lifeless objects; he manages to identify them in a vague way, but, on closer inspection, he sees that they do not really conform to anything familiar in shape, color, volume, or sound." Dreamlands of abstractions are a dime a dozen these days; what works in Palo Alto is assumed to work in Penang.

It's not that solutions proposed are unlikely to work but that, in solving the "problem," solutionists twist it in such an ugly and unfamiliar way that, by the time it is "solved," the problem becomes something else entirely. Everyone is quick to celebrate victory, only no one remembers what the original solution sought to achieve.

The ballyhoo over the potential of new technologies to disrupt education—especially now that several start-ups offer online courses to hundreds of thousands of students, who grade each other's work and get no face time with instructors—is a case in point. Digital technologies might be a perfect solution to some problems, but those problems don't include education—not if by education we mean the development of the skills to think critically about any given issue. Online resources might help students learn plenty of new facts (or "facts," in case they don't cross-check what they learn on Wikipedia), but such fact cramming is a far cry from what universities aspire to teach their students.

As Pamela Hieronymi, a professor of philosophy at the University of California, Los Angeles (UCLA), points out in an important essay on the myths of online learning, "Education is not the transmission of information or ideas. Education is the training needed to make use of information and ideas. As information breaks loose from bookstores and libraries and floods onto computers and mobile devices, that training becomes more important, not less." Of course, there are plenty of tools for increasing one's digital literacy, but those tools go only so far; they might help you to detect erroneous information, but they won't organize your thoughts into a coherent argument.

Adam Falk, president of Williams College, delivers an even more powerful blow against solutionism in higher education when he argues that it would be erroneous to pretend that the solutions it peddles are somehow compatible with the spirit and goals of the university. Falk notes that, based on the research done at Williams, the best predictor of students' intellectual success in college is not their major or GPA but the amount of personal, face-to-face contact they have with professors. According to Falk, averaging letter grades assigned by five random peers—as at least one much-lauded start-up in this space, Coursera, does—is not the "educational equivalent of a highly trained professor providing thoughtful evaluation and detailed response." To pretend that this is the case, insists Falk, "is to deny the most significant purposes of education, and to forfeit its true value."

Here we have a rather explicit mismatch between the idea of education embedded in the proposed set of technological solutions and the time-honored idea of education still cherished at least by some colleges. In an ideal world, of course, both visions can coexist and prosper simultaneously. However, in the world we inhabit, where the administrators are as cost-conscious as ever, the approach that produces the most graduates per dollar spent is far more likely to prevail, the poverty of its intellectual vision notwithstanding. Herein lies one hidden danger of solutionism: the quick fixes it peddles do not exist in a political vacuum. In promising almost immediate and much cheaper results, they can easily undermine support for more ambitious, more intellectually stimulating, but also more demanding reform projects.

Kooks and Cooks

Once we leave the classroom and enter the kitchen, the limitations of solutionism are delineated in even sharper colors. Political philosopher Michael Oakeshott, conservative that he was, particularly

9

liked emphasizing that cooking, like science or politics, is a very complex set of (mostly invisible) practices and traditions that guide us in preparing our meals. "It might be supposed that an ignorant man, some edible materials, and a cookery book compose together the necessities of a self-moved (or concrete) activity called cooking. But nothing is further from the truth," he wrote in his 1951 essay "Political Education." Rather, for Oakeshott the cookery book is "nothing more than an abstract of somebody's knowledge of how to cook; it is the stepchild, not the parent of the activity." "A cook," he wrote in another essay, "is not a man who first has a vision of a pie and then tries to make it; he is a man skilled in cookery, and both his projects and his achievements spring from that skill."

Oakeshott didn't much fear that our cooking habits would be destroyed by the proliferation of culinary literature; interpreting that literature was only possible within a rich tradition of cooking, so perusing such books might even strengthen one's appreciation of the culinary culture. Or, as he himself put it, "the book speaks only to those who know already the kind of thing to expect from it and consequently how to interpret it." He was not against using the book; rather, he took issue with people who thought that the book—rather than the tradition that produced it—was the main actor here. Whatever rules, recipes, and algorithms the book contained, all of them made sense only when interpreted and applied within the cooking tradition.

For Oakeshott, the cookbook was the end (or an output), not the start (or an input), of that tradition. An argument against rationalists who refused to acknowledge the importance of practices and traditions, rather than a celebration of cookery books, it's a surprisingly upbeat moment in Oakeshott's thought. However, one can only wonder if Oakeshott would need to revise his judgment today, now that cooking books have been replaced with the kinds of sophisticated gadgetry that would have Buckminster Fuller, the archsolutionist who never stopped fantasizing about the perfect kitchen, brimming with envy.

Paradoxically, as technologies get smarter, the maneuvering space for interpretation—what Oakeshott thought would bring cooks in touch with the world of practices and traditions—begins to shrink and potentially disappear entirely. New, smarter technologies make it possible to finally position, as it were, the cookery book's instructions outside the tradition; almost no knowledge is required to cook with their help. Today's technologies are no longer dumb, passive appliances. Some of them feature tiny, sophisticated sensors that "understand"—if that's the right word—what's going on in our kitchens and attempt to steer us, their masters, in the right direction. Here is modernity in a nutshell: We are left with possibly better food but without the joy of cooking.

British magazine *New Scientist* recently covered a few such solutionist projects. Meet Jinna Lei, a computer scientist at the University of Washington who has built a system in which a cook is monitored by several video cameras installed in the kitchen. These cameras are clever: they can recognize the depth and shape of objects in their view and distinguish between, say, apples and bowls. Thanks to this benign surveillance, chefs can be informed whenever they have deviated from their chosen recipe. Each object has a number of activities associated with it—you don't normally boil spoons or fry arugula—and the system tracks how well the current activity matches the object in use. "For example, if the system detects sugar pouring into a bowl containing eggs, and the recipe does not call for sugar, it could log the aberration," Lei told *New Scientist*.

To improve the accuracy of tracking, Lei is also considering adding a special thermal camera that would identify the user's hands by body heat. The quest here is to turn the modern kitchen into a temple of modern-day Taylorism, with every task tracked, analyzed, and optimized. Solutionists hate making errors and love sticking to algorithms. That cooking thrives on failure and experimentation, that deviating from recipes is what creates culinary innovations and pushes a cuisine forward, is discarded as whimsical and irrelevant. For many such well-meaning innovators, the context of the practice they seek to improve doesn't matter—not as long as efficiency can be increased. As a result, chefs are imagined not as autonomous virtuosi or gifted craftsmen but as enslaved robots who should never defy the commands of their operating systems.

Another project mentioned in *New Scientist* is even more degrading. A group of computer scientists at Kyoto Sangyo University in Japan is trying to marry the logic of the kitchen to the logic of "augmented reality"—the fancy term for infusing our everyday environment with smart technologies. (Think of Quick Response Codes that can be scanned with a smartphone to unlock additional information or of the upcoming goggles from Google's Project Glass, which use data streams to enhance your visual field.) To this end, the Japanese researchers have mounted cameras and projectors on the kitchen's ceiling so that they can project instructions—in the form of arrows, geometric shapes, and speech bubbles guiding the cook through each step—right onto the ingredients. Thus, if you are about to cut a fish, the system will project a virtual knife and mark where exactly that it ought to cut into the fish's body. And there's also a tiny physical robot that sits on the countertop. Thanks to the cameras, it can sense that you've stopped touching the ingredients and inquire if you want to move on to the next step in the recipe.

Now, what exactly is "augmented" about such a reality? It may be augmented technologically, but it also seems diminished intellectually. At best, we are left with "augmented diminished reality." Some geeks stubbornly refuse to recognize that challenges and obstacles—which might include initial ignorance of the right way to cut the fish—enhance rather than undermine the human condition. To make cooking easier is not necessarily to augment it—quite the opposite. To subject it fully to the debilitating logic of efficiency is to deprive humans of the ability to achieve mastery in this activity, to make human flourishing impossible and to impoverish our lives. A more appropriate solution here would not make cooking less demanding but make its rituals less rigid and perhaps even more challenging.

This is not a snobbish defense of the sanctified traditions of cooking. In a world where only a select few could master the tricks of the trade, such "augmented" kitchens would probably be welcome, if only for their promise to democratize access to this art. But this is not the world we inhabit: detailed recipes and instructional videos on how to cook the most exquisite dish have never been easier to find on Google. Do we really need a robot—not to mention surveillance cameras above our heads—to cook that stuffed turkey or roast that lamb?

Besides, it's not so hard to predict where such progress would lead: once inside our kitchens, these data-gathering devices would never leave, developing new, supposedly unanticipated functions. First, we'd install cameras in our kitchens to receive better instructions, then food and consumer electronics companies would tell us that they'd like us to keep the cameras to improve their products, and, finally, we'd discover that all our cooking data now resides on a server in California, with insurance companies analyzing just how much saturated fat we consume and adjusting our insurance premiums accordingly. Cooking abetted by smart technology could be a Trojan horse opening the way for far more sinister projects.

None of this is to say that technology cannot increase our pleasure from cooking—and not just in terms of making our food tastier and healthier. Technology, used with some imagination and without the traditional solutionist fetishism of efficiency and perfection, can actually make the cooking process more challenging, opening up new vistas for experimentation and giving us new ways to violate the rules. Compare the impoverished culinary vision on offer in *New Scientist* with some of the fancy gadgetry embraced by the molecular gastronomy movement. From thermal immersion circulators for cooking at low temperature to printers with edible paper, from syringes used to produce weird noodles and caviar to induction cookers that send magnetic waves through metal pans, all these gadgets make cooking more difficult, more challenging, and more exciting. They can infuse any aspiring chef with great passion for the culinary arts—much more so than surveillance cameras or instruction-spewing robots.

Strict adherence to recipes can produce predictable, albeit tasty, dishes—and occasionally this is just what we want. But such standardization can also make our kitchens as exciting as McDonald's franchises. Celebrating innovation for its own sake is in bad taste. For technology truly to augment reality, its designers and engineers should get a better idea of the complex practices that our reality is composed of.

As the molecular gastronomy example illustrates, to reject solutionism is not to reject technology. Nor is it to abandon all hope that the world around us can be ameliorated; technology could and should be part of this project. To reject solutionism is to transcend the narrow-minded rationalistic mind-set that recasts every instance of an efficiency deficit—like the lack of perfect, comprehensive instructions in the kitchen—as an obstacle that needs to be overcome. There are other, more fruitful, more humanistic, and more responsible ways to think about technology's role in enabling human flourishing, but solutionists are unlikely to grasp them unless they complicate their dangerously reductionist account of the human condition.

Pasteur and Zynga

I'll be the first to acknowledge that the problems posed by solutionism are not in any sense new; as already noted, generations of earlier thinkers have already addressed many related pitfalls and pathologies. And yet I feel that we are living through a resurgence of a very particular modern kind of solutionism. Today the most passionate solutionists are not to be found in city halls and government ministries; rather, they are to be found in Silicon Valley, trying to take the lessons they have learned from "the Internet"—and there's never been a more deceptively didactic source of great lessons about "life, the universe and everything" (to use Douglas Adams's memorable phrase)—and put them into practice in various civic initiatives and plans to fix the bugs of humanity.

Why the scare quotes around "the Internet"? In the afterword to my first book, *The Net Delusion*, I made what I now believe to be one of its main, even if overlooked, points: the physical infrastructure we know as "the Internet" bears very little resemblance to the mythical "Internet"—the one that reportedly brought down the governments of Tunisia and Egypt and is supposedly destroying our brains—that lies at the center of our public debates. The infrastructure and design of this network of networks do play a certain role in sanctioning many of these myths—for example, the idea that "the Internet" is resistant to censorship comes from the unique qualities of its packet-switching communication mechanism—but "the Internet" that is the bane of public debates also contains many other stories and narratives—about innovation, surveillance, capitalism—that have little to do with the infrastructure per se.

French philosopher Bruno Latour, writing of Louis Pasteur's famed scientific accomplishments, distinguished between Pasteur, the actual historical figure, and "Pasteur," the mythical almighty character who has come to represent the work of other scientists and entire social movements, like the hygienists, who, for their own pragmatic reasons, embraced Pasteur with open arms. But anyone interested in writing the history of that period cannot just deploy the name "Pasteur" as an unproblematic, objective term; it needs to be disassembled so that its various parts can be studied in their own right. The story of how these disparate parts—including the actual Louis Pasteur—have become "Pasteur," the national hero of France whom we see in textbooks, is what the history of science, at least in its Latourian vision, should aspire to uncover.

Now, I do not set out to write history in this book. If I did, I would indeed try to show the contingency and fluidity of the very idea of "the Internet" and attempt to trace how "the Internet" has come to mean what it means today. In this book, I'm interested in a much narrower slice of this story; namely, I want to explore how "the Internet" has become the impetus for many of the contemporary solutionist initiatives while also being the blinkers that prevent us from seeing their shortcomings.

In other words, I'm interested in why and how "the Internet" excites—and why and how it confuses. I want to understand why and how iTunes or Wikipedia—some of the core mythical components of "the Internet"—have become models to think about the future of politics. How have Zynga and Facebook become models to think about civic engagement? How have Yelp's and Amazon's reviews become models to think about criticism? How has Google become a model for thinking about business and social innovation—as if it had a coherent philosophy—so that books with titles like *What Would Google Do?* can become best sellers?

The arrival of "the Internet" both boosted and vindicated many of the solutionist attitudes that I describe in this book. "The Internet" has allowed solutionists to significantly expand the scope of their interventions, running experiments on a much grander scale. It has also given rise to a new set of beliefs—what I call "Internet-centrism"—the chief of which is the firm conviction that we are living through unique, revolutionary times, in which the previous truths no longer hold, everything is undergoing profound change, and the need to "fix things" runs as high as ever. "The Internet," in short, has supplied solutionists with ample ammunition to ratchet up their war on inefficiency, ambiguity, and disorder, while also providing some new justification for doing so. But it has also supplied them with a set of assumptions about both how the world works and how it should work, about how it talks and how it should talk, recasting many issues and debates in a decidedly Internet-centric manner. Internet-centrism relates to "the Internet" very much like scientism relates to science: its epistemology tolerates no dissenting viewpoints, while all recent history is just about how the great spirit of "the Internet" presents itself to us.

This book, then, is an effort to liberate our technology debates from the many unhealthy and erroneous assumptions about "the Internet." In this, it's much more normative than history aspires to be. Following the work of Latour and Thomas Kuhn, many historians of science have come to accept that, while the idea of "Science" with a capital *S* is even more chock-full of myths than the idea of "the Internet," they have made peace with this discovery, reasoning that, as long as there are scientists who think there is this "Science" with a capital *S* out there, they are still worth studying, regardless of whether historians of science themselves actually share this belief.

It's an elegant and reassuring approach, but I find it very hard to pursue when thinking about "the Internet" and the corrosive influence that this idea is beginning to have on public discourse and the kinds of reform projects that are getting priority. In this sense, to point out the many limitations of solutionism without also pointing out the limitations of what I call "Internet-centrism" would not be very productive; without the latter, the former wouldn't be half as powerful. So before we can embark on discussing the shortcomings of solutionism in areas like politics or crime prevention, it's worth getting a better grasp of the pernicious intellectual influence of Internet-centrism—a task we turn to in the next chapter. Revealing Internet-centrism for what it is will make debunking solutionism much less difficult.

CHAPTER TWO

The Nonsense of "the Internet"— and How to Stop It

"The internet is not territory to be conquered,
but life to be preserved and allowed to evolve freely."
—Nicolas Mendoza, AlJazeera.com

"What made Blockbuster close? The Internet. What made At the
Movies get canceled? The Internet. Who went tromping across my
lawn and ruined my petunias? The Internet."
—Eric Snider, cinematical blog

These days, "the Internet" can mean just about anything. "The Next Battle for Internet Freedom Could Be over 3D Printing," proclaimed the headline on TechCrunch, a popular technology blog, in August 2012. Given how fuzzy the very idea of "the Internet" is, derivative concepts like "Internet freedom" have become so all-encompassing and devoid of any actual meaning that they can easily cover the regulation of 3D printers, the thorny issues of net neutrality, and the rights of dissident bloggers in Azerbaijan. Instead of debating the merits of individual technologies and crafting appropriate policies and regulations, we have all but surrendered to catchall terms like "the Internet," which try to bypass any serious and empirical debate altogether.

Today, "the Internet" is regularly invoked to thwart critical thinking and exclude nongeeks from the discussion. Here is how one prominent technology blogger argued that Congress should not regulate facial-recognition technology: "All too many U.S. lawmakers are barely beyond the stage of thinking that the Internet is a collection of tubes; do we really want these guys to tell Facebook or any other social media company how to run its business?" You see, it's all so complex—much more complex than health care or climate change—that only geeks should be allowed to tinker with the magic tubes. "The Internet" is holy—so holy that it lies beyond the means of democratic representation. That facial-recognition technology developed independently of "the Internet" and has its roots in the 1960s research funded by various defense agencies means little in this context. Once part of "the Internet," any technology loses its history and intellectual autonomy. It simply becomes part of the grand narrative of "the Internet," which, despite what postmodernists say about the death of metanarratives, is one metanarrative that is doing all right. Today, virtually every story is bound to have an "Internet" angle—and it's the job of our Internet apostles to turn those little anecdotes into fairy tales about the march of Internet progress, just a tiny chapter in their cyber-Whig theory of history. "The Internet": an idea that effortlessly fills minds, pockets, coffers, and even the most glaring narrative gaps.

Whenever you hear someone tell you, "This is not how the Internet works"—as technology bloggers are wont to inform everyone who cares to read their scribblings—you should know that your interlocutor believes your views to be reactionary and antimodern. But where is the missing manual to "the Internet"—the one that explains how this giant series of tubes actually works—that the geeks claim to know by heart? Why are they so reluctant to acknowledge that perhaps there's nothing inevitable about how various parts of this giant "Internet" work and fit together? Is it really true that Google can't be made to work differently? Tacitly, of course, the geeks do acknowledge that there is nothing permanent about "the Internet"; that's why they lined up to oppose the Stop Online Piracy Act (SOPA), which—oh, the irony—threatened to completely alter "how the Internet works." So, no interventions will work "on the Internet"—except for those that will. SOPA was a bad piece of legislation, but there's something odd about how the geeks can simultaneously claim that the Internet is fixed and permanent and work extremely hard in the background to keep it that way. Their theory stands in stark contrast to their practice— a common modern dissonance that they prefer not to dwell on.

"The Internet" is also a way to shift the debate away from more concrete and specific issues, essentially burying it in obscure and unproductive McLuhanism that seeks to discover some nonexistent inner truths about each and every medium under the sun. Consider how Nicholas Carr, one of today's most vocal Internet skeptics, frames the discussion about the impact that digital technologies have on our ability to think deep thoughts and concentrate. In his best-selling book *The Shallows*, Carr worries that "the Internet" is making his brain demand "to be fed the way the Net fed it— and the more it was fed, the hungrier it became." He complains that "the Net . . . provides a high-speed system for delivering responses and rewards . . . which encourage the repetition of both physical and mental actions." The book is full of similar complaints. For Carr, the brain is 100 percent plastic, but "the Internet" is 100 percent fixed.

Does "the Net" that Carr writes about actually exist? Is there much point in lumping together sites like Instapaper—which lets users save Web pages in order to read them later, in an advertising-free and undisturbed environment—and, say, Twitter? Is it inevitable that Facebook should constantly prompt us to check new links? Should Twitter reward us for tweeting links that we never open? Or punish us? Or do nothing—as is the case now? Many of these are open questions—and the way in which technology companies resolve them depends, in part, on what we, their users, tell them (provided, of course, we can get our own act together). There may be some business hurdles to making the digital services we use less amenable to discussion, but this is where one has to explore the world of political economy, not that of neuroscience, even if the latter is the much more fashionable of the two. Carr, however, refuses to abandon the notion of "the Net," with its predetermined goals and inherent features; instead of exploring the interplay between design, political economy, and information science, he keeps telling us that "the Net" is, well, shite. Alas, it won't get any better until we stop thinking that there is a "Net" out there. How can we account for the diversity of logics and practices promoted by digital tools without having to resort to explanations that revolve around terms like "the Net"? "The Net" is a term that should appear on the last—not first!—page of our books about digital technologies; it cannot explain itself.

Like Marshall McLuhan before him, Carr wants to score, rank, and compare different media and come up with some kind of quasi-scientific pecking order for them (McLuhan went as far as to calculate sense ratios for each medium that he "studied"). This very medium-centric approach overlooks the diversity of actual practices enabled by each medium. One may hate television for excessive advertising—but then, a publicly supported broadcasting system may have no need for advertising at all; TV programs don't always have to be interrupted by ads. Video games might make us more violent—but, once again, they can do so many other things in so many different ways that it seems unfair to connect them only to one function. There's very little that the *New York Times* has in common with the *Sun* or that NPR shares with Rush Limbaugh.

Likewise, there's nothing inevitable about Google making information available permanently or Facebook trying to pitch unneeded products or not limiting the number of links it shows users to, say, ten a day. These are not "inherent" properties of "the Net"; these companies have chosen to do these things—perhaps for business reasons or out of sheer arrogance and self-confidence—but they could have easily chosen otherwise. In fact, all these companies seem to be adding or subtracting at least one feature per week; if anything, this is the best argument for not assuming that their platforms are somehow just a way in which "the Net" speaks to us. If "the Net" does have a voice when it speaks to us, it's that of a schizophrenic.

Given his McLuhanesque medium-centrism, it's not surprising that Carr has little to say about fighting all the digital distractions he identifies: his notion of the ever-permanent and rigid "Net" prevents him from identifying structural reforms that can result in less destruction ("My interest is description, not prescription," Carr told the *New York Observer*). In Carr's universe, we can only arm ourselves with software that can cut our Internet connections.

Or we can all move to the silent sanctity of the mountain ranges of Colorado, as Carr himself did when writing his book. Tinkering with "the Net" itself is not just impossible, it's unthinkable: its logic cannot be reversed; it can only be (occasionally) circumvented.

Against the Internet Grain

As it happens, Internet skeptics and optimists share quite a lot of common ground; both depend on some stable notion of "the Internet" to advance their arguments. Remove that notion, along with its simplistic assumptions about the inherent benefits of openness or publicness, and the pundits are suddenly forced to confront complex empirical matters, to inquire into the politics of algorithms, to grapple with the history of facial-recognition technologies, to understand how techniques like "deep packet inspection" actually work. As long as Internet-centrism rules supreme, our technological debate will remain lazy, shallow, and unproductive: "the Internet," no matter how many TED talks and Kindle singles are dedicated to it, will not tell us whether we need regular public audits of search engine giants like Google. Of course, pundits might say that such audits are "a war on Internet openness"—but this is precisely the kind of discourse we ought to avoid, as it makes claims about what appears to be a mythical entity.

It's not surprising then that imagining life after "the Internet" is so often an exercise in despair, a one-way ticket to irrelevance, cynicism, or madness. "The Internet," it seems, has arrived for good, and its finality is hardly contested; "the network," as its foremost theorist Lawrence Lessig assures us in the pages of the *New Republic*, "is not going away." It's not just that we no longer remember the world before Google, Facebook, and Wikipedia; it's also that large chunks of that world either no longer exist or, as is the case with the print edition of *Encyclopaedia Britannica*, are in the process of liquidation. Some might feel nostalgic for the time when they actually flipped through those hefty and dusty tomes, but overall it seems that humanity has placed its bet on the younger, leaner, and more efficient offspring.

Still, there's something peculiar about this failure of our collective imagination to unthink "the Internet." It is no longer discussed as something contingent, as something that can go away; it appears fixed and permanent, perhaps even ontological—"the Internet" just is and it always will be. To paraphrase Frederic Jameson on capitalism, it's much easier to imagine how the world itself would end than to imagine the end of "the Internet."

Of course, some claim that they can still imagine what it's like to go without "the Internet" and its toys for a week or two. What they don't realize is that this experience of the "offline" is also profoundly affected by the experience of the "online"; that we think of technology through the lens of this bifurcation between the two is also a contingent fact of history, not a God-given fact of nature. It is possible to think about activities like search and social networking without positing any such split between two seemingly different worlds. But even if we bracket concerns over this bifurcation, such withdrawal from "the Internet" is not the same as imagining a completely different world—a world where withdrawal itself is no longer required, for the coveted object itself is no longer available. A world in which there is no "Internet" to withdraw from eludes our creative faculties.

Even more peculiar is the fact that our smartest technologists—the guys who basically see the future in their bathroom mirror every morning—are equally helpless in this endeavor. These techies, who worship the god of creative destruction and pray on the altar of innovation and see industries come and go without shedding a tear, might be spending their weekends mining asteroids and jogging on other planets—but even they can't imagine how "the Internet" would die, let alone suggest what might succeed it. Their predictive models can anticipate and simulate the odds (and probably the consequences) of a global porcupine rebellion, but the basic outline of a world without cables, switches, and URLs still remains beyond their computing abilities.

Was it always like this? Could the Victorians imagine life after the telegraph or the steam engine? Could Marconi and his disciples imagine life after radio? Could the people of 1950s America imagine life after television? Could the French imagine life after Minitel? Science fiction and utopian literature of those eras do contain many a fine testament to that effort. Of course, one might counter, such analogies are imperfect, unfair even. For one, radio and television are still with us, and only in June 2012 did the French finally pull the plug on Minitel.

Besides, radio, television, even the telegraph—for what is e-mail if not better telegraph?—have reinvented themselves online. But this only adds confusion to our inquiry, for now that most other technologies are mediated by "the Internet," it's even harder to imagine how the whole enterprise might be supplanted by something else. If "the Internet" goes, it seems, the entire armament of our technologies—all those artifacts on display in our museums of science and technology and history textbooks—would go with it.

But perhaps we can't imagine life after "the Internet" because we don't think that "the Internet" is going anywhere. If the public debate is any indication, the finality of "the Internet"—the belief that it's the ultimate technology and the ultimate network—has been widely accepted. It's Silicon Valley's own version of the end of history: just as capitalism-driven liberal democracy in Francis Fukuyama's controversial account remains the only game in town, so does the capitalism-driven "Internet." It, the logic goes, is a precious gift from the gods that humanity should never abandon or tinker with. Thus, while "the Internet" might disrupt everything, it itself should never be disrupted. It's here to stay—and we'd better work around it, discover its real nature, accept its features as given, learn its lessons, and refurbish our world accordingly. If it sounds like a religion, it's because it is.

This very notion of "the Internet" is on display when Google's Eric Schmidt, for example, says that "policymakers should work with the grain of the Internet rather than against it," or when Rebecca MacKinnon, a prominent commentator on digital politics, notes that "without a major upgrade, [our] political system will keep on producing legal code that is Internet-incompatible." It's the same notion of "the Internet" that popular technology blogger and author Jeff Jarvis invokes when, discussing Germans' complex feelings about privacy, he writes of a "nagging fear Germans harbor that their heritage is coming into fundamental conflict with internet culture—with the future."

All these thinkers take "the Internet" to be fixed and unified, meaningful and didactic, powerful and unconquerable. And, as Jarvis puts it, it's "the future." In a similar vein, popular technology investor Paul Graham writes, "Web 2.0 means using the Web the way it's meant to be used. The 'trends' we're seeing now are simply the inherent nature of the Web emerging from under the broken models that got imposed during the Battle." "The Internet," thus, is believed to possess an inherent nature, a logic, a teleology, and that nature is rapidly unfolding in front of us. We can just stand back and watch; "the Internet" will take care of itself—and us. If your privacy disappears in the process, this is simply what the Internet gods wanted all along.

Perhaps one last example of this quasi-religious sentiment about "the Internet" would suffice. David Post, one of the early champions of the idea that "the Internet" represents a unique and unprecedented stage in human history, argues that "the Internet" might be propelled by laws and regulations as firm as those of nature. Rejecting Lessig's reasonable claims that "the Internet" has no inherent nature or purpose and that we should try to avoid an "is-ism" mentality whereby we believe that "the Internet" will always be as free as it is now, Post sees "the Internet" as something preternatural and autonomous. (Curiously, Lessig's point here is the exact opposite of what he wrote in the *New Republic* about the network "not going away," but this is hardly surprising: Lessig's academic self knows that there's nothing fixed about "the Internet," but his activist self also knows that claiming that it's here to stay will make his advocacy much easier). This is what Post actually writes:

> There are laws of Nature. . . . There are laws of growth, and scale, and organization, reasons why website visits, Internet connectivity, the population of cities, and the frequency of words all follow the same pattern, reasons why the one global network is the one with end-to-end design and distributed routing, though we probably understand those laws . . . not very well. And they matter. . . . We can shake our fists at the law of gravity all we like, but if we don't pay close attention to it when building our bridges, they will all fall down. . . .

It is not, as Lessig would have it, "is-ism" to keep looking for them and trying to understand how they work.

Eric Schmidt's "grain of the Internet," in other words, is real—for all we know, it might be as real as gravity—and we should keep looking for it by peeking deep inside "the Internet's" soul. How did we reach a point where "the Internet" is presumed to develop according to laws as firm and natural as those of gravity? That a serious legal academic can write this without anyone suspecting him of being slightly delusional is one indication of just how uncritical discussions about "the Internet" have become.

The Faux Didacticism of "the Internet"

Does "the Internet" have a message to impart to humanity? Does it contain important lessons that we all need to heed and perhaps incorporate into our institutions? Does it help us rediscover long-forgotten truths about human nature? More and more people—not just ivory tower intellectuals but also regular soldiers in the Internet war, people who join Anonymous and vote for representatives of Pirate Parties in elections—are answering these questions in the affirmative. It's this propensity to view "the Internet" as a source of wisdom and policy advice that transforms it from a fairly uninteresting set of cables and network routers into a seductive and exciting ideology—perhaps today's über-ideology.

Science and technology writer Steven Johnson has offered perhaps the sharpest summary of this ideology in *Future Perfect*. For Johnson, "the Internet" is much more than just a cheap way of sending Skype messages or adding hilariously unfunny captions to photos of cats. Rather, it's an intellectual template for how society itself should be reorganized; it's not "the solution to the problem, but a way of thinking about the problem." Thus, writes Johnson, "one could use the Internet directly to improve people's lives, but also learn from the way the Internet had been organized, and apply those principles to help improve the way city governments worked, or school systems taught students." Not surprisingly, he believes that in their political significance, major developments in Internet history are comparable to, say, the French Revolution or the fall of the Berlin Wall. Hence, "the creation of ARPANET and TCP/IP . . . should also be seen as milestones in the history of political philosophy." To Hobbes and Rawls, now we must add ARPANET and TCP/IP.

Why? Well, Johnson believes that sites like Wikipedia and Kickstarter, a popular fund-raising platform for aspiring artists and geeks, work because they embed the decentralizing spirit of "the Internet"—the same spirit that runs through and regulates its physical networks. And it's, of course, the spirit of victory: everything that "the Internet" touches automatically gets better, smarter, prettier. "Slowly but steadily, much like the creation of the Internet itself, a growing number of us have started to think that the core principles that governed the design of the Net could be applied to solve different kinds of problems—the problems that confront neighborhoods, artists, drug companies, parents, schools," writes Johnson.

What does this mean in practice? Take just one example: Johnson thinks that a site like Kickstarter offers a much better model of funding arts than, say, the National Endowment for the Arts (NEA); in fact, he thinks it's just a matter of time before Kickstarter overtakes the NEA. "The question with Kickstarter, given its growth rate, is not whether it could rival the NEA in its support of the creative arts. The new question is whether it will grow to be ten times the size of the NEA." Elsewhere in the book, Johnson writes that he doesn't want to scrap the NEA, only to make it work more like Kickstarter; what's most interesting about his argument, however, is that he doesn't spell out why the NEA should become like Kickstarter and what makes the latter's model superior. Perhaps, Johnson simply doesn't have to, as his audience can anticipate the argument that is implied: the Kickstarter approach is simply better because it comes from "the Internet."

This odd and shortsighted claim focuses on the mechanics of the platform rather than on the substance of what institutions like the NEA actually do. Kickstarter works as follows: creators—they can be start-ups that want to build a cool app or new gadget or artists who want to make a music video—post their fund-raising appeals on the site; if and when enough people chip in, the creators get the money to embark on their project. Many projects don't meet the fund-raising target and get no money; those that do sometimes fail to deliver what was expected (Kickstarter's most famous failed alumnus is Diaspora, an ill-fated start-up that wanted to take on Facebook and offer users better privacy; started in April 2010, the project had collapsed by August 2012, with one of its co-founders committing suicide). Some projects do deliver, but most are at the mercy of "virality"; if the online crowd finds their proposal appealing, money does pour in—often much more than was asked for originally.

Now, this is a very different model from the top-down hierarchical model of the NEA, in which a bunch of artsy bureaucrats make all the decisions as to what art to fund. But the fact that Kickstarter offers a more efficient platform for some projects to raise more money more effectively—bypassing the bureaucrats and increasing participation—does not mean it will yield better, more innovative art or support art that, in our age of cat videos, might seem old-fashioned and unnecessary. Sites like Kickstarter tend to favor populist projects, which may or may not be good for the arts overall. The same logic applies to other governmental and quasi-governmental institutions as well: if the National Endowment for Democracy worked like Kickstarter, it would have to spend all its money on funding projects like the highly viral Kony 2012 campaign, which, all things considered, may only be of secondary importance to both democracy promotion and US foreign policy as a whole.

Besides, it's not at all obvious whether this new system will promote fairness and justice. Contrary to what most Internet cheerleaders think, virality is hardly ever self-generated and self-sustaining. Memes are born free, but everywhere they are in chains—those of PR agencies and freelancing solo artists. Both have perfectly adapted to this new digital world and found ways to reverse engineer virality by manipulating the economics of social media. They know how to feed the right stuff to bloggers to generate buzz on important, even if niche, platforms, and since so many in the professional media now read sites like Gawker and The Huffington Post, extending their reach far beyond social media.

Thus, while Kickstarter might give us the illusion of more efficient distribution of arts funding than the NEA, it would be naïve and very shortsighted not to take note of the fact that we'll also get—and this is much more important than the efficiency of the platform—very different art.

How so? Danish academic Inge Ejbye Sørensen has studied how crowdfunding has affected documentary filmmaking in the United Kingdom. Britain stands out among other countries in that most of its documentaries are produced and fully funded by one of its four main broadcasters (BBC, ITV, Channel 4, and Channel 5), which dictate the terms to the filmmaker. In this context, crowdfunding and Kickstarter seem liberating, even revolutionary.

But, as Sørensen points out, this revolution has a few mitigating circumstances. First, Kickstarter might produce many new documentaries, but the odds are that they will be of a very particular kind (this critique also applies to other sites in this field, like indiegogo.com, sponsume.com, crowdfunder.co.uk, and pledgie .com). They are likely to be campaign-and issue-driven films in the tradition of *Super Size Me* or *An Inconvenient Truth*. Their directors seek social change and tap into an activist public that shares the documentary's activist agenda. A documentary exploring the causes of World War I probably stands to receive less online funding—if any—than a documentary exploring the causes of climate change. Second, some films have significant start-up costs (think drama documentaries or history movies) or involve considerable legal risks that may be hard to price and account for. Say you are making a film that includes an undercover investigation of the oil industry. When you have the BBC's lawyers backing you up, you'll probably take many more risks than if you are relying on crowdfunding. But if Kickstarter is your platform of choice, you'll probably forgo venturing into the thorny legal issues altogether.

Both of these arguments show the danger of viewing the nimble and crowd-powered Kickstarter as an alternative (rather than a supplement!) to the behemoth that is the BBC, or in the American context, the NEA. This might fit quite nicely with David Cameron's rhetoric of the "Big Society"—whereby individuals take on the roles formerly performed by public institutions—but it would be a mistake to treat the two approaches as producing the same content through different means. Some content is simply unlikely to get crowdfunded.

Johnson, however, does not want to make his case for reforming the NEA on aesthetic grounds; for him, Kickstarter is better because it's more Internet-like and more participatory. That these may be irrelevant considerations when it comes to funding art does not seem to bother him. This is Internet-centrism at work: the putative values of "the Internet"—be it openness or participation—become the prized yardstick for assessing every field of human endeavor, regardless of its own goals and standards.

But there's one more problem. Defining Internet values is notoriously tricky. Take someone like Internet pundit Jeff Jarvis, who in his first book, *What Would Google Do?*, argues that other institutions—both for-profits and nonprofits—should copy Google's business philosophy. His reasoning goes like this: "The Internet" seems open, public, and collaborative. Google seems so, too, and it's prospering. Hence its values are openness, publicness, and collaboration; these are also Internet values, and they bring profits and efficiency. So, reasons Jarvis, "the Internet" tells us something very important about Google, and Google tells us something very important about "the Internet." This logic is so circular, there's no way for pundits like him ever to be wrong.

But as the last few years show, Google is not driven by an ideology of either openness or publicness; at this point it seems to care only about market competition. When it felt so far ahead of Facebook and Apple, it built open platforms and launched unprofitable but useful services. But those days are long gone: it has shut down many of the platforms celebrated by Jarvis and become much more cautious, now charging for some services and eliminating others altogether. In 2010 it all but gave up on its nominal commitment to "openness" when it struck a deal with Verizon regarding traffic management on mobile networks. It's true that for a very long time Google stayed out of the content business—positioning itself as a platform for accessing the content of others—but today it owns the restaurant guide Zagat and the travel guide Frommer's and actively serves its own content in search results. Is Google less of an Internet company today than it was when Jarvis published his book? Or could it be that it never actually had any genuine lessons to impart about "the Internet" and that such lessons are always transitory and in flux?

Or take Wikipedia, which is easily the solutionists' favorite template for rebuilding the world; books with titles like *Wikinomics* and *Wiki Government* are a testament to the role this one website plays in solutionists' imaginations. The problem with using Wikipedia as a model is that nobody—not even its founder, Jimmy Wales—really knows how it works. To assume that we can distill life-changing lessons from it and then apply them in completely different fields seems arrogant to say the least. Worst of all, Wikipedia is itself subject to many myths, which might result in Wikipedia-inspired solutions that misrepresent its spirit.

"The bureaucracy of Wikipedia is relatively so small as to be invisible," proclaims technology pundit Kevin Kelly, confessing that "much of what I believed about human nature, and the nature of knowledge, has been upended by the Wikipedia." But what did Kelly believe before Wikipedia? Kelly writes that "everything I knew about the structure of information convinced me that knowledge would not spontaneously emerge from data, without a lot of energy and intelligence deliberately directed to transforming it." What a reasonable thing to have believed! Only there's no reason to stop believing this today. Wikipedia, as it turns out, has a huge—not small—bureaucracy; its rules cover the most arcane issues (just consider WP:MOSMAC, which regulates how Wikipedia articles should discuss "the Republic of Macedonia and the Province of Macedonia, Greece"). One estimate from 2006 posited that discussions about Wikipedia's governance and editorial policies—the stuff of which bureaucracy is made—constituted at least one-quarter of the whole site. Its bureaucracy is anything but small—and to start applying Wikipedia's lessons before actually grasping them is a recipe for disaster. That it's invisible to the likes of Kelly only means that they are looking at it the wrong way; the task of sound technological analysis—which is not beholden to Internet-centrism—is to make the seemingly invisible visible.

The best explanation of Wikipedia is what its own insiders like to say: Wikipedia works in practice but not in theory. It's a great line, and in addition to being funny, it also shows that we simply have no adequate theories to understand Wikipedia. Perhaps we shouldn't even strive for such theories, as they will inevitably gloss over the rich world of practices and mediators that make it tick.

There's nothing wrong with being humble and acknowledging the limitations of our understanding. Obviously, that something doesn't fit a grand theory of "how the Internet works" does not make it ineffectual, as the Wikipedia example shows so well. Given just how limited our knowledge of Wikipedia is, to expect that we can magically "pull a Wikipedia" whenever confronted with a burning issue is dangerously naïve.

If Internet Theorists Were Bouncers

Internet-centrism has found its way into regulatory thinking as well. One of the most attractive contemporary theories of Internet regulation, advanced by Harvard's Jonathan Zittrain, revolves around the idea of generativity. It starts from the premise that openness of the platform is the main reason why "the Internet" has unleashed so much innovation. On "the Internet," no one has to ask for permission to start a new service. Google could build a search engine without negotiating with ISPs. Wikipedia could build an encyclopedia without negotiating with the likes of Microsoft or AOL. Skype could build its impressive software without negotiating with AT&T.

As an explanation of what has happened in the last two decades, Zittrain's is a very elegant and pithy theory. However, generativity also prescribes how things should be done in the future: if we want this great wave of innovation to continue, the argument goes, we should maintain—even proactively defend—the openness of "the Internet." Any development that introduces a set of gatekeepers into "the Internet's" ecosystem—like the recent fascination with apps for smartphones and tablets—is to be scrutinized and, in most cases, resisted, for the new gatekeepers, greedy as they are, might not have "the Internet's" best interests in mind. In my book, a hallmark of a good theory of technological change and innovation is whether it can predict—or at least anticipate—how incumbent technology itself would be disrupted. It doesn't seem extraordinary to expect that theorists of innovation would at least be prepared for the eventual possibility that whatever incumbent technology they are celebrating at the moment might itself get undone by the very same forces of disruption that made it incumbent in the first place. In other words, if we were to travel back in history and apply what we know about "the Internet" to write better rules for regulating the telephone industry, we would probably put more emphasis on the possibility that the telephone would not be around forever. The same goes for the telegraph, the radio, and even television. If they had a second chance, good theorists of innovation in each of those industries would spend far more time trying to anticipate the death of their object of inquiry—be it the telegraph, the radio, or television—rather than articulating criteria and conditions that could allow those objects to live forever. This, at any rate, is what follows if one assumes that innovation should be platform independent and that maximizing it across all platforms—including future, unanticipated ones—should be the ultimate goal of effective regulation.

But the theory of generativity doesn't preoccupy itself with the thorny subject of how "the Internet" itself will die—not least because Zittrain, under the sway of Internet-centrism, badly wants "the Internet" to be eternal. His theory is a recipe for how "the Internet" can live forever. This, of course, is never expressed directly, for Zittrain assumes—quite correctly—that his geeky audience shares his desire to make its fetish object immortal. However, we shouldn't mistake our infatuation with "the Internet" for a genuine theory of innovation. Any robust theory, instead of treating "the Internet" like a permanent gift to civilization, would find a way to compare the innovation potentials of many different platforms and technologies, including those that might eventually threaten to supplant "the Internet."

Of course, there may be other strong social, political, and even aesthetic concerns about the challenge that the rise of apps presents to digital "forms of life." However, to claim that Apple—one of Zittrain's culprits—is bad for innovation because it's bad for "the Internet" is like claiming that "the Internet" is bad for innovation because it's bad for the telephone. Well, it might have been bad for the telephone—but when did the preservation of the telephone become a lofty social goal? Such teleological Internet-centrism should have no place in our regulatory thinking. But, alas, the preservation of "the Internet" seems to have become an end in itself, to the great detriment of our ability even to imagine what might come to supplant it and how our Internet fetish might be blocking that something from emerging. To choose "the Internet" over the starkly uncertain future of the post-Internet world is to tacitly acknowledge that either "the Internet" has satisfied all our secret plans, longings, and desires—that is, it is indeed Silicon Valley's own "end of history"—or that we simply can't imagine what else innovation could unleash.

The irony is that Zittrain's theory of generativity, while very critical of gatekeepers like Apple, is itself a gatekeeper. While generativity green-lights good, reliable, and predictable innovation, the kind that promises to stay within the confines of "the Internet" and leave things as they are, it frowns upon—and possibly even blocks—the unruly and disruptive kind that might start within "the Internet" but eventually transcend, supplant, and perhaps even eliminate it. Zittrain attempts to universalize what he takes to be the operating principles of "the Internet" and present them as objective, eternal, and uncontroversial foundations on which innovation theory itself could run from now on. Thus, if openness has supposedly been one of the defining features of "the Internet," it gets magically transformed into an objective benchmark for the future of innovation. Aggressive expansion into other domains is one of the hallmarks of Internet-centrism; it colonizes entire theories and domains, imposing its own values—openness, transparency, disruption—on whatever it touches. However, if we put the well-being of "the Internet" aside, absolutely nothing about Apple's hands-on approach to running its app store or controlling its gadgets suggests that it's bad for innovation. Its approach may not be "open"; it may not even be "Internet compatible." But these criteria only make sense in a world where the well-being of "the Internet itself" is the alpha and omega of everything, the summum bonum. This may even be a world in which Jonathan Zittrain and many other geeks would actually want to live; ideologies do have a tendency to present other worldviews as irrelevant or impossible. In reality, though, control and centralization are not inherently antithetical to innovation; if we have come to believe the opposite, then "the Internet" is partly to blame.

Woody Allen once wrote a hilarious satire titled "If the Impressionists Had Been Dentists," written in the form of a letter from Vincent van Gogh to his brother ("Theo . . . Mrs. Sol Schwimmer is suing me because I made her bridge as I felt it and not to fit her ridiculous mouth! . . . She claims she can't chew! What do I care whether she can chew or not!"). The world of Internet theory still awaits its Woody Allen, but an analogous satire—something along the lines of "If Internet Theorists Had Been Nightclub Bouncers"—would be quite useful. If Jonathan Zittrain's theory is any indication, his Apple nightclub would be run as an oasis of openness—what does he care that some patrons show up drunk or carrying drugs and weapons?—and this openness would make everyone inside the club happy. It's a nice theory, but there is a reason why real clubs don't preach the ideology of radical openness: it spoils the clubbing experience. But, Internet theorists might counter, what do we care about the clubbing experience if there's such a great atmosphere of openness inside the club? Well, good luck to them.

Zittrain's thought is a manifestation of a broader paradox that has become ubiquitous in our Internet debates. Rare is a reader of technology blogs or an attendee of technology conferences who has not heard the admonition that some dark, evil force—Hollywood, the National Security Agency, China, Apple—is about to "break the Internet." Technologists and geeks—the group that spends the greatest amount of time philosophizing about "the Internet" and its future—constantly remind us that "the Internet" is unstable and might fall apart. Save for the occasional proclamation that the world will stay as it is minus all the fun and convenience, no one seems to know what awaits us once "the Internet" does break. But break it will—unless some drastic change is taken to maintain its current state. Hence the greatest irony of all: one day we are told that "the Internet" is here to stay, and we should reshape our institutions to match its demands; another day, we are told that it's so fragile that almost anyone or anything could deal it a lethal blow.

It would be tempting to write this paradox off as a mere contradiction in geek logic. Or, as in Lessig's case, it might be just a rhetorical trick, a clever ruse that bolsters some important activist cause—say, copyright reform, net neutrality, or opposition to surveillance and censorship—while also nudging our seemingly obsolete political and legal institutions to experiment with technology and innovation. Such an interpretation certainly seems plausible. But it's also plausible that we have become utterly confused about "the Internet" and its presumed nature, that we are dead wrong about its finality, that the very idea of "the Internet" has impoverished our thinking about the world, and that we are worshiping false gods and ideologies. So, which is it?

Of Epochs and Epochalisms

Before examining Internet-centrism's corrosive influence on solutionism, a few words about its origins are in order. Even though its leading proponents may not be aware of it—being too young or inexperienced with books—Internet-centrism, for all its boasting about the truly revolutionary and exceptional nature of the modern era, overlaps with and feeds on several earlier fetishes and discourses about technology, information, innovation, and digitality. Plenty of books on the inevitable arrival of the information age and the postindustrial era, on the virtues and perils of automation, and on the transformational potential of cybernetics and artificial intelligence have all prepared the grounds—and our minds—for the current discussion. To present the discourse on Internet exceptionalism as exceptional would itself be a great error, for it's anything but.

Technological amnesia and complete indifference to history (especially the history of technological amnesia) remain the defining features of contemporary Internet debate. As British historian of technology David Edgerton points out, "When we think of information technology we forget about postal systems, the telegraph, the telephone, radio and television. When we celebrate on-line shopping, the mail-order catalogue goes missing. Genetic engineering, and its positive and negative impacts, is discussed as if there had never been any other means of changing animals or plants, let alone other means of increasing food supply." Only a hopelessly brave and optimistic soul would conclude that as "the Internet" comes to dominate and overtake many of these earlier debates, our respect for historical detail will somehow magically increase. If anything, the "Internet turn" in the technology debate will only aggravate this forgetfulness.

Of course, if one's knowledge of history is reduced to tweet-length CliffsNotes, it's natural to feel triumphant and unique, to believe one is living in truly exceptional times—an intellectual fallacy I call "epochalism." It's not a preserve of Internet optimists only; the pessimists love epochalism as well. After all, their criticisms matter only if the phenomena they are criticizing are seen as unprecedented. Thus, a self-proclaimed Internet pessimist like Andrew Keen can proclaim starkly that the growth of social media is "the most wrenching cultural transformation since the Industrial Revolution" without bothering to produce much evidence. Keen simply presumes that the unprecedented scale of today's transformations is self-evident—a hallmark assumption of epochalism.

By presuming that we are living through revolutionary times, epochalism sanctions radical social interventions that might otherwise attract a lot of suspicion and criticism. But in truly revolutionary times, everything goes; why not model politics on Wikipedia after all? All this talk about revolutions is just a clever way of legitimizing radical agendas that few would accept in normal times. The paralyzing influence of epochalism induces passivity and limits our responses to change, for the unfolding trends are perceived to be so monumental and inevitable that all resistance seems futile. It blinds us to the banal and highly fleeting nature of the "revolutionary" trends under consideration.

After all, it's much easier to proclaim yet another digital revolution—and to coin a requisite buzzword—than to wait and see if the observed change, instead of being a complete overthrow of established practices and principles, is just a shift in order and magnitude. But the trickery doesn't stop here, for the novel buzzword—coined only because we are apparently on the brink of a new era—is fed back into the system as a definite proof that the era is indeed new. Such circularity—whereby "the Internet" is seen as revolutionary because of Factor X, but Factor X is seen as revolutionary because of "the Internet"—is silly, but in an era of profound and revolutionary change, this passes for deep insight.

Take the fake novelty of a term like "crowdsourcing"—supposedly, one of the chief attributes of the Internet era, an idea that gave us that great source of didactic knowledge, Wikipedia. "Crowdsourcing" is certainly a very effective term; calling some of

the practices it enables as "digitally distributed sweatshop labor"—
for this seems like a much better description of what's happening
on crowdsource-for-money platforms like Amazon's Mechanical
Turk—wouldn't accomplish half as much.

But effective euphemisms come with trade-offs; they don't always
capture the historical complexity of the processes they purport to
describe. Didn't the British government turn to "crowdsourcing"—
in 1714!—to solve the "longitude problem" and solicit proposals for
how to better navigate at sea? Didn't the Smithsonian Institution—
in 1849!—turn to a network of over six hundred volunteer observers (in Canada, Mexico, Latin America, and the Caribbean) to
submit monthly weather reports (published in 1861 as the first of
a two-volume compilation of climactic data)? Didn't Toyota hold
a contest—in 1936!—to redesign its logo, only to receive 27,000
entries in return? Didn't Zagat turn to a form of "crowdsourcing"
to generate its restaurant reviews long before Yelp made online reviews fashionable? Granted, today it's much easier and cheaper to
do such things, but a revolution in knowledge gathering it isn't—
not if we want the word "revolution" to retain any meaning at all.

This message, however, is lost on our Internet pundits, who
think that "the Internet" has fundamentally altered how knowledge
is produced—nay, it has even altered what counts as knowledge. This,
at any rate, is what David Weinberger of Harvard's Berkman Center argues in his recent book *Too Big to Know*. Like Eric Schmidt,
Weinberger has seen the grain of "the Internet" and never looked
back since. "Knowledge is taking on the shape of the Net—that
is, the Internet," he proclaims, with unabashed enthusiasm.
"Knowledge now lives not just in libraries and museums and academic journals. It lives not just in the skulls of individuals. Our
skulls and our institutions are simply not big enough to contain
knowledge. Knowledge is now property of the network, and the
network embraces businesses, governments, media, museums, curated collections, and minds in communication."

This is heady stuff, but it couldn't be more wrong. It seems that
Internet-centrism turns our most insightful analysts into Martians,
who have just landed on Earth and have a hard time imagining
how things are run over here. So, in their doomed quest to understand these quirky humans, they venture into a modern university,

where they encounter professors, who spend hours coauthoring papers with strangers on other continents, browsing academic journals housed on servers miles away, giving Skype presentations at international conferences. "Ah," say the Martians, "we get it: this Internet thingy is the network that generates all your knowledge. Let's drink to that!"

Poor Martians: they'd never understand that the real knowledge-generating networks lie elsewhere—they tie together scholars, universities, conferences, computer servers, books, norms and practices, the phenomena they study and the tools and laboratories that allow them to do so. "The Internet" may be strengthening and occasionally weakening some of these networks—and it is certainly creating conditions for new networks to emerge—but it doesn't *fundamentally* change anything about what counts as knowledge or how it's made. By Weinberger's logic, we can also say that knowledge used to be the property of the airport or the post office—those did facilitate its production in the past—but that would be an insight far more trivial than the role Weinberger fashions for "the Internet."

Contrary to his claim that "knowledge is now property of the network," knowledge has always been property of the network, as even a cursory look at the first universities of the twelfth century would reveal. Once again, our digital enthusiasts mistake impressive and—yes!—interesting shifts in magnitude and order with the arrival of a new era in which the old rules no longer apply. Or, as one perceptive critic of Weinberger's oeuvre has noted, he confuses "a shift in network architecture with the onset of networked knowledge per se." "The Internet" is not a cause of networked knowledge; it is its consequence—an insight lost on most Internet theorists.

But even more disturbing about Weinberger's account is that it seeks to carve "the Internet" from the complex sociotechnical relations that it embodies and to analyze it on its own terms, as if it were a widget that fell from the sky and hence has no history or connections of any sort. This is a recurring feature of modern Internet discourse—yet another instance of vulgar McLuhanism—for it allows its practitioners to juxtapose "the Internet"—in optimistic accounts, it's the avatar of everything modern and progressive; pessimistic accounts usually hold the very opposite—against some social force or group, be it the mainstream media, Hollywood, dictators, or dissidents. Only by severing "the Internet's" ties with its context and presenting it as a McLuhanesque "medium" does any kind of simplistic score keeping—that never-ending game of trying to determine whether "the Internet" is good or bad for one thing or another—become possible.

It's time to put an end to this score-keeping game, for it generates nothing but confusion. It enables Weinberger to write, "At the very same time [that "the Internet" is blamed for all sorts of problems], sites such as Politifact.com are fact-checking the news media more closely and publicly than ever before." Score one for "the Internet"? After all, Politifact.com is a site, and a site is something that belongs on "the Internet's" side of the ledger. This is plain silly: Politifact.com might be a website, but it's also a project of the *Tampa Bay Times*, a venerable newspaper operation. Yes, we should talk about the new forms of fact checking made possible by new technologies, but to imagine that somehow Politifact.com tells us something of interest about the nature of "the Internet"—assuming, for a moment, that such a nature exists—is dead wrong.

With Models Like This . . .

Weinberger's commitment to Internet score keeping points to one of the great dangers of relying on "the Internet" as a causal explanation. Once commentators know what they want to say about the universe—that the world is flat, that knowledge is no longer contained in books, that Apple is bad for innovation, that dictatorships are crumbling everywhere, that no one reads serious fiction anymore—"the Internet" can always be invoked to provide a quick and easy (and invariably wrong) explanation. However, the ready availability of such Internet-driven explanations in itself needs to be explained. For both tech boosters and tech critics alike, "the Internet" is like George Soros in Glenn Beck's diagrams: once you plug it in, the great conspiracy suddenly makes sense. Fiction-wise, it's a brand new genre all in itself: a Webdunit.

Worse still, what many take to be original Internet theory—that is, a brave attempt to explain the world by accounting for the role of "the Internet" in it—is often just a derivative mishmash that borrows from some of the stalest, most banal approaches of modern political science and economics. If these approaches were not served with the tasty sauce of Internet-centrism, the explanations they generate would be questioned, opposed, and dismissed far more often. Alas, the conceptual novelty of "the Internet" as a field of inquiry, combined with the irresistible pull of Internet-centrism, renders the highly problematic areas of the underlying theoretical frameworks almost invisible.

Take Clay Shirky's *Here Comes Everybody*, which enjoys a cult status in geek circles as a seemingly original argument about the falling costs of collaboration. For much of his theoretical apparatus, Shirky draws on two sources: Susanne Lohmann's explanation of the 1989 protests in East Germany by means of rational-choice theory (from which Shirky borrows the notion of information cascades) and Ronald Coase's theory of the firm (from which Shirky borrows the notion of transaction costs). Alas, neither of them is an unambiguously good or neutral guide to understanding digital technologies once we liberate ourselves from Internet-centrism.

Like most scholars in the rational-choice tradition, Lohmann— whom Shirky misidentifies as a historian (she's a political scientist)— doesn't explain collective action of East Germany by attending to historical and cultural factors or tracing the emergence of new attitudes or ideologies. Such analysis requires far more extensive on-the-ground knowledge than most political scientists can boast. They have been trained to use data to build models—very much like those that failed to predict the collapse of the Soviet Union or anything of even minor significance in the last few decades—so their case studies are stripped of much local color by design.

Thus, in order to explain the 1989 protests, Lohmann comes up with a comprehensive and mostly context-independent theory of information signals and incentives that allow people to synchronize their behavior; since the people in Lohmann's models are one-dimensional and ahistorical characters, a theory of information cascades works as well in Calcutta as it does in Cairo (which is to say that, beyond offering some banal generalizations, it mostly doesn't work at all). Thus, the theory goes, if people see other people who are already protesting in the streets, they will be inclined to join in, but only after the protests reach a certain calculable high point.

That such a bland approach might help us explain the revolutions of 1989—or of 2011, for that matter—is highly disputed, not least because by focusing on the information strategies of social movements, such analysis inevitably pays short shrift to the dynamics of the state institutions they were opposing. As Steven Kotkin and Jan Gross, two distinguished historians of Eastern Europe, note about Lohmann's work, "Generalizing about social movements from the Communist experience can be hazardous because of the nature of the Communist state." Shirky, however, doesn't just generalize; he uses Lohmann's theory of information cascades to explain the political effects of "the Internet" everywhere: "the Internet" makes for better information signaling; as such, citizens should be expected to rebel more often. One of Shirky's pithy sayings—that "behavior is motivation that has been filtered through opportunity"—is as good a slogan that the bland theorists of rational-choice theory are ever likely to get.

How well does rational-choice theory explain political change? After several decades, the jury is still out, but its promoters have little to boast of. As Donald Green and Ian Shapiro note in their devastating critique of rational-choice theory—which also takes aim at Lohmann's work—its leading proponents "share a propensity to engage in method-driven research, and . . . this propensity is characteristic of the drive for universalism." In other words, since model building is their hammer and their only tool, the proponents of rational-choice theory see everything as a nail—and so they attempt to explain any kind of behavior, no matter complex or culturally specific, using the dry talk of incentives and opportunities. It's no wonder that Clay Shirky can explain the behavior of anorexic girls, open-source communities, revolutionaries in East Germany, and rebellious teenagers in Belarus through one clean theory of information cascades. It's a theory that can explain everything—but in its generality and disregard for details, it actually ends up explaining nothing. As Green and Shapiro point out, there's more to political behavior than just incentives and opportunities. In fact, "it may be shaped by enthusiasm for the collective objectives, attitudes toward leaders and prominent symbolic figures in the movement, and feelings of personal adequacy and obligation to participate." The choice of the explanatory model depends on what needs to be explained; it can't just follow from one's preference for building models or studying incentives and opportunities—even if digital platforms and technologies offer plenty of data on what one's opportunities and incentives may have been. To criticize Lohmann for her explanation of the 1989 protests or Shirky for his explanation of the political protests of the last few years is not to deny the importance of technology, let alone to question the need for protests, but to point out that another, richer, more intellectually stimulating way of discussing the same set of events is possible.

To quote Green and Shapiro again, rational-choice theory turns "a dispassionate search for the causes of political outcomes into brief-writing on behalf of one's preferred theory. If one is committed—in advance of empirical research—to a certain theory of politics, then apparent empirical anomalies will seem threatening to it and stand in need of explaining away." This is perhaps the best summary of what's so wrong with much of contemporary Internet-biased theorizing about politics. The models that Shirky and his disciples rely on, while nominally about "the Internet," do smuggle in a "certain theory of politics"—a theory of citizens responding to incentives and clinging together if they get the right signals and have the right tools—which is awfully simplistic to account for political developments in much of the world.

Nowhere does Shirky allude to the heavy intellectual baggage that comes with his methods; in fact, he just recasts Lohmann as a historian, so a theory of information cascades becomes something of a legitimate historical narrative rather than a reductionist model of human behavior. Any anomalies that do turn up—the findings that dictators are extremely smart in using the same technologies, or that people don't always respond to incentives, or that forces like nationalism and religion are exerting a profound and unpredictable influence on how people behave and are themselves transformed by technology—are simply dismissed as technophobic pessimism. In a true Hegelian dialectic spirit, Internet-centrism sustains itself through the binary poles of Internet pessimism and Internet optimism, presenting (and eventually consuming) any critique of itself as yet another manifestation of these two extremes. To challenge this ideology and this way of talking and thinking is to be immediately dismissed as too pessimistic or optimistic, as if no other type of critique were even conceivable. It's one of the hallmarks of Internet-centrism—at least as it manifests itself in the popular debate—that it brooks no debates about methodology, for it presumes that there's only one way to talk about "the Internet" and its effects.

Shirky's veneration of Ronald Coase's theory of the firm—and its accompanying discourse on transaction costs—may seem harder to dismiss, not least because Coase is a Nobel Prize–winning economist. References to Coase pop up regularly in the work of our Internet theorists; in addition to Clay Shirky, Yochai Benkler also draws heavily on Coase to discuss the open-source movement. There is nothing wrong with Coase's theories per se; in the business context, they offer remarkably useful explanations and have even helped spawn a new branch of economics. But here is the problem: thinking of a Californian start-up in terms of transaction costs is much easier than pulling the same trick for, say, the Iranian society. While it seems noncontroversial to conclude that cheaper digital technologies might indeed lower most so-called transaction costs in Iran, that insight doesn't really say much, for unless we know something about Iran's culture, history, and politics, we know nothing about the contexts in which all these costs have supposedly fallen. Who are the relevant actors? What are the relevant transactions?

In the absence of such knowledge about Iran, the natural reflex is to opt for the simplest possible model: imagine a two-way split between the government and the dissidents and then think through how their own transaction costs may have fallen thanks to "the Internet." This seems like a rather perfunctory way of talking about a rather complex subject. Cue Don Tapscott, a popular Internet pundit, proclaiming that "the Internet not only drops transaction and collaboration costs in business—it also drops the cost of collaboration in dissent, rebellion and even in insurrection." Okay—but is no one else in these countries collaborating or engaging in transactions? Is it just the dissidents? Are the dissidents united? Or do they all have different agendas?

Internet-centric explanations, at least in their current form, greatly impoverish and infantilize our public debate. We ought to steer away from them as much as possible. If doing so requires imposing a moratorium on using the very term "Internet" and instead going for more precise terminology, like "peer-to-peer networks" or "social networks" or "search engines," so be it. It's the very possibility that the whole—that is, "the Internet"—is somehow spiritually and politically greater than the sum of these specific terms that exerts such a corrosive influence on how we think about the world.

Hype and Consequences

Ahistorical thinking in Internet debates is too ubiquitous and persistent to be written off as ignorance or laziness. It's not that history books are not consulted because our Internet theorists are lazy; rather, it's that history itself is deemed irrelevant, for "the Internet" is seen as representing a distinct rupture with everything that has come before—a previously unreachable high point of civilization. Such "rupture talk"—an essential ingredient without which epochalism would be impossible—itself has a history. For example, University of Michigan historian Gabrielle Hecht sees similar themes and undertones in debates surrounding the advent of nuclear weapons and nuclear electric power in the 1950s, adding that both epochal discoveries were seen as marking "a historical break, the dawn of a new era—here, 'the nuclear age'—in which everything, everywhere, was forever different."

Under closer scrutiny, "rupture talk" appears everywhere in our Internet discourse. One can't think of a better example than the remark from Jonathan Zittrain at a 2011 conference on Internet governance in Toronto. Noting the challenges facing states, Internet companies, and their users, Zittrain asserted that there was a special reason for the audience to debate the issues of "the Internet," for, back in the day, "we wouldn't really have a conference here about electricity and the ways in which it could be used for good and evil." It's hard to think of a sentiment that better captures the naïveté of Internet triumphalism and the utter contempt in which it holds the history of technology.

The debates over electricity were, in fact, as dramatic and bizarre as the debates we are currently having about "the Internet," its democratic potential, and its effect on our brains. How else to explain the publication of a book like *The Silent Revolution, or the Future Effects of Steam and Electricity upon the Condition of Mankind*—in 1852!—which promised "social harmony of humanity" on the basis of a "perfect network of electric filaments." Or what to make of the fact that Patrick Geddes, Petr Kropotkin, and other nineteenth-century thinkers believed that electricity would usher in a brand-new age of neotechnics, where, to quote French historian Armand Mattelar, "town and country, work and leisure, brain and hand" would be reconciled? Or what to do with Nazi engineers like Franz Lawaczeck, a founding father of the National Socialist engineers' association, who believed that the Third Reich could promote small farms and businesses, thus encouraging a decentralization of society, by generating an abundance of cheap electricity? This is not to mention the complex and controversial history, itself full of protracted battles and rancorous debates, over the physical infrastructure that made electricity widely available. Only by papering over and suppressing such history can we see "the Internet" as unique and exotic.

It's not that our Internet thought leaders are insincere or inclined only to say things that will secure them better consulting projects— even though, occasionally, this seems like a factor. Rather, they themselves believe their own epochalist rhetoric. This, as we'll see later in the book, explains both the religious zeal with which they embark on and justify their quest to ameliorate the human condition as well as their lack of empathy for industries and institutions that are currently in crisis. Ruptures, after all, often involve sacrifices— or, as Clay Shirky likes to say, "it's not a revolution if nobody loses."

In order to be valid, any declaration of yet another technological revolution must meet two criteria: first, it needs to be cognizant of what has happened and been said before, so that the trend it's claiming as unique is in fact unique; second, it ought to master the contemporary landscape in its entirety—it can't just cherry-pick facts to suit its thesis. Under these conditions, very few of the contemporary declarations about the profound revolutionary impact of "the Internet" would survive close scrutiny. The examples are numerous, but perhaps one will suffice.

Like many other commentators on how the young people use technology, Don Tapscott and Anthony Williams, authors of

Wikinomics and its sequel, *Macrowikinomics*, argue that "the Internet" has produced an entirely new generation—the so-called digital natives. Tapscott and Williams find so much to love about these chaps! They are "bringing a new ethic of openness, participation, and interactivity to workplaces, communities, and markets." Moreover, "rather than being passive recipients of mass consumer culture, the Net generation spend time searching, reading, scrutinizing, authenticating, collaborating, and organizing (everything from their MP3 files to protest demonstrations)." They are "a generation of scrutinizers" who are "more skeptical of authority as they sift through information at the speed of light by themselves or with their network of peers." Best of all, "today young people are authorities on the digital revolution that is changing every institution in society."

How much of this is true? It's hard to say. Several studies show that, of all age groups, young people tend to be least informed about many aspects of digital culture. For example, a 2010 study that investigated what users know about online privacy found that "among all age groups, higher proportions of the eighteen–twenty-four-year-olds had the poorest understanding of the meaning of the privacy policy label and the right of companies to sell or share their data with other firms." As one of the study's authors put it, "The online savvy many attribute to younger individuals (so-called digital natives) doesn't appear to translate to privacy knowledge." In other words, it's not that young people don't care about privacy—they do—they just don't have the digital savvy that Tapscott and Williams attribute to them. These conclusions are echoed in a recent study from the European Commission that also found young people lacking in many digital competencies. A 2009 empirical study of students at five British universities found that "it is far too simplistic to describe young first-year students born after 1983 as a single generation. . . . [They are] not homogenous in [their] use and appreciation of new technologies and . . . there are significant variations amongst students that lie within the Net generation age band." But conducting such studies, of course, is not as sexy as musing on "the digital revolution that is changing every institution in society." The latter probably pays better, too.

Gutenberg in the Kingdom of Geekistan

If what we are witnessing today is not an "Internet revolution," does that mean the changes we are observing are trivial and unimportant? This, after all, is the charge that Internet cheerleaders levy against their opponents: the curmudgeons, we are told, must be blind, for they keep denying the importance of faster and cheaper communications, despite the self-evident benefits. Alas, these cheerleaders fail to notice that, while there is only one way to deny the importance of latest technologies, there are multiple ways to acknowledge it. A quest to tell a different story, composed of different characters and accents, requires no curmudgeonly passion to proceed.

Do historians of science who challenge the popular accounts of the scientific revolution deny that the discoveries of Newton and Galileo had something important to contribute to humanity? They certainly do not; instead, they acknowledge them in a different, subtler manner, pointing out that continuities between, say, seventeenth-century natural philosophy and its medieval predecessors were much more numerous than discontinuities. As historian of science Steven Shapin argues, "The past is not transformed into the 'modern world' at any single moment: we should never be surprised to find that seventeenth-century scientific practitioners often had about them as much of the ancient as the modern." Our contemporary framing of those changes as an event or series of events— as a well-contained "revolution" with start and end dates—is a relatively recent phenomenon; the very phrase "scientific revolution" was probably coined by philosopher Alexandre Koyré in 1939.

Or consider historians of medicine who refuse to entertain the notion that the numerous changes that happened in the science of bacteriology in the second half of the nineteenth century constitute a "bacteriological revolution"—still a popular term in the discipline. It would be silly to deny that important changes did happen in that period, but rejecting a label like the "bacteriological revolution" means acknowledging them in a different manner.

For example, historian Michael Worboys, writing of the supposed bacteriological revolution in 1880s Britain, identifies four interlinked changes often invoked to support its existence. Having closely studied evidence for all four of these changes, Worboys concludes that "historians have read into the 1880s changes that occurred over a much longer period, and that while there were significant shifts in ideas and practices over the decade, the balance of continuities and changes was quite uneven across medicine." Note that Worboys doesn't deny the importance of contributions made by Robert Koch or Louis Pasteur (well, "Pasteur" is probably more like it)—he just points out that the actual way in which these discoveries transformed the medical practice was much more convoluted; it was anything but predetermined or inevitable.

Such subtle accounts that seek to acknowledge important changes without falling into the epochalist mode are very hard to find in Internet studies. Perhaps it's time to turn the tables on Internet pundits; instead of having them explain "the Internet," we must try to understand why they explain digital technologies in this particular way, with constant invocations of "the Internet" and its inherent nature. Why do rupture talk and revolutionary rhetoric tend to displace all other forms of analysis? Why do we label old activities as new, imagine incompetent youngsters as possessing complete mastery over technology, and believe that nothing matches "the Internet" in terms of the complexity of the debate that it triggers? Isn't it time to inquire into what we are *not* talking about when the debate itself—that is, the issues it attends to and the questions it formulates—is constructed in revolutionary terms?

No one exemplifies the temptations and limitations of the rupture talk better than Clay Shirky, so perhaps it's worthwhile to return to his theories. Shirky sees the digital revolution everywhere, but it's especially pronounced in the media business. "When someone demands to know how we are going to replace newspapers, they are really demanding to be told that we are not living through a revolution. . . . They are demanding to be lied to," he declares. Revolutions, according to Shirky, are unpredictable—they can only be diagnosed, in real time. Hence, "the more serious you are about believing something is a revolution, the more you are confessing that you can't predict the future. That if it's a revolution it can't be predictable. And if it's predictable it can't be a revolution." It's a curious admission that insulates our techno-futurists from criticism. If they get things wrong—which they do all the time—they can write off such mistakes as the cost of doing business in our hyperrevolutionary times.

But Shirky, who also works as a consultant, knows the mantra of his trade: every crisis is to be recast as an opportunity. Thus, we hear that "nothing will work, but everything might. Now is the time for experiments, lots and lots of experiments." This, however, is Shirky the good cop—the one who thinks resistance is not futile. Shirky the bad cop, however, is not so sure and often succumbs to a weird form of digital fatalism, which borders on digital defeatism: "There is never going to be a moment when we as a society ask ourselves, Do we want this? Do we want the changes that the new flood of production and access and spread of information is going to bring about?" For Shirky the bad cop, everything has already been determined by the information gods; all we can do is accept the inevitable and enjoy the revolutionary ride.

These days there's so much anxiety in so many industries that Shirky, using his bad cop/good cop routine, provides just the right mix of flagellation and counseling. But something else makes his style of rupture talk so appealing. Oddly enough, it's his clever use of history—in a debate that is traditionally ahistorical—in order to establish some kind of equivalence between the invention of the printing press and the advent of "the Internet."

And it's not just fake history of East Germany, which is actually just rational-choice theory in disguise. References to the printing press are also ubiquitous in Shirky's writings. He dedicates several pages of his *Cognitive Surplus* to drawing an explicit analogy between Gutenberg's invention and the proliferation of social media. Elsewhere, he notes, "We're collectively living through 1500, when it's easier to see what's broken than what will replace it." He argues, "It is too early to tell whether the Internet's effect on media will be as radical as that of the printing press. It is not too early to tell that there is nothing that happened between 1450 and now that comes close."

But why not? Take the very opposite perspective—that "the Internet" changes nothing. As historian Marshall Poe puts it: "It's not much of an exaggeration to say that the Internet is a post office, newsstand, video store, shopping mall, game arcade, reference room, record outlet, adult book shop and casino rolled into one. Let's be honest: that's amazing. But it's amazing in the same way a dishwasher is amazing—it enables you to do something you have always done a little easier than before." This seems to downplay some of the structural changes that have happened in the last few decades, but it's not self-evident why the Shirky-style triumphalist explanation offers a more accurate interpretation than Poe's.

The shifts triggered by the proliferation of digital technologies must be investigated through a careful empirical and historical analysis; we can't just claim that some glorious event in the past— whether it's the invention of printing or the revolutions of 1989 or 2011—is functionally equivalent to the contemporary situation. Still, the idea that "the Internet" is the new printing press seems to have hijacked the public imagination. It's one of the core precepts of Internet-centrism. Thanks, in part, to Clay Shirky, Gutenberg's invention has now become one of the original myths of "the Internet"—never mind the more than five hundred years in between.

Two recent books—neither written by a historian—explicitly present Gutenberg as the geek extraordinaire. John Naughton, a technology columnist for the *Observer*, has penned a book with the self-explanatory title *From Gutenberg to Zuckerberg*. Gutenberg, we learn, "must have been an archetypal geek," who had to deal "with the early stirrings of venture capitalism, an experience at least as traumatic as anything encountered by Silicon Valley hopefuls five centuries later because it left him without ownership of the thing that he had created." Not surprisingly, Naughton concludes that "by looking in more detail at the transformations that printing brought about, we can perhaps get an idea of where we should be looking for the longer-term impact of the Net."

Another book in this vein is a Kindle single by Jeff Jarvis with the even more self-explanatory title *Gutenberg the Geek*. According to Jarvis, Gutenberg, "possibly the world's first technology entrepreneur," should be seen as "the patron saint of Silicon Valley, for he used technology to create an industry—perhaps the genesis of industrialization itself—and to improve his world." There's more: "Gutenberg—just like a modern-day startup—depended on exploiting new efficiencies, achieving scale, reusing assets, dividing specialized labor, and setting standards." In fact, "the parallels between his enterprise and those of Silicon Valley startups today is [*sic*] striking. He faced similar challenges and grappled with apparently timeless business dynamics. He, too, operated in a climate of disruption and, like his entrepreneurial descendants, caused profound change of his own."

Navigating the bogs of contemporary Internet hype, one has to be careful not to assume that such hype is itself unique to "the Internet." The printing press, for example, has long been useful to technology boosters—not least because we know how the print story ends: literacy, science, progress. Observe Daniel Boorstin, America's most overrated historian, writing in the late 1970s: "The democratizing impact of television has been strikingly similar to the historic impact of printing." Once Boorstin makes this dubious statement— have you watched television lately?—the rest follows quite naturally, with the kind of bombast that one could expect from Clay Shirky or Jeff Jarvis: "The era when television became a universal engrossing American experience, the first era when Americans everywhere could witness in living colors the sit-ins, the civil rights marches, was also the era of a civil rights revolution, of the popularization of protests on an unprecedented scale, of a new era for minority power, of a newly potent public intervention in foreign policy, of a new, more publicized meaning to the constitutional rights of petition, of the removal of an American President." The shorter Boorstin: move over, Martin Luther King Jr.—it was television, the natural successor of the printing press, that gave us the Civil Rights Act!

There may be other reasons why Gutenberg is in such high demand. Geeks and technologists have a very soft spot for the Protestant Reformation; the printing press plays an extremely important role in that narrative. Christopher Kelty, an anthropologist at the University of California, Los Angeles, who has studied geek cultures inside various open-source communities, has written brilliantly about this tendency in *Two Bits: The Cultural Significance of Free Software*. According to Kelty, many geeks, united by their common struggle against the Microsofts of this world, regularly exploit various usable pasts, myth-like stories that draw on historical events, not in order to remember the past but, rather, to make sense of the present and the future.

The story of the Protestant Reformation—with its allegorical battles between Catholic and Protestant churches, laity, clergy, and high priests and the accompanying images of control and liberation—is one such usable past. Kelly notes that "the Protestant Reformation makes for good allegory because it separates power from control; it draws on stories of catechism and ritual, alphabets, pamphlets and liturgies, indulgences and self-help in order to give geeks a way to make sense of the distinction between power and control, and how it relates to the technical and political economy they occupy." This is why, in many a geek debate, the state is recast as the monarchy, large corporations as the Catholic Church, start-ups and programmers as Protestant reformers, and the laity as "lusers" and "sheeple." Kelty believes that such stories are popular with geeks because they "explain a political, technical, legal situation that does not have ready-to-narrate stories."

From Bad Book History to Bad Blog History

But while Kelty's insights might explain why Gutenberg stories spun by Shirky and Jarvis appeal to technologists and geeks, it's still not clear why such stories are misleading or inappropriate or why they circulate beyond the Kingdom of Geekistan. Neither Jarvis nor Shirky is a historian, so in discussing the impact of the printing press—which they think is comparable to the impact of "the Internet"—both turn to the same source: Elizabeth Eisenstein's landmark two-volume study *The Printing Press as an Agent of Change*, first published in 1979. Without understanding the limitations of Eisenstein's highly disputed account of the "revolution" that followed the invention of the printing press, it's impossible to make sense of contemporary claims for the significance of "the Internet," not least because the stability that her account lends to "the Internet" makes her a favorite source of Internet optimists and pessimists alike (Nicholas Carr draws on Eisenstein's work in *The Shallows*). Much like with rational-choice theory, what many fellow scholars believe to be rather problematic scholarship is presented as universally admired and entirely uncontroversial. To use Eisenstein as our guide to "the Internet" is to commit to a very particular way of thinking about digital matters.

Drawing heavily on the work of Marshall McLuhan, Eisenstein argues that the importance of printing in triggering all the subsequent social transformations had not yet been sufficiently credited (hence she dubbed it the "Unacknowledged Revolution"). But while trying to do justice to the role of the printing press in history, Eisenstein embraces a rather limiting view of print media, over-emphasizing what she believes to be the inherent qualities of this technology: fixity (i.e., its ability to preserve texts that might otherwise get lost or badly damaged), ease of dissemination, and the tendency toward standardization. According to Eisenstein, the very technology of print endows texts with these new qualities—and the rupture is so significant that she elevates those qualities to the status of "print culture." The latter gives us the Reformation, the scientific revolution, the Big Mac, Steve Jobs, and LOLCats.

Many scholars have noted the limitations of Eisenstein's approach, which are extremely pertinent to the contemporary Internet debate. The first to ring alarm bells—in 1980, just a year after the book was published—was intellectual historian Anthony Grafton, who berated Eisenstein for pulling "from her sources those facts and statements that seemed to meet her immediate polemical needs." More problematic, in Grafton's view, was the fact that Eisenstein, in her quest to emphasize the radical nature of the break between the age of scribes and that of printers, minimized "the extent to which any text could circulate in stable form before mechanical means of reproduction became available." In other words, all these efforts to draw sharp distinctions between different cultures and ages smack of unabashed epochalism; many features of the "print culture" were in place—even if on a smaller scale—well before this culture sprang up out of nowhere.

More recently, literary scholar Mark Warner and historian Adrian Johns have offered much more devastating critiques of Eisenstein's account. Warner, in his *The Letters of the Republic* (1990), argues that the technology of printing should not be seen as lying outside of culture or history. It certainly didn't come equipped with its own "logic" or "nature"; the "inherent" characteristics identified by Eisenstein were hardly universal and were not there from the start. Wherever they did appear, these features were the product of complex negotiations and contingent historical processes, not the natural attributes of printing technology. "No hard fact of technology dictates what counts as printing," notes Warner. In a somewhat Oakeshottian vein, he adds, "We know what we mean when we talk about printing, but we know that because we are in a tradition; we have a historical vocabulary of purposes and concepts that gives identity to printing, and meaningfully distinguishes for us between books that have been impressed with types and those that have been impressed with pens."

Thus, Eisenstein's account holds only if one accepts a sharp separation between technology on the one hand and society and culture on the other—and then assumes that the former shapes the latter, never the other way around. The way Eisenstein inquires about the historical effects of print on society automatically brackets out the question of how society and culture made print what it is politically, materially, and symbolically. For Eisenstein, "print culture" just happens; it comes already prepackaged in its crustacean cage, its "inherent" characteristics intact and ready for immediate deployment. As Warner observes, by affording the print culture such a mysterious role—remember, she is a McLuhan disciple, after all—Eisenstein loses far more than she gains. "Politics and human agency disappear from this narrative . . . and culture receives an impact generated outside itself. Religion, science, capitalism, republicanism, and the like appear insofar as they are affected by printing, not for the way they have entered into the constitution and meaning of print in the first place."

Johns, writing in his *The Nature of the Book* (2000), is even more scathing. "[Eisenstein's] press is something 'sui generis' . . . lying beyond the reach of conventional historical analysis. Its 'culture' is correspondingly placeless and timeless. It is deemed to exist inasmuch as printed texts possesses some key characteristic, fixity being the best candidate, and carry it with them as they are transported from place to place. The origins of this property are not analyzed." As a result, notes Johns, Eisenstein tends to invoke the print culture or one of its characteristics to fill whatever gaps open up in her analysis or the history itself. Thus, Eisenstein's approach "identifies as significant only the clearest instances of fixity. It regards instances when fixity was not manifested as exceptional failures, and even in the successful cases it neglects the labors through which success was achieved. It identifies the results of those labors instead as powers intrinsic to texts. Readers consequently suffer the fate of obliteration: their intelligence and skill is reattributed to the printed page. To put it brutally . . . Eisenstein's print culture does not exist."

This is much more than an arcane debate between historians of the book. At stake here is how the history of the printing press—and of technology more broadly—should be done. Eisenstein's approach is to treat technology and its qualities as fixed, ahistorical, and unproblematic—and, by operating with such an impoverished notion of technology, to trace its effects on culture, society, and history. It's the same McLuhanesque approach that Nicholas Carr employs when he writes about "the Net" and compares it to "the book." Warner and Johns propose something quite different; instead of placing technology outside society, we can study how technology and society shaped each other, accounting for any local variations, tracing subtle shifts in the meanings that different communities attached to different technologies, exploring how those differences emerged, explaining how communities went about exploiting these technologies, and so on. This is not a matter of denying that the printing press matters—only of doing its history in a different, more informative and intellectually stimulating manner. It's an attempt to go beyond medium centrism—be it the book-centrism of Eisenstein or the Internet-centrism of Shirky—in order to achieve a richer, more accurate view of book history and Internet history.

As far as the contemporary debate goes, then, the discussion should focus on whether Shirky's Eisenstein-inspired account of "the Internet"—which is really an account of the presumed social effects of "Internet culture" rather than of the underlying physical infrastructure—is the best way to describe and acknowledge the role that these technologies are playing in the world at large. In other words, if we tried hard enough, we might find another way of talking about these technologies that would provide more nuance and not paper over important local differences.

Of course, Shirky and Jarvis show no sign that their accounts of "the Internet," for all their ostensible historicism, might ultimately be based on bad history. Both recast their critics as pessimists, conservatives, and curmudgeons, as people simply opposed to change—the most typical way in which Internet-centrism sidesteps criticisms of itself. Thus Shirky writes, "There is no intellectually coherent conservative position with regard to the printing press.

Most of the defenders of current culture don't even try to explain why it was OK that the printing press destroyed scribal production, but not OK that the internet threatens newsprint, or why a proliferation of new creators and experimentation with new forms was good in 1508 but bad in 2008. It is simply assumed that revolutions in the past were good but those in the future are bad." Of course, there is no coherent conservative position with regard to the printing press—this would also be an antiliteracy position—but as the numerous critiques of Eisenstein show, there are many alternative ways of talking about the printing press and its effects (one of Johns's many rejoinders to Eisenstein is titled "How to Acknowledge a Revolution"). If one doesn't see events described by Eisenstein as a "revolution," then perhaps one will also be less inclined to draw false equivalences between them and whatever is happening today.

Jarvis goes even further in recasting this important debate over how to talk about technology as a black-and-white, pessimism-versus-optimism battle, with the implication, of course, that anyone who suspects that Eisenstein-like accounts might be limiting our debate is out of touch with the modern world. Here is how he summarizes Adrian Johns's challenge to Eisenstein: "[Johns] accuses . . . Eisenstein . . . of giving too much credit to the printing press. . . . I'm a befuddled [*sic*] over the roots of the curmudgeons' one-sided debate. Why do they so object to tools being given credit? Are they really objecting, instead, to technology as an agent of change, shifting power from incumbents to insurgents? Why should I care about their complaints? I am confident that these tools have been used by the revolutionaries and have a role. What's more interesting is to ask what that role is, what that impact is." Jarvis's fundamental mischaracterization of Johns's critique of Eisenstein is only part of the problem. The Jarvis-Eisenstein view of the world presumes tools are fixed. They lie outside culture and history—an approach that characterizes much of Jarvis's writings about "the Internet" itself. Jarvis's contemporary revolutionaries invariably turn to "the Internet," but "the Internet" they find is unproblematic and unchanging, its democratic nature fixed in stone.

In presenting important methodological critique as technophobia, Jarvis and Shirky are doing their best to hide the fact that a very different debate about "the Internet"—one that wouldn't assume a revolution and wouldn't cut corners with clever buzzwords—is both possible and badly needed. Their notion of "the Internet" is far too broad, fixed, and abstracted from local context. This is the overlap between the Internet debate and the printing press debate. But there's also a crucial difference between the two: how the former debate is resolved will have far more influence on our future; its ramifications will extend far beyond the community of historians who have been battling with Eisenstein. Moreover, how we choose to resolve the unfolding Internet debate will determine how future historians will study it as well. Too much ink has been spilled in the last few decades to correct for Eisenstein's inaccuracies; we don't want future historians to take the same lengthy detour with "the Internet."

Recycle the Cycle

If Eisenstein's print culture is an example of how clumsily history can be appropriated to frame the present debate about "the Internet," the traffic occasionally goes in the other direction as well—as in when our Internet commentators start with contemporary anxieties and travel back in history to show how many of the modern debates associated with "the Internet" are themselves just a subset of much greater, longer debates about networks, information, and technology. There is nothing wrong with their mission per se—some might even argue that this is what history is for—but most such accounts are peculiar in that, in their quest to tell a certain story about "the Internet," they misrepresent and badly mangle the past, leaving us with an impoverished reading of history and a confused game plan for the future.

This should make us pause to ponder if Internet-centrism—whatever its own origins in bad history—might be nudging us to rewrite the history of other, pre-Internet periods with one simple purpose: to establish a coherent teleological account of how all other technologies paved the way for "the Internet" and how their own governance failed to embrace "Internet values" and may have delayed the arrival of this "network of all networks." This is the ideology of Internet-centrism at its purest: it suggests what kinds of questions we could and should be asking of the past. As an ideology, it has no need to dictate the answers, for we already know what we need to find in order to complete the grand narrative of "the Internet" itself.

A troubling example of what Internet-centrism does to history—in terms of both mangling the content and giving a second life to arcane, long-forgotten methodologies—can be found in Tim Wu's much-acclaimed *The Master Switch*. Wu, a legal scholar who coined the term "net neutrality," is a leading contributor to unfolding debates about "the Internet"; *The Master Switch* is his attempt to explore the history of other technologies—the telegraph, telephone, radio, cinema, television—and illuminate what those technologies can tell us about our current predicaments. This sounds like a noble mission, but anyone undertaking it should be aware of the immense difficulty of engaging with the past on its own terms. At worst, an attempt to illuminate the present by studying the past can turn into a fishing expedition, where the past becomes just a giant toxic aquarium, storing enough factoids and exotic characters to buttress any interpretation of virtually any contemporary trend or phenomenon.

Wu's argument in *The Master Switch* goes like this: There's something peculiar about information industries, for they tend to be dominated (and intellectually ravaged) by "information emperors"—Steve Jobs–like personalities who strive for absolute control. The dictatorial rule of such emperors and several structural qualities of their information empires usually lead to what Wu calls "the Cycle," which is the inevitable closing of the once open and innovative industries. It happens either because the information emperors are clever but ruthless businessmen or because they co-opt the government into giving them protection from competition. This is how we got Hollywood's studio system, which exercised unprecedented control over what films to make and what issues to censor; a closed telephone network, where AT&T banned users from plugging in their own devices, thereby potentially delaying the advent of "the Internet"; and, more recently, Apple's world of apps, in which a politburo sitting somewhere in Cupertino reviews and approves the apps it likes and deletes those it doesn't.

Wu's proposed solution to this problem is to prevent companies in the information business from integrating vertically—that is, to prohibit companies that create information from owning or creating infrastructure for its dissemination and vice versa. But the government's involvement would end there: Wu's reading of history suggests that government involvement has been mostly detrimental to the growth of information industries. His ideal is to keep both big government and big business out of the information industries; this, according to Wu, is how all successful information industries have developed, including "the Internet," and this is how it should be in the future. Amen.

This might seem like an appealing and elegant argument, but in reality it's just an attempt to come up with one of those "theories of everything." In this instance, "everything" is to be explained by a fixed set of concerns—in Wu's case, concerns over openness and innovation—that have come to dominate our thinking about "the Internet." First of all, Wu conveniently leaves aside those information industries—like book publishing—in which no dominant information emperor has emerged. The Cycle doesn't go there; it's too crowded. Curiously, one such emperor might emerge very soon—his name is Jeff Bezos, and he runs a small start-up called Amazon—but Wu himself seems to be enamored of Amazon and the price efficiencies it brings. Second, by limiting his history only to America—and why would "the Cycle," if it were real, unfold in America only?—he misses many foreign cases in which information emperors have done much good.

Wasn't André Malraux, France's powerful minister of cultural affairs under Charles de Gaulle and the godfather of New Wave cinema, one such emperor, albeit perhaps of a public-service variety? Zooming in on Malraux's career would reveal that the success of the French film industry in the 1960s was the direct consequence of the government's eagerness to subsidize risky low-budget films and support *maisons de la culture*, where such films could be shown. It's not a story of market-led innovation; quite the opposite. Information emperors don't have to be seen as evil (perhaps they don't have to be seen at all; Internet-centrism, in Wu's hands, has miraculously resuscitated the much discredited "great-man-of-history" style of narrating the past). Likewise, governments, despite the many conspiratorial suspicions that geeks harbor about them, can be powerful and benevolent players in the information industry.

One doesn't have to travel to France to see that; in fact, a more comprehensive look at the history of information empires in America reveals as much. As Paul Starr has shown in his devastating review of *The Master Switch* in the *American Prospect*, even a cursory look at the history of the post office—a communications network created by the government to foster free expression—is enough to disprove many of Wu's theories. The post office was conceived of as a monopoly, and it's been extremely successful in its mission. According to Starr, "The government didn't invite rival postal firms to compete; in fact, it created a monopoly. That monopoly, however, was conducive to free expression because of the policies Congress adopted, which subsidized the circulation of newspapers irrespective of their viewpoint and spread postal service throughout the country." But on "the Internet," no one likes monopolies— they smack of Microsoft and IBM—so this chapter of telecommunications history simply gets thrown overboard. Internet-centrism tolerates no competing hypotheses.

As Starr points out, had the US government followed Wu's dictum that "government's only proper role is as a check on private power, never as an aid to it," it "would not have created the Post Office or fostered the rapid development of newspapers, and American democracy would have suffered. More recently, the United States would not have developed the Internet or public broadcasting"—both of which required massive public financing. Such strong antigovernment sentiment—that it's always a parasite on innovation—is a recurring feature of the geek mentality, which is partly responsible for the disgust many geeks feel toward politics. As Starr notes, "Government policy, in Wu's distorted recounting, is mostly a record of regulatory capture and craven mistakes that Americans should be ashamed of—even though, strangely enough, the United States has for much of its history been a leader in communications, partly because of the constructive role government has played." Is it really that surprising, then, that a recent column on the technology site InfoWorld was titled "Why Politicians

Should Never Make Laws about Technology"? If geeks learn their history from Tim Wu, this sentiment follows quite naturally.

Methodologically, Wu's treatment of information industries is very close to Eisenstein's treatment of print culture: he starts by simply projecting the qualities he associates with "the Internet" back into the past and assuming that the industries and technologies he studies have a nature, a fixed set of qualities and propensities, then proceeds to celebrate selectively those examples that support those qualities and discard those that don't. So Wu starts with the hunch that the openness of "the Internet" is under threat, travels back in history to find trends that suggest all information industries have experienced similar pressures, and returns to the present to announce that history reveals that openness is indeed under threat on "the Internet."

That this is the very premise on which he starts his intellectual journey doesn't much matter in the end because such history has a very clear activist bend; the goal is not to understand the history of technology but to find enough historical arguments in order to—just like in Jonathan Zittrain's case—make "the Internet" live forever. Such Internet-centrism would be bad in itself, but it is also exerting a very unhealthy influence on technology and media history, where everything that transpired before "the Internet" is now reexamined according to its benchmarks. Historical accounts inspired by Internet-centrism are simply bad history, even if they occasionally make for effective policy advocacy on issues like net neutrality. That Internet-centrism makes us blind to this reality is a reason to worry, not celebrate.

***

So our survey of Internet-centrism paints a rather depressing picture. The very idea of "the Internet" has not merely become an obstacle to a more informed and thorough debate about digital technologies. It has also sanctioned many a social and political experiment that tries to put the lessons of "the Internet" to good use. It has become the chief enabler of solutionism, supplying the tools, ideologies, and metaphors for its efficiency crusades. Internet-centrism has rendered many of us oblivious to the fact that a number of these efforts are driven by old and rather sinister logics that have nothing to do with digital technologies.

Internet-centrism has also mangled how we think about the past, the present, and the future of technology regulation. It has erroneously convinced us that there are no other ways to talk about these issues without downplaying their importance. Internet-centrism has been tremendously helpful for activist purposes—it has rekindled (and occasionally created) geek religious movements that have been crucial to opposing government regulation of digital technologies. But what has been gained in activist efficacy has been lost in analytical clarity and precision. Internet-centrism's totality of vision, its false universalism, and its reductionism prevent us from a more robust debate about digital technologies.

Internet-centrism has become something of a religion. To move on, we need, as French media scholar Philippe Breton put it, "a 'secularization' of communication." Such secularization can no longer be postponed. We need to find a way to temporarily forget everything we know about "the Internet"—we take too many things for granted these days—roll up our sleeves, and work to ensure that technologies do not just constrain human flourishing but also enable it. The chapters that follow apply this secularized approach to contexts as different as politics and crime prevention not just to illustrate what happens once solutionism meets Internet-centrism but also to think through a more productive civic use of technologies so beloved by solutionists.

CHAPTER THREE

So Open It Hurts

"Owning pipelines, people, products, or even intellectual property is no longer the key to success. Openness is."
—JEFF JARVIS

"Radical transparency for firms and governments is not just a decision but a technological fact of life."
—DON TAPSCOTT

S unlight might be the best disinfectant, as US Supreme Court Justice Louis Brandeis famously said in 1913, but disinfectants, alas, are of little use to sunburn victims. As more of our personal information finds its way into easily accessible databases—an unfortunate consequence of ever-growing demands for more transparency, more sunlight, more disinfection—the risks of digital sunburn have substantially increased, while awareness of such risks seems still to be quite rudimentary. Although Internet-centrists like to imagine that Internet-enabled transparency will give us a more vibrant and responsible civic life, this is hardly a foregone conclusion. Once we abandon the notion of "the Internet" and start paying attention to individual digital technologies of which it is made, we are likely to discover a reality that is less stable.

Consider the plight of thousands of Californians who had donated money to Proposition 8, the ballot measure to ban same-sex marriage in the state. True, most of them are unlikely to win awards for their tolerance of diversity. But they should still be commended for expressing their political views—however parochial they might seem to their opponents—using the country's political system. Ballots not pogroms: that is how this country is supposed to work.

As is typical of other campaign-finance laws across America, California's Political Reform Act of 1974 stipulates that recipients of donations in excess of $100 must disclose the donor's name, address, and employer for the whole world to see. Well, perhaps not the whole world—not initially at least. When the act was passed in the mid-1970s, the lawmakers couldn't possibly imagine that such information might soon become easily accessible to anyone with a smartphone. The disclosures had to be made "public" in theory but not in practice: the hassle of finding those forms in some dusty, forlorn town hall archives had guaranteed them a life of practical obscurity.

Fast-forward to 2008. An enthusiastic computer virtuoso—whose identity remains unknown to this day—set up Eightmaps .com, a website that takes publicly available donor information about Proposition 8 and puts it on a Google map, placing a marker—along with the donor's name and occupation—next to the address. With these personal details out in the open, it doesn't take much effort to establish where these donors work and embarrass them in front of their coworkers. This is exactly what happened to a University of California college professor after he donated $100 to the Proposition 8 campaign. Not only did he become the target of several angry missives, but one such message was copied to his university colleagues and supervisors.

The obvious problem with sites like Eightmaps.com is that, in exploiting our rarely examined admiration of transparency, they can be used to suppress virtually any kind of political cause, regardless of where it falls on the liberal-conservative spectrum. It's naïve to think that this is just a conservative problem, as some pundits have maintained; now that sites like Eightmaps.com can be set up in a matter of minutes—both the data and the technological infrastructure are available for free—many other important social debates can be greatly affected. As one commentator put it, "Would you give to the Council on American-Islamic Relations, La Raza or Planned Parenthood if you thought right-wing goons would Eightmap you, as these left-wing goons have Eightmapped social conservatives?"

There are several responses to the civic challenges posed by sites like Eightmaps.com. One is to proclaim that "the Internet" has once and forever transformed how information is produced, accessed, and distributed. Short of establishing some kind of Internet kill switch, we have to accept rather than fight this new reality. As Internet pundits like Jeff Jarvis would advocate, we simply ought to upgrade our norms and learn how to live with this increased level of publicness, hoping perhaps that the disclosure benefits from total transparency will outweigh the costs imposed on civic participation. Those with a penchant for law might go further and propose that we tinker with the regulations in question. In the California case, this might mean raising the minimum on donations that require disclosure from $100 to, say, $1,000, or even removing the disclosure requirement altogether.

The hope (at times presented as a fact of life) that underpins both these responses—that is, to upgrade the norms or change the regulations—is that, to quote Lawrence Lessig again, "the network is not going away." Instead of disaggregating "the Internet," isolating its various parts and trying to understand which of them exhibit democracy-enhancing and democracy-suppressing tendencies, Lessig's preferred method is to treat "the Internet" as a unified whole, something with a logic and a spirit and not amenable to targeted policy interventions. Lessig wrote that "the network is not going away" while musing on various democratic challenges brought on by increased transparency, and his arguments are worth studying in greater detail, for they nicely show the blinkers that Internet-centrism could impose on otherwise immensely smart and talented thinkers.

In October 2009, the *New Republic* published "Against Transparency," Lessig's controversial essay (which Lessig expanded on in his 2012 book, *Republic, Lost*). The crux of Lessig's argument is that improved access to political information—which "the Internet" provides—is not enough to fix politics and may even break it, especially if this information, once misinterpreted, feeds into the numerous cynical and paranoid narratives that have become a permanent fixture of American public life.

Much of the information explosion of the last few decades, argues Lessig, has been uncoordinated. An army of "civic geeks" has been scanning government documents, building databases to store them, visualizing connections between donors and politicians, and honing many other forms of technologically mediated muckraking. According to Lessig, the kinds of inferences these geek initiatives have made possible—that is, that Company X has given money to Senator Y, which might explain her vote on issue Z—may be too simplistic and incorrect. Thanks to digitization, many more facts and factoids are widely accessible, but by themselves, they mean little; they need to be interpreted. But even then we may not have absolute certainty that Senator Y's vote on issue Z was really the result of Company X's donation. Simply publishing information about donations and insinuating that it can explain the voting record could serve only to make voters more cynical, as the information tidbits they see might fit into their already established opinions about corruption in politics.

All of this rings true, and Lessig is correct to emphasize that information has a social life, and the political context in which it is disseminated and interpreted matters a great deal. Publishing doesn't happen in a political vacuum, and most transparency schemes would only benefit from greater attention to the often deeply ironic unintended consequences that they bring about. Where Lessig goes astray, revealing his own Internet-centrism, is in his discussion of solutions to the problems he's just identified— yet another proof that the pathologies of Internet-centrism and solutionism are intertwined. According to Lessig, the problems that transparency poses for our political process are similar to the challenges that file sharing posed for the music industry and that sites like Craigslist posed for the classified sections of newspapers. Lessig's is a powerful narrative about power and control, and all these stories, because they are about "the Internet," are part of that narrative. Here is how he puts it:

> These troubles with transparency point to a pattern that should
> be familiar to anyone watching the range of horribles—or
> blessings, depending upon your perspective—that the Internet
> is visiting upon us. So, too, does the response. The pattern is
> familiar. The network disables a certain kind of control. The
> response of those who benefitted from that control is a frantic

effort to restore it. Depending upon your perspective, restoration seems justified or not. But regardless of your perspective, restoration fails. Despite the best efforts of the most powerful, the control—so long as there is "an Internet"—is lost.

For Lessig, "the Internet" is like a force of nature—perhaps like a hurricane—"visiting" all sorts of "horribles" upon us. We shouldn't resist, only cut our losses. Thus, the music industry shouldn't have gone after platforms like Napster—this, for Lessig, is anti-Internet—and the newspaper industry shouldn't complain about sites like Craigslist or Google News or hide their stories behind paywalls for exactly the same reason. Instead, the music industry should perhaps be saved by a flat consumer tax on culture, and newspapers should be turned into nonprofits. Why does Lessig think that these solutions are good? Well, because they have "the singular virtue of accepting the architecture of the Internet as it is, and working out how best to provide the goods we need given this architecture." It is in this context that Lessig's quote about "the network . . . not going away" appears. Close scrutiny of the quote in context, however, reveals how easily Lessig's brand of Internet-centrism mutates into hopeless technological defeatism: "But the network is not going away. We are not going to kill the 'darknet' (as Microsoft called it in a fantastic paper about the inevitable survival of peer-to-peer technologies). We are not going to regulate access to news, or ads for free futons. We are not going back to the twentieth century."

In the context of challenges induced by transparency, Lessig proposes that it would be better to tinker with the laws and embrace publicly funded elections so that citizens wouldn't even entertain the notion that politicians might be bought off. The reasoning that makes Lessig opt for the legal rather than the technological solution is of particular importance here: the network is sacred and permanent, so any tinkering with its nodes is out. However, Lessig's essay reveals a certain disingenuousness about what actually constitutes "the Internet" that he is writing about (perhaps it's not accidental that Lessig himself writes of "an Internet" in scare quotes). When Lessig writes of the need to accept the "architecture of the Internet," one might be led to believe that he's actually talking about the physical infrastructure—this is, after all, what "architecture" means most of the time. But nothing about the physical infrastructure of "the Internet" dictates whether the *New York Times* should run a paywall or whether Google News should pay newspapers a fee for aggregating their stories. These may be stupid proposals—even though the paywall, despite all the naysaying from our Internet gurus, seems to be working fine for the *New York Times*—but their supposed "stupidity" does not derive from their inherent incompatibility with the "architecture of the Internet." To suppose that "the Internet," like the Bible or the Koran, contains simple answers to how we should regulate access to news or music or "ads for free futons" is to believe that it operates according to laws as firm as those of gravity.

Ironically, this is the position that Lessig the academic has made a career out of opposing. But Lessig the activist and public intellectual has no problem embracing such a position whenever it suits his own activist agenda. As someone who shares many of the ends of Lessig's agenda, I take little pleasure in criticizing his means, but I do think they are intellectually unsustainable and probably misleading to the technologically unsavvy. Internet-centrism, like all religions, might have its productive uses, but it makes for a truly awful guide to solving complex problems, be they the future of journalism or the unwanted effects of transparency.

It's time we abandon the chief tenet of Internet-centrism and stop conflating physical networks with the ideologies that run through them. We should not be presenting those ideologies as inevitable and natural products of these physical networks when we know that these ideologies are contingent and perishable and probably influenced by the deep coffers of Silicon Valley. Instead of answering each and every digital challenge by measuring just how well it responds to the needs of the "network," we need to learn how to engage in narrow, empirically grounded arguments about the individual technologies and platforms that compose "the Internet."

If, in some cases, this would mean going after the sacred cows of transparency or openness, so be it. Before the idea of "the Internet" hijacked our imaginations, we made such trade-offs all the time. No serious philosopher would ever proclaim that either transparency or openness is an unquestionable good or absolute value to which human societies should aspire. There is no good reason why we should suddenly accept the totalizing philosophy of "the Internet" and embrace the supremacy of its associated values just because its cheerleaders believe that "the network is not going away." Digital technologies contain no ready-made answers to the social and political dilemmas they create, even if "the Internet" convinces us otherwise.

Bad for the Databases, Good for Democracy?

In 2010 Manuel Aristarán, a young programmer from Bahía Blanca, a town in southern Argentina, used free, open-source tools to build an innovative website called Gasto Público Bahiense, which loosely translates as "Bahia Blanca's Public Expenditures." Aristarán's site was subversive in its simplicity: it pulled spending data already available on the municipality's website and presented it in straight-forward visualizations that made it possible to discern spending patterns. Finally, citizens could trace how much money went to individual contractors or determine whether education or transportation ate a greater share of the municipality's resources.

The country's nascent open-government-data movement had good reason to celebrate. It's not that this data wasn't available before—it was—but to get it, users had to perform individual searches for every item. This was not exactly hard work, but anyone who wanted to see the big picture would find it tedious; few citizens bothered as a result.

The celebrations, it turned out, were short-lived: a year after Aristarán's site was launched, the municipal government redesigned its website. This would normally be good news, but the redesign was a much more ambitious affair than the usual invasion of shiny buttons and flashing banners. The municipality also tweaked access to its databases; now those who wanted to access its data had to prove they were human by filling in a CAPTCHA (you have prob-ably encountered CAPTCHAs when opening a new e-mail account or leaving a blog comment; you are usually asked to enter hardly legible text that computer scripts supposedly cannot read). Thus, while anyone could still access the data and even copy it from the municipality's website, computer scripts—which had allowed

Aristarán to feed the data into Gasto Público Bahiense—were no longer of any help.

The geeks, of course, were enraged. David Sasaki, an open-government activist who documented this episode on his blog, called it "a major step backward for open government in Argentina." As it happens, several other Argentinian activists were contemplating using Aristarán's software to set up similar sites for their own cities, but they eventually decided against it as the system was too dependent on the whims of municipalities and the activists preferred to work with officials rather than present themselves as adversaries (in retrospect, this was a very wise move). But, to return to Sasaki's criticism, does it matter that the redesign was a "a major step backward for open government"? Does a step backward for open government also mean a step backward for Argentinian politics or democracy? Has the municipality committed the deadly sin—at least in Lawrence Lessig's cosmology—of not "accepting the architecture of the Internet as it is"?

It might seem that the answer to all these questions is a resounding yes: more open government is better for politics, and inserting artificial barriers between users and government portals is very much an anti-Internet, antinetwork move. Before jumping to conclusions, though, let us not forget that the Bahía Blanca case is just one of many possible instances of enacting "openness from below"; it just happens that the main protagonist is a noble-minded geek with no political agenda.

But imagine a more sinister scenario. Suppose that Aristarán's elaborate charts, as well as the aggregate statistics they rely on, are likely to be hijacked by some populist and media-savvy movement that seeks to cut funding to schools and shift all that money to, say, a nearby rum-making factory or simply to spend it on some annual celebration, and the government knows it is too weak to resist such pressure. In these circumstances—hardly alien to the tumultuous political culture of Latin American twenty-five years ago—it seems reasonable that the interests of "open government" should defer to those of preserving democratic government, with all its messy and universally detested compromises and evasions. An inefficient democracy is always preferable to a well-run dictatorship. If all these

conditions hold, allowing humans to see the numbers while ex-
cluding computer scripts seems like a reasonable compromise.

This is not to say that Bahía Blanca, with or without Aristarán's
website, was on the verge of a coup; far from it. But nor does it
imply that the threat of a coup is the only legitimate excuse for tinkering with the accessibility settings of the municipal website. If
the authorities did indeed overreact, the only legitimate way to
criticize their response would be to evaluate it from the perspective
of demands imposed by local Argentinian politics. In other words,
it shouldn't matter whether their actions lived up to global and
supposedly neutral standards of "open government"—a term that,
in the hands of activists like Sasaki, is suffused with Internet-centrism
even though it never mentions the word "Internet."

Whether the actions of the Bahía Blanca municipality posed
a threat to Lessig's "never going away network" should be an even
lesser concern. Of course, the solution was technological, and if
one rigorously follows Lessig's logic, it did go against the "network"
and its spirit of openness and transparency. But so what? Why is
this a bad idea, especially when its impact on the network itself
seems so trivial? Why would a nontechnological solution—of the
kinds that Lessig proposed in response to the newspaper crisis or
music piracy—be preferable here?

One can imagine that the Argentinian authorities could have
tweaked the laws (or their interpretation of the laws) and simply
stopped publishing the spending data altogether. This, however,
would surely be a worse outcome for democracy than publishing
such data in the limited humans-only format. Of course, to do
nothing and simply let Aristarán continue with his site might be
an appropriate response as well, but this conclusion must be arrived
at after some extensive empirical analysis of the local politics, not
simply assumed based on how well the proposed solution matches
"the spirit of the Internet." This spirit is a powerful myth concocted
by overzealous legal activists, and the sooner we bury it, the better.
Whatever its usefulness for activist purposes—and the goals of
many such campaigns have been anything but laudable—this myth
of a singular, interconnected, and fragile network also constrains
our imaginations and ties our hands in responding to very real

problems that have emerged as various data platforms have become interconnected and easily accessible.

Escaping the Double Click

Liberated from this myth of a singular network, we can regain numerous policy options we thought we had lost to Internet-centrism. If we are lucky, we might even find ways to address challenges posed by sites like Eightmaps.com without necessarily sacrificing the genuine opportunities for transparency that have indeed opened up in the last few decades. Deborah Johnson, Priscilla Regan, and Kent Wayland—respectively, an ethicist, a privacy scholar, and an anthropologist—offer some excellent interdisciplinary first thoughts on how this can be done in their fascinating 2011 article "Campaign Disclosure, Privacy and Transparency." As one might glean from its title, the article investigates the social and political consequences of making various campaign disclosure records—very much like those exploited by the developers of Eightmaps.com—available online.

The authors' key insight is that the new electronic systems that mediate access to such forms—from online databases to search engines—are anything but the unproblematic and highly predictable purveyors of information that we often take them to be. These platforms actually transform and modify the information they carry; it's one of the few cases in which Marshall McLuhan's famous dictum that the medium is the message is actually worth heeding, at least partially, for it forces us to confront the information infrastructure that gets us the information we want. There is a certain shallow attitude toward such infrastructure—an attitude that French philosopher Bruno Latour calls "double click"—that treats communication and the production of knowledge as relatively uncomplicated and frictionless affairs that could happen without mediators like databases and search engines. As regular computer users, we have become used to the idea that information can appear effortlessly in our browsers in a matter of clicks; how it gets there from the original source—on what proverbial cloud does our e-mail reside?—and what happens to it in the process is often far more interesting than the actual content of whatever it is we are clicking. But, alas, we rarely bother to investigate such minutiae.

In a similar vein, information systems that mediate our access to campaign data are not like transparent glasshouses but, rather, more like houses of mirrors. "Instead of [allowing] others to see what is happening inside . . . they pull data about people and institutions into a house of mirrors in which the observer can 'see,' at best, a partial construction—a mediated glimpse—of what those being watched are doing." Thus, our new infrastructure affects the information that travels through it in at least four ways. The two that are most relevant for us here are what the authors call "bouncing"—which occurs whenever information collected for one purpose, like a person's reflection in a house of mirrors, is used for another purpose on another site—and "highlighting and shading"—whereby some pieces of the disclosed information take on unintended, disproportionate roles in defining the person's reputation and hiding other, more pertinent pieces, much like how the reflection in a house of mirrors distorts various aspects of a person's body.

Eightmaps.com is a straightforward example of "bouncing"—campaign disclosure forms were not envisioned to feed data into vigilante sites—but "highlighting and shading" is a bit trickier to grasp. Suppose you once gave money to an election campaign, and this information was duly posted online on the associated website. Eventually, by way of "bouncing," this information finds its way to a popular aggregator like The Huffington Post, which hosts a section on campaign donations. As The Huffington Post is very smart about its search engine optimization strategy—it writes clever headlines that secure it higher results on Google—its links tend to appear near the top of Google search results for many queries. Thus, anyone googling your name will see, as the first or second link in Google's search results, The Huffington Post's minipage about you—which contains nothing but your campaign contributions.

Consider the plight of law professor James Gardner, which he himself documented in a recent article. Gardner donated money to various campaigns, and The Huffington Post culled this information from the website of the Federal Election Commission (FEC). While the first result for his name is his faculty page at the institute where he teaches, scrolling down the first page of results usually reveals the Huffington Post entry. Gardner is not too worried that some nutty supporter of the candidates he opposes will get angry with him. Rather, he is concerned about his ability to do his job properly—that is, teach. As it happens, Gardner teaches constitutional law, a politically loaded subject, and students might dismiss their professor's scholarship if they think that it's driven by ideology. "I take great pains in this course to maintain an appearance of ideological and partisan neutrality, and I am convinced that it heightens my effectiveness for a very wide range of students." Maintaining such neutrality is no longer an option as Gardner's political identity can be discovered on page one of his search results.

But imagine that Gardner had made only one donation in his entire life and quickly forgotten about it, disengaging from politics to the extent that his friends described him as "apolitical." The tight (albeit informal) relationship between Google and The Huffington Post all but assures that anyone searching for his name would be tempted to believe otherwise, for his political "side" would be blown out of proportion and "highlighted," while other, more pertinent parts of his personality were "shaded."

How does this new taxonomy of "bouncing" and "highlighting" help us deal with some of the unintended consequences of highly networked and easily available information platforms? Unlike Lessig, with his fanatical dedication to the religion of Internet-centrism, Johnson, Regan, and Wayland believe that a different configuration of the technological infrastructure would produce a different outcome. Campaign-finance disclosure records posted online could be "read-only" so that, while accessible on the FEC website, they would not be easy to download or reproduce elsewhere. This, of course, is very similar to what the Argentinian bureaucrats did; such measures might reintroduce some of the practical obscurity that is now under threat.

Another way to fight "bouncing" is to make the published data harder to find or at least to try to ensure that anyone searching for it ends up on the FEC website, which has fewer incentives to shade and amplify information than commercial publishers. Or one can think of ways to "tie" database fields together so that highlighting and shading particular aspects of information by "untying" them becomes problematic. Or—the unthinkable!—one can explore ways to limit the influence that The Huffington Post, abetted by Google, has on one's reputation (some legal scholars have even proposed the radical step of giving users the right to respond to search results about them). Or one might impose expiration dates on campaign-finance data, letting it self-destruct, say, five years after the election. If the data carries a "self-destruct" code that recreates the expiration date in every new instance of republication, it might even help deal with third-party sites like The Huffington Post.

Why hasn't any of this happened? Johnson, Regan, and Wayland speculate it's because the free circulation of donor data nicely fits within the broader intellectual assumptions we make about the importance of transparency in politics. This rings true, but the dominance of Internet-centrism in debates about privacy and regulation may be an even more pertinent factor. Our inaction is not just the result of our fetish for transparency—it's also the direct result of our fetish for "the Internet." Ironically, in addition to sanctioning the hideous ideology of "solutionism," with its never-ending quest for solutions to often nonexistent problems, Internet-centrism is beginning to block our ability to think of effective technological solutions to problems that do exist. Solutions are not assessed based on their merits but rather on how well they sit with the idea of a free, open, transparent "network" and its "architecture." This is the other, darker side of epochalism: while new solutions are generated because we think that we are living in unique and exceptional times and anything Internet-incompatible ought to be swept away, we also believe that whatever problems "the Internet" presents ought to be dealt with in a manner that won't affect "the Internet."

From Sunburn to Solar Power

The contrast between the two approaches—between a willingness to roll up our sleeves and tinker with "the Internet" and Lessig's technological defeatism—is striking. Granted, Lessig is trying to solve a somewhat different problem; his real target is cynicism in our political culture, not the gradual erosion of privacy or the chilling effect that sites like Eightmaps.com have on public life. Lessig doesn't even see flag bouncing—the easy migration of information from its original source to third parties—as something to worry about. But many of his other concerns—especially the possibility that citizens might draw incorrect inferences from the political information they encounter online—do overlap with those related to highlighting and shading, even though he never actually uses those terms.

These problems won't magically go away even if America opts for publicly funded elections—Lessig's preferred solution—for our digital houses of mirrors are built of much more than just election data. The digitization of court records, for example, offers a similar, if not more formidable, challenge. If you agree to serve as a witness in a mildly controversial case, you probably do not expect that this item of information will also be at the very top of search results for your name on Google, courtesy of The Huffington Post's search engine optimization algorithms.

This problem has attracted considerable interest—and concern—from many scholars. Peter Winn, a law professor at the University of Washington School of Law, warns that the availability of such information online might make many parties to the judicial process less eager to cooperate. "When participants start getting burned or hurt after disclosing their sensitive information to the court, when the information is used for other purposes than resolving the dispute, litigants, witnesses, and jurors are going to be less and less inclined to tell the truth in the first place," he notes. Joel Reidenberg, another cyberlaw luminary, shows that the problem of highlighting and shading is something to wrestle with in this context as well: "If information about individuals is extracted from court filings and exploited through data mining or combined with additional information acquired from data brokers, from other public databases or from other publicly available information, the original context is lost and the data mining leads to the development of behavior profiles on individuals, to stereotyping." "In effect," cautions Reidenberg, "by making all this information about the citizen so transparent, the public does not really know what happens to their personal information and, ironically, the accuracy of the information describing individuals can be compromised through out-of-context compilations and profiling."

A 2012 study in *Maryland Law Review* investigates how the privacy interests and rights of everyone involved in the legal system can be balanced with the social benefits of providing easier public access to court records. Technology, as it happens, can be of great help in reaching this objective, but only if designers of the information systems are prepared to impose some constraints on and grant selective access to various parties based on the privileges those parties are entitled to. The data might still be available online, but instead of everyone seeing everything, it's more like everyone sees something. Thus, note the authors, "a policy with a default to redact from a publicly accessible record the names of all non-parties, including members of juries, witnesses, and those inadvertently implicated through the case, which may have been practically impossible in the past, becomes quite routine with the technical tools available."

This, of course, would be bad for Internet openness, as well as for the Huffington Posts and Googles of this world—not to mention the well-being of the "network"—but why should their well-being alone set the course of public policy? Or why should we opt for purely legal solutions that, in trying not to violate the openness of the network, might actually lead to even less overall openness, as files that might otherwise be published online in redacted form are suddenly confined to physical court archives? Why should the defense of some vague Internet values distract us from caring about balancing values that actually matter? (And "balancing" is the right word here; we can't have it all.) And would the "network" really get hurt if we experimented just a little?

It's striking that Lessig, who earned his reputation promoting the idea that there are four distinct modes of regulation—technology (or code), law, markets, and norms—would be so reluctant to consider how technology can be enlisted to solve some of the thorny problems triggered by the increasingly digitized and networked status of our information infrastructures. Internet-centrism seems to provide very convenient defeatist narratives for almost all social problems: if some proposed technological solution didn't work with file sharing, then it certainly won't work with newspapers or court records. Why? Because all three have an "Internet" angle, and in true Internet-centrist fashion, everything that has an "Internet" angle is suddenly seen as governed by Internet rules and objectives. Everything becomes interconnected; everything is part of an "Internet ecology"—that dreaded metaphor so beloved by theorists of cybernetics. Eventually, nothing that involves even a basic manipulation of how online technologies function is permitted.

And, then, of course, there is the uncomfortable truth that all of the technical solutions proposed to mitigate the consequences of our newly found openness—putting data in "read-only" mode, blocking search engines from indexing sensitive data, attaching expiration dates to files—closely resemble what the entertainment industry expects from Silicon Valley as part of its own war on online piracy. For advocates like Lessig, to accept such techniques as reasonable mechanisms for dealing with increased transparency would be tantamount to endorsing Hollywood's favorite tool kit. In addition, accepting some technological solutions in one context while rejecting them in another might puncture the view of a unitary, singular "Internet," where certain solutions are discarded on purely ideological grounds.

Hence, all these technological fixes are currently rejected without much by way of empirical investigation of their efficacy; they are snubbed for going "against the grain of the Internet" and violating the "remix" or "read/write" spirit that Lessig associates with Internet culture in much the same doctrinaire manner that print scholar Elizabeth Eisenstein associates fixity and standardization with that of the printing press.

Thus, we get curious statements like "The network is not going away," as if the network were indeed like gravity. In reality, the network is not going away because Lessig has spent a good decade giving hundreds, if not thousands, of talks to convince everyone that the "network" should not be tinkered with and that its remix-inducing features should be preserved and respected. This was very effective in opposing Hollywood's demands—some of which were, in fact, excessive—but such a way of thinking, in which the "network" becomes a giant abstract concept that includes both the fifteen-year-old making cat videos and the Argentinian government municipality tinkering with its website, is not a helpful way of navigating our way out of the intellectual maze we are in.

Why, one might ask, should the local politics in Bahía Blanca make sacrifices so that a fifteen-year-old in Palo Alto can remix cat videos without going to jail? This, in essence, is what Internet-centrists like Lessig demand. I'd be the last person to want fifteen-year-olds to end up in jail for piracy, but I also think that we need to find better, more persuasive ways of making that case—ways that would have no need for the simplistic truths of Internet-centrism and wouldn't shy away from tinkering with the technologies we build just because doing so would go against the grain. To refuse to tinker with and care for the technological infrastructures we have built is to succumb to an impulse far worse than the technophobic ambition to shut them down or the Internet-centrists' ambition to always preserve "the Internet" as it is.

We don't deal with sunburn by refusing to sunbathe. But nor do we accept it as inevitable and campaign for laws that ensure better, faster, cheaper sunburn treatment. Instead, we tinker with technology—buy sun lotion and put up an umbrella—and get on with life. Despite Brandeis's admonition about disinfectants and the promises of green energy, most of us have not fallen for the weird ideology of "sun-centrism," which sees technological interventions as illegitimate simply because they help us manipulate the effects of sunlight, exploiting them in some cases and neutralizing them in others. We can have both solar batteries and sunglasses, sun creams and blinds, greenhouses and air conditioning: to assume that either somehow impinges on the "architecture of sunshine" or contradicts its spirit of enlightenment and disinfection is ridiculous. Of course, you might counter, we can break "the Internet," and climate change aside, we cannot "break" the sun; thus we should treat "the Internet" with care and elevate it to a unique status. This, I argue, is the root of the delusion: "the Internet" that can be all but shattered by a trivial change on a website in Argentina is not worth defending; it's a myth—and quite a damaging myth at that.

When Transparency Hurts

It's hard to say which is worse: Lessig's unconditional surrender to "the Internet" or the blind enthusiasm of his fellow geeks, who, by reading too much into "the Internet," embrace the most extreme solutionist mind-set and become convinced that its arrival gives them the right—perhaps even the duty—to promote transparency in all walks of life, never stopping to inquire into the darker, less explored side of transparency crusades. In their universe, transparency can only deliver—it can never take anything away.

British transparency theorist David Heald draws a useful distinction between transparency as an intrinsic value, as an end in itself, and transparency as an instrumental value, as merely a means to some more important goal, like accountability. Thus, writes Heald, "the 'right' varieties of transparency are valued because they are believed to contribute, for example, to effective, accountable, and legitimate government and to promoting fairness in society." This means, among other things, that there are also "wrong" varieties of transparency, which might lead to populism, thwart deliberation, and increase discrimination. It's hard to believe that when Vladimir Putin orders workers to install Web cams at polling stations across Russia, his invocation of transparency rhetoric serves functions other than legitimizing his own stay in power by pretending that Russian elections are even more democratic and transparent than those of Russia's Western critics (the trick here, of course, is to find ways to rig the elections while on camera—not exactly a very challenging task for Russian bureaucrats).

In Germany, the Pirate Party—the newcomers to the country's political scene who run on a platform of Internet-centrism—have received harsh criticism from other parties for aspiring to publicize deliberations inside the Council of Elders, a high-level deliberative body tasked with managing the Bundestag's internal affairs. This would certainly be in the interests of transparency—holding it to be an intrinsic value—but what would it do to the quality of deliberations inside the council? Evidence from other institutions does not support the Pirates' case. In 1993, the Federal Open Market Committee (FOMC), a unit of the Federal Reserve System that is primarily responsible for setting America's monetary policy, gave in to pressure from Congress and began releasing transcripts of deliberations that preceded committee votes (until then, FOMC released only individual votes of committee members and summary minutes of meetings). A victory for transparency? Perhaps—but the new requirements may have also significantly affected the quality of debate. A 2008 study compared levels of dissent voiced before and after the new transparency requirements and found that "Fed policymakers appear to have responded to the decision to publish meeting transcripts by voicing less dissent" with some of the chair's proposals.

This may be explained by committee members trying to anticipate the impact of their deliberations on their careers and images and mitigating them accordingly, which may actually undermine honest debate about policy. Critics of the Federal Reserve System know very well that transparency can be politics by another means and thus have paralyzing effects on the Fed's ability to function. No wonder, then, that Fed bashers like Ron Paul keep demanding more and more audits of its policy making, even when the Fed points out that these are likely to force it to spend more time on fighting off political attacks and to distract it from economic policy.

Recent research in cognitive science and psychology shows that concerns over accountability and transparency greatly affect our decision-making process. How does the quality of our decisions change if we are held accountable for them? In a 1999 study, Jennifer Lerner and Philip Tetlock found that as long as decision makers do not know the views of those who will scrutinize their decisions later on, they will engage in "preemptive self-criticism" and soul-searching—most likely, a positive development. But if the views of the audience are indeed known, then decision makers are likely to engage in some "attitude shifting" and to bring their publicly stated views and decisions in line with what the audience expects. With the proliferation of social media and various data-mining techniques for detecting public opinion in the smallest of clusters, we can no longer expect that politicians and other decision makers will not try to conform to their own interpretations of the vox populi.

Another set of studies in psychology has found that, having stated our initial position publicly, we are less likely to change our minds through subsequent deliberations, as we want to be seen as consistent decision makers. James Madison voiced that concern in the context of deliberations at the 1787 American Constitutional Convention, writing that "had the members committed themselves publicly at first, they would have afterwards supposed consistency required them to maintain their ground, whereas by secret discussion no man felt himself obliged to retain his opinions any longer than he was satisfied of their propriety and truth, and was open to the force of argument." In other words, a quest for transparency has costs; occasionally, those costs could be far more significant than the expected benefits, and there is often no good reason to sacrifice the quality of deliberation in the name of making it more transparent.

The relationship between transparency and trust is also quite complicated. Philosopher Onora O'Neill has been an especially perceptive observer of how various transparency schemes might erode—rather than strengthen—trust. In O'Neill's view, fostering trust is a much more important public objective than fostering transparency, and if the latter undermines the former, perhaps we should curb our enthusiasm about what the world of networks and databases has to offer. O'Neill writes that "increasing transparency can produce a flood of unsorted information and misinformation that provides little but confusion unless it can be sorted and assessed. It may add to uncertainty rather than to trust. . . . Transparency can encourage people to be less honest, so increasing deception and reducing reasons for trust; those that know that everything that they say or write is to be made public may massage the truth."

This is where the distinction between transparency as an intrinsic and an instrumental value is particularly important. When we seek to increase or decrease transparency in some aspect of our public or private lives, we should do it not because we value transparency (or, for that matter, opacity) as such but because transparency promotes or undermines other, higher goods. The fact that digital technologies can make it easier to subject more elements of our lives to external scrutiny is not an argument in favor of more transparency. Caring for the well-being of the imaginary "network" so dear to Internet-centrists should never be seen as a higher good than, say, the project of fostering trust.

To think otherwise would be to let some amorphous concerns over the well-being of our means determine the very ends that we ought to be pursuing. Solutionists, as you might remember, assume problems rather than investigate them; armed with the idea of "the

Internet," they are assuming very particular problems in a particularly Internet-centric way. "The Internet" can increase transparency? Fine, this means that transparency is important and is worth pursuing in its own right. This could work wonders as a strategy to legitimize "the Internet" and cement its reputation as a transparency-boosting medium, but it doesn't necessarily work as a prescription for smart reform, which requires a thorough empirical investigation into the world of politics.

Such an investigation is likely to reveal that citizens—that is, real citizens who live and breathe, not the imaginary automatons of rational-choice theory—may not actually desire more transparency in politics or have the bandwidth to take advantage of it. As John Hibbing and Elizabeth Theiss-Morse show in *Stealth Democracy: Americans' Beliefs about How Government Should Work*, their landmark study of actual beliefs and aspirations that Americans have about how the country's democracy should function—as opposed to what political theorists imagine those beliefs and aspirations to be—most citizens are not interested in making political decisions themselves or providing input to those who do or even knowing the intimate details of the decision-making process. Rather, Americans want what the authors call "stealth democracy," whereby democratic procedures (much like stealth aircraft such as B-2 bombers) do exist but are not visible to the public on a routine basis.

It's a fascinating thesis, but its application to transparency is of most interest to us here. Hibbing and Theiss-Morse caution that exposing citizens to how the government works is not likely to make them feel any better about politics, for politics is not something they are necessarily interested in to begin with. Thus, they argue, "we should not look to new ways of exposing people to every nook and cranny of the decision-making process as a solution to people's negative views of government. People do not need and do not want to be satiated in politics."

Occasionally, such satiation can even be a hindrance to politics. Hibbing and Theiss-Morse compare the practice of keeping roll-call votes, which have traditionally been part of the public record, to that of calculating attendance rates, which publications like *Congressional Quarterly* have begun doing relatively recently.

Now that the numbers are out there, a politician's less-than-sterling attendance record is likely to feature in negative ads from his or her contenders in the next election. However, as Hibbing and Theiss-Morse point out, "the difference between a 100 percent attendance record and a 95 percent attendance record is invariably a smattering of inconsequential quorum calls." All of a sudden, politicians can no longer make decisions about how to balance their obligations, and politics as a whole suffers as a result. Thus, write *Stealth Democracy*'s authors, "members would be doing something much more beneficial to the greater good by remaining in their offices or committee rooms, meeting with constituents, studying, or discussing issues with fellow committee members. But the pressures of publicity force them to dash off to vote on every non-issue, no matter how foregone the conclusion."

This is an apt illustration of how the merits of transparency "solutionism"—regardless of whether it's based on cutting-edge databases and visualizations or pen and paper—cannot be evaluated separately from the nature, tempo, and constraints of the field in which it's to be applied as a remedy. The same transparency solution would have very different effects in constituencies where negative advertising is allowed than in those where it isn't. It would be a mistake for transparency enthusiasts, of which there are quite a few in geek circles, to disregard the subtle differences and indeterminacies that politics introduces into their magnificent and abstract schemes to improve the world.

But it's not just politics that suffers once transparency is recast from an instrumental value into an intrinsic one; many other institutions have experienced similar pressures. Michael Power, in his classic study on the rise of "the audit society," points to two troubling consequences of auditing—in the context not just of corporations but of public institutions also—both of which are likely to accompany the quest for more transparency. The first, which Power dubs "decoupling," can be filed under the "perversity" part of Albert Hirschman's "perversity-futility-jeopardy" triad. Think of politicians or business executives who, facing increased pressure to document everything they say, return to their secret confines and opt to communicate verbally so as to avoid putting anything on paper. Arguably, in such a case, demanding more transparency might produce less. Or they do the opposite and pursue a response known as "snowing," whereby they generate so much data of such poor quality that they effectively make it impossible to understand what is really going on. Thus, actual performance becomes decoupled from the artificial performance captured by audits and transparency schemes. Those might offer us the illusion of objective and unproblematic "double-click" access to "truth," but in reality they often introduce their own incentives to circumvent transparency. This insight is hardly novel; Jean-Jacques Rousseau, in *Discourse on Inequality* (1754), was already complaining that "books and auditing of accounts, instead of exposing frauds, only conceal them; for prudence is never so ready to conceive new precautions as knavery is to elude them."

Power also points to a second unintended consequence of transparency, which he dubs "colonization." This maps nicely onto the "jeopardy" part of Hirschman's triad, so that the will to improve, pursued blindly, ends up corroding other important values. The requirement to strive for a perfect attendance record now that the attendance statistics are closely watched by reporters and one's political opponents fits under this category. Anyone who has watched the popular crime series *The Wire* knows what colonization does to organizations: police forces start chasing the wrong criminals to improve their statistics and thus improve a mayor's electability, while schools concentrate all their efforts on improving test scores, even if children learn much less as a result. Of course, the growing public fascination with standardization and quantification shares as much blame here—we can't fault transparency alone for such trends—but the quest for transparency as a worthy end in itself, with little to no regard for what the practice being made transparent is all about, does create the right conditions for these problems to flourish. And it doesn't much matter whether such transparency is produced by professional auditors or amateurs armed with an Internet connection.

The Perils of Information Reductionism

The Audit Society was published in 1997, but the audit temptation has arguably only gotten worse since. The problem is that, now that digital technologies allow us to collect and store data on the cheap, it might be tempting to skip the complex philosophical and empirical analysis that is essential to analyzing the purposes transparency and opacity serve in a given context. However, it would be incorrect to put the blame squarely on the transformations in the new technological environment, for, as already noted, one can easily imagine how such a technological environment could be built differently, without automatically genuflecting before the gods of transparency and the "network." Thus, we also need to explain the attitudes and ideas that sustain this technological environment, allowing it to quietly expand even further, while presenting all these developments as inevitable, permanent, and natural.

Internet-centrism and solutionism feed on Enlightenment-era attitudes toward the liberating power of information. More information is always presumed to be better than less; having more ways to analyze the same piece of information is always preferable to having fewer ways. Legal scholar Julie Cohen calls this set of attitudes "the information-processing imperative" and argues that it gives rise to a mind-set that equates information gathering with a "single, inevitable trajectory of forward progress."

Technology companies have long understood that our Enlightenment-era pro-information bias works in their favor. This is one reason they are perceived as doing something far nobler than the rest of corporate America; unlike ExxonMobile or McDonald's, Google is in the enlightenment business—and that in itself entitles it to different treatment. Google knows this too—hence its mission "to organize the world's information and make it universally accessible and useful." This mission betrays no awareness that perhaps some information, even if it's in the public domain already, shouldn't be organized or "made useful." Questions of ethics—of whether it's right or wrong to organize information and increase its usefulness—are never posed. Instead, Google is preoccupied solely with questions of efficiency, for it presumes—and given our Enlightenment bias, rightly so—that few could challenge its ends.

In his final book, the late Tony Judt spoke of the dismal "discursive shift . . . towards economics" that had taken over the public debate in the late 1970s. "Intellectuals don't ask if something is right or wrong, but whether a policy is efficient or inefficient. They don't ask if a measure is good or bad, but whether or not it improves productivity," lamented Judt. He continued, "The reason they do this is not necessarily because they are uninterested in society, but because they have come to assume, rather uncritically, that the point of economic policy is to generate resources." Judt wasn't writing of Silicon Valley, but its preoccupation with questions of efficiency over those of morality is hard to deny. In the latter case, it's not the abstract resources of economic theory but information being generated (it's hardly surprising that Google has a chief economist on its staff). As long as information is produced and processed efficiently, the legacy of the Enlightenment is believed to be in good hands.

The problem with Silicon Valley's quest to organize the world's information (Google is only one of the many culprits here) is that it tends to succumb to the worst excesses of "information reductionism"—a tendency to view all knowledge through the prism of information that sociologist Nikolas Tsoukas faults for assuming that "a set of indices" can "adequately describe, to represent, the phenomenon at hand." The quest to organize the world's knowledge cannot proceed without doing at least some violence to the knowledge it seeks to organize; making knowledge "legible," to borrow James Scott's phrase, is tricky regardless of whether a totalitarian government or a Silicon Valley start-up does it.

According to Tsoukas, information reductionism thrives whenever humans start thinking of ideas as autonomous objects that can be exchanged between the sender and the recipient in their original form, without any distortion that might be introduced by the communications channel or the nodes doing the sending and the receiving. It's the ultimate double click: ideas are seen as completely independent not just of the infrastructures that transport them but also of each other. This is a very naïve view of how humans and institutions communicate. Once popular with theorists of cybernetics, it was all but forgotten but is now enjoying an intellectual renaissance of sorts thanks to the epochalist claims of Internet-centrists.

Legal scholar Mark Fenster has argued that "at its core . . . transparency theory takes the form of a classic, linear model of communication that posits a simple process of information transmission from a source to an intended audience via the medium of a message." Such shallow and one-dimensional cybernetic interpretation of communication blinds transparency enthusiasts to, as Fenster puts it, "the modern government's sprawling, often incoherent bureaucracy; the slippery nature of 'information'; the elusive and frustrating capacities of the public; and, ultimately, the difficulties of the communications process itself." In reality, alas, information uncovered by various transparency inquisitions rarely exists in the objective, virgin state that information reductionists imagine. Thus, as Fenster argues, "any 'message' that government information comprises is produced and only exists within a political and regulatory framework that shapes its creation and only circulates within a mediated environment that reshapes it in the process of making it available." The flawless and perfect communication process assumed by cybernetics simply doesn't exist.

Another critical fallacy that underpins information reductionism is its belief that an item of information can come into existence on its own, in a fully autonomous and independent fashion, without first involving an act of human interpretation. As linguist George Lakoff argued long ago, information presupposes a purposeful subject. That Americans, on average, spend two years of their lives struggling with thirst might be an accurate description of reality (it isn't), but it becomes information only when someone—perhaps Coca-Cola—starts actively looking for it. As Tsoukas points out, "To reduce something to allegedly objective information and then treat that information as if it was [*sic*] an adequate description of the phenomenon at hand, is to obscure the purpose behind the information, a purpose that is not made explicit in the information as such."

To put it in simpler terms, all attempts to measure and describe, say, the openness of a government already start with some basic, even if implicit and invisible, model of what governments are and what they ought to be. To fully understand whether promoting government transparency in a particular context is a worthy undertaking, we need to make these models—that is, the underlying theoretical assumptions about what could and should be measured—explicit.

We should resist the temptation to view such models as natural and objective stand-ins for the phenomena they are measuring or making transparent. As recent work in anthropology and sociology shows, only by suppressing the inherently unstable, subjective, and controversial nature of what we are making transparent can we reduce it to information that can be manipulated, optimized, and tinkered with. This temptation will undoubtedly increase as social-networking sites, search engines, and mobile phones allow us to generate or collect even more information. Reductionism in itself is not bad and can even be intellectually liberating—as long as we find a way to remind ourselves constantly about what is being reduced and what parts of reality are being shed off in order to zoom in on a particular indicator or model of politics.

Openness and Its Messiahs

Perhaps some of the worst problems of information reductionism could be avoided if only the solutionists' transparency vocabulary didn't brim with ambiguous terms. Appeals for "transparency" no longer look problematic once solutionists start to talk about "openness." It's bad enough that our cultural and intellectual heritage makes us view those concepts as worth pursuing in their own right. Solutionists—especially those of the geek persuasion—regularly develop and consume their own myths about how "openness" contributes to progress and success, which only adds to the confusion.

It might be tempting to view this openness fetish as originating in communities promoting open-source software. But according to Chris Kelty, the UCLA anthropologist who studies geek cultures, there is not much agreement about the value of openness—about whether it's worth pursuing as its own end or only instrumental to some higher goods—even in geek circles. As Kelty points out, "Open tends toward obfuscation. Everyone claims to be open, everyone has something to share, everyone agrees that being open is the obvious thing to do—after all, openness is the other half of 'open source'—but for all its obviousness, being 'open' is perhaps the most complex component of Free Software." Thus, as we have already noticed with the transparency rhetoric, it is never quite clear whether being open is a means or an end.

As a result, notes Kelty, there is no geek consensus on the merits of openness at all. "Is openness good in itself, or is openness a means to achieve something else—and if so what? Who wants to achieve openness, and for what purpose? Is openness a goal? Or is it a means by which a different goal—say, 'interoperability' or 'integration'— is achieved? Whose goals are these, and who sets them? Are the goals of corporations different from or at odds with the goals of university researchers or government officials?" So, if Kelty is to be believed, the community that has done the most to infuse technology debates with respect for "openness" is itself torn about its merits and meanings.

Our Internet debates, in contrast, tend to be dominated by a form of openness fundamentalism, whereby "openness" is seen as a fail-safe solution to virtually any problem. Instead of debating how openness may be fostering or harming innovation, promoting or demoting justice, facilitating or complicating deliberation— the kinds of debates we are likely to have about the uses of openness in the messy world that we live in—"openness" in networks and technological systems is presumed to be always good and its opposite—it's quite telling that we can't quite define what that is—always bad.

This Manichean tendency to view every technological issue in open-versus-closed terms leads to almost religious celebration of companies that embrace openness for tactical purposes and use it to their own advantage. The tactic here is once again very similar to what Elizabeth Eisenstein did with attributing qualities like fixity to "print culture." Openness is presumed to be an "Internet" value, so whenever it can be read into the actions of "Internet ambassadors"—the Googles and Facebooks of this world—it's invoked to explain their success. Then, this success is itself invoked to prove that "openness" is indeed an Internet value. This explains why our Internet theorists are never wrong.

Take Tim Wu, who celebrates Google, an arch-open company in his view, as if it were a divine creature. In *The Master Switch*, Wu writes that Google's birth was "audacious" and its ideas are "vaguely messianic." Its founders—perhaps like Jesus?—"style themselves the challengers to the existing order, to the most basic assumptions about the proper organization of information, the nature of property, the duties of the American corporation, and even the purpose of life." Google represents nothing less than the "utopia of openness," which aims to "plant the flag of openness deep in the heart of the telephone territory" and never dares to "resist or subdue the Internet's essential structure" (remember: resistance is futile; the network, with its "essential structure" and "architecture," is not going away). It is "the greatest corporate champion of openness," the leader of the "openness movement," and "the incarnation of the Internet gospel of openness." Wu's Google is also one of the "apostles of openness"—very much unlike Steve Jobs, the "apostle of perfectibility"; former FCC chairman Reed Hundt, who is a "competition apostle"; and former Time Warner CEO Gerald Levin, who is "an apostle par excellence of [the] control model."

Gospel, messiah, apostle, incarnation—Wu writes as if he had some kind of spiritual awakening while visiting Google's temple in the holy city of Mountain View. Oddly enough, he never mentions that he himself has been an (unpaid) adviser for Google and helped greatly to shape its early strategy on, well, "openness." (In 2007 Chris Sacca, then head of special initiatives at Google, told *Businessweek*, "Tim helped us catalyze a strategy. . . . He's a singular force in this space. You're just seeing the start of what he's going to accomplish.") Such disclosures make it difficult at times to tell whether Wu is praising Google's genius or his own.

Wu's effervescent analysis portrays Google's predilection for openness as natural and inevitable; its executives simply saw the structure of the network and couldn't resist it. It's the print debate all over again, with Google's "openness" being just a by-product of "the Internet's essential structure," much like fixity, in Elizabeth Eisenstein's account, was just a manifestation of some eternal quality of print. That Google may have played a role in shaping or maintaining this very structure of "the Internet," positioning it as "essential" rather than "contingent," that it might have spent a lot of marketing and think tank money to be seen as an "evangelist of openness," that it surrounded itself with an army of "openness" evangelists—none of this enters Wu's analysis (but then, he's one of the evangelists in question).

Compare Wu's messianic pronouncements with a very different kind of empirical analysis that makes no a priori assumptions about Google's divine status in the pantheon of openness gods and instead tries to explain what that status does for Google and how it has been achieved. Kimberley Spreeuwenberg and Thomas Poell, two Dutch academics, conducted a detailed study of how Google has created, managed, and positioned the work done within the Open Handset Alliance—a consortium of eighty-four companies that develop software and hardware for Google's Android platform. Google and its executives never miss a chance to brag that their approach to mobile platforms, unlike that of Apple, is dominated by "openness."

Yet, as the Dutch study points out, "open" in Open Handset Alliance might be something of a misnomer, for "it is highly questionable whether Android, in the light of the ideals of open source, can in fact be characterized as an 'open source project.'" Thus, the authors note, "while Android was publicly introduced as a project aimed at preventing any 'industry player to restrict or control the innovations of any other,' within the Android ecology Google clearly has control over the other involved actors."

This control is achieved through tricky software licenses and restrictive technological specifications for how software and hardware should be designed, all of them wrapped in the stale language of "compatibility." Furthermore, leaked communication between Google and one of the hardware partners in the Open Handset Alliance illustrated that Google can exercise control over its partners in a nominally "open" ecosystem by tinkering with various carrots and sticks, for instance, by allowing well-behaving partners to acquire certain features ahead of the competition or threatening to disable certain features for partners that do not behave.

Likewise, since Google's interest in expanding into mobile handsets is partly driven by its desire to remain a powerful player in advertising, the company has no strategic interest in following the "open-source" playbook down to the last rule. Instead, it picks the rules it wants to follow based on its own corporate strategy (e.g., it won't let independent developers code the operating system itself, as this might weaken its control over development and, indirectly, its utility for harvesting user data—which would make achieving its advertising goals much harder).

This is not unexpected, but instead of celebrating what Google does for openness, it's important to investigate what openness does for Google. As one perceptive observer noted of Google, "'Openness' and 'connectedness' are not the principles on which it is organized so much as the products that it sells." Why this market for openness and connectedness exists, how it relates to other tenets of Internet-centrism, and how this market is manipulated: all of these are not the kinds of questions one is likely to ask when the occurrence of "openness" on "the Internet" is presumed to be natural and unproblematic. To use the dreadful language of social theory, ideas like "openness" and "the Internet" are constructed—and mutually co-constructed at that—and they do not drop down on us from the sky. Unless we are prepared to trace how such construction happens, not only will we write bad history of technology, but we will end up with extremely confused policy making that treats contingent and fluid phenomena (which, of course, might be worth defending) as permanent and natural fixtures of the environment.

Thus, while Internet-centrists assume that Google is "open" by default, their opponents—let's call them Internet realists—assume that Google does a lot of work to look "open" and investigate what that work involves. While Internet-centrists tend to be populist and unempirical, Internet realists start with no assumptions about the intrinsic values of "openness" and "transparency"—let alone their inherent presence in digital networks—**and** pay particular attention to how these notions are involved **and m**anifested in particular debates and technologies. While Internet-centrists believe that "openness" is good in itself, Internet realists investigate what the rhetoric of "openness" does for governments and companies— and what they do for it.

Who Put "Open" in "Open Government"?

The ambiguity of a term like "openness" in part explains the confusion, excitement, and disappointment generated by various recent campaigns to promote "open government" and liberate "open-government data." Of course, no one quite knows what these campaigns are about: put five "open-government" experts in a room, and you'll get six different opinions (and god knows how many tweets). This confusion hasn't prevented governments from declaring their commitment to this vague ideal. President Barack Obama's first directive in office was to require executive branch agencies to make information available online in open formats. In September

2011, the United States and seven other governments even signed a multilateral "Open Government Declaration," which, after noting that "people all around the world are demanding more openness in government," committed the signatories to the timely release of high-value data in open formats.

The definitional complexity may not be immediately obvious, but it's immense. Harlan Yu (Princeton) and David Robinson (Yale) have offered perhaps the smartest analysis of the sources behind this confusion. With a term like "open-government data," it's not obvious whether we are talking about data that could make governments more "open"—in the sense of reducing secrecy—or about innocent data that could be liberated from some obscure government archive where it has languished, with little to no effect on the political process and secrecy as such. Does "open government" refer to making train schedules and city maps more accessible? Or does it refer to publishing data that could embarrass politicians and end careers?

If it's just about maps and trains, there are few reasons to be excited (or worried) about the political consequences of this supposed reform. If this is all there is to open-government data, Obama perhaps could have chosen something more symbolic as his first directive. If, however, the scope of "open-government" reform is much wider, then we need to scrutinize its logic much more closely. After all, a shift toward "open government" that only seeks to put train schedules on our iPhones need not imply or trigger any changes in the level of political freedom. For all we know, since the Nazis had an enviable train system, they'd be all for making their train data universally accessible.

As Yu and Robinson argue, "A government can provide 'open data' on politically neutral topics even as it remains deeply opaque and unaccountable. The Hungarian cities of Budapest and Szeged, for example, both provide online, machine-readable transit schedules, allowing Google Maps to route users on local trips." Isn't such data both open and governmental? It surely is. But it may not make Hungary any more democratic. In fact, while the country has been nudging ever closer to authoritarian rule, it might have also emerged as one of the successes of "open government."

This, as we have seen earlier, is a common problem with Internet-centrism: it redefines a term like "open" in accordance with the supposed values of "the Internet," only to feed it back into the public conversation, with few people noticing that the meaning of "openness" has shifted. Of course, if North Korea were to publish its train schedules, no one would mistake it for a democracy. But in borderline cases like Hungary, there is a risk that governments will exploit our new fetish for digital openness to present themselves as far more democratic, transparent, and legitimate than they actually are. When better train maps earn you points on human rights and secrecy indexes, something must be profoundly wrong with our scoring system.

Even democracies cannot resist such temptations. Just look at America: under Obama's direction—nominally the era of "more open and transparent government"—his administration aggressively prosecuted leakers and whistle-blowers, expanded the government's classification program, and even forbade reporters from disclosing the names of federal workers championing its open-government work!

However, there is another reason to be cautious. Obama's open-government directive included Data.gov, the repository of high-value agency information. "High-value," like "open government," is an extremely ambiguous term; as far as the Obama administration was concerned, it also meant data sets that "improve public knowledge of the agency and its operations" or "create economic opportunity." In other words, "high-value" doesn't necessarily mean "inducing transparency or accountability." So, predictably, the agencies flooded Data.gov with all sorts of irrelevant data—no one can question the zeal with which American bureaucracy can produce paperwork—while some of this data was actually already available online. What exactly has this done for transparency?

Yu and Robinson studied some of the declarations and manifestos of the "open-government lobby," the assortment of well-meaning technology activists who helped shaped the Obama administration's early work on "open government." In spelling out eight important principles behind open-government data—timeliness, completeness, freedom from license restrictions, and so on—the activists were primarily concerned with technicalities of the disclosure process and raised few questions about politics; as a result, note Yu and Robinson, "an electronic release of the propaganda statements made by North Korea's political leadership . . . might satisfy all eight of these requirements, and might not tend to promote any additional transparency or accountability on the part of the notoriously closed and unaccountable regime."

Just as it's very important to understand what "openness" does for Google, it's important to understand what "openness"—and the broader narrative of "the Internet" that feeds and enables it—is doing for governments that preach the virtues of "open government." As already noted, both "transparency" and "openness" have their limits and, taken too far, can easily reduce the democratic process to a sham. Of course, in small doses—especially in problematic regimes with few other checks on government—increased transparency and openness would never hurt. But if we don't subject highly ambiguous terms like "open government" to closer scrutiny, if we don't cleanse them of Internet-centrism and the double meanings it generates, we might unwillingly allow some governments to claim progress where there is none, while stalling more important reforms.

Nathaniel Heller of Global Integrity, an international anti-corruption NGO, has been suspicious of the Kenyan government's immense enthusiasm for "open government." Of course, the bureaucrats don't like all of it—government secrecy is not on the agenda—so they opt for uploading the least damaging databases instead. As Heller points out, "It's much cooler (and frankly less politically controversial) for any government to put government health databases online . . . than it is for the same government to provide greater transparency around the financing of political parties in the country." As long as the open-government solutionists are so preoccupied with the means—with the quality of standards and databases—and not the actual content that these standards and databases seek to disseminate, little progress will occur.

In the United Kingdom, the coalition government has also been extremely enthusiastic about the promise of "open government." David Cameron and his ministers have even commended the work of "armchair auditors," promising to publish many of the government data sets online (which, to their credit, they did). At the same time, the government has launched an attack on freedom-of-information laws—Cameron complained that they are "furring up the arteries of government"—while flirting with the idea of charging for any such requests that members of the public file with the government. There have also been some rhetorical attempts in conservative circles to use the rise of "armchair auditors" as an excuse to cut funding for professional investigators at the BBC. It's worth asking whether Cameron's hip credentials when it comes to "open-government data" will make it easier for him to wage war on freedom-of-information requests, if only because he's already seen as a champion of "openness." It would be a pity if the well-meaning solutionists and geeks end up getting caught in crossfire.

But even Cameron's embrace of "open-government data" in its most unproblematic variation may not be just about efficiency. Adding to the ambiguity, "open government" might just be a euphemism for "small government." After all, its rhetoric is continuous with some ideas of an older administrative philosophy of new public management, one popular during the Margaret Thatcher era, that argued for maximizing the efficiency of public institutions by turning them into consumer-oriented for-profit entities while outsourcing supervisory, quality-checking, and auditing functions to third parties, of which citizens are now just one emerging part. When everything can be run like Wikipedia, why bother with big government? It's far better to rely on Cameron's "big society," starve the public sector, and expect that the "armchair auditors" will be as effective as the Leveson Inquiry.

Noticing the disturbing similarity between the rhetoric surrounding "open government" and new public management, governance expert Justin Longo speculates that the former might be just a Trojan horse for the latter; in our excitement about the immense potential of new technologies to promote openness and transparency, we may have lost sight of the deeply political nature of the uses to which these technologies are put. Thus, notes Longo, "support for more open data aims at building coalitions of citizen consumers who are encouraged to use open data to expose public service decisions, highlight perceived performance issues, increase competition within the public sector, and strengthen the hand of the citizen as customer." Alas, if any of the geeks working on "open-government" projects in the United States are concerned about the political uses of their movement's rhetoric, they are hiding these concerns really well.

Open-data schemes are born into a world torn apart by numerous political struggles; it's not surprising, then, that the warring factions find ways to exploit such schemes to their own advantage. Building data sets and hoping that they will be used for "good" purposes only is no longer enough. The data sets enter a world inhabited by real people, who have many competing concerns and aspirations. Solutionist schemes that have no way to understand and act upon those concerns and aspirations are unlikely to deliver on their sweet promises.

Take maps that visualize crime statistics across different neighborhoods; "open-government" enthusiasts are very passionate about them. In theory, their logic is sound. The maps could help the police to be more effective and identify problematic areas; they could also help the public make more informed decisions about where to go and live. The reality, not surprisingly, is a bit more complicated. While better crime statistics might help some people avoid buying properties in dodgy neighborhoods, they would also make it harder for other people to sell those properties. As a result, those who already live in these dodgy neighborhoods might be less willing to report crimes in the first place. In fact, in a 2011 survey by an insurance company, 11 percent of respondents claimed to have seen an incident but chose not to report it, worried that higher crime statistics for their neighborhood would significantly reduce the value of their properties. David Hand, a professor of mathematics at Imperial College, notes that "the open data initiative ignores such feedback effects—[that is,] that the very act of publishing the data will influence the quality of future data." Perhaps we want data to be open—but not too open.

In India, recent digitization of land records and their subsequent publication online, while nominally an effort to empower the weak, may have actually empowered the rich and powerful. Once the digitized records were available for the whole world to see, some enterprising businessmen discovered that many poor families had no documents to prove ownership of their land. In most cases, this was not the result of some nefarious land grab; local culture, with its predominantly oral ways of doing business, pervasive corruption, and poor literacy, partly explains why no such records exist.

In other words, the fact that no claims of ownership are available online may be the result of a poorly designed and selective digitization effort; it doesn't necessarily mean that the current occupants have no claims to the land. Of course, having discovered that many current dwellers cannot actually prove their ownership, some of the richer families have hired lawyers and aggressively pushed to kick them out. In hindsight, this could have been prevented by embracing a different way of recording and accepting claims to the land (e.g., accepting old family photographs or maps tracing ownership in addition to official land titles) or by selectively limiting access to what kinds of data can be studied by third parties with no obvious need to examine it.

The point here, as with most open-government schemes, is not that information shouldn't be collected or distributed; rather, it needs to be collected and distributed in full awareness of the social and cultural complexity of the institutional environment in which it is gathered. Sometimes preserving the social relations that enable that environment to exist—for example, to make policing of crimes possible—might require producing data that is only half transparent or half accessible, much like in the Argentinian example. Such a compromise is not the end of the world, and it's not a capitulation of "openness" and certainly not of democracy, for democracy thrives on compromise and the art of reconciling seemingly irreconcilable interests. The tyranny of openness—the result of our infatuation with Internet-centrism—must be resisted.

CHAPTER FOUR

How to Break
Politics by Fixing It

> *"We are not politicians.*
> *We made our revolution to get the politicians out.*
> *We are social people. This is a social revolution."*
> —Fidel Castro

> *"What we're offering is not a program, but an operating system."*
> —Marina Weisband, then political director
> of the German Pirate Party

> *"Wikipedia is just the beginning . . . we can learn from*
> *its success to build new systems that solve problems*
> *in education, governance, health, local communities, and*
> *countless other regions of human experience."*
> —Steven Johnson

Internet-centrism may be a relatively new phenomenon, but it already boasts a political party of its own: the Pirates. While they still have a very marginal presence in North America, the Pirate Parties have already made substantial noise in Europe, even dispatching a number of their representatives to the European Parliament. The Pirate movement emerged in Sweden and initially focused almost exclusively on reforming copyright and patent law.

Gradually, however, it has expanded beyond these two issues, taking on issues like anonymity, privacy, and freedom of expression.

All of this would have been laudable had the Pirates not lumped these issues under the extremely amorphous banner of "Internet freedom," which takes one rather ambiguous term—"the Internet"—and marries it to an ill-defined term like "freedom." "Internet freedom" has become a highly emotional but completely meaningless shibboleth that hucksters of all stripes have begun to exploit for their own purposes.

Is there much analytical vigor left in the idea of "Internet freedom," when Kim Dotcom, the notorious millionaire founder of the file-sharing site Megaupload, has emerged as one of its greatest champions, strategically deploying the rhetoric of "freedom" and "innovation" to deflect attention from his site's role in facilitating wide-scale violations of copyright? The claim that going after Megaupload is an attack on "Internet freedom" makes as much sense as saying that going after people who steal books from libraries is an attack on "literary freedom." Today, the notion of "Internet freedom" mobilizes Anonymous activists to launch cyberattacks, ensuring good press coverage for their heroes, like Dotcom.

There's a good chance that today's copyright laws are unjust and inadequate—but this needs to be empirically demonstrated, not simply assumed from their supposed incompatibility with the spirit of "the Internet." The reason why copyright reform and protection of anonymity are important is very simple: backed by smart legislation, they would provide many more opportunities for human flourishing. It's the flourishing of humans—not of "the Internet"—that should preoccupy the Pirates.

Yes, digital technologies simultaneously threaten and enable such human flourishing, and it's important to bring new, younger, more knowledgeable voices to help improve policy making about their future, but the Pirates are on the wrong path with their aim to defend "Internet freedom." The term's ambiguity aside, its value will always be instrumental, not intrinsic: we value "Internet freedom" because, in many cases, it will lead to "human freedom." Occasionally—as with sites like Eightmaps.com—it will not, in which case there is nothing pathological or regressive about curtailing it.

While Internet-centrism has shaped the range of problems pursued by the Pirates, solutionism has greatly influenced how they go about solving them. The Pirates do not just try to defend "the Internet"; they also work to make their own party mimic its mythical "architecture," as if "the Internet" were a template for how party work should be organized in the twenty-first century. In Germany such efforts have reached a very advanced stage: the German Pirates use a panoply of tools to improve communication flows inside their party. In addition to chats, wikis, and mailing lists, they also use a collaborative text editor known as PiratePad, which allows hundreds of people to edit a document simultaneously. Campaign posters are not designed by a professional advertising firm; rather, supporters can upload their own designs to a wiki. Twitter is used to generate campaign slogans.

The benefits that the Pirates derive from such openness are not immediately clear. *Der Spiegel,* one of the country's most respected publications, got to the heart of the matter when it asked whether the party's embrace of "the Internet" was actually harming its cause. "What other party streams the meetings of its national committee live on the Internet or allows people to watch sessions of its parliamentary groups? Is there another party where it's possible to find its members' cell phone numbers via a Google search?" As *Der Spiegel* notes, "The constant chatter of the crowd also has negative consequences: It makes it difficult for the party to be taken seriously as a political actor."

The Pirates' most advanced and widely discussed technological innovation is an online system called LiquidFeedback, which allows the party to better understand what its members think about issues of the day. Here is how it works: Any member of the party can register (with the option of using a pseudonym) with LiquidFeedback and propose that the Pirates should do *x*. If more than 10 percent of other members find this proposal intriguing, it passes to the next stage, in which party members can vote for or against it.

After the proposal has been submitted, and before it has moved to the voting stage, other party members can launch counterproposals on a similar subject or make suggestions about how to improve the original one. What's interesting is that party members can transfer their votes to those they consider more knowledgeable about a given subject; thus, someone recognized as an expert on transportation policy might end up casting ten votes rather than one. To prevent some such experts from accumulating and abusing power, transferred votes can be recalled to their original "owners." The votes cast in LiquidFeedback are not binding; they simply inform party officials about the views of the grass roots. Big policy proposals are still discussed and voted upon at the party congress. LiquidFeedback thus aims to provide the intellectual inputs to the Pirates' work; the outputs are still determined by rather conventional means.

This all sounds great in theory—what a marvelous way to boost participation!—but the reality is much grimmer. In one German region, reports *Der Spiegel*, the Pirates used LiquidFeedback to gather general opinions on only two issues, while only twenty votes were cast in the online poll about the controversial law on circumcision—that in a federal state with nearly 18 million inhabitants. "It's a grassroots democracy where no one is showing up to participate," as *Der Spiegel* summed it up. Other German parties have accused the Pirates of appropriating their ideas while pretending that they come from "the Internet." As Volker Beck, a senior member of the Green Party, told NPR in June 2012, "The ridiculous truth about the Pirates is that they take our proposals from parliament and put it into their liquid feedback system to discuss about it. . . . They are taking up our content and propose them as their own." But Beck's concerns aside, it's not obvious what is so new and revolutionary about LiquidFeedback. Mechanisms for gauging what the party base makes of the issues of the day have always existed. The focus group, the poll, and the survey have all performed many of the same functions as LiquidFeedback, with one difference: the latter is much more open-ended in that genuinely new issues—provided they are not stolen from the Green Party— can appear on the party's agenda. This is all well and good, but a revolution in party building it isn't; well before blogs and wikis, there existed outlets—from party newspapers to actual meetings of local party cells—in which ordinary party members had plenty of opportunities to express their views.

There's something eerily utopian about the Pirate project, originating in its assumption that the old, well-tested ways of doing politics—driven by hierarchies, leaders, rules, and bureaucracies—are simply the unfortunate result of an imperfect communications infrastructure. Now that the infrastructure can be improved, why not get rid of those legacy costs as well? If today's blogs, wikis, and social networks allow instantaneous and infinite deliberation, if they allow us to replace leadership with some flexible rotation of duties and get rid of bureaucracy in its entirety, why bother with the old system at all? This is epochalist thinking at its worst: the new is presumed to be better because, well, it's new, while the old is discarded because the new is so easily available.

The greatest irony, then, is the fact that, despite the perfect infrastructure the Pirates have at their disposal, they are still hopelessly apolitical. Wikis cannot make up for the lack of strategic direction, the absence of catchy slogans, and the inability to discipline transgressors. Not surprisingly, support for the Pirates is waning, as the infrastructure alone does not give birth to spectacular reform ideas. In Germany, support for the Pirates dropped from 13 percent in April 2012 to just 6 percent in August 2012. As Klaus-Peter Schöppner, a German pollster, told *Der Spiegel*, "The Pirate phenomenon was so fascinating at the beginning, but people are ultimately yearning for strong individuals who want to take responsibility and stand for something. The model of an ominous, gray mass quickly loses momentum." Being successful at party politics requires a very different set of skills, attitudes, and organizational structures than successfully editing Wikipedia; small and tiny contributions by everyone might be enough to produce a decent article, but they may not be enough to build an effective political party.

For all their reliance on the wisdom of crowds, the Pirates have not yet produced any meaningful positions on issues that do not touch upon the purely digital. The Pirates have little to say on matters of social inequality, the European debt crisis, or the future of climate change, not to mention gender inequality, a problem to which their own male-dominated party is a living testament. That everyone can submit a proposal and a counterproposal on the most trivial of matters also means that the Pirates spend a lot of time assessing issues' that may not be terribly important, especially in comparison with the debt crisis or the war in Afghanistan (consider their recent discussion on whether to abolish Germany's list of the most dangerous dogs). LiquidFeedback creates an impression of political activity and widespread participation, but it's as important to inquire what all this activity and participation is directed at.

Granted, with time, LiquidFeedback might enable the Pirates to understand what their members actually want on each of those issues. However, given the complexity of today's politics, it seems rather naïve to expect ordinary citizens to have well-formed views on how to restructure Greece's euro debt or regulate nanotechnology. Of course, citizens could and should be involved in deliberations over such matters, but such deliberations need much more than just a fancy platform for soliciting and aggregating opinions. Such interventions will require far more innovation in institutional design than just providing voters with an opportunity to leave their comments in a suggestions box or give a proposal a quick thumbs-up or thumbs-down.

The Pirates' ideal of political representation seems to be the old delegate model articulated by James Madison, where politicians are supposed to blindly follow the wishes of their constituencies. An alternative, Burkean view treats representatives as trustees who, once elected, do what they think is best for their constituency, even if occasionally they have to go against its immediate preferences. Over the last half century, many a political philosopher has shown that both these models are inadequate and rely on paradoxes that, as political theorist Hanna Pitkin argued in *The Concept of Representation*, we should not even try to resolve. The Pirates seem to rely on a rather outdated, even fundamentalist concept of representation. Or perhaps their embrace of the delegate model is simply due to the fact that they don't feel ready to take responsibility for complex issues that lie outside the digital domain—often their only domain of expertise. But if that's the case, then it's really worth asking if they should be in politics at all.

While the pirates try to model themselves on the idea of "the Internet," it's now common for commentators to urge other parties to start modeling themselves on the Pirates; such feedback loops have become very common in our Internet-centric world. In May 2012, the *New York Times* published an op-ed by German journalist Steve Kettmann, expressing regret that Barack Obama didn't use LiquidFeedback when he entered office. After all, he had an immense online following after the 2008 elections; all these people could have helped him with policy making as well. "If Mr. Obama had followed the Pirate method, he would not only have sent updates via Facebook and Twitter, but he would have involved larger numbers of supporters in an extensive dialogue and given them an actual say in determining such priorities as which issues to pursue in his first months in office and how much to reach out to conservatives," wrote Kettmann.

In fact, the Obama administration did attempt many such experiments; they accomplished very little. One of the most popular questions in its 2009 Open for Questions initiative—in which anyone online could submit and vote on questions to be asked of President Obama—related to the legalization of marijuana. Another similar outlet is a section on the White House's website called "We the People," where anyone can submit and vote on petitions urging Obama to take action; if petitions reach 25,000 votes in thirty days, the White House will respond to the questions they raise. Among the popular petitions in early September 2012 were requests like "Clarify the President's position on Michael Vick," "Advise the TSA administration to save their Explosives Detecting Puppy Program," and "Enforce women's equal right to go topless in public wherever men have this privilege." These might be very important issues, but it's hard to understand what to make of the votes behind them. A tweet urging support for a given petition from, say, Justin Bieber, with his 30 million Twitter followers, can all but guarantee a quick and easy 25,000 votes for the most trivial issues. Should the White House drop everything and start responding to these queries?

Or what about the idea that LiquidFeedback could have told Obama "how much to reach out to conservatives"? It's hard to know whether Kettmann is simply naïve about the American political system or too enthusiastic about what software like Liquid-Feedback can accomplish. Knowing that 51 percent of his supporters who use LiquidFeedback think Obama needs to be "nice" to the Republicans, what exactly should the president do? Kill health-care reform and see what the LiquidFeedback crowd says in response? In the American context, LiquidFeedback is a solution to a problem that doesn't exist; both parties already rely on sophisticated microtargeting tools to uncover and appeal to our most secret wants and desires. Arguably, we need the very opposite: a way for leaders to show a bit of courage and take some radical steps, even if they go against what the public wants at the moment.

Future Perfect—Democracy Isn't

The Pirates, for all their naïveté and faith in software, should be commended for not losing faith in politics altogether. They may not be the world's leading experts on representative democracy, but at least they are ready to commit to the rituals of politics; they are prepared to campaign, get elected, and push for different laws. They may not look like conventional politicians—fellow parliamentarians like to complain that the Pirates wear shorts to legislative sessions—but, unlike, say, the Anonymous movement, the Pirates seek to operate within the system. They may despise particular parties and their elected representatives, but they still seem to believe that parties and representatives have important roles to play.

In this, the Pirates are not as extreme as some modern solutionists, who seek to improve politics by getting rid of political parties and complex systems of representation altogether. Inspired partly by the Pirates' LiquidFeedback software and partly by the success of Wikipedia and various peer-to-peer projects, Steven Johnson, in his *Future Perfect*, celebrates the benefits of switching to what he calls "liquid democracy." In a traditional democracy citizens elect representatives to legislate on their behalf; in a liquid democracy, citizens don't have to elect representatives—they can simply transfer their vote to whoever they think is more knowledgeable about the issue. Thus, writes Johnson, "in a liquid democracy, you can transfer your vote to your friend, and authorize her to 'spend' it as she sees fit."

In essence, Johnson is proposing to take the mechanism through which the Pirate Party identifies the issues that matter to their community and make it the core of our new political system. And if the Pirate Party claims that it was inspired by "the Internet," so does Johnson. "Proxy voters are like the influential bloggers and aggregators that have carved out a new space between media consumers and big news organizations."

Why should anyone bother with this plan? Johnson explains its numerous advantages. First of all, it can help avoid the traps of partisanship; thus, he notes, "by transferring your vote to your more knowledgeable friend, you've weakened the funnel of simplified, party-line voting: your proxy voter might well support candidates from other parties if she thinks they're the most qualified." Second, it can reduce the information burden on each particular voter so that "you don't need to be an expert in everything for your vote to matter. You can pick your targets, and let the people you trust in other fields make the remaining calls." Third, Johnson thinks that "liquid democracy" will create new spaces for participation that go far beyond the voting booth. As a result, he notes, "instead of choosing a candidate once every few years, ordinary citizens have a platform by which to participate in the decision-making process directly, according to their interest and their expertise."

The guiding spirit of Johnson's proposal is not new. "Liquid democracy" may sound fancy and contemporary, but the practices it describes have been with us for quite some time under the names of "proxy voting" and "delegate voting." Lewis Carroll wrote one of the first papers that broached the subject in 1884; many subsequent commentaries—produced mostly by adherents of rational-choice theory—appeared in the mid-twentieth century. "Liquid democracy" is an interesting example of a set of old, solutionist ideas that have acquired new currency with the rise of Internet-centrism.

Excitement over the possibilities that new technologies open up for direct participation has a long history of its own. In a 1969 article in *Public Choice*—the primary publishing outlet of public-choice theorists (public-choice scholarship is a subset of rational-choice scholarship)—James Miller III, a future high-ranking appointee in the Reagan administration, argued that "we must face up to the fact that communication costs have been falling and it is now possible for a large number of people to express their opinions simultaneously." In particular, he marveled at "the advancing technology of electronic computers, indicating devices, and recording equipment . . . [which] could be used to record political decisions, giving each voter an opportunity to cast his ballot on every issue and have it recorded through the machine." Miller, like Johnson more than forty years after him, wanted to use these computers for proxy voting. "Instead of electing representatives periodically for a tenure of two years or more, why not allow citizens to vote directly or delegate proxy to someone else for as long as they like." In another striking similarity to Johnson, who writes of a "gradient of participation," Miller argued that there would be some kind of gradation, with some voters choosing to delegate their votes over certain issues and choosing not to delegate them over others: "The most concerned voter would vote on every issue at his personal console. Another may delegate proxy to someone he feels would vote as he would if only he had the time and knowledge to partic004ipate directly. Most voters, however, would utilize some combination of these extremes."

As we know in retrospect, Miller's proposal didn't take off. Given the pull of both Internet-centrism and solutionism, however, it very well might flourish, especially now that it has cheerleaders like Steven Johnson. But, as is typical of solutionism, neither Miller nor Johnson displays any basic understanding of the intricacies of the political process, reducing it to the only variable under solutionists' control: votes. Neither of them mentions that the legislative process also involves discussion, bargaining, compromise, and deliberation; voting is just the final stage of a much longer sequence of events, which, for the most part, remains conventional and predominantly invisible (unless, of course, something goes wrong and media get hold of the story).

Miller and Johnson's model of politics is essentially a referendum, where it's only possible to vote thumbs up or thumbs down— much like in some of those news aggregators that Johnson quotes as his inspiration. Take California, where people really like to vote on every single issue under the sun, often to their own detriment. Such plebiscites exert a paralyzing effect on the state, draining its coffers and producing a stream of numbered propositions that most Californians cannot remember. Those of us convinced that this is a dysfunctional system wouldn't see proxy voting or liquid democracy as an adequate step toward reforming it. Is switching to the California system with a minor, liquid twist really a good way to reform American politics?

In Johnson's "liquid democracy," experts, who end up accumulating votes from less-informed voters, are presumed to be omniscient; they know the "truth" and thus need not deliberate, bargain, or compromise. No wonder voting is all that's left. This is a very immature view of politics. It's also extremely utopian in assuming that the less-informed voters will be able to find experts on every subject that they do not know about and verify their credentials in a given field. And why is evaluating someone's expertise in, say, climate change or macroeconomic policy presumed to be an effortless affair? Evaluating expertise about expertise is not easy.

Furthermore, it's much more likely that thousands of other voters, along with journalists and other candidates running for office, will notice the tiniest discrepancy in a candidate's credentials; when you are evaluating whether your friends are knowledgeable about a given issue, no one else is looking but you. And what about issues that are too arcane? Or should we assume that citizens have enough friends who can moonlight as experts on all issues that matter? Johnson seems to think so, arguing that, since we habitually turn to our foodie friends for recommendations on where to have dinner, we can do the same when it comes to political decisions. How odd. Am I the only one with no friends who are experts on the economic situation in Honduras and the effects of climate change on Alaska? Should I just call my foodie friends instead?

Go to the iTunes of Politics to Download Your Welfare

Johnson's interpretation of a new political philosophy inspired by "the Internet" does contain strong hints about his distaste for the modern party system—especially when he rails against "simplified, party-line voting"—but his distaste is not as pronounced as in some other solutionist initiatives to "fix" politics once and for all. For example, a number of civic start-ups have tried to replace America's seemingly dysfunctional two-party system with something more effective. Americans Elect was one such group that believed "the Internet" could help find a third-party candidate to stand in the 2012 presidential elections. Americans Elect, enthused Thomas Friedman in the *New York Times*, can do to American politics "what Amazon.com did to books, what the blogosphere did to newspapers, what the iPod did to music, what drugstore.com did to pharmacies."

Friedman wrote this in July 2011. By May 2012, Americans Elect could not even be counted on to do for American politics "what pets.com did to pet stores"—which is to say, not much. Friedman, of course, was not alone; many other pundits, intoxicated by "the Internet," thought that Americans Elect would change the country's politics forever. Lawrence Lessig, never passing up an opportunity to remind us of just how revolutionary all this Internet stuff is, proclaimed that "10,000 clicks from 10 states could begin a candidate in the process towards winning the Americans Elect nomination." Well, it wasn't meant to be: Americans Elect, for all the promise of "the Internet," couldn't find a suitable candidate, discovering that getting anyone of note to enter the race is hard to pull off with tweets alone.

But the recent solutionist push extends far beyond the efforts to disrupt the presidential process; the party system itself is increasingly under attack, with many Internet renegades gearing up to replace it with nimble, Internet-based organizing. Much of this new rhetoric can be traced back to Clay Shirky's populist and anti-organizational thinking in *Here Comes Everybody*; the book carries the telling subtitle "The Power of Organizing without Organizations." Cue the Shirky-esque tone of Mark Zuckerberg's remarks in 2008: "We are at a point now with the Internet, with a lot of these applications, where communication should be efficient enough [so] that . . . people should be able to have a voice . . . without having a large organization with millions of people that has been organized and raised millions of dollars in order to fight for a specific cause." Because people can now organize without organizations— be they parties or trade unions—why bother with those slow and ineffective institutions at all?

Such anti-institutional and antiparty rhetoric has quickly found its way into specific solutionist projects that aim to fix politics by ridding us of parties. The most visible player here is Ruck.us— whose tagline is "No Parties. Just People"—a start-up cofounded by Nathan Daschle, the thirty-eight-year-old son of former senator Tom Daschle and a onetime executive director of the Democratic Governors Association. The site's mission is as ambitious as it gets: to supplant the two parties—those have become "outdated and antiquated," as Ruck.us's other cofounder, Ray Glendening, told the *Washington Post*—and make "the Internet" the main outlet for political expression in the country.

Here is how it works: When you register on the site, you are asked to supply some basic information about your interests (e.g., do you care about foreign policy more than taxation?) and your core political beliefs (e.g., do you think the government has a role to play in education?). Ruck.us then calculates your "political DNA" in order to match you with similar users and encourage you to join relevant "rucks" (according to the site, "the word comes from rugby, where players form a ruck when they loosely come together to fight the other team for possession of the ball."). Ruck.us is like Netflix for politics, with its cause-recommendation engine essentially encouraging you to, say, check out a campaign to ban abortion if you have expressed strong opposition to gun control, much in the way that Netflix would recommend that you check out *Rambo* if you liked *Rocky*.

Once in a "ruck," members can simply follow news posted by other members or be more proactive and share information themselves: links to relevant petitions, organizations, and events are particularly encouraged. As the site learns more about the user, new questions are posed, and new rucks are recommended; membership in each ruck is always in flux, and there is little sense of community, as each Ruck.us member might belong to dozens of them. The focus, thus, is on individual action around specific issues—never on such outdated notions as collective pursuit of shared goals or solidarity. None of this sounds particularly profitable, so Ruck.us also carries "sponsored rucks"—campaigns funded by the likes of the National Wildlife Foundation and Livestrong—where the causes and information flows are partly dictated by the sponsor. (It may not be a revolution in politics, but Ruck.us is certainly a revolution in lobbying!)

Back in April 2012, when its most die-hard fans still believed that Americans Elect might transform American politics, Nathan Daschle wrote an op-ed for CNN, touting the revolutionary changes brought on by technology. "Whereas 30 years ago we were blissfully ignorant about our limitations, we now expect options, tailoring, customization and immediacy, none of which is available in the 19th century creation that is our two-party system," he lamented. He went on to proclaim that "the Americans Elect innovation is so exciting . . . because it relieves us of anachronistic structures that harm our political system. It's the iTunes of politics." For Daschle, too, the network is not going away: "The trends are undeniable. Change it is a-coming, and it's likely to be in the form of a composite mash of Americans Elect, Ruck.us, and all of the other disruptive technologies." Democracy as a mash-up is not quite what de Tocqueville described in *Democracy in America*.

If all these ideas had come from some wild, *Wired*-reading cyberlibertarian from California, they wouldn't have merited much attention. But Daschle is firmly embedded in the very structures that Ruck.us seeks to disrupt. At issue here is not only the damage that Ruck.us might do to politics but the way in which the very idea of an "iTunes of politics" could have emerged in the mind of what must be a seasoned political operator. This is where the dominance of Internet-centrism can perhaps shed some light.

Much of the impetus behind Ruck.us does come from the idea that we are living in unique times, when everything is possible, since everything is in flux. "Politics is the last sector of American culture that has yet to be revolutionized by technology. When you look around, every sector of our lives has a plethora of options except for our outlets for political engagement: We still have these two binary options," notes Ruck.us cofounder Glendening. But what does "iTunes of politics" even mean? All iTunes has disrupted is the ability of the music industry to sell songs in bulk and call them albums. Does it mean that, if Daschle has his way, only "blockbuster issues"—those that get the most "rucks" or the best sponsors—will be campaigned on, while those that are less popular but perhaps more important will not? How is this a good thing, especially for those holding unpopular and minority views? Or is "iTunes of politics" just a cursory reference to the global supermarket of causes, where citizen-consumers will be able to shop for the cause that maximizes their emotional well-being without demanding much in return? Can there really be a better way to capture the consumerization of modern politics than to compare it to iTunes?

Predictably, not everyone is excited about Ruck.us. As Dave Karpf, a George Washington University communications professor, told *Politico*, "Plots to disrupt the two-party system through technology tend to all have the same basic flaw: They treat politics like commercial markets." However, according to Karpf, "our two-party system doesn't form out of a market problem; it forms out of an electoral-system design. The party coalition that attracts a plurality of voters wins everything. The party coalition that comes in second wins nothing. That yields two parties. Every time. New information technologies haven't made that irrelevant." The kinds of deep structural issues that reduce American politics to just two parties have little to do with technology or lack of information; thus, it's naïve to expect that digital platforms could help deal with them. Here, once again, "the Internet" is a great solution to a problem that doesn't exist.

The ultimate irony is that Internet-centric solutionists, in misdiagnosing the problem and trying to fix it in a rather perfunctory manner, may breed problems of their own. Of course, modern politics—and certainly American politics—is not perfect. But here, too, our well-intentioned geeks need to develop a deeper appreciation of both the role that parties play and of the many positive aspects of partisanship throughout US history. Antipartyism is not unique to our modern, Internet-centric times; it's a recurring sentiment in American political and social thought, with many an earlier thinker believing that party politics is just a symptom of a broken, divisive system that has fallen from grace and lost its unity and wholeness. The efforts to bypass parties—either in Steven Johnson's "liquid democracy" kind of way or through what Ruck.us offers—are not new either; they very much align with the philosophy of voluntarism, which emerged during the Progressive Era and argued that citizens can bypass parties, form their own small groups and voluntary association, and fight off the special interests.

In *On the Side of the Angels: An Appreciation of Parties and Partisanship*, a seminal defense of partisanship in American politics, Nancy Rosenblum celebrates what she dubs "the creativity of party politics and the moral distinctiveness of partisanship" and points out that parties not only reflect but actively create the political interests and opinions of their members. Parties are easy to criticize: voters find them off-putting; special interest groups and rich donors find it all too easy to exploit them; parties can be too slow to respond to public opinion and prevent their members from tackling important problems on their own. But, for all those faults, parties also play an important—and often invisible role—in making political life both more reasonable and more creative. They regulate rivalry and mediate deliberation, throwing weight behind important issues of the day.

Above all, parties help create conditions in which partisanship can flourish—and whatever centrist pundits like to believe, partisanship has many beneficial uses as well. It entrenches pluralism as the only game in town, forcing the ruling party to acknowledge that its own "truth" may be just one way to tell the story. Partisanship, according to Rosenblum, "does not see pluralism and political conflict as a bow to necessity, a pragmatic recognition of the inevitability of disagreement. It demands severe self-discipline to acknowledge that my party's status is just one part in a permanently pluralist politics, and hence the provisional nature of being the governing party and the charade of pretending to represent the whole."

The attempt to replace partisanship with something less flawed and less contentious, Rosenblum contends, might only make things worse, for, as she eloquently puts it, "rescuing politics from the unreasonable is unreasonable." Likewise, historian Sean Wilentz argues that for all the bad rap partisanship receives in today's public debate, we shouldn't forget that "the anti-party current is by definition anti-democratic, as political parties have been the only reliable vehicles for advancing the ideas and interests of ordinary voters." In other words, while digital technologies might one day make it easier to disrupt the party system and eschew partisanship—and start-ups like Americans Elect and Ruck.us will surely persevere in this mission—this hardly makes the project worth pursuing. That we have found a powerful "solution" to the problem of partisanship does not mean that partisanship is a "problem." This is where solutionism together with Internet-centrism forces us to assume problems based on the sheer awesomeness of our digital tools, not on the needs and requirements of democratic politics itself. As political theorist Bernard Crick once wrote, "Boredom with established truths is the great enemy of the free man."

Learning to Love the Imperfections

The main problem with solutionism is that it refuses to accept that a striving for perfection, regardless of whether it manifests in demands that politicians ought to be completely honest and transparent or in actual efforts to transcend the supposed limitations of partisanship, might be exerting a negative influence on our political culture. Perfection shouldn't be pursued for its own ends; democracy is a complex affair in which, in the absence of disappointments, there would never be any accomplishments.

Letting go of perfectionism would reveal politics in a very different light. If one assumes that politics is always imperfect—and that such imperfection is a good thing—then the solutionists' quest for transparency seems misguided for one simple reason: pursued in an unreflexive manner, it recasts compromises like lower attendance rates at voting sessions or occasional recourses to hypocrisy and ambivalence as sins, while any realistic model of politics should at least occasionally treat them as virtues.

Solutionists do not understand that politicians are not like inflatable mattresses or hair dryers that can be easily ranked on a five-star scale, as we are wont to do with our Amazon purchases. It's not that we do not evaluate them at all—we do—but such evaluations boil down to a binary choice, which we express, every few years, at the voting booth. A politician who has mastered the art of compromise and accepted the inevitability of imperfection might get another term in office, but a hair dryer that has mastered those very arts will never receive five stars. Polish dissident Adam Michnik was onto something when he defined democracy as "eternal imperfection, a mixture of sinfulness, saintliness, and monkey business." Try marketing a hair dryer with that slogan.

If disappointment with politics is to become more visible—which it might, given the changes in the information environment—then we desperately need to find new ways to have citizens appreciate its imperfections. A stream of "bad" numbers will look bad and disheartening only if we stick to simplistic, reductionist criteria of what counts as "success" in politics to begin with, if we fetishize the means, attendance rates, over the ends, the bargaining outcomes of legislative sessions.

When John Wonderlich of the Sunlight Foundation—a bastion of technosolutionism that aims to use digital tools to promote government transparency—enthuses that "there is a cultural change in what people expect from government, fuelled by the experience of shopping on the internet and having real-time access to financial information," this is something to be mourned, not celebrated. The mentality of the Amazon shopper is that of someone who prizes immediate payoffs and rarely wants to make sacrifices in the name of others. Try telling that shopper that not all of his or her desires can be satisfied because someone else has equally compelling interests and those have to be taken into account as well; the market simply doesn't work that way.

But politics thrives on mediocrity, real and perceived; one day everyone is bound to be disappointed. If bargaining could always lead to win-win situations, no politics would be necessary. As the French philosopher Bruno Latour once put it, "What we despise as political 'mediocrity' is simply the collection of compromises that we force politicians to make on our behalf." To accept the mediocrity of politics is to accept that the citizen, unlike the consumer, is not always right: where consumers can pay their way through, be treated like emperors, and expect to get the best possible hair dryer, citizens need to accept a certain humility and be prepared to make sacrifices, if only out of solidarity with others.

To import the mentality of the consumer—even of the activist consumer—into the realm of politics is to make politics so disappointing that few will tolerate it at all. Most public institutions should not be held to the same standards as their private counterparts simply because their mission is to provide goods and services that markets cannot or should not provide. This work is often challenging enough, even without constant reminders about their suboptimal performance by peeved consumers. As Catherine Needham cautions in her 2003 book *Citizen Consumers*, "The fundamental danger is that consumerism may foster privatized and resentful citizens whose expectations of government can never be met, and cannot develop the concern for the public good that must be the foundation of democratic engagement and support for public services."

However, it's not just the solutionists at the Sunlight Foundation who expect "the Internet" to deliver what perhaps shouldn't be delivered at all. Noted political theorists have been championing the idea of "monitorial democracy," whereby politicians operate under constant scrutiny—by citizens, NGOs, commissions, and agencies—for, as we all know, politicians tend to be imperfect, inefficient, and corrupt. It's not that this effort is wrongheaded—the stories of corruption and bureaucracy run amok often invoked in this context are certainly not fairy tales—but theories of "monitorial democracy" rarely spell out what political activities should be left unscrutinized, unmonitored, and unrated. The danger here, as is often the case with transparency schemes, is that additional sunlight is presumed to be good in itself, not as an enabler of other, higher goods.

In *Defending Politics*—perhaps the smartest defense of the practice of politics published in the last few years—Matthew Flinders finds that "monitorial democracy" suffers from many of the same problems that Michael Power identified in the "audit society" more broadly. The chief preoccupation of monitorial democracy, charges Flinders, is not with fostering social goods but, rather, with "controlling, monitoring, and scrutinizing politicians and decision-makers, based upon the assumed 'self-evident truth' that politicians are not to be trusted."

A recent *Guardian* article got a very representative opinion of the vox populi when it quoted one regular voter complaining that "my idea of a politician is a thief, a liar and a cheat." This is a bad-faith, aggressive model of politics that holds politicians in contempt, celebrates "gotcha"-style reporting, and "rejoices in the taking of political scalps." Most disturbingly, it says precious little about the responsibilities of citizens, focusing instead on their rights (mostly, just one right actually: the right to know). As Flinders points out, treating citizens as consumers leads them to think that politics can deliver the same "standards of service that they would commonly expect from the private sector . . . [which] is the political equivalent of suicide."

As old newspaper and TV archives are digitized, as all speeches are recorded and transcribed for posterity, as one's early tweets and pokes are scrutinized, the temptation to succumb to solutionism and to reveal politicians and public institutions as the frauds they are becomes irresistible. Politicians used to be shamed with their unflattering attendance statistics; soon, they will be confronted with various "truthfulness" indexes based on everything they have ever said. The recent preoccupation with fact checking and the corresponding proliferation of projects like PolitiFact.com (of the *Tampa Bay Times*), FactCheck.org (of the Annenberg Public Policy Center), and the *Washington Post*'s Fact Checker (which grades the accuracy of politicians' statements on a one-to-four "Pinocchios" scale) offer a foretaste of things to come. Right now, such projects still require humans to do both the analysis and the ranking, but as our technologies get smarter and our archives grow bigger, fact checking will probably be outsourced to algorithms.

In Truth We Trust?

The Truth Goggles project, developed by an MIT graduate student and widely celebrated in the media, is one step toward automating at least some of the steps involved in fact checking. This tiny piece of software can be integrated with your browser. Once you visit an article on the *New York Times* website, you can click the "Truth Goggles" icon in your browser, and the software will scan the article for factual claims. If the article contains any of the more than 6,000 (and growing) items in PolitiFact's database of fact-checked claims, those facts will be highlighted in yellow while the rest of the text will be blurred. On clicking the highlighted claim, a user will see a pop-up window showing what PolitiFact thinks of this particular claim—that is, whether it's true, half true, mostly true, mostly false, false, and so on—and providing some contextual information as well.

Thus, we meet the double-click mentality once again: "truth" magically creeps into our browsers, while the noble efforts of truth hunters at PolitiFact and innovators at MIT mostly remain invisible and, for the most part, unscrutinized. But who will watch the truth hunters and the innovators? The extremes of the spectrum look rather unproblematic; statements labeled as absolutely "true" or absolutely "false"—provided they are not about climate change or evolution— may not be too controversial. But what about all the statements in between? Can we really trust PolitiFact's decision to label something "mostly false" when perhaps it should be "mostly true"?

In December 2011, prominent blogger and journalist Glenn Greenwald pointed out that for at least some of its judgments on the accuracy of statements about the war on terror and illegal detention of terrorist suspects, PolitiFact reaches out to supposedly "centrist" foreign policy experts, who seem neutral and ideology-free (PolitiFact's fact-checks include a section on sources used in assessing a statement's accuracy, which lists the experts spoken to). In one such case, PolitiFact labeled as "mostly false" a Ron Paul claim that "American citizens are vulnerable to assassination" by their own government after the Department of Defense's operational definition of al-Qaeda and the Taliban had been rephrased in a very vague manner. As Greenwald noted, Paul was hardly alone in making this assumption; many prominent lawyers and the American Civil Liberties Union shared such views. And yet PolitiFact chose to reach out to two supposedly neutral "experts," who, if Greenwald is to be believed, are anything but neutral and are simply neoconservatives in disguise. Greenwald, a terrific polemicist, does have a tendency to overstate his case, but here he is on firm ground: the two experts in question do have a history of supporting many of the elements of the global war on terror.

But PolitiFact operates in its own ideological bubble, which it is not always able to detect. Once they put their stamp of approval or disapproval on controversial claims—and once those stamps find a permanent place in our browsers—the faux centrism of "Washington experts" becomes even more entrenched in our public conversation. So semiautomated fact checking does offer some solutions—it may uncover factual errors—but those solutions might come at the expense of sustaining ideological frames that ought to be questioned and perhaps even overturned. This particular shortcoming can be overcome once PolitiFact and its geek friends abandon the double-click idea and accept that they deserve as much scrutiny as the politicians they aspire to fact-check, perhaps even more.

In the next few years, projects like Truth Goggles are likely to proliferate and become even more sophisticated. To begin with, it will be impossible to get any public statement—even those made before one embarked on a political career—to disappear. Most politicians have already accepted that everything they say—and tweet—is likely to live forever, but the geeks never miss a chance to remind them that this so: Politwoops, a project of the Sunlight Foundation, collects and highlights tweets deleted by politicians, as if they should never be granted an opportunity to regret what they say. Perhaps the Sunlight Foundation would prefer that politicians say nothing at all.

Technologies that store, search, and retrieve text are important, but they are just the beginning. Soon, it will be trivially cheap to analyze both audio and video files for signs of dishonesty; the ability to "decipher" loudness, pauses, and changes in pitch will be crucial in analyzing the former, facial expressions in analyzing the latter. Many decades of research on how emotions can be automatically "read" off our faces—the work of famous psychologist Paul Ekman, whose research inspired Fox's television series *Lie to Me*, stands out in particular—are beginning to bear fruit, as computer power gets cheaper, algorithms get better, and the photo archives get bigger thanks to social media. These techniques will enable far more than just analyzing the accuracy of particular statements; they will indicate whether politicians are genuinely serious about their promises, whether they are confident about their own proclamations, or whether they themselves might be harboring suspicions that their much-celebrated reform plans will not work.

This is where solutionists ought to be very careful. A project like Truth Goggles seems to embrace a model of politics that treats hypocrisy, inconsistency, and ambiguity as inherently bad and harmful to good politics, as something that ought to be eliminated. But is it really the case? We need to challenge not just the idea that the truthfulness of a statement can be boiled down and evaluated in "Pinocchios" but also the notion that hypocrisy, mendacity, and ambiguity are ruining our politics. In extremely large doses, they certainly do; but in small doses, they are more virtues than vices. They enable our political process to function; if they go, something genuinely important will be lost. Thus, while newer and smarter technologies can eventually help eliminate all three of these vices almost in their entirety, this doesn't change the truths that political philosophy discovered long ago. In fact, hypocrisy, mendacity, and ambiguity have all claimed a number of influential supporters, and many of those arguments, written as they were before our obsession with "the Internet," still hold true today.

Political philosopher Judith Shklar wrote a whole book, *Ordinary Vices*, in which she argued that a war on hypocrisy is a futile and counterproductive endeavor, for hypocrisy is a structural condition that makes liberalism possible. The liberal reformers, she argued, should stop fixating on hypocrisy and go after other problems—most of all, cruelty. "The paradox of liberal democracy is that it encourages hypocrisy because the politics of persuasion require . . . a certain amount of dissimulation on the part of all speakers. On the other hand, the structure of open political competition exaggerates the importance and the prevalence of hypocrisy because it is the vice of which all parties can, and do, accuse each other. It is not at all clear that zealous candor would serve liberal politics particularly well."

Several decades after Shklar, political philosopher Ruth Grant, in another important defense of hypocrisy, argued that some kinds of hypocrisy are actually positive, even necessary. Thus, she argued, "the blanket condemnation of hypocrisy must be seen as a political vice—and particularly so if what passes for honest politics is not principled politics but the frank self-interestedness of those 'realists' who are, in fact, merely cynics." More recently, political theorist David Runciman advanced similar arguments, proposing that some types of political hypocrisy are even desirable and worth encouraging. His explanation of the recent preoccupation with rooting out hypocrisy rings true: it's not that there's more hypocrisy today; it's just that, with twenty-four-hour political exposure in the media, it's much easier to find.

Mendacity has received less attention from political theorists, but historian Martin Jay, in his *Virtues of Mendacity*, has made up for this intellectual deficit. Truth can disempower and is not always worth airing; or, as Jay puts it, "truth-telling can . . . be a weapon of the powerful, while lying is a tactic of the weak." A politics without lies and hypocrisy wouldn't be politics at all. According to Jay, "Politics, however we chose to define its essence and limit its contours, will never be an entirely fib-free zone of authenticity, sincerity, integrity, transparency, and righteousness. And maybe . . .

that's ultimately a good thing too." To expect politicians to always tell the truth is to subject our deliberately mediocre politics to perfectionist standards that would drain politics of any meaning. This doesn't mean that we should encourage our politicians to lie, just that we should remember that lies can often serve enabling functions, and while in many cases they will be enabling corruption and laziness, in others they will enable compromise and hope.

One unintended consequence of our turbo-charged fact-checking culture might be that ambivalent and ambiguous political statements will give way to more concrete, numerically obsessed accounts. This might work well for some purposes—cue Bill Clinton's speech at the National Democratic Convention in 2012, which stood in stark contrast to the predominantly fact-free performance of the Republican camp—but this too might have a debilitating effect on our politics. As political scientist Deborah Stone has argued in her seminal *The Policy Paradox*, ambivalence has many positive uses in democratic politics; it's more of an art than a science. "Ambiguity enables the transformation of individual intentions and actions into collective results and purposes. Without it, cooperation and compromise would be far more difficult, if not impossible," argues Stone.

For example, defining a policy in rather ambiguous, vague terms might help politicians to garner support from many different quarters; precision might come later on. "'Defending American interests' is an ambiguous idea around which everyone unites," she notes. Ambiguity makes it possible to actually get things done, giving politicians some breathing space to work on a problem without getting distracted by the attention of the media and the public. Thus, writes Stone, "legislators can satisfy demands to 'do something' about a problem by passing a vague statute with ambiguous meaning, then letting administrative agencies hash out the more conflictual details behind the scenes." Most importantly, without ambiguity, conflicts might never get resolved, and compromise might never be achieved. "Ambiguity facilitates negotiation and compromise because it allows opponents to claim victory from a single resolution," concludes Stone.

Demanding that our politics gets more precise, asking politicians to commit their thoughts to tweets, pokes, and blog posts, and forcing them to be specific to the point that they would rather say and do nothing at all—all of this is unlikely to improve the state of our democracy. We must resist the temptation to accept "the Internet's" gift, which might be little more than a curse in disguise. We must not fixate on what this new arsenal of digital technologies allows us to do without first inquiring what is worth doing.

Networks, Leaders, Hierarchies

The idea that "the Internet" can rid us of political parties or fix deep structural problems in democratic politics goes back to the early 1990s. A 1994 article in *Wired* quoted Esther Dyson, the prominent technology investor and commentator, as saying that "organized political parties won't be needed if open networks enable people to organize ad hoc, rather than get stuck in some rigid group." Even Dyson's sentiment, of course, is only part of a broader geek unease with modern politics—and of the potential of "the Internet" to fix it. As Josh Quittner, author of the *Wired* article, put it, "The Net is merely a means to an end. The end is to reverse-engineer government, to hack Politics down to its component parts and fix it." Solutionism met Internet-centrism a long time ago.

Still, every new technology—be it some fancy cryptographic tool or a WikiLeaks copycat or a gimmick to visualize otherwise useless data—rekindles the solutionist urge and gives rise to yet another wave of epochalism, which, in turn, is used as evidence to justify some radical intervention or simply to sanction inaction. As a result, we are often reminded how "the Internet" and its various components can serve as a pattern for reshaping political institutions—regardless of what their current structure does to the advancement of diverse human interests.

Thus, Heather Brooke, a campaigner for government transparency, follows Larry Lessig's dictum and proposes that "instead of re-engineering the Internet to fit around unpopular laws and unpopular leaders, we could re-engineer our political structures to mirror the Internet. Instead of putting our faith in state intervention to control the Internet for our protection, we trust in the good that comes when individuals can speak and come together freely." The state and its institutions are treated with suspicion, as if "the Internet" itself can somehow defend its users against violations of privacy or cybercrime. The message here is unequivocal: the Network is here; get used to it! Last time I checked, much of this proverbial "Internet" was built by for-profit companies with the explicit objective of making money, not defending human rights. Why should we be reengineering our political institutions with this model in mind?

In a similar vein, Beth Noveck, a law professor and former deputy chief technology officer at the White House, warns that "if institutions don't work with the networks, networks will work around them, rendering government practices increasingly disconnected, ineffectual, and brittle." Not surprisingly, she proposes that "democratic theory and the design of governing institutions must be rethought for the age of networks." Well, at least it's not an epoch.

Most likely, Internet-centrism accounts for much of this fascination with networked, decentralized, and leaderless structures—and their supposed superiority over centralized hierarchies and their leaders (of which the political party is just one type). Much of this network fetish can be explained by undue excitement over the ease and speed with which such networks can be formed. That networks might be inferior to hierarchies when it comes to getting things done doesn't bother our Internet-centric pundits; for them, the task is to celebrate "the Internet" everywhere they see it, not to engage in analysis of what kinds of organizational structures would be more appropriate for a given reform agenda.

Cue Clay Shirky deploying his trademark lingo of rational-choice theory in *Here Comes Everybody*: "Newly capable groups are assembling, and they are working . . . outside the previous strictures that bounded their effectiveness. These changes will transform the world everywhere groups of people come together to accomplish something, which is to say everywhere." "Previous strictures" are cast as obsolete and unnecessary—they are something that thwarts the self-realization of groups. It's groups and networks—which are distributed and often span borders—that hold power; hierarchies and states, confined as they are to fixed territories and programs of action, are outfoxed at every turn.

This notion of the almost God-given superiority of networks informs Shirky's interpretation of WikiLeaks, the one transnational network to rule them all. Thus, in a later speech, Shirky argues that "there was no way the State Department could go to WikiLeaks and have a conversation that hinged on or even involved anything called the national interest. Julian [Assange] is not a U.S. citizen, he is an Australian citizen. He was not operating on U.S. soil, he was in Iceland. The Pentagon Papers conversation took place entirely within the national matrix, and the WikiLeaks conversation took place outside of it." Groups win; nation-states lose. Networks good; hierarchies bad. Global good; local bad.

The problem here is that Clay Shirky believes that global affairs now work according to the demands of "the Internet," while, in reality, the story is much more complicated. A conversation about the national interest between the transglobal network that is (was?) WikiLeaks and the US government actually did take place. In fact, according to at least some credible reports, WikiLeaks did offer the State Department the opportunity to review the diplomatic cables and highlight what should be redacted—an opportunity that the ugly and messy hierarchy of the State Department reportedly declined (Mark Stephens, one of Assange's numerous ex-lawyers, once claimed that two cables were actually removed at their request). Assange himself often complains that the US government thwarted his highly mobile, distributed, and transnational network, not least because Washington can target—not directly but through rhetoric—the very intermediaries, from credit card companies to technology providers, that enable such networks. If there's a didactic story about the death of hierarchies and the onset of the transnational networked age, the story of WikiLeaks certainly isn't it.

It would be incorrect to say that the current fashion for networked and horizontal modes of political organization is solely due to Internet-centrism. A brief foray into the history of economics and ecology would reveal that the preference for horizontal solutions developed much earlier—and not necessarily as a coherent philosophy but as a response to the much-hated hierarchical ways of governing. Digital networks have simply provided the appearance of an infrastructure in which horizontal modes of governance could be enacted. But here, once again, these new possibilities may have imposed themselves as preferred solutions to every organizational challenge, even if the task at hand requires a more vertical, hierarchical structure; gradually reform movements have come to accept such horizontalism as always being a more superior option. This is precisely what social theorist David Harvey means when he complains that "unfortunately . . . the idea of hierarchy is anathema to many segments of the oppositional left these days. A fetishism of organizational preference (pure horizontality, for example) all too often stands in the way of exploring appropriate and effective solutions."

Leaders, like hierarchies, are seen as a burden, as something that "the Internet" has eliminated—only to make political struggle more effective. Alec Ross, a senior State Department official who oversees technology and innovation, is very optimistic about the Arab Spring. "If you think about revolutionary heroes of the past—whether it was Lech Walesa in Poland or Vaclav Havel in the Czech Republic or Nelson Mandela in South Africa—we don't see those kinds of figures in these revolutions taking place in the Middle East right now and that is in part because the Internet has distributed leadership." Or could it be that we simply didn't see those figures because Hosni Mubarak's government had been systematically jailing and torturing its opponents, often with Washington's tacit approval? Ross doesn't say.

Even those who participated in the revolution seem under the illusion that "the Internet" has upended all political truths that held before. Wael Ghonim, the Google executive who became one of the public faces of the youth revolt in Egypt, writes that "the older style of revolution was to have a leader. But in our revolution, and other revolutions that took place in the Arab world, it was a leaderless movement. Everyone was contributing." This, of course, is how most people describe Wikipedia—and "the Internet" is, in fact, Ghonim's operating metaphor. "It was the difference between Web 1.0, where most of the internet was content that users just read and watched, to Web 2.0, where users have started to communicate and collaborate with one another on content. In Revolution 2.0, no one is a leader—everyone is a leader," he said in an interview given in early 2012. Here is a man who lives and breathes Internet-centrism.

Such logic works only if one presumes that the revolution ended the moment Mubarak stepped down. If you take a longer view of the situation—and don't confuse the end of the uprising with the end of the revolution itself—it's not at all obvious that such leaderless revolutions are a welcome development. Later events in Egypt highlighted the immense naïveté of Ghonim's thinking. Squeezed between one hierarchy, the army, and another, the Muslim Brotherhood, the liberal and pro-Western youth, with their unbending belief that politics is just like Wikipedia, were essentially locked out of the political process. Furthermore, the absence of clear leadership and common goals further splintered this "network," so that its opponents didn't even have to try very hard. As Hazem Kandil, a political sociologist and expert on Egypt, noted in *Dissent* more than a year after the Arab Spring, "as long as revolutionaries cannot organize their ranks and encourage their fellow citizens to make difficult choices, take risks, and accept short-term instability, then there is little hope that the people themselves will be able to turn their gallant uprising into a complete revolution."

Some in the youth movement belatedly understood the challenge of being a network fighting against two powerful hierarchies. As Ahmed Maher, a leader of the April 6 Youth Movement, told the *New York Times* in June 2012, "We are the spark that ignites the world; we know how to inflame things. . . . But when we have a strong entity that can stand on its own feet—when we can form a government tomorrow—then we become an alternative. We didn't understand that the media isn't an alternative to the streets." According to Maher, building such an alternative—a real political movement that can transcend the limitations of a network—is what his group plans to do in the next five years. "The Internet" may have made the revolutions of the Arab Spring possible, but "the Internet"—at least the blind, unquestioning faith in the superiority of decentralized and horizontal networks—is making those revolutions very difficult to complete.

Technoescapists versus Technorationalists

The geeks' confusion about politics is not exhausted by their utopian plans to get rid of important intermediaries and dismantle the stifling hierarchies. An equally disturbing inclination is to ditch politics altogether and hope that technology—especially "the Internet"—can rid us of problems that politics can no longer solve or, in a milder version, that we can replace politicians and politics with technocrats and administration. The former are the technoescapists, who think that technology, exemplified by "the Internet," can make politics obsolete; the latter are the techno-rationalists, who think that technology and "the Internet" can shrink what makes politics political and instead boost its technocratic dimension. Both are extremely dangerous.

The best ambassador of the technoescapist camp is German-born investor Peter Thiel, who made his fortune with PayPal and was the first outside investor in Facebook. Thiel cuts a very odd figure: a self-proclaimed libertarian who bankrolled much of Ron Paul's presidential campaign, he also chairs the board of Palantir, a leader in intelligence-gathering and data-mining solutions that mostly caters to the interests of America's defense community—a community that devoted libertarians like Paul actually want to dismantle.

Palantir is also a big believer in open government, having given money to the Sunlight Foundation, its primary promoter. That Palantir caters primarily to the interests of the intelligence community, which is responsible for the culture of government secrecy in America, does not discourage its support of "government openness." This might seem quite weird, but it isn't; a video on Palantir's YouTube channel shows how to export "open-government" databases set up by the Sunlight Foundation into the company's open-source intelligence software. Note the irony here: the "open-government" crusade is feeding the intelligence industry with better data, which, in turn, bolsters the main enemies of government openness.

But Thiel is no stranger to controversy. He's received plenty of media attention for his support of quixotic causes. One of his most controversial ideas is to pay promising young people $100,000 each to encourage them to drop out of college and pursue entrepreneurial ideas, many of them with a social-change bent. This is solutionism at its purest: the world's problems are seen to be so urgent and the technologies in our hands so mighty that it's imprudent to wait a few more years and see those young people graduate. Another of Thiel's many quixotic initiatives is to support permanent, autonomous ocean communities, where geeks work, live, and experiment outside the jurisdiction of the state. To that effect, he's donated more than $1 million to support the Seasteading Institute, run by Milton Friedman's grandson Patri, which is building one such government-free zone 199 miles (320 kilometers) off the coast of San Francisco, where US regulations—from gun-control laws to building codes—no longer apply. Why all this effort? Perhaps, as one sharp wit put it, "because the first place most of us want to experiment with looser building codes is 320 kilometres out to sea."

In a 2009 essay for the Cato Institute, a libertarian think tank, Thiel explained why his brand of technoescapism is a serious endeavor. "In our time, the great task for libertarians is to find an escape from politics in all its forms—from the totalitarian and fundamentalist catastrophes to the unthinking demos that guides so-called 'social democracy.'" Thus, he writes, "the critical question then becomes one of means, of how to escape not via politics but beyond it. . . . The mode for escape must involve some sort of new and hitherto untried process that leads us to some undiscovered country; and for this reason I have focused my efforts on new technologies that may create a new space for freedom." Thiel then proceeds to outline how cyberspace might be one such space, pointing out that "in the late 1990s, the founding vision of PayPal centered on the creation of a new world currency, free from all government control and dilution—the end of monetary sovereignty, as it were."

Now, viewed in the abstract, PayPal does seem to fulfill the dream of technoescapism: finally, people are no longer tied to banks and states and can engage in transactions as they wish. But this, of course, is true only if one assumes that platforms like PayPal operate in an absolute power vacuum, completely immune to pressures that countries, institutions, and hierarchies might exert on those engaged in the transactions as well as on PayPal itself. PayPal may have obviated the theoretical need for banks—but its investors still need a bank to cash their checks from PayPal, so no technoescape actually takes place.

Consider the role that PayPal has played in the WikiLeaks saga: yes, it was initially a great tool to raise money for Assange's cause, but the moment WikiLeaks took on the US government, PayPal ran away from Assange (freezing WikiLeaks's account) in much the same way that Peter Thiel wants to run from reality. Likewise, as of July 2012, PayPal had revised how it deals with file-sharing sites, requiring any sites that want to use PayPal to solicit membership fees from users to ensure that they host no illegal files. Instead of subverting the power of the entertainment industry—as Thiel's belief in technoescapism would suggest—PayPal has become a useful tool in perpetuating that power. Geeks' power myopia is scandalous.

Another recent manifestation of technoescapism can be found in *Abundance*, a new book cowritten by Peter Diamandis, a wealthy entrepreneur and cofounder of the Singularity University. The latter is an outlet that promotes Ray Kurzweil's idea that computers will one day be as smart as people, who in turn will live forever, and presents it, along with some other key ideas of technogospel, in an easy-to-absorb manner, suitable for busy executives eager to foot the university's $25,000-for-ten-weeks tuition bill. (Thiel is an avid supporter of singularity as well, having given money to Kurzweil; it's not very likely that he pays anyone to drop out of the Singularity University.) *Abundance*'s basic message is that technology is perpetually making things better and more abundant, for "when seen through the lens of technology, few resources are truly scarce; they're mainly inaccessible." Thus, we'd better defer to technophilanthropists like Diamandis to solve all of the world's most pressing problems, from hunger and authoritarianism to education and health care. "The high-tech revolution created an entirely new breed of wealthy technophilanthropists who are using their fortunes to solve global, abundance-related challenges," he writes.

Diamandis promises us a world of abundance that will essentially require no sacrifice from anyone—and since no one's interests will be hurt, politics itself will be unnecessary. In fact, all problems can be fixed locally, bypassing the entrenched interests; "in today's hyperlinked world, solving problems anywhere, solves problems everywhere," he argues, in what must be the book's most vacuous statement. (Why are Armenia and Azerbaijan still fighting over Nagorno-Karabakh if someone in Orange County can sort it out with a couple of tweets? Diamandis doesn't say.) The word "politics" appears only once—in the URL of a website listed in the bibliography (foodpolitics.com). That technology will replace politics, for it will sidestep questions of distribution and allocation and replace them with questions of production and application, is one of the core tenants of technoescapism. It doesn't naturally occur to technoescapists that without politics and some threat of coercion or punishment, some players, be it countries, corporations, or individuals, might not cooperate with the rest, refusing to cut production or install more efficient technologies or bear their share of costs for destroying the environment or the commons.

Not surprisingly, *Abundance* has very little to say about problems like climate change, for regardless of how many solar panels can be installed in Californian houses, this noble move won't much alter what the Chinese Communist Party thinks about the importance of economic growth, climate change be damned. As technology journalist Joe Gertner points out in his *New York Times* review of the book, *Abundance* might gloss over problems like climate change "because arresting its effects will necessitate not only a huge technological push but also the messy business of changing human behavior, radically altering government policies and brokering international accords. In other words, it doesn't begin to fit into the authors' paradigm of a problem that requires a D.I.Y. or techno-philanthropic fix." Likewise, hoping that distributing tablets or e-readers might solve Africa's problems with illiteracy is one thing, but actually getting governments to commit to choosing readers over textbooks or building new schools or hiring more teachers is quite another. The former is a problem of application; the latter, of allocation. No amount of technology will solve the latter problem, since this debate is animated by very different ideas about what teaching is and how government funds should be distributed—ideas that have little to do with the technology in question.

Unlike Thiel and his brand of technoescapists, technorationalists do not aim to rid us of building codes—they, like good technocrats, would prefer that such codes were adopted swiftly, without too much unnecessary consultation and debate. Politics, in this model, is imagined as consisting of little else but fixing potholes and dealing with stray dogs. Political matters are reduced to administrative matters—and those can be settled scientifically, so there is no need to waste time discussing their merits and perpetuating all the messiness of the political process. Thus, Jeff Jarvis tells us that "if the geeks take over—and they will—we could enter an era of scientific rationality in government." Sean Parker, Facebook's ex-president played by Justin Timberlake in *The Social Network*, enthusiastically proclaims that "to the extent that . . . new media are going to have a role in reforming politics, it's going to happen because . . . those systems will make politics more efficient."

Today's politics, by comparison, is seen as wildly inefficient and in need of repair, if not outright replacement. Katie Stanton, a former Google executive who briefly worked for the Obama administration and currently works for Twitter, compared her experience in Washington to that of "a vegetarian trapped inside the sausage factory." Her ex-boss, Google's Eric Schmidt, lambasts Washington as "an incumbent protection machine [in which] the laws are written by lobbyists" (this antilobbyist sentiment has somehow never prevented Google from rapidly expanding its own lobbying operation in Washington, DC).

So many geeks are impatient with politics because they think that it involves nothing but talk. For them, deliberation is the cancer in the body of modern democracy, and it would be so much more productive to replace talk with action, with doing things, for all this chatter is of little to no use. After all, no great apps have ever come out of a committee meeting. So Beth Noveck, the open-government advocate and author of *Wiki Government*, tells us—in the kind of language beloved by administrators—that "it is overdue to rethink the legitimacy of attenuated participation in a small number of representative institutions." Got it?

The actual meaning of this convoluted linguistic construct becomes clear later on, when she writes that "the digital environment offers new ways to engage in the public exchange of reason. With new tools, people can 'speak' through shared maps and diagrams rather than meetings." Maps and diagrams are so much better than debates and meetings! Thus, Noveck complains that "most of the work at the intersection of technology and democracy has focused on how to create demographically representative conversations. The focus is on deliberation, not collaboration; on talk instead of action; on information, not decision-making." This is a rather depressing view of wikigovernment: instead of articulating their grievances and concerns, citizens will be given an opportunity to contribute to mapping their neighborhood, Wikipedia style. Politics is out; technocracy is in. We'll check some online form to tell the government which potholes to fill, but we won't discuss whether the workers fixing them need better pay or we need better roads.

An even sharper antipolitical—and even antidemocratic—sentiment can be observed in the work of Parag Khanna, the geopolitics wunderkind who has recently reinvented himself as a technology visionary. In *Hybrid Reality*, coauthored with his wife, Khanna suggests that not just talk but even elections might need to go so that technocratic modes of governance can continue unabated. Drawing on the generativity theory of Jonathan Zittrain—Internet-centrism rears its ugly head again, lending support to crazy governance ideas—Khanna writes, in the euphemistic style of the Chinese politburo, that "a generative governance system can be designed to provide stability and positive change at the same time."

What does any of this mean? Well, "positive change" for Parag Khanna means that "using technology to deliberate on matters of national importance, deliver public services, and incorporate citizen feedback may ultimately be a truer form of direct participation than a system of indirect representation and infrequent elections." Thus, he continues, "we cannot be afraid of technocracy when the alternative is the futile populism of Argentines, Hungarians, and Thais masquerading as democracy. It is precisely these nonfunctional democracies that are prime candidates to be superseded by better-designed technocracies—likely delivering more benefits to their citizens." And here comes the clincher: "To the extent that China provides guidance for governance that Western democracies don't, it is in having 'technocrats with term limits.'"

All of this sounds more like "wicked government" than "wikigovernment." Deliberation and debate are silenced; technocrats and administrators are given free reign; deeply political, life-altering issues are recast as matters of improving efficiency. Politicians, as is to be expected, are hated for being partisan ideologues. The best articulation of geeks' distaste for politics and strong respect for administration comes from an interview given by Bill Maris, who heads Google's venture fund. The man deeply hates politics and badly wants it to be replaced with technocracy:

Thinking about government policy sends shivers up my spine. The gears are grinding together in government, and it's slow and complicated and no one understands it. Great things are usually not accomplished in Silicon Valley through government policy, they are accomplished by individuals who set out to change the world, invent something, create a better live [*sic*] for themselves and their children. . . . I have a hard time finding people I love, trust, and respect that do want to be in politics. Because what are the incentives? They are usually not financial—hopefully—but there's not much incentive to make a change, to make a difference. . . . There are people who spend their entire careers in government and policy, and I'd hate to do that and ask myself, "has the peanut been pushed one inch?" That's why I draw a distinction between politics and the government. There are people who are doing really hard work—in the military, building bridges, engineers, the NIH, versus what goes on at the highest level in Washington. And you've got to ask: "are you guys totally out of touch?"

This little tirade has everything: the worship of the individual hero, the entrepreneur; the myth of "the Internet" as created without much government intervention; the framing of political problems as a matter of providing adequate financial incentives (for what else might motivate people to get involved in politics, when all politicians are seen as liars?); the idea that all politicians do is push peanuts (inch by inch); the sharp distinction between politics and administration and a healthy disgust for the former.

Technocrats and Their Limits

One would think that by the second decade of the twenty-first century, the intellectual poverty of technocracy and the primacy of politics over it would be a well-established truth in need of no further defense. Back in 1902, Winston Churchill, in a letter to H. G. Wells, cautioned that "nothing would be more fatal than for the Government of States to get in the hands of experts. Expert knowledge is limited knowledge, and the unlimited ignorance of the plain man who knows where it hurts is a safer guide than any rigorous direction of a specialized character." Would it be too much to expect our geeks to know something about history?

Jeff Jarvis's enthusiasm for a geek-run government of scientific rationality is peculiar for its complete lack of awareness of the sheer unoriginality of such plans (Internet-centrism, as already noted, has the disturbing power to recast old, discarded, and retrograde ideas as unique, original, and progressive sheerly by virtue of their association with "the Internet"). Is Jarvis's demand for a government of "scientific rationality" really different from Saint-Simon's proclamation—in 1821—that "in the new political order . . . the decisions must be the result of scientific demonstrations totally independent of human will. . . . Under such an order we shall see the disappearance of the three main disadvantages of the present political system, that is, arbitrariness, incapacity and intrigue"?

Bernard Crick, in his *In Defense of Politics* first published in 1961, provided the best criticism of such wishful thinking—and its disrespect for arbitrariness, incapacity, and intrigue—to date. "Suppose the 'arbitrariness' which Saint-Simon hated to be no more than a product of diversity; 'incapacity,' simply some sense of limitations; 'intrigue,' no more than the conflict of differing interests in any even moderately free State . . . then we have a characterisation of politics itself, indeed a rather good one. . . . At heart what disturbs those hopeful for a science of politics is simply the element of conflict in ordinary politics; what excites them has been the prestige of science, its good reputation for—so it is thought—'unity.'" The idea underpinning the latter part of the argument—about the unity of science—has long been put to rest by a new generation of historians of science, who, following Thomas Kuhn's work on scientific paradigms, have shown that scientific disciplines rely on wildly different methods of thinking and argumentation and that much of the presumed unity is a myth. The idea that somehow conflict is bad for politics is even more suspicious. There is so much conflict in politics simply because people who are free to choose will be bound to pursue conflicting agendas. The arbitrariness of politics that Saint-Simon condemns derives from the fact that in truly free societies, there are few restrictions on what freedoms can be pursued. As such, no algorithm or set of laws can ever be designed to resolve the ensuing conflicts and clashes. Saint-Simon had some intriguing solutions to the problems he identified—not as good as "the Internet" but good enough—except that what he thought to be "problems" were not problems at all.

Writing in the early 1960s, Bernard Crick was prescient enough to foresee that technology was more than just a collection of artifacts and systems; it could also be a style of thought that would be invoked in the name of reforming politics and cleansing it of imperfection, a doctrine that could "rescue mankind from the lack of certainty and the glut of compromises . . . [and] rehouse and redevelop mere politics." The key to this doctrine, wrote Crick, was the belief that "everything in society is . . . capable of rational manipulation if the techniques of power and production are understood." Crick, in other words, was an early critic of solutionism; his own peeve, Internet-centrism, was present as well—it went by the name of "scientism."

Many scholars of technocracy echo Crick's conclusions. Thus, as sociologist Jean Meynaud wrote in his study of technocrats in France, "one of the most important components of the technician's mentality is his belief that rational analysis and interpretation of facts are liable to bring about unanimity, at least among men of good will. The technician who believes that he has arrived at a full understanding of a question is always surprised and often grieved when he encounters opposition to his theories; inevitably, he is tempted to attribute this to ignorance or ill-will." When the benefits of one's solutions look so obvious, how can people fail to recognize them?

Meynaud's speculation that technocrats believe they have superior access to truth, seeing those who disagree with them as ignoramuses, can help us explain, among other things, Google's befuddlement over the massive opposition to its quest to scan all the world's books. Here is how Douglas Edwards, Google's brand manager between 1999 and 2005, describes it: "For Larry [Page] and Sergey [Brin], truth was often self-evident and unassailable. The inability of others to recognize truth did not make it any less absolute. Obviously, it's a good idea to make as much information as possible available to as many people as possible. Obviously, a lot of valuable information is in books. Obviously, helping people find that information is good. Obviously, an author only benefits if people find out that his or her book contains useful information. There are no shades of grey in this. Truth is, after all, a binary function."

But is truth really a binary function? It might be—if one arrogantly assumes that one's values and interests are the only "correct" values and interests out there. Technocratic thinking views pluralism as an enemy, not an ally—or, in geeks' own parlance, it's a bug, not a feature. As two scholars of technocracy observe, its fundamental assumption "is that disagreements occur not because people are bound to differ but because they are misinformed." The paradox is that, while technocracy itself is an ideology, most technocrats try their best to distance themselves from any insinuation that they might be driven by anything other than pragmatism and the pursuit of efficiency.

Unfortunately, Crick's attack on technological thinking has received less attention than several other similar attacks by his contemporaries: Jane Jacobs's attack on unimaginative urban planning, Isaiah Berlin's attack on "procrusteanism," Friedrich Hayek's attack on central planning, Karl Popper's attack on historicism, and Michael Oakeshott's attack on rationalism come to mind. Most of these important critiques of the arrogance and self-conceit of the planner and the reformer are united by a common theme: something about the experience of living in the polis with other human beings is essentially irreducible to formulaic expression and optimization techniques. Thinking and deliberation are unavoidable; even the most perfect algorithms won't spare us those—not without impoverishing our political culture as a result.

Thus, the mind-set of the modern-day reformer—much like his or her critical disposition—has an extensive intellectual tradition; "the Internet" here is merely an enabler and cunning concealer of impulses and urges that have been around for a very long time. However, it would be futile to deny that the last two decades have also unleashed an unprecedented wave of innovation and the proliferation of countless new ways to fix politics.

Good intentions, even when clothed in exciting mash-ups, don't justify naïveté. What hasn't changed since Crick wrote his critique of technological thinking is the fact that fixing politics without first getting a thorough understanding of what it is and what it is for is still a very dangerous undertaking. Or, to put it bluntly, it's never been cheaper to act on one's stupidity. Political thinking, as well as political morality, needs to be cultivated; it doesn't occur naturally—not even to geniuses in Silicon Valley. As Princeton sociologist Miguel Angel Centento put it so well in his 1993 study of the technocratic mind-set, "While advanced degrees may help our modern Leviathans construct societies in which our lives will be longer and less nasty, there is no reason to suspect that such expertise will keep them from making our existence even more brutish."

CHAPTER FIVE

The Perils of
Algorithmic Gatekeeping

"Yes, the internet is democratizing in that sense that the cheap equipment is democratizing. But just because a football is cheap and anyone can kick one around, it doesn't mean that everybody is Ronaldo."
—FRANNY ARMSTRONG, BRITISH DOCUMENTARY FILMMAKER

"Do you remember 'books'? A book is basically thousands of tweets printed out and stapled together between pieces of cardboard."
—ADRIAN CHEN, GAWKER.COM

J oel Whitney, then editor in chief of a highbrow online magazine called *Guernica*, was surprised to receive an e-mail from Google. A magazine of politics, literature, and art, *Guernica* has published a wide range of authors, from Noam Chomsky to Amitav Ghosh and from Amartya Sen to Meghan O'Rourke. This is not your average anonymous Tumblr, but it's not a lavishly funded literary outlet either; somehow, they do a lot—with very little.

Google's e-mail sought to inform Whitney that *Guernica*'s membership in the AdSense program—a Google-run program that allows participating websites to earn money by running automatically generated ads that target site content and audience—was being revoked. For a site like *Guernica*, with its middle to low six-figure readership per month, AdSense was a small but stable source of income—just one of the many less visible positive effects that Google has on the literary world.

Google's angry e-mail was triggered by a short story called "Early Sexual Experiences" that had appeared in *Guernica* a few weeks earlier. It ran in a special series on innovative memoir writing edited by the acclaimed author Deb Olin Unferth. The short story— written by the equally renown author Clancy Martin, whose work has been published in the *New York Times* and *Harper's*—was a first-person, 1,500-word account of, well, early sexual experiences, which mentioned, among other things, masturbation and the loss of virginity. Google—or rather its prudish algorithms—flagged the story as inappropriate and in violation of Google's decency rules. Google's algorithms believed that *Guernica* was pornography— and the company deferred to their judgment.

Now that *Guernica* had been informed of the decision, the Google ads on its site were soon turned off. There is an appeal process, but in *Guernica*'s case, it led nowhere. Whitney says that "even after consulting a friend—a benefit supporter who bought a ticket to our fundraiser the year before, a Google employee who told us it's all what the algorithm decides—Google rejected our appeal." What sane small online publisher will now dare publish a memoir like Clancy Martin's if it means foregoing a stable stream of income?

Guernica's is not an isolated case. In late 2011, Omoyele Sowore, a Nigerian exile living in New York, got a similar e-mail from Google. Sowore runs a website called Sahara Reporters, which mixes editorial writings on the state of affairs in Nigeria with reported stories contributed by a network of citizen journalists on the ground. One such story focused on police brutality in the region and included a number of graphic photos. Google's algorithms found the images too violent and informed Sowore that it was suspending the site's participation in AdSense. Pleas to Google were met with silence. Only after an intervention from a well-placed staffer with the Committee to Protect Journalism did Google agree, perhaps sensing that the story would yield very bad publicity if pushed by activist free speech NGOs, to reconsider its treatment of Sahara Reporters.

On the surface, both cases don't look all that controversial. After all, Google is a private company, and it can run its advertising business any way it likes; inevitably, there will be people trying to exploit its advertising system to make money from illegal activities.

Sites promoting ethnic violence or pedophilia perhaps should not be allowed to make money with Google's help. Thus, it is not the fact that Google selects whom it does business with that is so worrisome here. It's not even Google's prudish attitude toward innovative fiction—even though, one presumes, James Joyce wouldn't much profit from Google AdSense had he chosen to serialize *Ulysses* on his blog. It's not even the fact that Google outsources such important decisions to algorithms. What's truly rankling here is Google's insistence on the supposed neutrality and objectivity of its algorithms. Instead of acknowledging that its algorithms might have shortcomings and biases that ought to be corrected, Google behaves as if introducing humans to occasionally review the work of its algorithms would be tantamount to abandoning all faith in artificial intelligence as such.

Google's reluctance to acknowledge that its algorithms can occasionally malfunction allows it to extricate itself from a number of tricky ethical aspects of its work. Take Google Autocomplete—a useful feature that proposes ways to finish one's search query based on just a few typed characters. By drawing on what other users have searched for in the past, Autocomplete can anticipate that whenever you type "Rome was not," you will very likely finish with "built in a day." Why not just spare you the few seconds it takes to type in the whole sentence? Why not let users save their precious time, given that so many of their search queries are similar?

Alas, we are not just patrons of Google's information library—we are also the protagonists of many of its books. And those books keep changing, as Google keeps tinkering with its algorithms and adding new features. One indirect consequence of a service like Google Autocomplete is that now anyone can see what kind of searches about a given subject are most popular. When I type "Britney Spears is" into Google, Autocomplete gives me four suggestions for how most other users have completed that query. Thus, others have inquired if Britney is a "hot mess," whether she is "dead" or "ugly," and—my favorite—whether she is a "three-headed alien" (which, on further investigation, turns out to be the title of a book).

Britney Spears is a public figure, and the controversy here seems moot at best. But suppose that an enemy of yours, in a deliberate effort to smear your reputation, starts paying users to search for your name followed by the word "pedophile." An army of eager contributors, recruited through sites like Craigslist and Amazon's Mechanical Turk, are now generating enough search volume to make this new query replace a few other, more positive terms associated with your name. Now, everyone who searches for your name is also informed that you might be a pedophile—and, remember, you have no way to appeal, for Google's algorithms are in charge, and they never get things wrong.

It's hard to say if Bettina Wulff, Germany's former first lady, has been the victim of a similar crowdsourced hit job, but in September 2012 she sued Google for "autocompleting" searches for her name with terms like "prostitute" and "escort." Wulff's is only one of the many legal challenges facing the search engine giant. Google, insisting that its algorithms offer an unmediated and objective access to Truth, keeps running into legal trouble in Europe and Asia, where it has already lost several cases in court. The cases are usually brought by peeved individuals and institutions who find their names and brands associated with all sorts of nasty terms and insinuations. In Japan, Google was ordered to modify its Autocomplete results after a Japanese man complained that they linked him to crimes he had never committed. Likewise, in France, Google was ordered to modify its Autocomplete results after it suggested that a man was a "satanist" and "rapist"; Google also lost a similar case in Italy.

In virtually all such cases, Google invokes the neutrality of its algorithms and claims that its Autocomplete results simply reflect what others have searched for. As the company's spokesperson said in response to one of the lawsuits, "We believe that Google should not be held liable for terms that appear in Autocomplete as these are predicted by computer algorithms based on searches from previous users, not by Google itself." Google, of course, knows that its algorithms can be gamed: in 2010, a marketer named Brent Payne turned to the cheap human labor available on Amazon's Mechanical Turk and offered to pay small amounts to individuals who would agree to conduct the searches he specified. As a result of his clever manipulation, anyone searching for "Brent P" on Google would see "Brent Payne manipulated this" as one of the Autocomplete suggestions. The trick worked—until Payne went public with his experiment.

Not everyone affected by Google's Autocomplete would take the search engine giant to court. It's not immediately obvious how a different, more humane policy would hurt anyone (except perhaps Google's bottom line). It's not really a freedom-of-expression issue, because no one is asking Google to remove offensive information from its search index; if they exist, the pages containing actual accusations will still be findable. But Google can, for example, proactively refuse to show negative suggestions—those of the "idiot" and "Satan" variety—for queries; those who want results for "John Smith is evil" can just type in the whole query—why save them the time? In fact, this is already Google's attitude toward file-sharing sites; if you want Google to serve you links that come from, say, The Pirate Bay—the notorious platform for swapping pirated content—Google's Autocomplete won't suggest anything; you have to type the whole query yourself.

Alternatively, Google could find a way to have companies and individuals claim their identity online and choose which negative autosuggestions about themselves they'd like to remove. At the very minimum, it could set up a way to complain about the suggestions—which would be easier now that Google also runs its own social network, Google+. This might be of particular importance to small businesses who have no money to spend on maintaining their online reputation; when one of their competitors can turn to Craigslist or Amazon's Mechanical Turk to generate new ways to "autocomplete" queries about them, this can make or break their business (something similar happened with another, now-defunct Google service—Places—where some firms reported their competitors' businesses as "closed," which, once fed into Google's information empire, could discourage thousands of potential customers).

But none of this will happen as long as Google maintains that its algorithms are just an objective reflection of reality. In fact, the rhetoric of mirrors and reflections is ubiquitous in Google's presentations of itself to the outside world. Marissa Mayer, a longtime Google senior executive who jumped ship to lead Yahoo!, once said of her former employer, "We're trying to build a virtual mirror of the world at all times." Asked to explain the role that digital platforms played in the riots that swept the United Kingdom in 2011, Google's Eric Schmidt also invoked the mirror imagery. "It is a mistake to look into the mirror and try to break the mirror. Whatever the problem was [that caused the riots,] the internet is a reflection of that problem," he said.

Note how invoking "the Internet" as a unified social force out there allows Schmidt to avoid any meaningful debate about its components. (Here Google is hardly alone; Facebook, too, likes to hide behind such mirror rhetoric: "Our role in the system [is] to constantly be innovating and be updating what our system is to reflect what the current social norms are.") But the mirror is a poor metaphor for capturing Google's role in today's public sphere; the company doesn't just reflect, it also shapes, creates, and distorts—and it does so in numerous ways that cannot be reduced to one singular logic of "the Internet." What sociologist Donald MacKenzie wrote of financial models applies to Google as well: it's more like an engine than a camera in that how it initially chooses to present and slice reality also creates a new reality in its own right.

Compare Google engineers to journalists. The latter might like the idea that they too only reflect or document what's happening in the world at large. But naïve is the journalist who believes that journalism doesn't also transform reality, introducing new (and often disturbing) incentives—for example, to talk in sound bites or highlight the most populist parts of one's message—into the political process. Reality might be recorded all right—but newspapers, radio stations, and TV channels are also complex sociotechnical systems, where thousands of actors are pursuing their own agendas, which, quite often, have nothing to do with the recording of reality per se.

Better awareness of how the practice of journalism is constrained by various conditions of modern capitalism—from the constant anxiety over the security of one's career to the growing pressure to produce content that might hit it big online—might actually give us better, more responsible journalism. Instead of hiding behind labels like "objectivity" or "neutrality" and pretending that anyone carrying a press card automatically shares in these values, it would be much more productive to investigate what kinds of obstacles—be they cultural or economic—stand in the way of those values. And if both "objectivity" and "neutrality" are still seen as useful in the context of doing journalism, then an effort to sustain them, against all the obstacles, can begin in earnest.

Google likewise should stop hiding behind the rhetoric of mirrors and reflections, acknowledge its own immense role in shaping the public sphere, and start playing that role in a more responsible manner. Being "objective" is hard work; it doesn't just happen naturally once all the important work has been delegated to the algorithms. Our new algorithmic overlords should not aspire to act like ethical automatons; only by being self-reflexive and morally imaginative can they live up to the heavy burden of their civic responsibilities.

Alas, their current attitude is nowhere near that ideal. *Wired's* Steven Levy, in his hagiographic biography of Google, observes that "Brin and Page both believed that if Google's algorithms determined what results were best—and long clicks indicated that the algorithms were satisfying the people who did the searching— who were they to mess with it." Believe this they did—but why didn't Steven Levy bother to inquire why? It's time our technology reporters learn to control their hagiographic impulses and start challenging the just-so narratives spouted by Silicon Valley.

We need to explain, not take for granted, why Brin and Page believed this or that and how they got almost everyone else to believe it. The validity of such beliefs cannot be presumed to be self-evident, as if the very technological efficacy of a given algorithm were enough to explain its success. As every engineer knows, there are usually multiple ways of achieving the same objective. Why some such ways, even if they are presented as merely technological and unproblematic, cannot just be explained away with appeals to seemingly timeless concepts like efficiency; why such concepts impose themselves as timeless and worth pursuing; how the idea of "the Internet" modifies the appeal of such concepts; why "the mirror," rather than, say, "the engine," becomes the preferred metaphor to explain Google—these are the puzzles our public conversation about technology must try to solve.

Drowning in the Algorithmic Sea

Once we go beyond the heroic but vapid stories that technologists tell outsiders about their work, we might be in a better position to understand the inner workings of technologies, their civic impact, and how to reform and regulate them. Google's own rhetoric makes for a nice target of investigation—and not just because of its constant references to mirrors and reflections. Google also likes to invoke noble terms like "democracy" to show that what its algorithms compute is not just objective but also just. Thus, in explaining why they present search results the way they do, Google's website tells us that "democracy on the Web works"—by which they mean that everybody gets a say by voting for their favorite website with links, which are then counted by Google's PageRank algorithm in order to determine which results should come on top.

Theirs is a very peculiar definition of "democracy." For one, the idea of equality on which Google search is based is quite shallow: yes, everyone can vote with "links"—but those who have the resources to generate more links, perhaps by paying influential sites to link to them, or to game the system through search engine optimization have much more power than those who don't. It's anything but "one person, one vote." At best, this is more of an oligarchy than a democracy. Besides, Google's ranking algorithm considers at least two hundred other factors—for example, the loading speed of the website—in addition to how many other sites link to a particular page. For the democracy metaphor to work in this context, "democracy" itself needs to be redefined. Google's Kafkaesque reading of democracy goes something like this: you enter a booth to cast a vote only to discover that the electoral commission is also going to consider your fashion taste, your accent, the weather outside, and many other factors—of which, predictably, you cannot be informed.

Consider how Google likes to highlight its scientific credentials to justify its innovative, can-do attitude. It's not just that Google never misses a chance to tout its roots in Stanford's nerdy environment but it also actively positions itself as belonging in the very pantheon of science, where exceptions can be granted and blame can be withheld, for the noble mission is nothing less than Enlightenment itself. "We're scientists. So if it works, great. If it doesn't, we'll try something else," says Eric Schmidt in an effort to bolster the legitimacy of Google's products—who would be crazy enough to oppose the march of science and suggest that perhaps some of those products need to be modified?—and present Google's curiosity and ability to try things as just an extension of the scientific method.

But science, of course, does have a moral code, which would be apparent to anyone who's ever tried to conduct experiments involving humans. Many such experiments would need to be approved by various human subject panels and institutional research boards. Scientists don't just spontaneously "try things"; they are forced to think through the social and political consequences of their work, often well before entering the lab. What institutional research board would approve Google's quixotic plan to send a fleet of vehicles to record private data floating through WiFi networks or the launch of Google Buzz, the company's disastrous stab at social networking, which ended up compromising the privacy of many of its users? What institutional research board would be satisfied with the excuse that Sergey Brin produced after the Google Buzz fiasco: "It never occurred to me as a privacy thing." Well, yes—that's why no company, certainly not a company of Google's size and clout, should be "trying things" without first establishing an institution-wide respect for ethical dilemmas.

Perhaps Google doesn't feel comfortable in its new position as guardian and gatekeeper of our public life. Most likely, complex ethical dilemmas are not what it signed up for originally. Its commercial ethos is in constant tension with its public responsibilities, and so far the former almost always wins. When Eric Schmidt says he doesn't want to "criticize the consumer for doing things that are idiotic. . . . We love our consumers even if I don't like what they're doing," there's no doubt that Google doesn't fancy itself as a successor to the *New York Times* or NPR. Schmidt doesn't talk of Google's users as citizens; rather he frames them as "consumers," which at once takes much pressure off his company's shoulders. Consumers, after all, are always right, even if occasionally idiotic. Google can pretend that its civic role doesn't exist as long as it wants; this doesn't simply make that role go away. The neutrality defense is bunk—and the sooner Google itself acknowledges this and finds a way to exercise its newly found powers responsibly, the fewer mistakes of the Google Buzz or WiFi variety it will commit in the future.

We must stop thinking of the new filters and algorithmic practices promoted by the new digital intermediaries (and their digerati cheerleaders) as unproblematic, objective, and naturally superior to the filters and practices that preceded them. These new filters might be faster, cheaper, and more efficient, but speed, cost, and efficiency are only peripherally related to the civic roles that these filters and algorithms will be playing in our lives. Without subjecting these faster, cheaper, and more efficient filters to the close ethical scrutiny they deserve, we risk committing one of the many fallacies of solutionism and celebrating improvements related to less important problems while completely neglecting more burning, but less obvious, issues.

David Weinberger of Harvard's Berkman Center is dead wrong when he writes of "the Internet" that its "filters no longer filter out. They filter forward, bringing their results to the front. What doesn't make it through a filter is still visible and available in the background." Likewise, to argue that "instead of reducing information and hiding what does not make it through, filters now increase information and reveal the whole deep sea" (as Weinberger does) is not just to give Silicon Valley a free pass on morality but also to give in to one of the core beliefs of Internet-centrism—the idea that just because these new filters originate on "the Internet," they must somehow be divine, free from the biases of their creators, and completely immune to the power context in which they are designed and deployed.

Another danger of Internet-centrism in this context is that, in assuming that digital filters are different from their analog predecessors, we risk blurring immense theoretical and conceptual differences among them. This is the inevitable consequence of imagining "the Internet" as a culture that, much like print culture, replicates its coherent, stable qualities in its products (not surprisingly, Weinberger identifies five "most basic properties" of "the Internet," which he then proceeds to locate in individual platforms). In reality, some of these new digital filters don't just refuse to reveal "the whole deep sea" but conceal it in very different ways; the idea of a coherent Internet culture precludes us from noticing these differences (it's in this sense that anyone who is desperately trying to understand how today's digital platforms work is much better off simply assuming that "the Internet does not exist"). Even a brief empirical study of filters employed by popular social media platforms would reveal as much; they all rely on very different filters that produce very different regimes of visibility.

Consider Twitter's Trends feature, a filter that relies on several signals and algorithms to determine which topics are "trending" across the platform. Whether something becomes a trend on Twitter is important for one simple reason: once the story achieves this much coveted status, it attracts even more attention, spilling into national and global conversations far beyond Twitter. In this sense, Twitter too is an engine, not a camera; it doesn't just reflect realities—it actively creates them.

Consequently, when some important discussion generates a lot of buzz but never rises to the status of a trend, it's very common to see Twitter accused of censorship. This was the case with the Occupy Wall Street discussion—much of it happening under the #occupywallstreet tag—which continuously failed to register on Twitter's radars. Many users and commentators assumed that this must have happened for political reasons and immediately cried foul. There's something peculiar about such claims, for they seem to assume that, at all other times, Twitter's "trend-finding" engine works flawlessly.

Every time accusations of censorship are aired (especially when they concern Justin Bieber's disappearance from trends), someone working for Twitter steps forward and points out that trends are identified based on many factors other than the volume of tweets. For example, whether the topic discussed is new to Twitter users counts as well. What about other factors? Well, we don't know: Twitter, like Google, does not disclose the signals it monitors for fear that, once this knowledge is out, the system will be gamed by manipulators.

Tarleton Gillespie, a professor of communications at Cornell, investigated numerous censorship complaints made about Trends and published an interesting study about Twitter's trending algorithms. He pointed out that, even though people who complain about censorship think they "know" what Trends measures, in reality, it's impossible to say for sure. Thus, he writes, the fact that #occupywallstreet is not trending could mean that

(a) it is being deliberately censored (b) it is actually less popular than one might think (c) it is very popular but consistently so, not a spike (d) it is popular and spiking, but not in a way the algorithm is designed to measure (e) it is popular and spiking, but not as much as some pop culture phenomena that has crowded it off the list (f) it is popular and important, but not as popular as the pop culture phenomena that have been strategically gamed onto the list (g) it has not Trended because it has not Trended, thereby not enjoying the amplification Trends itself offers.

Twitter doesn't say which set of factors it relies on, and the ambiguity that ensues only contributes to making a given trend look organic and natural. It's the double-click mentality in action once again: highly contingent outcomes of human decisions over which factors to prioritize in labeling something a trend are recast as just inevitable and objective outcomes of leaving computers on and having the scripts do their work.

In *Engineering the Revolution*, historian Ken Alder writes of how French military engineers adopted what he calls a "technocratic pose"—an attitude whereby "technology-makers [claim to be] neutral conduits who passively mediate between the epistemological and social world around them"—which allowed them to navigate different warring factions after the 1789 revolution and design cutting-edge guns at the same time. Twitter, like many other technology companies, also frequently adopts such a "technocratic pose," pretending that it is just doing objective, neutral measurements. As Gillespie points out, "Trends promises a mathematical and an exhaustive analysis of what is being talked about, while presenting it as automatically generated and self-evident facts about the discussion."

Twitter makes certain assumptions about what aspects of the public discussion constitute a trend, decides on how those aspects are to be measured, and having measured them, feeds them back to the public. The company doesn't just "reflect"—in Silicon Valley's lingo—the public's interests but actively shapes them. And it doesn't shape them in accordance with some "basic features of the

Internet"; instead, it starts with some basic vision of what public debate is and what it should be—and it's those visions that we risk missing if we give in to Internet-centrism and naïvely believe that all these decisions reflect the nature of "the Internet" and are guided by the gradual unfolding of its spirit.

Thus, Gillespie notes that "a term that has trended before has a higher threshold before it can trend again. The implication is that the algorithm prefers novelty in public discourse over phenomena with a longer shelf-life. This is a longstanding critique of broadcast journalism, reappearing in social media." This, if anything, should undermine the presumed rupture and discontinuity between new and old media that the epochalist purveyors of Internet-centrism love to celebrate. Perhaps Twitter is much more like Fox News than it appears at first sight. But such insights are not just useful analytically; they are also immensely useful for media activism and reform. Such highly empirical investigations of various biases introduced by Twitter's algorithms—rather than facile, populist, and unsubstantiated claims of censorship—provide much better grounds on which to reform Twitter and perhaps push the company toward a different metric.

Many users—if only they knew!—might feel uncomfortable with how Twitter measures the popularity of discussions across clusters. Here, Twitter believes that discussions that occur within clusters—between users in the same region, who already follow each other or share the same demographics—are less worthy of appearing on Trends than discussions that span different clusters and demographics. You might hate global inequality or love equal rights for gays, but if your "meme," regardless of how intense it is, doesn't break out of your cluster, the odds are it won't make it to Trends. But, as Gillespie points out, this preference for breadth over depth is in itself a highly political choice that rests on a certain vision of how public debate should function.

Instead of treating the new filters as unproblematic and objective, we need to understand what other approaches to conducting the public debate they might be making impossible or less common. Moreover, we want coders and engineers who, refusing to adopt yet another "technocratic pose," are brave enough to defend their own preferred vision of how public debate should function. Assumptions of such a nature are inevitable—all designers eventually need to endorse at least some weak vision of who will be using their products—but, intoxicated with Internet-centrism, we have let too many designers off the hook far too easily.

The Meme Industry Will Make You Famous

Once we start paying attention to how digital filters and algorithms actually function, once we grapple with what they hide and reveal, many of the founding myths of Internet-centrism might no longer look tenable. Few of these myths have been more detrimental to our public discourse than the idea that, "on the Internet," ideas go viral, predominantly of their own will, and that the most viral of such memes—the term of art for these rapidly propagating units of culture—are worth reporting on.

It's one thing to bring news from Bujumbura to Washington; it's quite another to bring news from Twitter or Facebook to the "offline" world. The former rests on a tenable and useful distinction between "there" and "here"; the latter is just the by-product of Internet-centrism. Once the distinct separation between the "online" and the "offline" collapses, and we no longer treat "the blogosphere" and "social media" as independent entities that somehow exist outside the real action, we might treat the mediators of our public life with the sobriety and empiricism they deserve.

Sociologist Nathan Jurgenson has an apt term for this tendency to establish a firm split between the online and the offline; he calls it "digital dualism" and argues that it underpins much of contemporary debate about digital technologies, particularly evident in widespread concerns that "the virtual" is impinging on "the real" or that online connections are somehow inferior to offline ones. In reality, however, things are never that neat, and the universe we live in is rather a hybrid of the two worlds—moreover, it has always been that way (Jurgenson's arguments, while limited to various digital technologies, fit within a broader intellectual critique, advanced most persuasively by historians and sociologists of science, holding that the splits between humanity and technology and nature and society are themselves artificial and have a history). When advertisers use our social-networking data to customize the ads we see when watching TV, defending the split between the online and the offline is simply analytically suffocating. Likewise, when Facebook has already developed a way to check what products advertised on the site we end up buying in, well, "offline" supermarkets—it does so by partnering with a firm that tracks purchases on supermarket loyalty-card programs—it's not so obvious what is gained by positing this great online-offline divide.

Consider a term like "the blogosphere," which, when used in the public debate these days, often has pejorative connotations. Cue controversial Harvard historian Niall Ferguson responding to the numerous critics of his much-discussed anti-Obama *Newsweek* cover story in August 2012. "I really can't stand America's liberal bloggers," writes Ferguson. "The spectacle of the American liberal blogosphere in one of its almost daily fits of righteous indignation is not so much ridiculous as faintly sinister." Now, who are these bloggers, and what blogosphere do they belong to?

Among the "liberal bloggers" Ferguson mentions in his piece are Nobel Prize–winning economist Paul Krugman, another distinguished economist and former government official, Brad De-Long, and former Jimmy Carter speechwriter and prominent journalist James Fallows. To believe that these people share some core identity as "bloggers" and that it should override their other identities—as prominent academics and public intellectuals—just because they used a blog to respond to Ferguson is the height of Internet-centrism. Why not attack them for using a keyboard or sitting in a chair? Even Andrew Sullivan, whom Ferguson also mentions in his response, is a very unconvincing "blogger": with a PhD from Harvard and a stint as the editor of the *New Republic*, Sullivan challenged Ferguson as a fellow conservative intellectual, not as a pajama-wearing "blogger." Imagine for a moment that the split between the "online" and the "offline" doesn't exist—and suddenly Niall Ferguson needs to put much more work into discrediting his critics. This is one way in which the idea of "the Internet," with all of its associated myths, corrodes our public debate and results in an overuse of lazy shortcuts.

No one benefits more from the idea of "online" being a distinct intellectual space of its own than the public relations industry, which skillfully exploits this digital duality to dress bland press releases up as exciting and autonomously generated "memes." "Online" is how Madison Avenue and K Street get the traditional media to cover people, products, issues, and events they would never bother covering otherwise. What often sanctions such coverage today is the fact that so many people "online" are talking about it.

Consider the numerous memes—for instance, the "Invisible Obama" (a reference to Clint Eastwood's performance at the Republican National Convention) or the "Big Bird" (Mitt Romney's reference to cutting funding to PBS)—that emerged in the 2012 presidential campaign. Although it might be tempting to think of them as emerging organically and autonomously and to treat them as a natural aggregation of the vox populi, reality is far more complex—and not just because of the ways in which the algorithms of Twitter and Facebook have "produced" their virality.

Take the "Invisible Obama" meme. According to a report in *USA Today*, "Within 15 minutes after the first tweet by @Invisible Obama, the account had been mentioned on Twitter by *Mental Floss* magazine, the news website *Salon*, and *Washington Post* political reporter Chris Cillizza and columnist Ezra Klein." Those four Twitter accounts have more than a million followers combined. This is the kind of influence that major national columnists enjoy in print—Twitter just allows the bigwigs to act on that influence momentarily instead of waiting for several days. There's nothing criminal about it per se; we simply shouldn't presume that something is "trending" on "the Internet" simply due to natural and autonomous forces. Likewise, while it might be tempting to celebrate the viral success of the @RomneyBinders Twitter account—a reference to Mitt Romney's poorly-worded remark on "binders full of women"—we shouldn't forget that this same account was called @FiredBigBird (and already had a sizable number of followers from the very first presidential debate) right before Romney's blunder; its owner renamed it to capitalize on the "binders" buzz.

As Ryan Holiday, a marketing wunderkind who got fed up with the dark and exploitative world of Internet public relations, writes in his eye-opening tell-all *Trust Me, I'm Lying: Confessions of a Media Manipulator*, "I don't think someone could have designed a system easier to manipulate if they wanted to." The account that emerges from Holiday's book is quite frightening and confirms that, memes, for the most part, are made, not born. This is not to say that all memes are generated that way; some people do in fact enjoy watching and linking to photos and videos of other people eating strange things and filling their blenders with odd gadgets—but such "authenticity" is much rarer than we think. The goal of the PR industry is, as Holiday puts it, to "create the perception that the meme already exists and all the reporter (or the music supervisor or celebrity stylist) is doing is popularizing it." There are multiple strategies to achieve this; Holiday himself has perfected the art of what he calls "trading up the chain," where he first feeds a story to a small blog—for example, by setting up fake e-mail accounts and sending tips or even leaks (with grainy photos, to achieve maximum authenticity) to its authors. If the blog bites— and why wouldn't it as, in its quest for more traffic, it has nothing to lose—then it becomes a matter of convincing a somewhat larger blog to link to the smaller one.

The small blog may even take the initiative and start promoting its own post on Facebook and Twitter and submit it to various news aggregators, like Reddit. This is where the PR agency might step in and, having established multiple accounts on Reddit, help vote up the submission to the front page. Getting it there is key, because both the authors of large blogs like Gawker and reporters for national media peruse such aggregators in search of story ideas. Even if the story ends up on Gawker only, this is already an accomplishment: it might not be the most highly visited blog in the world, but it's read by media elites who have their own columns and TV shows to fill with, well, "ideas."

For Holiday, blogs (and by "blogs" he primarily means for-profit sites like Gawker or The Huffington Post) are just "beachheads for manufacturing news." Because of their very distinct economic model, whereby the more controversial their story and their headline, the more money they can make from boosted traffic, blogs fall for anything even remotely controversial. Holiday tells a very revealing anecdote about how during a lawsuit involving a company he represented as a PR agent, he needed to feed some information into the public sphere and generate certain debates. "I dashed off a fake internal memo, printed it out, scanned it, and sent the file to a bunch of blogs as if I were an employee leaking a 'memo we'd just gotten from our boss.' The same bloggers who were uninterested in the facts when I informed them directly gladly put up EXCLUSIVE! and LEAKED! posts about it." Suddenly something that, just a minute ago, was mind-numbingly boring has been turned into exciting, meme-ready material.

If Theodor Adorno and Max Horkheimer, the doyens of the Frankfurt School and formidable cultural critics, were writing their seminal book *The Dialectic of Enlightenment* (1944) today, they would surely need to revise its most famous chapter, replacing the "culture industry" with the "meme industry." The main problem here is that the hidden initial manipulations of the PR industry are only made worse by the business incentives of platforms like YouTube and Facebook, which have their own reasons to promote memes: they create some shared culture and, more importantly, lead to more page views, more user interaction (i.e., users reveal more about their interests to the company), and, eventually, more and better advertising. Memes, then, are what happens when one greedy industry meets another.

Just like in the case of Twitter's Trends, it's important to inquire what roles the filters and algorithms of a particular platform play in shaping the conditions under which memes are made. Here is, for example, what Felicia Williams, former entertainment content manager at YouTube, told technology writer B. J. Mendelson: "No one knows exactly how the YouTube algorithms work, but I've noticed that if a video has a big buzz when released and sustains a steady popularity in the first few months it is somehow marked as very relevant to audiences and is displayed at a heavy rotation as 'buzzed about,' 'popular,' or 'related video.' This relevance ranking increases popularity, which results in more promotion and an exponential growth in viewership."

In other words, the PR industry just needs to spend enough money to sustain a video's popularity for a short period; if they are lucky, YouTube will create the impression that the meme is spreading autonomously by recommending this video to its users. Eventually, this will turn the video into a meme—and legitimize countless reports about it in the media, most of which will be of the "and now to the odd news from the Internet community" variety. Such news accounts should, in fact, read "and now, to the odd news from the most creative PR agencies," but Internet-centrism allows our news outlets to deploy the most outrageous euphemisms with no fear of prosecution.

And YouTube, of course, is hardly the only culprit here. Facebook's filters are also designed to notice the already popular, frequently clicked items while disregarding other, less meme-worthy ones. Those may never appear in your news feed at all. This is what Norwegian media scholar Taina Bucher discovered on studying Facebook's EdgeRank algorithm. EdgeRank chooses which news items—from the thousands shared by your friends—you should see when you log into the site. According to Bucher's research, Facebook wants to feed us stuff with high meme potential; thus, it studies what kinds of stories—from which friends? on which subjects?—users tend to click on most often. Bucher even writes of "the algorithmic bias towards making those stories that signify engagement more visible than those that do not." There is nothing wrong with this attitude per se, but as with Twitter, it does embody a certain vision of how public life should function and what it should reward, and it does make meme manufacturing easier. To invoke neutrality here, to argue that Facebook just reflects what's happening and that memes arise organically and naturally, without its active involvement, simply contradicts empirical evidence.

The larger problem with the "memefication" of public life is that when editorial decisions are made with an eye to what might and might not become an "online hit," this invariably affects both what is reported and how. Media scholar C. W. Anderson notes that the latest tech-savvy generation of news-publishing outlets that heavily rely on vast troves of quantified information about their current and potential readers tends to think of them as "algorithmic audiences"—these are people with easily identifiable needs and desires that can be identified and catered to with the right algorithms. In contrast, the more publicly spirited earlier generation of news publishers thought of their audiences as primarily "deliberative" and tried to involve readers in conversations over what they thought was in the public interest regardless of how well it fit with what the audience actually desired. At least in theory, those conversations and public debates were to be settled solely through the force of the better argument, not based on how many page views each argument got.

Compare this to the news environment that Ryan Holiday describes. At one point, he quotes Jonah Peretti, founder of BuzzFeed and the unrivaled king of memes, saying that it's hard to build memes around content that makes people sad. "If something is a total bummer, people don't share it. . . . The problem is, after looking at that you feel depressed. . . . It's almost like you're sending a bad feeling to your friends so why would you want to send a bad feeling to your friends?" notes Peretti. It's hardly surprising then, as Holiday observes in his book, that of two collections of photos from the recession-stricken Detroit that hit "the Internet" around the same time, only one went viral.

What explains the difference? The one that didn't go viral had shots of rather unhappy local people in it; the one that did was all buildings and local color. One, thanks to The Huffington Post, became a meme; the other one went nowhere, receiving only 29 comments versus The Huffington Post's 4,000 plus (not to mention the 25,000 "likes" on Facebook). The memefication of public life is something that Holiday contemplates with horror—and perhaps for good reason. "The economics of the web make it impossible to portray the complex situation in Detroit accurately. . . . Simple narratives like the haunting ruins of a city spread and live, while complicated ones like a city filled with real people who desperately need help don't," he writes (given the urgency of his message, he can perhaps be forgiven for occasionally falling for Internet-centrism).

Such meme logic—the tendency to assess everything in terms of how the intended audience is likely to react according to what is known about that audience—is rapidly intruding on other parts of our culture as well. In the music industry, record labels are increasingly relying on complex algorithms that can analyze any given song across multiple dimensions and score it according to how likely it is to conquer the charts based on a long history of earlier hit-making songs. As Christopher Steiner points out in his *Automate This*, start-ups like Music Xray, which allow musicians to upload their songs online and have them analyzed for hit potential, introduce the music industry to such great "efficiencies and the new breadth of artists . . . that it's only a matter of time until the major labels—all labels, really—come to rely on an algorithm to pick the musicians they sign and the songs they market."

This might seem like liberation to artists who had to be "found" by the previous human-led model of talent discovery. Now the process is recast as more objective as human judgment is minimized; the method is part of what historians of science Peter Galison and Lorraine Daston would call "mechanical objectivity." But we should not lose sight of the benefits that subjectivity plays in art; much good art is meant to shock and provoke. It's not meant to collect "likes" on Facebook or raise money on Kickstarter. To make the process of discovering new musicians a prisoner of the algorithms is to slow artistic innovation. A lot of this music will sell—but it won't necessarily be music that anyone will care about twenty years down the road.

As Steiner notes, "Algorithms may bring us new artists, but because they build their judgment on what was popular in the past, we will likely end up with some of the same kind of forgettable pop we already have. It's a clear foible of the technology that all these years of so-so music are included in its analysis." Of course, algorithms can be configured differently—and some independent labels might choose to release music that is bound to remain unpopular—but it's hard to expect the major labels to pass up the opportunity to make more, and safer, money by deploying the algorithms.

Surviving Big Data

As we transition into the meme-saturated world of "algorithmic audiences," it becomes very hard to remember the time when serious news media didn't obsess over whether something was a "total bummer" and reported news that was important and worth caring about, regardless of how it affected the emotional well-being of the audience. To celebrate "the age of big data" and acquiesce to the ongoing invasion of journalism by various statistical measures and indicators is to give in to solutionism and endorse a very different, complacent kind of journalism. Ignorance of one's audience—and a certain inefficiency that this introduces into the world of journalism—is not necessarily a problem that needs to be solved, even if the latest tools make the solutions trivial and obvious. Overcoming solutionism and resisting the temptation to solve this problem of ignorance—especially when the tools are so readily available—will not be easy, especially when the epochalist rhetoric of Internet-centrism seeks to convince us that revolutionary times demand drastic and revolutionary measures.

It's not so hard to see where the pressure to generate this new data about audiences comes from. As Joseph Turow points out in his revealing book *The Daily You*, publishers of high-quality content simply cannot sell as much advertising on their own sites as they'd like. So they turn to ad networks, which can supply them with infinite ads, but those ads pay considerably less—often by multiples in double and triple digits—than the ads that are sold directly by the publisher and thus tied to a particular publishing brand like the *New York Times* or the *Guardian*. So the publishers are tempted to turn to another set of intermediaries—these sneaky, evil intermediaries somehow always survive the insurmountable challenge that is "the Internet"!—which promise to supply publishers with detailed information about their readers. This information is often collected on other sites and social-networking sites and is recorded either by means of storing cookies on readers' computers or turning to newer and fancier techniques, like "device fingerprinting," which allows publishers to observe even those users who delete or simply never store their cookies (it's particularly effective with mobile phones).

Armed with this extensive information, publishers are then tempted to maximize the "time that their readers spend on their sites," for this too may entitle them to earn better rates from advertisers. One way to do this is to show users silly slide shows of cats and buildings in Detroit. Another is to show them highly personalized slide shows based on what the publisher knows about their interests—some might like cats, but what about dog lovers?—which will guarantee that readers will keep clicking.

Consider a service like The Daily Me, which allows online publishers to present new visitors to their websites with stories and ads that are customized based on what these visitors have read on other sites. Turow interviewed the founder and CEO of The Daily Me, who offered him the example of a reader who typically reads the

Boston Globe but, on following a link found on a blog or a search engine, ends up on the website of the *Dallas Morning News*. Since both newspapers do business with The Daily Me, and since the visitor has already read soccer stories in the *Boston Globe*, a cookie somewhere on his computer, after some magic from The Daily Me, tells the *Dallas Morning News* that it ought to be serving him soccer stories as well. But this is not all, for the ads get personalized as well. Turow notes that "when an ad is served along with the story, its text and photos are arranged instantly to include soccer terminology and photos as part of the advertising pitch." Thus, while the soccer fan gets soccer-relevant ads, "a basketball fan receiving an ad for the same product will get language and photos familiar to people with hoop interests." If The Daily Me's CEO is to be believed, all of this generates much better click-through rates and results in many more pages being viewed on the website.

Now, making certain stories more visible and modifying ads to reflect user interests may seem innocent enough. But Turow notes that such practices are rapidly expanding into the editorial part of the news publishing business as well, not least because of the economic pressures to get people reading and clicking. Turow quotes one digital publishing insider who says that because personalization is now widely used in other industries—from travel to finance—users and publishers might be more eager to experiment with it in news as well. Turow quotes another executive—then president of digital efforts at Time Inc.—who tells him that companies like his are "trying to figure out how to carry out editorial personalization in a manner that wouldn't cause audiences to freak out." The executive seems dead certain that it can work: because "lots of firms are beginning to create content for specific audiences," the goal for his firm—this is *Time* magazine we are talking about!—is to "be nimble in the use of data when creating content."

Turow draws a rather depressing conclusion from all of this, but it's hard to disagree: "We are entering a world of intensively customized content, a world in which publishers and even marketers will package personalized advertisements with soft news or entertainment that is tailored to fit both the selling needs of the ads and the reputation of the particular individual." It might start with something seemingly innocent: customizing headlines and perhaps lead paragraphs to reflect what the site knows (or can find out) about the reader. But soon enough—and in parallel with what Amazon might do with books—such practices might also expand to include customizing the actual text of the articles. Thus, the language, for example, might reflect what the site can guess about the education level of the reader (*Economist*-like vocabulary for the educated few; *New York Post*-like vocabulary for the uneducated masses). Or perhaps a story about Angelina Jolie might end with a reference to her film about Bosnia (if you are into international news) or some gossipy tidbit about her life with Brad Pitt (if you are into Hollywood affairs). Many firms—with names like Automated Insights and Narrative Science—already employ algorithms to produce stories automatically. The next logical step—and probably a very lucrative one—will be to target such stories to individual readers, giving us, essentially, a new generation of content farms that can produce stories on demand tailored for particular users.

The implications of such shifts for our public life are profound: the kind of personalization described above might destroy the opportunities for solidarity and informed debate that occur when the entire polis has access to the same stories. But it's even more important to keep certain modes of debate about these issues alive; we cannot just give in to the temptation to view such problems from the perspective of efficiency alone. Under the old system, where there was no way to measure the audience's reaction to particular articles, the advertisers were engaging in practices that were terrifically inefficient—they had to place their ads in the newspaper without seeing the breakdown of how many people read each article—but this inefficiency was rather beneficial.

As journalist Jacob Weisberg points out, ignorance-induced inefficiency was actually good for journalism as a civic enterprise: "I often wonder how many people read the coverage of the Albany state government in the *New York Times*. Not knowing the answer to that question may be what allows the *Times* to invest as much as it does in such coverage! In a Google world where nobody clicked on those stories, they would go down in priority." Or disappear. Communications professor David Karpf writes of "beneficial inefficiency" that accompanied traditional journalism in the past, when "the lack of information on advertising effectiveness, combined with scarce advertising space, inflated prices." Today, however, when every click can be recorded for posterity, "advertisers can measure impressions and clickthroughs. They can target their advertisements toward niche markets and populations. These greater efficiencies drive advertising prices downward. Legacy media organizations then have trouble paying for their existing overhead and infrastructure."

The language of efficiency—the one and only god of most geeks and economists—slowly but surely creeps into this debate as well. Here is Slate columnist Matthew Yglesias composing a love letter to targeted advertising: "Better-targeted ads produce economic benefits for consumers and advertisers alike. More efficient advertising creates incentives for firms to expend more resources on improving the real quality of their services. And more efficient advertising can create markets for content that otherwise might starve for lack of revenue." Got that?

It sounds great, but once you start looking at the actual pressures faced by online publishers, the immense power accumulated by advertising networks and exchanges, and the growing pressure to get people to click so that one can make more money from targeted ads, it's hard to share Yglesias's optimism. It's all but impossible to agree with him that "in a world of user tracking, the precise nature of content is less important. The editorial job becomes to find an audience—any audience—and then the tracking will target ads for shoes or apps or kitchen gadgets or car insurance or whatever it is that the other information about the reader as an individual suggests he's interested in." Yglesias's is a fairy tale that, in some abstract quest for efficiency, overlooks the actual dynamics of the contemporary digital publishing world and operates simply by projecting the positive features of a technology—targeted advertising in this case—onto some highly theoretical economic model of the world.

"Down with the Gatekeepers!" . . .
Say the Gatekeepers

Faith in the neutrality, objectivity, and self-evidence of filters and algorithms is not the high point of cybernaïveté, though. That dubious honor goes to the widespread belief that "the Internet" is ridding us of gatekeepers and intermediaries. "Disintermediation"— easily one of the ugliest words in the English language—is often heralded as the defining feature of the digital age. Thanks to innovative new technologies, middlemen of all stripes are believed to be going the way of the dodo. Once editors, publishers, and bookstores wither, the story goes, our public life will finally be liberated from their biases, inefficiencies, and hidden agendas. There are elements of truth to this, but we shouldn't miss a far more important and less visible development: the digitization of our public life is also giving rise to many new intermediaries that are mostly invisible—and possibly suspect.

Consider blogging. When the first generation of bloggers got online in the late 1990s, the only intermediaries between them and the rest of the world were their hosting companies and Internet service providers. People starting a blog in 2012 are likely to end up on a commercial platform like Tumblr or WordPress, with all of their blog comments running through a third-party company like Disqus. But the intermediaries don't just stop there: Disqus itself cooperates with a company called Impermium, which relies on various machine learning tools to check whether comments posted are spam. It's the proliferation—not elimination—of intermediaries that has made blogging so widespread. The right term here is "hyperintermediation," not "disintermediation."

Impermium's new service goes even further: The company claims to have developed a technology to "identify not only spam and malicious links, but all kinds of harmful content—such as violence, racism, flagrant profanity, and hate speech—and allows site owners to act on it in real-time, before it reaches readers." Impermium says it has 300,000 websites as clients (which is not all that surprising, if it's incorporated into widely used third-party tools like Disqus). As far as intermediaries go, this sounds very impressive: a single Californian company makes decisions over what counts as hate speech and profanity for some of the world's most popular sites without anyone ever examining whether its own algorithms might be biased or excessively conservative. Instead of celebrating the mythical nirvana of disintermediation, we should peer inside the black boxes of Impermium's spam algorithms.

The belief in the emancipatory potential of disintermediation is most pronounced in the vast literature on the future of book publishing, a field that is itself constantly defying the trends it predicts (someone ought to publish a book about the doomsayers who keep publishing books about the end of publishing).

The questions occasioned by the Internet-centrist perception of a new epoch are many: Who needs libraries and bookstores when books can be borrowed and bought online? Who needs publishers when authors can self-publish? Who needs editors when articles and even books can be personalized to match the interests of the reader? And, in the extreme, who needs authors when algorithms can write prose? The reason this bashing of gatekeepers enjoys such tremendous popularity with geeks might have to do with the already mentioned cult of the Protestant Reformation—the original myth of today's Internet culture. Just as the church was seen as an unnecessary and corrosive gatekeeper that interfered with direct communication with God, so are publishing institutions seen as essentially precluding unmediated access to the world of memes and ideas. "The Internet," say the hopeful, will liberate the memes from the oppression of the creative elites—the very elites who dare claim that not all memes are created equal and some are so bad that they should perhaps not be created at all.

No one is more enamored of this highly democratizing development than Jeff Bezos, founder and CEO of Amazon. He likes to boast that he's dedicated himself to eliminating the gatekeepers, for they "slow innovation" and stand in the way of "self-service platforms"—where everyone can publish a book in minutes—that Amazon itself has been so keen to promote. Bezos's populist rage against institutions—in the best traditions of Martin Luther's fulminations against the church—is on full display when he boasts that the Kindle best-seller list "is chock-full of books from small presses and self-published authors, while the *New York Times* list is dominated by successful and established authors." Why this is an achievement worth celebrating is not explained and presumed to be self-evident, as if the method of a book's production is as important as the quality of its ideas. How many books on the Kindle best-seller list will still be read twenty years from now? Bezos, like his solutionist brethren in the meme industry, seems to think that the goal of publishing is to produce the maximum number of books and have the maximum number of people read them. It's some kind of perverse utilitarianism for the literati. Whether those books are Sudoku puzzles or Tolstoy novels doesn't matter at all, for it's all about the number of books downloaded, pages flipped, and memes created.

Amazon's promise rests on two rhetorical strategies that are beloved by solutionists. The first strategy is that of "innovation talk," whereby all innovation is treated as inherently good in itself, regardless of its social or political consequences. After all, innovation is progress—and how can progress be bad? The second strategy is "tool talk," which aims to recast any debate about technology as a debate almost exclusively about tools and, by extension, about ways in which these tools can empower users. Both kinds of talk impoverish our debate about digital technologies; both must be recognized early on and resisted.

The perils of innovation talk may not be immediately obvious. Innovation might be one of the defining buzzwords of our times, but it has not received the critical attention it deserves, and we usually take its goodness for granted, oblivious of how obsession with innovation twists our accounts of the past. Historian David Edgerton notes in his *The Shock of the Old* that much of the recent history of technology is dominated by accounts that prioritize invention and innovation rather than actual use of technologies and devices. We tend to forget that most innovations and inventions have no consequences—and those that do usually require significant repairs and maintenance to keep working. Moreover, we tend to dismiss the important role that older technologies play once newer, faster, and shinier alternatives are introduced. We view World War II as the war of the motorized vehicle, while, if anything, it may have been the war of the horse: as Edgerton points out, Nazi Germany used 625,000 horses in its invasion of the Soviet Union.

However, it's not just the historiography of technology that gets deformed by the contemporary veneration of innovation. Future policy often suffers as well. The problem is this: since innovation is seen as having only positive effects, few are prepared to examine its unintended consequences; as such, most innovations are presumed to be self-evidently good. A study by a team of Scandinavian researchers that aimed to review all academic articles about innovation published since the 1960s found that of all the studies under examination—thousands of them—only twenty-six articles addressed the negative or undesirable consequences of innovation. This is roughly 1 per 1,000 articles, a proportion that hasn't changed since the 1960s. Overlooked statistics like this reveal the "pro-innovation bias" of most academic literature on the subject.

Such pro-innovation bias is responsible for the establishment of a clear boundary between the study of innovation and its various boosting factors—this field of inquiry is mostly pursued in business schools—and the study of the consequences of innovation, which is usually done in disciplines such as public policy and science and technology studies but very rarely under the umbrella of "innovation studies" as such. Thus, innovations that fail or lead to disastrous results are naturally not considered part of the innovation vocabulary; technologies are innovative only if they are successful and risk-free. Moreover, the consequences of innovation that are considered tend to be rather linear and direct. When Jeff Bezos writes of "innovation" associated with the Kindle, he knows that his intended audience is not likely to consider any consequences that may not be direct, anticipated, or desirable; most of us suffer from some form of "pro-innovation bias" as well.

It wasn't always like this. According to Benoit Godin, the Canadian scholar who has traced the intellectual history of "innovation" as a concept, for over 2,500 years, the word had negative connotations. "The innovator was a heretic, a revolutionary, a cheater," writes Godin. Then, something changed. "Innovation got a positive hearing when people started experiencing changes everywhere, above all 'revolutionary' changes, and worked deliberately to make still more changes." In the 1960s, Western governments, preoccupied with the modernization agenda and dominated by social scientists, economists, and consultants, stripped the word "innovation" of its political content, turning it into a boring synonym for novelty, invention, creativity, originality, usefulness, or whatever buzzword was popular at Harvard Business School's retreats that year.

Not surprisingly, few scholars are working on the ethics of innovation; the fruits of innovation are somehow presumed to benefit everyone equally, so considerations of justice are rarely brought to bear on such discussions. This is a mistake, and a closer analysis of, say, innovation in the pharmaceutical industry (and the claims to intellectual property that it entails) would reveal that consideration of global justice, of whether the quest for innovation risks shutting off the poor and the sick from access to medicines, should also affect how we discuss innovation. As three prominent scholars rightly point out in a recent article on justice in the diffusion of innovation, "Depending on what is created and to whom it becomes available, innovation can worsen existing injustices or create new injustices or it can lessen existing injustices." This requires going beyond preoccupation with novelty and efficiency and asking difficult, normative questions about power, legitimacy, and morality.

Tool talk presents challenges of a somewhat different nature. To better understand what they are, it might be useful to draw on the difference that communications scholar Majid Tehranian draws between "techoneutrals" and "technostructuralists." For Tehranian, technoneutrals "typically tend to be the consultants, who have few theoretical pretensions and considerable interest at stake not to alienate their clients. They often assume a neutral position with respect to question of effects: on the one hand this, but on the other hand that."

Technoneutrals are usually the first to acknowledge that "the Internet" can be bad and good and that it all depends on how people use it. They believe that technologies in themselves are entirely neutral, that they don't take sides, and that in the right hands they can do marvels. Little attention is paid to the hidden and not-so-hidden agendas of their creators or the specific conditions in which these technologies will be used. A gun found on the streets of Detroit is presumed to be as neutral and conducive to violence as a gun stored in a rare weapons collection in the Museum of Engineering: it all depends, we are told.

Technoneutrals of the more optimistic streak often end up advocating an extreme laissez-faire attitude toward individual technologies: since it all depends, let's just give technology a chance! That's why Jeff Jarvis demands that facial-recognition technology be given a fair trial: "Is it wise to ban a technology before it is even used and understood? Imagine how else such a combination could be beneficial: finding missing children or learning the fate of victims

in a disaster such a Hurricane Katrina or the 2011 Japanese earth-
quake and tsunami." Technoneutrals, for all their commitment to
balancing the pros and cons, don't actually engage in any profound
calculation: a technology that is likely to be used for "good" purposes
once in three years is as neutral as a technology that is likely to be
used for "bad" purposes every minute. They are much more likely
to advocate solutionist measures as, by definition, they are blind
to the multiple contexts in which solutions could be launched and
the many unpredictable ways in which those contexts would mitigate their effectiveness. Technostructuralists, on the other hand,
approach the world—not just technology's place in it—with a different philosophy. According to Tehranian, they believe that technologies "[develop] out of institutional needs and their impact is
always mediated through the institutional arrangements and social
forces, of which they are an integral part." Technostructuralists
view information technologies "neither as technologies of freedom
nor of tyranny but primarily as technologies of power that lock
into existing or emerging technostructures of power." Thus, any
given technology is allowed to centralize and decentralize, homog-
enize and pluralize, empower and disempower simultaneously.

The impact of a particular technology thus is not presumed to
be naturally flowing from some of its inherent or natural qualities
or assumed to be neutral, for it all depends on the context. Rather,
this impact is deduced from analyzing how particular aspects of a
given technology—and those aspects are themselves often in flux—
might restructure political and social relations, introducing entirely
new classes of actors into the game. Analysis ought to proceed
slowly, patiently, and without any grandiose assumptions about
"Technology" with a capital *T* or "the Internet" with a capital *I*.
Technostructuralists eschew the easy fixes of Internet-centrism
and solutionism.

It's easy to mistake technostructuralists for pessimists, but this
is not who they are. Their point is not that such liberation through
technology is illusory or inconsequential but, rather, that such liberation never happens in a vacuum and may, all things considered,
actually enslave. Yes, Google's self-driving cars would make driving
easier and perhaps even cut the number of deaths on the road, but
a reasonable transportation system ought to pursue many other

objectives. Would self-driving cars result in inferior public transportation as more people took up driving? Would it lead to even greater suburban sprawl as, now that they no longer had to drive, people could do e-mail during their commute and thus would tolerate spending more time in the car?

To technostructuralists, Amazon's foray into publishing cannot just be a tale of individual empowerment through new, better tools for reading and publishing. To accept this tale would be to focus on the direct, anticipated, and desirable consequences of innovation at the expense of indirect, unanticipated, and undesirable ones and to fetishize the tool over the practice it enables. To return to the late Tony Judt, occasionally it does help to ask what is wrong and what is right—and not just what is most efficient.

Once we are no longer committed to innovation and tales of individual empowerment, it becomes possible to see that, if Amazon's dream of a world without gatekeepers becomes reality, then the company itself will become a powerful gatekeeper. For one, by essentially abandoning the publishing process to the vagaries of the market, it will make certain book projects likelier—yes, we want more stories about bespectacled wizards!—and others less so—please, not another biography of some obscure Japanese general! It doesn't take a Karl Marx to realize that the economics of publishing—who gets paid what and when—dictate the scope of intellectual risks that can be taken. It's much likelier that the biography of that obscure Japanese general will be written if the author knows he'll receive an advance than if the author has to first spend a decade writing the book, while working odd jobs in the meantime, and hope that the project will recoup itself. Yes, now and then, Amazon might stumble on a submission worthy of a Pulitzer—but in a universe run by Amazon, most such books would simply never be written. Amazon might be a reluctant gatekeeper, but it's a gatekeeper nevertheless.

But we also need to understand where all this talk of gatekeeping ends. Would anyone really be surprised if, ten years down the road, Amazon decided that authors ought to follow the same path as some workers in its warehouses—that is, be replaced by robots? If one starts by assuming that gatekeeping is bad and efficiency is good, then authors too are gatekeepers of sorts: they temporarily imprison memes and ideas—and it's memes and ideas that buyers actually want from books (rest assured: Amazon won't eliminate the buyers, who also get to imprison memes and ideas—someone has to pay for the books in the end).

Thanks to its Kindle e-reader, Amazon already collects a wealth of information about individual readers as well as reading practices across entire demographics; it knows what words are looked up in Kindle's dictionary, what paragraphs are underlined most frequently, and how many readings it takes to finish the book. All of this, in the best tradition of tool talk, is presented as enhancing the reader experience—and Amazon is not lying here. But such statistics enhance many other things beyond reading—including Amazon's ability to engage in the kind of meme-driven publishing that knows the audience better than it knows itself and can pander, perhaps even subliminally, to its every whim.

Nothing prevents Jeff Bezos from taking such knowledge and churning out books automatically, bypassing the authors completely and offering such a personalized offering—pushing all the right emotional and intellectual buttons for each reader—so that no bought book goes unread. A growing number of newspapers and magazines already turn to companies like Narrative Science to supply them with articles—mostly about sports and finance—produced by algorithms. There's no reason to believe that Amazon can't do this job better—and in long form. Smaller start-ups already cull and sell books that are written without any human involvement (and, of course, they are mostly sold on Amazon.com).

If one thinks that the goal of literature is to maximize the well-being of memes or to ensure that all readers are satisfied (and why wouldn't they be, given that the books they read already reflect their subconscious inclinations and preferences?), then Amazon should be seen as the savior of literature. But if one believes that some ideas are worse than others, that some memes should be put to rest rather than spread around, that many authors are public intellectuals who serve important civic functions that surely cannot be outsourced to algorithms, and that one of the goals of literature is to challenge and annihilate, not just to appease and amplify— then there is very little to celebrate in Amazon's fantasy world without gatekeepers.

The Rise of Uncritical Critics

Solutionists run into the same set of challenges, regardless of whether they want to improve politics or literature. Such improvement schemes cannot start by celebrating the power (or the logic) of their tools, be it open-government databases or e-readers. The fact that such tools might remove inefficiencies or ambiguities can be seen as a good thing only by forgetting or ignoring the goals and aspirations of activities that solutionists want to improve; to hope that journalism or publishing could be made better with more numbers is to have a very confused view of what either of them is about.

A site like Yelp might claim to offer more extensive, more numerous, and seemingly more objective reviews of a given restaurant than a professional restaurant critic on staff at one of the metropolitan newspapers. But to view opinions from Yelp as superior is to forget what critics actually do; their actual practice of food criticism is underpinned by a very different set of goals and ideas that are not easy to replicate online. Yelp doesn't care whether you go to a restaurant once or a dozen times; nor does it care how many dishes you sample. It doesn't actually care if you go to the restaurant at all; the infamous owner of a pizzeria in Florida who was photographed lifting and hugging President Obama discovered that, as his business became national news, the number of his Yelp reviews jumped from 2 to 2,500, most of them by people who had never set foot inside his establishment.

More broadly, Yelp doesn't give you a way to evaluate food in Italian restaurants according to a set of criteria explaining what good Italian cuisine should be. Instead, you evaluate Italian cuisine in the same way that you would evaluate Japanese: it all boils down to a bunch of stars and, if you are in the mood for writing, a brief review. It doesn't really matter that the judgments of thousands of people can be aggregated in this way, for, already at the level of the individual review, it's impossible to capture things and qualities that matter to food critics.

As sociologist Grant Blank points out in *Critics, Ratings, and Society: The Sociology of Reviews*, a rich study of the actual practice of reviewing, most professional food critics will have at least three meals in a restaurant they are reviewing; some report making as many as seven visits. They will normally bring a few friends along so that they can sample a wide variety of dishes on the menu. To check for consistency—a major criterion for evaluating the chef's performance—they will order the same entrees on different occasions. To avoid being recognized and treated differently from other patrons, restaurant critics often employ camouflage. According to Blank, standard efforts "include wearing hats, wigs, glasses, dark glasses, pretending to be pregnant, making reservations under other names, having several credit cards in different names, and asking guests to pay using their credit card." Dennis Ray Wheaton, a longtime restaurant critic for *Chicago* magazine, would even wire himself and carry a hidden tape recorder so that he could dictate notes to himself without getting caught.

A main challenge for the critic is to evaluate just how well the food on offer matches the external standards established for a given cuisine. The rules and rituals of French cuisine have long been codified in books like Georges Auguste Escoffier's *Le Guide Culinaire*, which first appeared in 1903 and is still in print. "French cuisine is complex in its combinations of sauces and ingredients; flavors count but so do textures and colors. Even more complex is that reviewers must judge not just individual items but the balance and harmony of flavor, texture, and color on each plate," notes Blank. A critic like Craig Claiborne, who was instrumental in building up the practice of restaurant reviewing for the *New York Times*, wasn't just intimately familiar with the precise standards in Escoffier's book—he was also intimately familiar with the process of cooking: he used his GI benefits to attend a well-regarded cooking school in Switzerland and was himself regarded as an excellent cook.

Yelp, of course, is hardly the first start-up to pose a challenge to restaurant critics; Zagat, now owned by Google, got there first with its dinner questionnaires, which, according to its founders, offered "results as close to scientific as you can get" (they'll fit right in at Google). But the science that first Zagat and now Yelp offer is the science of aggregating opinions about food experiences; it's nowhere near the kind of restaurant criticism practiced by Wheaton or Claiborne, for it doesn't really have a way to speak of excellence in complex terms. Restaurants that receive poor aggregate ratings on Yelp are unlikely to receive good marks from restaurant critics—this much they do share—and bad service, like bad food, is easy to spot. But good restaurants can be good for a whole variety of reasons—from consistency to adherence to set culinary standards—that may not be obvious to nonprofessional reviewers. If the goal is to get consumers to go places and fill their stomachs with pleasant food between uploading photos to Instagram and posting updates to Twitter, then Yelp is perfect. But if one views cooking as an art that has its own standards of excellence and its own intellectual and artisan tradition, if one grants that cuisine also has a mission to educate and provoke, then Yelp perhaps falls short of the mark. For the food critic, even the "undatabased restaurants"—to use the colorful expression of writer Joshua Cohen—might be worth visiting; for your typical Yelp user, if it's not on Yelp, well, it doesn't really exist.

This doesn't have to turn into one of those "amateurs-versus-professionals" spats that animate so much of our Internet debate. The kind of expertise required to produce a news report or an encyclopedia article is probably quite different from what it takes to write a restaurant review. We shouldn't give in to Internet-centrism and imagine that "the Internet" ruins nothing or that "the Internet" ruins everything. Nor should we fetishize it for what it allows us to do.

But Internet pundits do turn any criticism of deficiencies embedded in sites like Zagat and Yelp into some grand metanarrative about the elites' disdain for the masses—a disdain that "the Internet," the logic goes, would all but destroy. Internet-centrism is at is most destructive when it recasts genuine concerns about the mismatch between what new digital tools and solutions have to offer and the problems they are trying to solve as yet more instances of Luddite and conservative resistance.

Consider the case of the food critic Steven Shaw, who in 2000 published a provocative essay called "The Zagat Effect" in *Commentary.* Shaw presented a whole litany of complaints about Zagat, highlighting some structural problems in its operation. One of Shaw's objections was that Zagat's definition of excellence is inappropriate for restaurant criticism. Shaw pointed out that the reason Union Square Café emerged as Zagat's number one restaurant in New

York was that it came first in response to this question in the survey: "What are your favorite New York restaurants?" There were restaurants that scored higher than Union Square Café on food, décor, and service—the hallmarks of traditional restaurant criticism—on Zagat's own ranking. Thus, concluded Shaw, "if you want to know how good a restaurant is, averages are seriously misleading."

Placing Union Square Café at the top is tantamount to saying that *American Pie* is the best film of 1999 because 40 percent of respondents listed it as their favorite film of the year while *American Beauty*, *The Matrix*, and *Fight Club*—all released the same year— only received 20 percent of the vote each. Shaw's point is not that such measurements are pointless but that whatever it is they are measuring is hardly the excellence that restaurant critics are after. Thus, writes Shaw, "Union Square Café is, indeed, a very good restaurant, one beloved by many New Yorkers for its compassionate service—it is perhaps the most unintimidating of the city's better restaurants—and its simple but intensely flavorful food. But with all due respect to that justly popular establishment, it is patently ridiculous to rank it ahead of a dozen other places, and in particular such world-class restaurants as Lespinasse, Jean Georges, and Daniel."

Clay Shirky tells the same story in *Cognitive Surplus*, and his version brims with populist, antiestablishment rage against professional critics and promises that, thanks to "the Internet," the masses can finally dispense with their highbrow pretensions. Shirky complains that "nowhere does Shaw spell out why preferring Union Square Café to Lespinasse is patently ridiculous—calling Lespinasse world-class simply begs the question." But Shaw does point out why this is ridiculous: according to Zagat's own ranking, Union Square Café loses to restaurants like Lespinasse on food, décor, and service—and yet it still comes out as the top restaurant in New York City. It's not that Shaw is an elitist who hates regular diners but that even regular diners give other restaurants higher scores on a host of criteria that appear most relevant to the dining experience.

Shirky, however, turns Shaw's critique of the biases inherent in Zagat's methods into an attack on the common people. So, in the best tradition of Internet-centrism, he launches into a tirade against elitist critics. Thus, Shirky complains that Shaw is "unwilling to condemn Union Square as a bad restaurant; it's just not the kind of restaurant people like him prefer, which is to say people who eat in restaurants professionally and are happy to have a little intimidation with their appetizers. But if he makes that complaint too visibly, he risks undermining his desire to be able to guide his audience." This Shaw smacking only clears the way for Shirky's passionate rupture talk—the one promising us that the old world is gone and the new digital world is already in the making. "Back when professional reviews were the only publicly available judgment of restaurants, this difference didn't matter much (and critical contempt for the audience wasn't so visible), but when we can all now find an aggregate answer to the question 'What is your favorite restaurant?' we want that information, and we may even prefer it to judgments produced by professional critics."

As is typical of Internet pundits, Shirky doesn't bother asking whether this trend is good or bad beyond its offering a vague sense of empowerment to individual consumers. Nor is he interested in understanding what made restaurant criticism of the pre-Zagat and pre-Yelp era valuable and perhaps worth defending. Compare Shirky's defeatism with Shaw's defense of cuisine as a social activity:

> It is the vision of great chefs that ultimately creates educated consumers and hence the demand for better and better cuisine. Under the sway of a Zagat-style survey . . . a restaurant that wants to . . . flourish will find itself pandering to average tastes the way an assistant professor of English saddled with the need to score high on student-evaluation forms inevitably finds himself assigning easier and more popular texts. One does not . . . gain the accolades of the Zagat constituency by presenting challenging, complex, or advanced cuisine. One gains the love of the Zagat reader by serving tuna burgers (as does the Union Square Café—and very good ones at that).

Now, one can disagree with Shaw about the goals, purposes, and social functions of cuisine, but it's noteworthy that Shirky does none of that; he's primarily interested in making an argument about "the Internet"—and with "the Internet" as his favorite causal explanation. The operating logic here is simple: pre-Internet meant expertise, post-Internet means populism; we are post-Internet, hence, populism. For Shirky, things just happen—remember, it's a revolution, so all resistance is futile!—and as long as the people seem to be in charge, it all must be a good thing.

By this logic—which celebrates massive cultural participation as worth pursuing in its own right, regardless of what it does to culture—even ratings of albums and songs that we generate on iTunes and Spotify might eventually be preferable to those of professional music critics. Solutionists would be delighted: such ratings not only produce more "objective" opinions of art, but they also involve the public in the very process of making (or at least rating) culture; thus they are more democratic and participatory. So even if music critics go, the logic goes, they won't be much missed.

There are several problems with such a view. First of all, it tends to prize participation in culture much more than culture itself. This approach is propelled by considerations of logistics, not mechanics. That is, it doesn't seem to matter what people are listening to—whether it's Justin Bieber or Stravinsky—as long as they have the means to vote it up or down and create a meme and a YouTube video out of it. Sociologist Nancy Hanrahan is particularly perceptive on this issue:

> It cannot be denied that the erosion of cultural expertise made possible by the new technologies is democratic in at least one sense, in that there is broader participation in making and evaluating culture. If democracy were as easily quantified as CD sales or the number of hits to a website, perhaps the argument could be left there. But it is not just participation but also the terms of participation that must be considered. If greater participation in culture through digital technologies and the network structures in which they are embedded favors the market, discourages artistic innovation, or is bought at the expense of critical reflection on art, on what grounds can that be considered democratic? If, on the other hand, democracy means the expansion of opportunities for deliberation, for

publicness, or for genuine diversity, the current situation falls short.

Another key point often missed by populist solutionists is that professional music critics—and this applies to film and book critics as well—serve many other functions that cannot be easily delegated to crowds. One such function is identifying innovative, perhaps even provocative, high-quality music acts and explaining to the public why they deserve appreciation, for, as Adorno once remarked, "without expertise, without a habitual knowledge of the familiar, the new that is taking shape can hardly be understood."

People who write reviews of songs on iTunes don't much bother comparing their every rated song to the canon or trying to predict what new styles might eventually emerge out of them. Media scholar Ryan Gillespie is right to worry that "the consumption mentality of reviews encourages the treatment of art and entertainment as merely means to the ends of pleasure, thereby eliminating the appreciation and contemplation of challenging, experimental, and avant-garde works."

In most cases, ordinary people don't write reviews for the same reasons as professional critics; they are mostly interested in reviewing their own experience, not in making sense of a given work. Writer Daniel Mendelsohn gets to the very heart of the difference when he writes that "all criticism is based on that equation: KNOWLEDGE + TASTE = MEANINGFUL JUDGMENT. The key word here is *meaningful*. People who have strong reactions to a work—and most of us do—but don't possess the wider erudition that can give an opinion heft, are not critics."

This is not to say that a world without iTunes reviews or Yelp would be a better one. Ideally, we would recognize the importance of extending public participation in culture while at the same time defending and perhaps even subsidizing the important civic functions performed by professional critics. To succumb to the solutionist temptation to recast the new digital platforms as just more objective and efficient versions of the older, inefficient, human-driven alternatives is to opt for an adversarial and counterproductive approach that refuses to acknowledge the immensely important roles that subjectivity, inefficiency, and ignorance have been playing in our culture and public life as a whole. "The Internet" cannot be a solution to those "deficiencies" because these are not deficiencies at all; rather, they are important but fragile accomplishments that we ought to defend.

CHAPTER SIX

Less Crime,
More Punishment

"Imagine what would have happened if Adam and Eve had not lived in a garden but in a smart building. The divine designer would probably have arranged it so that they never saw apples."
—Ursula Franklin

"What the utopian denounces is not so much evil in the moral sense, but the impudence of a world which is content to exist full of flaws and defects—an ontological condemnation rather than moral. . . . The world opposed is the world of darkness, utterly full of evil, of devouring fire, falsehood and deceit, a world of turbulence, of darkness, of death, a world in which the good things perish and plans come to naught."
—Thomas Molnar

As they embrace the latest technologies, police have a very bright future ahead of them—and not just because they can now look up potential suspects on Google. Several other, less visible trends are bound to make their work easier and more effective, raising thorny questions about privacy, civil liberties, and due process.

For one, policing is in a good position to profit from "big data." As the costs of recording devices keep falling, it's now possible to spot and react to crimes in real time. Consider a city like Oakland in California. Like many other American cities, today it is covered with hundreds of hidden microphones and sensors, part of a system known as ShotSpotter, which not only alerts the police to the sound of gunshots but also triangulates their location. On verifying that the noises are actual gunshots, a human operator then informs the police. These systems are not cheap—ShotSpotter reportedly charges $40,000 to $60,000 a year per square mile—but they are hardly the latest word in crime detection. Why bother with expensive microphones if smartphones can do the job just fine? It all boils down to designing an appealing and nonintrusive app and creating the right incentives—perhaps by appealing to the moral conscience of citizens or by turning crime reports into a game—so that citizens can take on some of the tasks of faulty sensors and easily distracted human operators.

It's not hard to imagine other ways to improve a system like ShotSpotter. Gunshot-detection systems are, in principle, reactive; they might help to thwart or quickly respond to crime, but they won't root it out. The decreasing costs of computing, considerable advances in sensor technology, and the ability to tap into vast online databases allow us to move from identifying crime as it happens—which is what the ShotSpotter does now—to predicting it before it happens. Instead of detecting gunshots, new and smarter systems can focus on detecting the sounds that have preceded gunshots in the past. This is where the techniques and ideologies of big data make another appearance, promising that a greater, deeper analysis of data about past crimes, combined with sophisticated algorithms, can predict—and prevent—future ones. This is a practice known as "predictive policing," and even though it's just a few years old, many tout it as a revolution in how police work is done. It's the epitome of solutionism; there is hardly a better example of how technology and big data can be put to work to solve the problem of crime by simply eliminating crime altogether. It all seems too easy and logical; who wouldn't want to prevent crime before it happens?

Police in America are particularly excited about what predictive policing—one of *Time* magazine's best inventions of 2011—has to offer; Europeans are slowly catching up as well, with Britain in the lead. Take the Los Angeles Police Department (LAPD), which is using software called PredPol. The software analyzes years of previously published statistics about property crimes like burglary and automobile theft, breaks the patrol map into five-hundred-square-foot zones, calculates the historical distribution and frequency of actual crimes across them, and then tells officers which zones to police more vigorously.

It's much better—and potentially cheaper—to prevent a crime before it happens than to come late and investigate it. So while patrolling officers might not catch a criminal in action, their presence in the right place at the right time still helps to deter criminal activity. Occasionally, though, the police might indeed disrupt an ongoing crime. In June 2012 the Associated Press reported on an LAPD captain who wasn't so sure that sending officers into a grid zone on the edge of his coverage area—following PredPol's recommendation—was such a good idea. His officers, as the captain expected, found nothing; however, when they returned several nights later, they caught someone breaking a window. Score one for PredPol?

Trials of PredPol and similar software began too recently to speak of any conclusive results. Still, the intermediate results look quite impressive. In Los Angeles, five LAPD divisions that use it in patrolling territory populated by roughly 1.3 million people have seen crime decline by 13 percent. The City of Santa Cruz, which now also uses PredPol, has seen its burglaries decline by nearly 30 percent. Similar uplifting statistics can be found in many other police departments across America. Other powerful systems that are currently being built can also be easily reconfigured to suit more predictive demands. Consider the New York Police Department's latest innovation—the so-called Domain Awareness System—which syncs the city's 3,000 closed-circuit camera feeds with arrest records, 911 calls, license plate recognition technology, and radiation detectors. It can monitor a situation in real time and draw on a lot of data to understand what's happening. The leap from here to predicting what might happen is not so great.

If PredPol's "prediction" sounds familiar, that's because its methods were inspired by those of prominent Internet companies. Writing in *The Police Chief* magazine in 2009, a senior LAPD officer lauded Amazon's ability to "understand the unique groups in their customer base and to characterize their purchasing patterns," which allows the company "not only to anticipate but also to promote or otherwise shape future behavior." Thus, just as Amazon's algorithms make it possible to predict what books you are likely to buy next, similar algorithms might tell the police how often—and where—certain crimes might happen again. Ever stolen a bicycle? Then you might also be interested in robbing a grocery store.

Here we run into the perennial problem of algorithms: their presumed objectivity and quite real lack of transparency. We can't examine Amazon's algorithms; they are completely opaque and have not been subject to outside scrutiny. Amazon claims, perhaps correctly, that secrecy allows it to stay competitive. But can the same logic be applied to policing? If no one can examine the algorithms—which is likely to be the case as predictive-policing software will be built by private companies—we won't know what biases and discriminatory practices are built into them. And algorithms increasingly dominate many other parts of our legal system; for example, they are also used to predict how likely a certain criminal, once on parole or probation, is to kill or be killed. Developed by a University of Pennsylvania professor, this algorithm has been tested in Baltimore, Philadelphia, and Washington DC. Such probabilistic information can then influence sentencing recommendations and bail amounts, so it's hardly trivial.

But how do we know that the algorithms used for prediction do not reflect the biases of their authors? For example, crime tends to happen in poor and racially diverse areas. Might algorithms—with their presumed objectivity—sanction even greater racial profiling? In most democratic regimes today, police need probable cause—some evidence and not just guesswork—to stop people in the street and search them. But armed with such software, can the police simply say that the algorithms told them to do it? And if so, how will the algorithms testify in court? Technoneutrals will probably overlook such questions and focus on the abstract benefits that algorithmic policing has to offer; technostructuralists, who start with some basic knowledge of the problems, constraints, and biases that already pervade modern policing, will likely be more critical. Legal scholar Andrew Guthrie Ferguson has studied predictive policing in detail. While he doesn't deny that it can be put to great uses,

Ferguson cautions against putting too much faith in the algorithms and succumbing to information reductionism. "Predictive algorithms are not magic boxes that divine future crime, but instead probability models of future events based on current environmental vulnerabilities," he notes.

But why do they work? Ferguson points out that there will be future crime not because there was past crime but because "the environmental vulnerability that encouraged the first crime is still unaddressed." When the police, having read their gloomy forecast about yet another planned car theft, see an individual carrying a screwdriver in one of the predicted zones, this might provide reasonable suspicion for a stop (that is, it might be hard to challenge the legality of the stop in court). But, as Ferguson notes, if the police arrested the gang responsible for prior crimes the day before, but the model does not yet reflect this information, then prediction should be irrelevant, and the police will need some other reasonable ground for stopping the individual. If they do make the stop, then they shouldn't be able to say in court, "The model told us to." This, however, may not be obvious to the person they have stopped, who has no familiarity with the software and its algorithms.

Then there's the problem of underreported crimes. While most homicides are reported, many rapes and home break-ins are not. Even in the absence of such reports, local police still develop ways of knowing when something odd is happening in their neighborhoods. Predictive policing, on the other hand, might replace such intuitive knowledge with a naïve belief in the comprehensive power of statistics. If only data about reported crimes are used to predict future crimes and guide police work, some types of crime might be left unstudied—and thus unpursued.

What to do about the algorithms then? It is a rare thing to say these days but there is much to learn from the financial sector in this regard. For example, after a couple of disasters caused by algorithmic trading in August 2012, financial authorities in Hong Kong and Australia drafted proposals to establish regular independent audits of the design, development, and modification of the computer systems used for algorithmic trading. Thus, just as financial auditors could attest to a company's balance sheet, algorithmic auditors could verify if its algorithms are in order. As algorithms are further incorporated into our daily lives—from Google's Auto-complete to PredPol—it seems prudent to subject them to regular investigations by qualified and ideally public-spirited third parties. One advantage of the auditing solution is that it won't require the audited companies to publicly disclose their trade secrets, which has been the principal objection—voiced, of course, by software companies—to increasing the transparency of their algorithms.

You've Been Arrested—by Facebook

The police are also finding powerful allies in Silicon Valley. Companies like Facebook have begun using algorithms and historical data to predict which of their users might commit crimes using their services. Here is how it works: Facebook's own predictive systems can flag certain users as suspicious by studying certain behavioral cues: the user only writes messages to others under eighteen; most of the user's contacts are female; the user is typing keywords like "sex" or "date." Staffers can then examine each case and report users to the police as necessary. Facebook's concern with its own brand here is straightforward: no one should think that the platform is harboring criminals.

In 2011 Facebook began using PhotoDNA, a Microsoft service that allows it to scan every uploaded picture and compare it with child-porn images from the FBI's National Crime Information Center. Since then it has expanded its analysis beyond pictures as well. In mid-2012 Reuters reported on how Facebook, armed with its predictive algorithms, apprehended a middle-aged man chatting about sex with a thirteen-year-old girl, arranging to meet her the day after. The police contacted the teen, took over her computer, and caught the man. Facebook is at the cutting edge of algorithmic surveillance here: just like police departments that draw on earlier crime statistics, Facebook draws on archives of real chats that preceded real sex assaults. Curiously, Facebook justifies its use of algorithms by claiming that they tend to be less intrusive than humans. "We've never wanted to set up an environment where we have employees looking at private communications, so it's really important that we use technology that has a very low false-positive rate," Facebook's chief of security told Reuters.

It's difficult to question the application of such methods to catching sexual predators who prey on children (not to mention that Facebook may have little choice here, as current US child-protection laws require online platforms used by teens to be vigilant about predators). But should Facebook be allowed to predict any other crimes? After all, it can easily engage in many other kinds of similar police work: detecting potential drug dealers, identifying potential copyright violators (Facebook already prevents its users from sharing links to many file-sharing sites), and, especially in the wake of the 2011 riots in Britain, predicting the next generation of troublemakers. And as such data becomes available, the temptation to use it becomes almost irresistible. That temptation was on full display following the rampage in a Colorado movie theater in June 2012, when an isolated gunman went on a killing spree murdering twelve people. A headline that appeared in the *Wall Street Journal* soon after the shooting says it all: "Can Data Mining Stop the Killing?" It won't take long for this question to be answered in the affirmative.

In many respects, Internet companies are in a much better position to predict crime than police. Where the latter need a warrant to assess someone's private data, the likes of Facebook can look up their users' data whenever they want. From the perspective of police, it might actually be advantageous to have Facebook do all this dirty work, because Facebook's own investigations don't have to go through the court system. While Facebook probably feels too financially secure to turn this into a business—it would rather play up its role as a good citizen—smaller companies might not resist the temptation to make a quick buck. In 2011 Tom-Tom, a Dutch satellite-navigation company that has now licensed some of its almighty technology to Apple, found itself in the middle of a privacy scandal when it emerged that it had been selling GPS driving data collected from customers to the police. Privacy advocate Chris Soghoian has likewise documented the easy-to-use "pay-and-wiretap" interfaces that various Internet and mobile companies have established for law enforcement agencies.

Publicly available information is up for grabs too. Thus, police are already studying social-networking sites for signs of unrest, often with the help of private companies. The title of a recent brochure from Accenture urges law enforcement agencies to "Tap the Power of Social Media to Drive Better Policing Outcomes." Plenty of companies are eager to help. ECM Universe, a Virginia start-up, touts its system, called "Rapid Content Analysis for Law Enforcement," which is described as "a social media surveillance solution providing real-time monitoring of Twitter, Facebook, Google groups, and many other communities where users express themselves freely." "The solution," notes the ECM brochure, "employs text analytics to correlate threatening language to surveillance subjects, and alert investigators of warning signs." What kind of warning signs? A recent article in the *Washington Post* notes that ECM Universe helped authorities in Fort Lupton, Colorado, identify a man who was tweeting such menacing things as "kill people" and "burn [expletive] school." This seems straightforward enough but what if it was just "harm people" or "police suck"?

As companies like ECM Universe accumulate extensive archives of tweets and Facebook updates sent by actual criminals, they will also be able to predict the kinds of nonthreatening verbal cues that tend to precede criminal acts. Thus, even tweeting that you don't like your yogurt might bring police to your door, especially if someone who tweeted the same thing three years before ended up shooting someone in the face later in the day.

However, unlike Facebook, neither police nor outside companies see the whole picture of what users do on social media platforms: private communications and "silent" actions—clicking links and opening pages—are invisible to them. But Facebook, Twitter, Google, and similar companies surely know all of this—so their predictive power is much greater than the police's. They can even rank users based on how likely they are to commit certain acts.

An apt illustration of how such a system can be abused comes from *The Silicon Jungle*, ostensibly a work of fiction written by a Google data-mining engineer and published by Princeton University Press—not usually a fiction publisher—in 2010. The novel is set in the data-mining operation of Ubatoo—a search engine that bears a striking resemblance to Google—where a summer intern develops Terrorist-o-Meter, a sort of universal score of terrorism aptitude that the company could assign to all its users. Those unhappy with their scores would, of course, get a chance to correct them—by submitting even more details about themselves. This might seem like a crazy idea but—in perhaps another allusion to Google—Ubatoo's corporate culture is so obsessed with innovation that its interns are allowed to roam free, so the project goes ahead.

To build Terrorist-o-Meter, the intern takes a list of "interesting" books that indicate a potential interest in subversive activities and looks up the names of the customers who have bought them from one of Ubatoo's online shops. Then he finds the websites that those customers frequent and uses the URLs to find even more people—and so on until he hits the magic number of 5,000. The intern soon finds himself pursued by both an al-Qaeda–like terrorist group that wants those 5,000 names to boost its recruitment campaign, as well as various defense and intelligence agencies that can't wait to preemptively ship those 5,000 people to Guantánamo.

We don't know if Facebook has some kind of Pedophile-o-Meter. But, given the extensive user analysis it already does, it probably wouldn't be very hard to build one—and not just for scoring pedophiles. What about Drug-o-Meter? Or—Joseph McCarthy would love this—Communist-o-Meter? Given enough data and the right algorithms, all of us are bound to look suspicious. What happens, then, when Facebook turns us—before we have committed any crimes—over to the police? Will we, like characters in a Kafka novel, struggle to understand what our crime really is and spend the rest of our lives clearing our names? Will Facebook perhaps also offer us a way to pay a fee to have our reputations restored? What if its algorithms are wrong?

The promise of predictive policing might be real, but so are its dangers. The solutionist impulse needs to be restrained. Police need to subject their algorithms to external scrutiny and address their biases. Social-networking sites need to establish clear standards for how much predictive self-policing they'll actually do and how far they will go in profiling their users and sharing this data with police. While Facebook might be more effective than police in predicting crime, it cannot be allowed to take on these policing functions without also adhering to the same rules and regulations that spell out what police can and cannot do in a democracy. We cannot circumvent legal procedures and subvert democratic norms in the name of efficiency alone.

Why You Should Ride the Metro in Berlin

Predictive policing may seem too restrictive, but compared with some other recent techniques, it actually looks humanistic and emancipatory. On learning that a crime is likely to take place, the patrolling officers simply go to the spot and do their usual police work; they don't lock up all potential offenders or build a wall around the potential crime zone. Doing so would be too draconian and too expensive, and they simply don't have the resources to pull it off.

But not all cases are so clear-cut anymore. Suppose that the police know that every Friday night there is an uptick in drunk drivers traveling from nightclubs (hopefully they can figure this out without predictive software). Police can simply dispatch more officers to patrol those zones. Will the police catch all of them? Probably not. Or they can use another strategy and try to prevent drunk people from ever getting behind the wheel. Perhaps anyone bringing car keys into the club would have to surrender them for the night on buying a drink. Or, more realistically, cars, equipped with the latest breath-analyzing gizmos, won't start if the gizmos detect that the driver has been drinking. Wouldn't this be a much better arrangement for the police? This way, they won't have to waste precious resources, enforcement rates will be 100 percent, and even indirect problems like discrimination and racial profiling will go away, because there's no longer any need to stop cars for checkups (not on suspicion of drunk driving anyway).

The idea that opportunities cause crime and the consequent belief that environments ought to be designed so that crime becomes impossible lie at the foundation of a criminological approach known as situational crime prevention (SCP), which has been shaping criminology since at least the early 1980s. Unlike earlier welfarist approaches that focused on reforming the individual criminal and changing the underlying social conditions—the presumed drivers of crime—SCP-inspired approaches do not preoccupy themselves with questions of morality and reform. Nor do they seek to rehabilitate criminals by telling them what they have done wrong. SCP treats crime as something normal and naturally occurring rather than deviant, assuming that it is bound to occur whenever barriers and controls are missing.

As criminologist David Garland puts it in his seminal *The Culture of Control*, theories like SCP, which he dubs "criminologies of everyday life," assume that "crime is an event—or rather a mass of events—that requires no special motivation or disposition, no pathology or abnormality, and which is written into the routines of contemporary social and economic life." Thus, the logic goes, by designing the environment in the right way, it might be possible to eliminate crime altogether or, at least, make it less severe. "Attention should centre not upon individuals but upon the routines of interaction, environmental design and the structure of controls and incentives that are brought to bear upon them. The new policy advice is to concentrate on substituting prevention for cure," notes Garland.

To see SCP-inspired logic in action, consider turnstile design in the subway systems of various cities. New York features plenty of full-body turnstiles (officially known as high entrance/exit turnstiles). Fake MetroCards aside, these turnstiles are nearly impossible to circumvent (in fact, when first installed in New York, they violated the state fire code, which requires greater capacity for exit). The inability to cheat the system can have drastic consequences during emergencies. In *Against Security*, sociologist Harvey Molotch describes a case in which New York police were delayed in responding to a platform shooting because they didn't have MetroCards and had no way of circumventing the full-body turnstiles. The victim died in the meantime.

The subway in Berlin is strikingly different: one is supposed to buy and validate a ticket, but because there are no turnstiles, one can also ride the subway without one. If caught, the free rider must pay a fine. The New York system leaves you no choice but to comply; the Berlin system, although threatening you with a penalty, also appeals to your civic duty. As two of its key theorists put it in their defense of SCP, "It is ethically more defensible to arrange society so that people are not readily tempted into crime, than to allow temptations to abound and then to visit punishment on those who fall." From this perspective, the New York system is not just more efficient; it's actually ethically preferable to Berlin's.

Cars that don't start because the driver is drunk, gated communities that tolerate no intruders, bridges that make it impossible to jump off, exact fare systems on public buses that spare drivers the need to carry cash and thus decrease robberies—all of these are examples of SCP in action. Broadly speaking, SCP has five policy levers—increasing risk, increasing effort, decreasing rewards, decreasing provocations, and decreasing excuses—and one or several such levers are usually translated into the material environment to prevent crime (e.g., getting riders to drop coins into a metal box as they board the bus increases effort, as the robber will need to break the box or at least move it, and decreases rewards, as the driver no longer has to carry cash for change, so there is less money to steal). SCP almost always involves some tinkering, engineering, and manipulation of technology; cars that won't start are impossible without breath-analyzing gizmos, and gated communities are impossible without video cameras, smart gates, and, more recently, advanced forms of biometric identification. Activities that are not heavily technologically mediated—say, reading a book—are less amenable to SCP interventions than technologically heavy activities like riding the subway or driving a car.

But this may change very soon as all of our activities become mediated in one way or another. If you switch from a physical book to an e-book, it suddenly becomes possible for an SCP engineer to intervene by, say, limiting what you can do with your e-reader. It can ban highlights, eliminate anonymity, or black out any obscenities in the text. Or say you stick with the physical book, but instead of putting on your old-fashioned reading glasses, you put on a pair of those fancy smart glasses designed by Google. The company has also patented technology that can recognize the objects present in videos without any human input. Combine the glasses and this new object-recognition technology, and the scope for potential interventions has expanded considerably; drunk males high on testosterone may be prevented from seeing the opposite sex. Or suppose you want to read the book on your computer, and since reading is now touted as one of those social activities that we are supposed to do with our friends, you open it inside Facebook. Suppose it's one of those interesting books that helped design the Terrorist-o-Meter, and your own terrorist score puts you perilously close to being a suspect. What good believer in SCP wouldn't want Facebook to ban you from accessing the text or to ping the Department of Homeland Security while you are still on Chapter 3?

Such highly personalized targeted interventions have been rare in the usual SCP context, as our technological environments were designed for the masses, not for individuals. But two recent trends are significant. First, the war on terror, with its panoply of risk-prevention-based measures, has all but normalized the idea—just look at our airports—that people who fit a certain profile deserve different treatment than everyone else; only through personalization can such individuals be identified and separated from others. In other words, it becomes possible to prevent not just actual crimes but even pseudo-crimes—that is, acts that become "criminal" simply because people meeting a certain profile engage in them (at which point, SCP might sound more like sorting than policing). Second, the proliferation of various commercial platforms, where ideas are created or distributed—YouTube, iTunes, the Kindle Store, Google Play—has made a lot of individual action (including speech) subject to the whims of companies, not governments. When Uncle Sam tells you to shut up, it's censorship; when Apple does, it's simply a contractual clause somewhere in the terms of service (which you never read anyway). The police need some probable cause to monitor your private Facebook communications, but Facebook itself can do this, well, just because it can—and it has the right algorithms.

But it's not immediately obvious why anyone should worry about SCP; after all, isn't eliminating crime—with or without digital technologies—a good thing? This is one case in which the narrow focus on efficiency might conceal the idea that perhaps the project of law enforcement should aspire to other goals as well. You might recall Albert Hirschman's elegant perversity-futility-jeopardy scheme discussed earlier in this book. All three themes appear in numerous critiques of SCP and go a long way to expose its numerous deficiencies. Once again, we should think twice before dismissing such complaints as reactionary and conservative, for, as we will see shortly, the "reforms" they attack might themselves be antithetical to liberalism. If liberalism itself is in jeopardy, it's hard to see the harm in assailing its so-called reformers.

Autotopia in Jeopardy

A common refrain in critiques of SCP—mostly a variation on the futility thesis—is that it provides a quick technological fix that doesn't address the root causes of crime and might make things worse. Thus, barred from one type of crime, criminals will simply pursue another. Or, barring universal adoption, they will pursue the same crime through different avenues: if some houses install sophisticated alarm systems, robbers will simply visit their alarm-free neighbors instead.

Perversity critique is even more intriguing: some scholars argue that as SCP schemes become ubiquitous, they make it harder to enforce rules and laws in situations that are not amenable to SCP solutions. If almost everything in your daily life is administered like the turnstiles in the New York subway, you might not feel the pressure to do the right thing in situations where the turnstile-like controls are missing. If you've been reared in an SCP-inspired environment, when you find yourself in a small grocery store that lacks a closed-circuit TV camera and a fancy antitheft system, how will you behave while the shopkeeper is distracted and almost blind? This is what is so perverse about SCP: schemes that intend to prevent crime might lead to more crime. Of course, SCP defenders usually point out that this won't be the case if SCP solutions become universalized; thus, there's more crime only if the quaint shopkeeper refuses to install the security camera. Once that is in place, everything is back to normal, and there's no crime.

Jeopardy critique has produced the most compelling and troubling arguments, for while acknowledging that certain SCP techniques might actually be effective, they also pose challenging questions about what we are likely to lose if they become the dominant approach to policing (and given the proliferation of new digital intermediaries, it's not hard to imagine how such dominance might come about). This critique of SCP sidesteps questions of means and efficiency; assuming that the means work as intended by their designers, it questions the moral and political appropriateness of the ends of such projects. Is a world without crime worth pursuing? What do we gain or lose by making it impossible to commit crimes rather than punishing the guilty after the fact? How does this approach affect important democratic values like solidarity, dissent, and deliberation?

The answers to such questions are rather gloomy. First of all, many critics argue that, at its core, SCP fosters and promotes feelings of distrust among fellow citizens; their guiding spirit, as one commentator put it, is that "the best policy is to regard most strangers and even neighbors with a moderate dose of benign suspicion." David Garland notes that the intellectual approach behind SCP not only "flies in the face of traditionalist ideas that see order as emerging out of moral discipline and obedience to authority" but also "subverts the old welfare state belief, that for society to work, solidarity must extend to all of its members who must be made part of an all-encompassing civic union." The world fostered by SCP is one of atomistic, selfish individuals, perpetually concerned about security and unable not only to trust others but to engage in moral reasoning at all. Such people do a great job of weighing the pros and cons of new alarm systems but struggle to weigh their own values.

Another concern is that our personal characters will fall victim to the ruthless efficiencies introduced via SCP. Thus, Canadian legal philosopher Ian Kerr warns of the dangers inherent in the quest to "automate human virtue," which he describes as "programming people to 'do the right thing' by constraining and in some cases altogether eliminating moral behavior through technology rather than ethics or law." Kerr's concern—and he limits his discussion mostly to recent technologies like "digital rights management" protection (found in electronic books and DVDs) and driverless cars—is that such schemes lead to a kind of "moral disability," whereby humans put morality on autopilot and no longer cultivate any disposition for honesty. Thus, notes Kerr, "digital locks would ensure particular outcomes for property owners but would do so at the expense of the moral project of honesty."

This "moral project of honesty" is not limited to our visits to the shopkeeper; it also regulates how we communicate with our peers in daily life. In other words, the favorite excuse of SCP proponents—that once SCP schemes are everywhere, they will help us transcend the "corroded morality" problem—may not hold. The only way to "universalize" SCP logic in the context of our everyday interactions with our friends—in which honesty, trust, and integrity are naturally expected—would be to supply everyone with a lie detector, which, disturbingly, might very well be the future we are heading toward. Once everyone is wearing Google's magic glasses, the costs of subjecting friends to a mini lie detector—perhaps one based in the cloud—are trivial.

Kerr furnishes numerous examples—from shopping carts that stop rolling once you leave the supermarket's parking lot to golf carts programmed not to drive too close to the green—that no longer give their human operators a chance to do the right thing. To Kerr, this all smacks of Disneyland's Autotopia—a popular attraction where kids drive specially designed little cars through an enclosed track. Well, "drive" may not be the right word. Kids, of course, sit in the driver's seat and even steer the car sideways, but a hidden rail underneath always guides them back to the middle. The Disney carts are impossible to crash; its drivers are simply duped passengers. Instead of training kids how to drive, notes Kerr, Autotopia actually untrains them, for no mistakes are permitted. The broader fear here is that the logic of Autotopia has slowly penetrated many other aspects of life and that we need to restore some decision making—even if it will result in more inefficiency and crime—back to humans.

Kerr's concerns are cogent, but something also feels amiss in his analysis. For one, he defines the scope of moral conduct too narrowly. Suppose you are an absent-minded college professor who loves to think of Schopenhauer—not other cars—at busy traffic intersections. But you are also a deeply moral and self-conscious person, and as life would have it, you must drive to work every day. So, given your absent-mindedness and your intention to avoid harming others, you opt for the safest possible car, in which virtually everything is automated. You can think about Schopenhauer all you like without running over your favorite undergraduate. It seems counterintuitive to suggest that a deliberate attempt to behave morally—even one that would require recruiting technology to help you with the mission—will somehow compromise your morality. Granted, you won't have a chance to express your impeccable morality at every left turn, but you have still expressed it when, unsure of your own driving abilities, you surrendered control to the car itself.

Of course, there may be other reasons to oppose automated and driverless cars; for instance, they might completely devastate whatever is left of public space in America, as urban sprawl might continue even more aggressively. But this is a very different type of critique from Kerr's concerns about automating virtue. There are perhaps good arguments to be made as to why mastering how to drive an unautomated car might be as intellectually and aesthetically stimulating as repairing a motorcycle. Likewise, some have argued that relying on natural navigation—from wind patterns to tide heights—might be preferable to relying on GPS, much in the same way that cooking without detailed instructions might be preferable to having a robot dictate the next step. As one author writes in a recent book celebrating natural navigation, "It is more important to understand why the methods work than to be able to use them." But this too is not really a concern about virtue; *GQ* readers notwithstanding, few people can excel at repairing motorcycles, natural navigation, and molecular gastronomy simultaneously. Choices need to be made, and such choices have more to do with aesthetics than with virtue.

It's too early to dismiss Kerr's concerns though; rather, we need to complicate them. Recent writings of legal theorist Roger Brownsword offer a great way to do this. According to Brownsword, regulators can use three registers to get us to do the right thing. They can go via the moral register and argue that something should or shouldn't be done because it's right or wrong relative to well-established community standards. Alternatively, they can go through the prudential register and appeal to our self-interest; thus, they can argue that we shouldn't do something because it will ultimately harm us. Finally, they can go through what Brownsword calls the register of practicability. For example, in the spirit of SCP theorists, they can make something technologically infeasible, obviating the need to appeal to our moral or prudential interests.

Although Kerr, fearful of Autotopia, would argue that only the first two registers preserve virtue and nurture our character, Brownsword notes that the third, technological register—provided it's used with moral or prudential considerations in mind—can do so as well. If you know that you are given to shopping sprees and ask the bank to block your credit card once you spend more than $100 in the same store, you are, in fact, shifting from the prudential to the technological register. Likewise, if you choose to drive a safer, fully automated car because you want to save lives or spare yourself legal trouble, you are not necessarily leaving the realm of morality or prudence, for moral and prudential considerations are driving your decision making.

Or to use a real example: some casinos now rely on facial-recognition technology to recognize and stop gambling addicts who have previously asked to be prevented from entering the premises. There may be some privacy-related concerns here—even though Canadian casinos have recently solved the most burning privacy issue with a creative use of encryption technology—but it's hard to see how fighting one's gambling addiction with the help of such technology is immoral. As long as you make this decision yourself—and don't have it made for you—there is no problem with delegating at least some enforcement to technology. Things get really tricky when a third party—a company or a regulator—does such register shifting for you. Why would the regulators want to do this? Perhaps shifting the registers will result in greater efficiency or utility or less crime—in which case we are back to SCP and Kerr's digital locks. Or perhaps the regulators believe that you are subject to the same cognitive biases and limitations as the rest of us humans; as such, you might be tempted to do the wrong thing even if you really don't want to.

This last set of assumptions accounts for the proliferation of what Cass Sunstein and Richard Thaler call "nudges": clever manipulations of default settings—what the authors call "choice architecture"—to get you to eat healthy foods or save money for retirement. Nudging is to manipulation what public relations is to advertising: it gets things done while making all the background tinkering implicit and invisible. The most effective nudges give agents a semblance of agency without giving them much choice.

Brownsword sees two problems with nudges. They appear to belong firmly in the prudential register; by tinkering with our "choice architecture," regulators try to appeal to our self-interest.

But in a truly democratic society, the choice of the appropriate register, as well as shifts across them, should be subject to public debate and scrutiny as well. In other words, it's not unproblematic to assume that the "right" reason to drive a more energy-efficient car is to save money on gas. Nor is it unproblematic to assume that the "right" reason to eat smaller portions is to stay thin and get a better job or find a prettier mate. Perhaps we want people to drive energy-efficient cars in order to fight climate change or stop conflicts in the Middle East. Or perhaps we want people to eat smaller portions because, as some recent studies speculate, increasing rates of obesity are linked to climate change. Or perhaps, as some activists in the fat-acceptance movement would argue, being overweight should not be stigmatized at all; we should really worry about "health"—and, as they would argue, one can be fit and healthy at any size.

Nudging is solutionism by other means. Turning something into a nudge by mere technocratic fiat presumes social consensus—over both ends and means—where it may not yet exist. As nudges proliferate, dissenting views over what needs to be done (and how) might indeed evaporate, but this should not be taken as an indication that the nudge in question has worked. Its presumed effectiveness is likely to be the result of a forced consensus rather than the outcome of genuine deliberation.

Another problem with nudging is even more insidious: nudges work only if they get us to behave in ways expected by regulators. At some point, however, this may require nudges that are not particularly gentle and make it impractical not to do what's expected of us. Perhaps you can still continue driving even as the alarm tells you that one of your passengers is not wearing a seat belt. Most people will surely find this annoying and simply ask the passenger to put it on. Thus, you might think that you are only letting the regulators tinker with the prudential register, when in reality you are allowing them to operate in the practical one.

Wither Moral Citizenship?

For Brownsword, then, the real problem is not that the moral and prudential registers are being overtaken by the technological one. Rather, it is that once laws and norms become cast in technology, they become harder to question and revise. They just fade into the background and feel entirely natural; indeed, they are often seen as an extension of the built environment rather than the outcome of deliberate planning by some wise social engineer. However, if we want to live in a world where norms and laws are constantly subject to revision and debate, then perhaps we should be wary of delegating so much regulation to technology. As Brownsword puts it, "Moral communities need to keep debating their commitments. In such a community, it is fine to be a passive techno-managed regulatee, but active moral citizenship is also required."

Brownsword does not draw the connection, but his concerns echo those that John Dewey expressed almost a century ago when he wrote about the importance of revising our theories—including those of what is and is not moral—in light of our practical experience in the world. For Dewey, moral rules are "intellectual instruments to be tested and confirmed—and altered—through consequences affected by acting upon them." Thus, we can't do without "honest acknowledgment of the uncertainty of the moral situation and of the hypothetical character of all rules of moral mensuration prior to acting upon them."

An example might bring clarity to what Dewey had in mind. Once it was perfectly acceptable to own slaves or limit participation in political affairs to white males of a certain class. The consequences of acting on such moral precepts proved devastating, and the rules were revised. From Dewey's perspective, the moral system worked well in both cases in that it allowed us to recognize its injustice and revise it accordingly. Morality, thus, is not about pursuing a set of fixed ends but about maintaining the legal and deliberative spaces for such ends to be embraced, debated, revised, and, if necessary, ditched. As Dewey himself put it, "Just as physical life cannot exist without the support of a physical environment, so moral life cannot go on without the support of a moral environment." Dewey's "moral environment" is simply an accumulation of the legal and deliberative spaces that allow arguments believed to have been resolved long ago to be reopened anew.

The shift to the practical, technologically enabled layer risks foreclosing some of those spaces. As we'll see in this book's last chapter, this doesn't have to be: technologies inspired by a different design ethic and philosophy might actually produce more, not fewer, such debates. Alas, the solutionist technologies that come out of SCP-inspired criminology and the burgeoning behaviorist literature on nudging are not focused on fostering or maintaining Dewey-style debate; they are focused on increasing utility and efficiency—they want to get things done.

Bruno Latour—himself a Dewey fan—once wrote, "To maintain the reversibility of foldings: that is the current form that moral concern takes in its encounter with technology" ("folding" in this context simply means forcing a tool or technology to perform only one particular function). The problem with solutionist technologies and designs is that, in pursuing irreversibility, they try to do the very opposite from what Dewey and Latour intend. Surrounded with such technologies, we have little choice but to behave in accordance with the seemingly universal norms of anonymous social engineers, ideally without ever coming to question the adequacy of those norms.

However, to practice active moral citizenship one needs to know that things could be otherwise; one needs to have at least some abstract grasp of their reversibility. This insight does not occur naturally; our technological environment, depending on how it's built, could make such questions more or less likely. If you have never visited more than a handful of stations in New York, you may think that using full-body turnstiles is the only way to run a modern subway system. Consequently, you are less likely to question whether the current arrangement is just and practice the kind of active moral citizenship that Brownsword and Dewey celebrate.

Compare this to Berlin's system, which operates primarily through the prudential and moral registers. Every time you see a free rider fined by the ticket controller, you have yet another opportunity to reflect on the appropriateness of the no-turnstiles approach. Perhaps you might conclude that the system is too lenient, or that the controllers are too tough, or that homeless people caught without tickets should not be prosecuted. Berlin's built environment lends itself to the kind of Deweyan moral environment that makes moral citizenship possible. In New York, by contrast, the system is perfectly efficient. As far as solutions go, it's all one can wish for; as Steve Jobs would say, it just works. That uncomfortable questions—about justice and inequality, race and public infrastructure—are never posed is presented as something to celebrate, not lament.

However, to laud such efficiency as an achievement is to fall for the most despicable and extreme form of solutionism. In this context, solutionism might optimize the current transportation system, but it can't think its way out of it; it cannot easily come up with a better scheme as it deliberately closes spaces for reflection on what such a transportation system might be. But here we should also avoid the temptation to blame everything on technology; technology is not in any sort of opposition to Dewey-style deliberation and moral life. Brownsword's account of the practical, technologically mediated register is too simplistic—it too must be complicated to account for a different set of technologies that actually stimulate (rather than block) deliberation. Properly designed, technology can expand—not just shrink—the deliberative spaces that make our moral life possible.

The problem is that, in the context of law enforcement, no one wants to advocate for technologies that are anything but perfect; a technology to root out pot smoking is not intended to trigger debate about the legalization of drugs—quite the opposite. In this sense, while technologies can facilitate deliberation, they often fall short of this objective when used by state institutions and official bureaucracies. Thus, because of the institutional logic of law enforcement, technological solutions tend to gravitate toward the nondeliberative, perfectly efficient pole of the spectrum. Once we have this in mind, the advantages of operating in the moral and prudential registers become clearer. Moreover, technology's gravitation toward perfection should also make us appreciate the deliberative spaces created by the imperfection of law.

The Perils of Preemption

If all of the above is true, why is there no rebellion against New York's full-body turnstiles, especially given that New Yorkers are also regularly exposed to other, more permissive turnstile designs? Most likely, few people see the issue of charging for subway rides as significant, controversial, or worthy of their attention. Consensus has been reached—perhaps even before the social engineers got into the act.

But not all laws and regulations are like that; as with nudges, in many cases what's being challenged is not just the choice of the appropriate register but the appropriateness of the law itself. In other words, whether you are prevented from burning the flag because it's illegal or because the new generation of smart matches won't ignite near anything that resembles a flag is an important subject for debate—but so is the very idea that flag burning should be illegal.

In an important article on digital preemption—an Internet-friendly synonym for situational crime prevention—legal scholar Daniel Rosenthal suggests that the technological register is troubling due to the immense difficulty involved in revising laws embedded in technological systems, which Rosenthal dubs "stasis." Digital-preemption schemes treat the laws they enforce as final and perfect; they constitute one fixed variable that such schemes won't tinker with. As Dewey recognized long ago, this is a rather naïve view, for bad laws are never in short supply, and even good laws tend to become outdated as practice informs our theory.

For example, many laws—against everything from marijuana possession to adultery—are technically on the books but are rarely enforced. It may even be that the public does not vehemently oppose the criminalization of certain activities—think of various vice crimes where only the individual who engages in them is harmed—because it knows that the police are unlikely to enforce the law. Delegate enforcement of such crimes to technology, however, and we'll end up with overenforcement of relatively unimportant crimes. Worse, the very process of technological enforcement, with its ensuing regime of impossibility, might prompt the public to revise their earlier views on the relative insignificance of such crimes. As Michael Rich, another legal scholar, notes, "If making certain conduct impossible . . . give[s] rise to self-reinforcing societal norms opposed to that conduct, the government decision-maker should be especially certain that impossibility measures target only behavior that society truly condemns."

The fact that so many people are violating a law might in itself prompt the government to revise or even scrap it. Remove the opportunity to break the law, and the government loses an important channel of learning from the citizens. This is a lesson well known to Prohibition scholars.

Of course, another important channel for challenging the law is civil disobedience. And yet, in a world where lawbreaking is impossible, no civil disobedience can take place, for the system provides no means of violating the law—regardless of the lawbreaker's reasons for doing so. This is a problem, for as many philosophers and legal theorists have argued, it's not so far-fetched to believe that we do have a right to civil disobedience. Ronald Dworkin, for example, has argued that this right derives from all the other rights that we have to challenge the government. Thus, whenever a law violates a right that is important to our dignity or some other personal value of consequence—say, freedom of expression—we have a right to disobey it. Considerations of utility are irrelevant here; the expected futility of our protest doesn't deprive us of this right.

For Dworkin, there is also a great signaling value to civil disobedience, as it can indicate that the law in question doesn't correspond to common belief or morality—which is one reason why we should investigate whether our smart, digital environments make resistance easier or harder to practice. Would opponents of the Vietnam War have accumulated as much symbolic capital if the draft cards they burned—in violation of federal law—were made from fireproof material? Or take what is perhaps the most symbolic act of civil disobedience in the twentieth century: Rosa Parks's refusal to give up her seat and move to the back of the bus with the other black riders. This courageous act was possible because the bus and the sociotechnological system in which it operated were terribly inefficient. The bus driver asked Parks to move only because he couldn't anticipate how many people would need to be seated in the white-only section at the front; as the bus got full, the driver had to adjust the sections in real time, and Parks happened to be sitting in an area that suddenly became "white-only."

Now, imagine that Parks is riding one of the smart buses of the near future. Equipped with sensors that know how many passengers are waiting at the nearest stop, the bus can calculate the exact number of African Americans it can transport without triggering conflict; those passengers who won't be able to board or find a seat are sent polite text messages informing them of future pickups. A smart facial-recognition scheme—powered by video cameras at bus stops—keeps count of how many people of each race are waiting to board and divides the bus into two white and black sections accordingly. The bus driver—if there still is one—can tap into a big-data computer portal that, much like predictive software for police, produces historical estimates of how many black people are likely to be riding that day and calculates the odds of racial tension based on the weather, what's in the news, and the social-networking profiles of specific people at the bus stop. Those passengers most likely to cause tension on board are simply denied entry.

Will this new transportation system be convenient? Sure. Will it give us a Rosa Parks? Probably not, because she would never have gotten to the front of the bus to begin with. The odds are that a perfectly efficient seat-distribution system—abetted by ubiquitous technology, sensors, and facial recognition—would have robbed us of one of the proudest moments in American history. Laws that are enforced by appealing to our moral or prudential registers leave just enough space for friction; friction breeds tension, tension creates conflict, and conflict produces change. In contrast, when laws are enforced through the technological register, there's little space for friction and tension—and quite likely for change.

Security expert Bruce Schneier makes a similar point when he celebrates "defection"—security speak for lawbreaking—as "an engine for innovation, an immunological challenge to ensure the health of the majority, a defense against the risk of monoculture, a reservoir of diversity, and a catalyst for social change." Advanced security systems tend to become institutionalized and integrated into vast bureaucratic systems; when policing functions are shifted to technology, with its aura of neutrality and seemingly natural origins outside human interests and institutions, such institutionalization can happen even quicker—and in a far less visible manner. As Schneier points out, societies protected by such measures are not necessarily moral or desirable; they can be—and are—rather awful. To build a technological environment where lawbreaking is impossible is to close the important social valves through which social change happens. "Sometimes a whistle-blower needs to publish documents proving his government has been waging an illegal

bombing campaign in Laos and Cambodia. Sometimes a pluto-
nium processing plant worker needs to contact a reporter to discuss
her employer's inadequate safety practices. And sometimes a black
woman needs to sit down at the front of a bus and not get up.
Without defectors, social change would be impossible; stagnation
would set in," notes Schneier. John Dewey would agree.

However, neither mass disregard for the law (as with the Prohibition) nor civil disobedience (as with Rosa Parks) needs to be
present for such change to occur. Sometimes it's enough for a law
to be broken. Sometimes being caught with marijuana in one's
pocket is better than being prevented from putting it there, simply
because an arrest is likely to generate media attention and trigger
a public debate about drug laws. Preemption, on the other hand,
is usually a silent and invisible business. Moreover, as Daniel Rosenthal argues, courts cannot do anything about cases that do not appear before them, which means that preemption diminishes their
role in reviewing bad and outdated laws. "[While] courts alter laws
through constitutional scrutiny, statutory interpretation, and the
common law mode of analysis . . . [they] cannot review laws that
are not brought before them, usually as a result of a person's violation of the law," he notes.

Michael Rich presents a whole list of crimes that, once they
reached the courts, resulted in the overthrow, or at least the significant modification, of unjust laws. "Virginia's anti-miscegenation
law was overturned through a challenge to the convictions of Mil-
dred and Richard Loving for violating the statute. Texas's prohibition on flag-burning was invalidated only after Gregory Lee Johnson
was convicted under the law. And the Supreme Court invalidated
Texas's criminalization of private, homosexual conduct only [after]
John Geddes Lawrence and Tyrone Garner challenged their convictions for engaging in such conduct," he writes. Logically, if violation of the underlying criminal statute is rendered impossible,
those who believe the statute unjust have no means to protest it.

Some laws seem more settled than others, while others circum-
scribe issues—think nuclear research—where even one tiny misstep
might have dire consequences. Not all crime-eliminating and preemption systems are equally evil; some might actually pass all the
right moral tests. As Michael Rich points out in his study of one

technology proposed to eliminate drunk driving, its potential to impinge on our expressive rights is minimal. It's also hard to think of many people who'd like to engage in civil disobedience by violating the laws against drunk driving in order to protest them. Although one can think of cases where drunk driving might perhaps be morally justifiable—you may be drunk but need to take your pregnant wife to the hospital—they seem relatively rare, especially compared to the number of deaths it causes. Here it's very important to avoid the totalizing antitechnology discourse that seeks to reject all technological interventions as illegitimate and inherently morally corrosive; this is not the case.

At the same time, we also need to be wary of the very opposite danger, especially when the number of digital intermediaries regulating our behavior—from e-books to smart glasses—is skyrocketing. The acceptance of one register-shifting effort shouldn't sanction the proliferation of other, more dubious efforts at preemption. As Rich puts it, if the drunk-driving program succeeds "with only a minimal perceived intrusion on the autonomy and privacy of innocent drivers, society may be less careful in assessing a program that seeks to prohibit speeding or one that leaves the realm of traffic offenses." The trick here is to resist the simplifying temptations of techno-optimism and techno-pessimism and to assess each case of technological intervention on its own merits.

Alas, Internet-centrism prevents us from grasping many of these issues as clearly as we must. To their credit, Larry Lessig and Jonathan Zittrain have written extensively about digital preemption (and Lessig even touched on the future of civil disobedience). However, both of them, enthralled with the epochalist proclamations of Internet-centrism, seem to operate under the false assumption that digital preemption is mostly a new phenomenon that owes its existence to "the Internet," e-books, and MP3 files. Code is law—but so are turnstiles. Lessig does note that buildings and architecture can and do regulate, but he makes little effort to explain whether the possible shift to code-based regulation is the product of unique contemporary circumstances or merely the continuation of various long-term trends in criminological thinking.

As Daniel Rosenthal notes in discussing the work of both Lessig and Zittrain, "Academics have sometimes portrayed digital preemption as an unfamiliar and novel prospect. . . . In truth, digital preemption is less of a revolution than an extension of existing regulatory techniques." In Zittrain's case, his fascination with "the Internet" and its values of "openness" and "generativity," as well as his belief that "the Internet" has important lessons to teach us, generates the kind of totalizing discourse that refuses to see that some attempts to work in the technological register might indeed be legitimate and do not necessarily lead to moral depravity.

In terms of theoretical warfare, the real enemy here is not criminology per se. Rather, what lends support to SCP-like approaches in criminology is our usual suspect: rational-choice theory (RCT). It's RCT that smuggles the cult of efficiency through the proverbial backdoor; it has no purchase on questions of morality, character, and virtue and sidesteps those questions entirely. Thus, we shouldn't delude ourselves into thinking that the current predicaments are unique or simply the result of new technologies or our confused and shallow thinking about them. In fact, the attempts to reign in digital technologies are the consequence of a much longer trend— perhaps they fall under the very culture of control theorized by David Garland—but that trend did not start in Silicon Valley.

So the worry that Apple and its tethered devices—Zittrain's bugbear-in-chief—might be giving us a world in which we have no choice but to do the right thing is both too late and too misguided. We already inhabit that world, and challenging its logic would require challenging it everywhere, not just in the iTunes store. We find Apple's model so appealing not because Steve Jobs hypnotized us—although that's part of it—but because Apple has embraced a model that we already encounter almost everywhere in our daily lives. We are gaining very little by continuing to imagine "the Internet"—or "cyberspace"—as some unique conceptual territory that develops and operates in accordance with its own trends and inclinations. Once again, "the Internet" is the consequence— rarely the cause—of the world we inhabit.

Bouncers Versus Vibes

Governments are not the only players having to choose which register to employ in enforcing their rules. Private actors have to make similar decisions, albeit in a different key and for reasons other than regulation. For private actors, such decisions often revolve around exclusion: whom to do business with and whom to avoid. Landlords, eager to lease their property, want to minimize the hassle of screening out problematic applicants. Nightclubs would rather bar entry to patrons who are unlikely to fit into the atmosphere. Top restaurants want some consistency among their patrons; most would probably prefer those with money and fame.

But note that even such seemingly similar establishments as bars and restaurants opt for differing approaches. Lior Strahilevitz, a legal scholar at the University of Chicago, came up with an elegant typology of different exclusionary strategies in his book *Information and Exclusion*. Nightclubs normally put a bouncer at the entrance and task him with deciding who gets in and who doesn't; Strahilevitz calls this strategy "the bouncer's right." Restaurants, in contrast, rarely hire bouncers and turn to an assortment of softer strategies— charging high prices, forcing patrons to make reservations, requiring a certain dress code, designing fancy menus that will put off many unsophisticated first timers—that often accomplish the mission as effectively. The former approach is about brute force; the latter is all about softer exclusion through language and aesthetics. There are several other exclusionary strategies—a property developer might develop a golf course next to the property to ensure that only those with an interest in golf choose to buy condos (an "exclusionary amenity" approach)—but they should not preoccupy us here.

It's tempting to file "the bouncer's right" under situational crime prevention. If you are drunk, a Breathalyzer won't allow you to drive; if the bouncer doesn't like you, he or she won't let you in. Exclusionary vibes, on the other hand, operate mostly out of Brownsword's prudential register: you are being persuaded that perhaps going to this fancy restaurant might not be good for you. Occasionally, the restaurant may even employ moral undertones, hinting that outlier guests will spoil the dining experience of other patrons. Still, "exclusionary vibes" are more Berlin than New York in that there is no technological enforcement. Nothing formally stops you from paying a visit to the restaurant in question; if you insist, you can go and suffer the consequences. If you can secure a reservation, there is no bouncer to keep you out.

Lior Strahilevitz argues that the choice of which exclusionary strategy to apply in each context is largely a factor of information costs. If the resource owner cannot easily obtain information about each prospective entrant's preferences and behaviors, then the exclusion function will be delegated to the entrant, and an exclusionary-vibes strategy is more likely. If the information is easily obtainable, then the resource owner will prefer to remain in charge and opt for a bouncer's-right strategy. Much—but certainly not all—of what the club owner needs to know can be learned at the entrance by the experienced bouncer; restaurants are trickier in that the dress code and first impressions don't necessarily say much about the fit between the diner and the institution.

The novelty of Strahilevitz's analysis lies in his insight that in an information-saturated environment like ours, it's much easier and cheaper to rely on bouncers than to send exclusionary vibes. It is no longer expensive for the restaurant to screen prospective patrons: it need only ask for their Yelp or Facebook credentials. This way, the restaurant can learn more—more quickly—than any bouncer. Not surprisingly, some clubs already ask patrons for their Facebook information at the door; even bouncers prefer more exhaustive sources of information. Strahilevitz overlooks yet another reason to choose the bouncer's-right over the exclusionary-vibes strategy: those positively identified as worthy of admission can also receive discounts and customized services once inside. Facebook already provides apps that, by relying on facial recognition, allow users to access discounts once they check into camera-fitted participating stores and bars.

Strahilevitz is an optimist and a disciple of Chicago's famed school of law and economics, and his rhetoric is, once again, firmly rooted in rational-choice theory. So he is naturally excited about such developments—and not just because of greater efficiency. One doesn't have to be a committed free marketer to find at least some of his arguments persuasive. For example, he argues that if we all had an extensive online reputation, some employers might stop discriminating based on race and gender and instead pay attention to our qualifications and previous achievements. Some interesting empirical studies lend support to this idea. One study published in the *Journal of Law and Economics*, for example, looked at how background checks influence hiring decisions at American firms. It found that firms that do not do background checks use the race of the applicant as a proxy for involvement in the criminal justice system. Because African American males are incarcerated at much higher rates than whites or Hispanics, they tend to be rejected much more frequently. But firms that do perform background checks are 8.4 percent more likely to hire African Americans than firms that do not. The conclusion here, then, is that the more information about applicants is out there, the less likely statistical discrimination is to occur.

Another recent study found that someone's Facebook profile is a good predictor of that person's job performance, especially for traits like conscientiousness, agreeability, and intellectual curiosity. The hope is that job applicants will have a harder time lying in front of their online friends, so Facebook might better reflect the candidate's personality. In theory, this, too, might reduce the need to make broad assumptions about candidates based on race or gender. If Facebook shows that the candidates are good, then they must be really good, whatever the stereotypes.

Many such arguments sound persuasive. However, the striving for appropriate, nearly perfect matches that lie at the heart of the bouncer's-right strategy also sounds terrifying. It does have the potential to imprison us inside our own worlds, making it harder and harder to peek out and mingle with people who are not like us. It might rid us of social awkwardness—everyone can be assured of always being in the right place at the right time—but this is also likely to preclude important avenues for social advancement.

One example of the exclusionary-vibes strategy given in Strahilevitz's book is elite beaches in Rio de Janeiro. They are divided in twelve posts (or *postos*), half a mile apart from each other, with each attracting its own crowd. Thus, the famed Ipanema is popular with entertainers and left-wing intellectuals, Posto 9, with homosexuals, and Posto 7, with surfers, while Postos 11 and 12 are frequented by upper-middle-class moms. Beaches are still public property, and nothing would prevent gay men from going to Posto 7 or upper-middle-class moms from going to Ipanema. But, notes Strahilevitz, "social norms and traditions are strong, and it is understandable that beachgoers who are wearing little clothing, are potentially vulnerable to thieves, and are susceptible to involuntary interactions with neighboring sunbathers would prefer to pitch their towels and umbrellas near like-minded folks."

Sounds good. But surely while the intermingling on those beaches might not be widespread, some still exists? I remember visiting half of those beaches as a tourist and, having not read my travel guide, I'm not sure I knew which was which. How would a switch from the exclusionary-vibes to the bouncer's-right strategy be in the public interest? Rio may not be the best example—this is public property after all—but there is no shortage of beach land in private hands around the globe. Do we really want to be asked for our Facebook credentials if we happen—or decide—to visit the favorite beach of a social group that we do not belong to?

The first season of HBO's *The Wire* features just such an awkward moment when the young, but not entirely heartless, drug dealer D'Angelo Barksdale takes his girlfriend to a fancy Baltimore restaurant. They look extremely uncomfortable and act like fish out of water, confusing courses and saying silly things to the waiter. However, it's clear that the restaurant also stands for the kind of honest society to which they badly want to belong—if only they can abandon the drug trade. Later in the series, *The Wire* features a similar experience, with police major turned teacher Howard "Bunny" Colvin taking his most problematic students to a formal dinner in a restaurant—it's obvious that none of them have been to one before—and they are so stunned that, for a moment, they forget about violence and drugs and cursing. Neither D'Angelo nor Bunny's students would ever make it inside if the restaurants they visited embraced the bouncer's-right over the exclusionary-vibes strategy (although, in the latter case, it was probably Bunny's presence that got them inside in the first place).

Or think of a newspaper geared toward the well-off. Its publisher might conclude that most of the negative comments on its website come from lower-class individuals who are envious of the rich. So it comes up with an innovative paywall: instead of charging everyone, it only charges those who make less than $30,000 a year—something that can be discerned quite accurately in a data-rich public sphere—on the assumption that only highly motivated poor people will pay the fee. This might rid the paper of bad comments, but it doesn't seem like a good way to promote a meaningful and all-inclusive public debate. The charm of exclusionary vibes lies precisely in the fact that they are circumventable, making otherwise impossible conversations, conversions, and insights happen.

A data-rich world, in which the bouncer's right rules supreme and digital preemption is the norm, would probably rob our childhood and teenage years of whatever sense of excitement and experimentation we associate with them. Smoking, drinking, sex, pornography, edgy music and film: if from now on it were no longer possible to experiment with these without first going through an information-hungry digital intermediary, then we would genuinely lose something valuable. Of course, much of this is already illegal, but such illegality is beside the point; the really pertinent question is whether such regimes can be circumvented.

Against Technological Defeatism

Viewed in the abstract, it may seem that the tides of digital preemption, situational crime prevention, and reputation-based controls are unstoppable and irreversible. Information is everywhere, and it's getting cheaper. All of us are carrying mobile phones. Technology seems to be moving in accordance with its own law—Moore's law—and we, the humans, can only conform and tinker with our laws to meet technology's demands.

This sentiment pervades our public debate about technology. Thus, the *Wall Street Journal*'s Gordon Crovitz writes that "whatever the mix of good and bad, technology only advances and cannot be put back." The *New York Times*'s Nick Bilton, writing of multitasking, notes that "whether it's good for society or bad . . . is somewhat irrelevant at this point." Parag and Ayesha Khanna argue in *Hybrid Reality* that "the flow of technology is at most slowed by reluctant governments, but it is more accurate to say that technology simply evades or ignores them in search of willing receivers." All these commentators adopt the stance of what I call "digital defeatism," which—by arguing that this amorphous and autonomous creature called "Technology" with a capital *T* has its own agenda—tends to acknowledge implicitly or explicitly that there's little we humans can do about it.

This view of technology as an autonomous force has its own rather long intellectual pedigree; in 1978 Langdon Winner offered perhaps the best summary in his *Autonomous Technology: Technics-out-of-Control as a Theme in Political Thought*. This view has been debunked hundreds of times as a lazy, unempirical approach to studying technological change, and yet it has never really left the popular discourse about technology. It has recently made a forceful appearance in Kevin Kelly's *What Technology Wants*, and Kelly's thought is not a bad place to observe technological defeatism up close, if only because he is a Silicon Valley maven and the first executive editor of *Wired*. Besides, very diverse thinkers about "the Internet"—from Tim Wu to Steven Johnson—cite Kelly's *What Technology Wants* as an influence. Thus, it won't be such a great stretch to say that Kelly's theories do provide the intellectual grounds on which Internet-centrism grows and flourishes.

The defining feature of Kelly's thought is its explicit denial of its own defeatism. Kelly, using a fancy word, "technium," as a stand-in for "Technology" with a capital *T*, reassures his readers that "the technium wants what we design it to want and what we try to direct it to do." This sounds like a rather uplifting, humanist message—but the very next sentence shatters it: "But in addition to those drives, the technium has its own wants. It wants to sort itself out, to self-assemble into hierarchical levels, just as most large, deeply interconnected systems do. The technium also wants what every living system wants: to perpetuate itself, to keep itself going. And as it grows, those inherent wants are gaining in complexity and force."

Kelly offers the best of all possible worlds: technology is both what we make it of it and an autonomous force with its own wants and desires and largely independent of humans. Kelly's thought is full of such doublespeak, by which we are simultaneously promised control over technology and assured that we need no such control because it's too late. Thus, he can write that "our concern should not be about whether to embrace [technology]. We are beyond embrace; we are already symbiotic with it," only to follow with "and most of the time, after we've weighed downsides and upsides in the balance of our experience, we find that technology offers a greater benefit, but not by much. In other words, we freely choose

214

to embrace it—and pay the price." So we get both mysticism—we are symbiotic with technology; we've already embraced it!—and radical empowerment—whenever we embrace technology, it's because we want to!—which is a rather odd combination.

But, promises Kelly, none of this actually matters, because technology wants the same things as evolution, for technology is just evolution by other means. Thus, he notes that "with minor differences, the evolution of the technium—the organism of ideas—mimics the evolution of genetic organisms." Technology is nature, and nature is technology; resistance is futile—who would want to challenge nature? With this simple insight, Kelly develops a whole theory that can explain literally every development—from malware like Stuxnet to Google glasses—by claiming that this is just what technology wants.

All we have to do is to develop the right listening tools—and the rest will follow. Hence, notes Kelly, "only by listening to technology's story, divining its tendencies and biases, and tracing its current direction can we hope to solve our personal puzzles." Elsewhere, he writes, "We can choose to modify our legal and political and economic assumptions to meet the ordained [technological] trajectories ahead. But we cannot escape from them." So, what he is saying here is this: technology has a story to tell; we should listen to it and modify our political and economic assumptions accordingly.

But why, one might ask, should we modify our political and economic assumptions if we can instead shape those trajectories? What if they are not ordained? Why alter our conception of privacy if we can regulate Facebook and Google? Why accept the proliferation of measures inspired by situational crime prevention and digital preemption everywhere if we can instead limit them only to instances in which they do not undermine dissent and deliberation? And how far should we go in modifying our assumptions? What if the voice of technology that Kelly pretends to hear is actually the marketing speak of Silicon Valley's public relations departments? Kelly doesn't bother with such questions; instead, he succumbs to the pro-innovation bias and declares that no meme should ever go to waste: "The first response to a new idea should be to immediately try it out. And to keep trying it out, and testing it, as long as it exists." Do you hear that, the land mine?

Concerns over distribution never appear in Kelly's analysis. Instead of discussing who should get to play the proverbial Aristotelian flute—the rich? the talented? the random?—Kelly imagines that technology will simply produce enough flutes so that questions of distribution will themselves become obsolete. Like Peter Diamandis, Kelly depicts a world in which technology will guarantee abundance, and abundance will make conflicts over resources unnecessary. This seems a rather shallow reading of human nature, for when everyone has a flute, some people will certainly want two, if only to stand out from their neighbors. Abundance in the absence of robust political institutions means little.

What's most disturbing about Kelly's ideas—and here he's quite representative of many other technology pundits—is that he thinks beyond local communities and even nation-states. His playing field is the whole of humanity, the entire cosmos. It's a philosophy best described as macroscopism: everything is analyzed based on how well it fulfills the needs of humanity as a whole. Thus, local communities that choose to restrict certain technologies or prohibit them outright are portrayed as essentially stealing something from humanity. By the same logic, Europeans are holding back possibilities for all of us because they regulate genetically modified food or have tougher environmental standards. It's one of those cases in which the vacuity of rhetoric surrounding global justice empties existing local practices of any meaning and space for maneuver.

This is most pronounced in Kelly's discussion of the Amish and their notoriously limited—some might say well-thought-out—use of technology. What bothers Kelly about the Amish is that, by refusing to use certain technologies, they are actually slowing down innovation everywhere: "By constraining the suite of acceptable occupations and narrowing education, the Amish are holding back possibilities not just for their children but indirectly for all." The idea never occurs to Kelly that political communities might be entitled to self-determination and that, as long as they arrive at some restrictions on technology in a democratic fashion—alas, this is not always the case with the Amish—it might actually be good for humanity. Instead of criticizing the undemocratic means, he is only concerned with the ends.

Likewise, when discussing restrictions on technology, Kelly views all of them as ineffective, even harmful. "If we take a global view of technology, prohibition seems very ephemeral. While an item may be banned in one place, it will thrive in another." He continues, "In a global marketplace, nothing is eliminated. Where a technology is banned locally, it slips away to pool somewhere else on the globe." But why should we take a global view of technology when we live in a world where technology is regulated by local communities? A certain technology might disappear in one place but appear in another because, in the former case, the community deemed it unacceptable and was powerful enough to enforce the ban, while in the latter case, the community either embraced the technology of its own will or was simply to weak or corrupt to resist the marketing talk of whoever came pitching.

The problem with Kelly's thought is that, while nominally about technology, it's actually deeply political; what's worse, it traffics in rather obnoxious politics. No one liked the idea that technology is just an extension of nature more than the Nazis (well, at least before the possibility of defeat forced them into a more pragmatic mode). Here is Kelly on nature and technology: "Technology's dominance ultimately stems . . . from its origin in the same self-organization that brought galaxies, planets, life, and minds into existence." Or consider this passage: "We tend to isolate manufactured technology from nature, even to the point of thinking of it as anti-nature, only because it has grown to rival the impact and power of its home. But in its origins and fundamentals, a tool is as natural as our life." Now compare Kelly's proclamations with philosophizing by the Nazi technology functionary Fritz Todt: "It would be paradoxical if the works of technology stood in contradiction to nature in their outward expression since the real essence of technology is a consequence of the laws of nature. . . . The works of technology must be erected in harmony with nature; they may not be permitted to come into conflict with nature as thoughtless, egotistical measures." The Nazis heard the voice of technology: it informed them about gas chambers.

Likewise, the laissez-faire part of Kelly's thought comes directly from Ayn Rand, even though he doesn't acknowledge the connection.

Rand's name rarely comes up in the context of technology theory, but she did write one essay, "The New Anti-Industrial Revolution," that addressed the subject of technology regulation head-on. The crux of Rand's argument can be boiled down to one pithy saying: "A 'restricted' technology is the equivalent of a censored mind." Thus, Rand writes, in the best tradition of macroscopism, that "restrictions [on technology] mean the attempt to regulate the unknown, to limit the unborn, to set rules for the undiscovered." Because we never know what new innovation a technology regulation might thwart, we should never attempt it in the first place. "Who can predict when, where or how a given bit of information will strike an active mind and what it will produce?" wonders Rand before warning that the "ecological crusade" would rid us of our toothbrushes, and "computers programmed by a bunch of hippies" (she actually wrote that—in 1971!) would retard human progress. By this logic, societies should not restrict the use of biological weapons or asbestos because we don't know what good might come of them.

To support the idea that technologies—and now "the Internet"—develop in accordance with their own rules, Kelly and other pundits usually invoke Moore's law. For Kelly, "the curve [behind Moore's law] is one way the technium speaks to us." The idea that Moore's law is akin to a natural law is widespread in Silicon Valley—it's one of the original myths of Ray Kurzweil's singularity movement—and it has long spread beyond the technology industry, frequently invoked to justify some course of action.

There are few empirically rigorous studies of Moore's law, but Finnish innovation scholar Ilkka Tuomi has done perhaps the most impressive work, digging up industry data, calculating actual growth rates, and tracking various expressions and references to Moore's law in the media. Tuomi's conclusion? "Strictly speaking there is no such Law. Most discussions that quote Moore's Law are historically inaccurate and extend its scope far beyond available empirical evidence," he writes. Furthermore, notes Tuomi, "sociologically Moore's Law is a fascinating case of how myths are manufactured in the modern society and how such myths rapidly propagate into scientific articles, speeches of leading industrialists, and government policy reports around the world."

In its original 1965 formulation by Intel cofounder Gordon Moore, the law stated that the number of components on chips with the smallest manufacturing costs per component would double roughly every twelve months. Ten years later Moore significantly revised his estimates, updating the growth rate to twenty-four months. But he also changed what was being measured. Thus, writes Tuomi, while still counting the number of components on semiconductor chips, Moore now no longer focused on optimal-cost circuits but rather mapped the evolution of the maximum complexity of existing chips. In 1979 he revised the law yet again. The industry, in the meantime, took his law to mean whatever it wanted, even embracing a different time estimate of eighteen months. As most media reports will attest, many still believe that eighteen months is what Moore said—even Intel's site used to claim this—but Moore never said any such thing, and he is usually the first to point it out ("I never said eighteen months. I said one year and then two years.").

By analyzing the actual growth rates, Tuomi found that while the semiconductor industry was experiencing significant growth, it was anything but neat and exponential. The growth in the 1970s exhibited different patterns from that in the 1980s; growth patterns in the 1990s differed again. There was even more diversity across individual microprocessors. To question Moore's law, then, is not to deny that important changes have happened over the last five decades but only to see how well those changes fit a singular pattern that a "law" predicts. As Tuomi points out, Moore's law has always been about the future, not about the past; historical accuracy has never really bothered the semiconductor industry.

One intriguing interpretation of Tuomi's work is that the semi-conductor industry greatly benefited from the rhetoric surrounding Moore's law, for it promised ever-cheaper semiconductors and helped ease concerns about where they would actually be used, thus boosting the initially weak demand for the industry's products. In retrospect, this may have been for the better. "The industry has been continuously falling forward, hoping that Moore's Law will hold, economically save the day, and justify the belief in technical progress," notes Tuomi. "Instead of filling a market need, the semi-conductor industry has actively and aggressively created markets."

But we shouldn't mistake the clever marketing and rhetorical tricks of the semiconductor and computer industries for divine laws that inform us about the future.

A concept like Moore's law doesn't just fall from the sky; nor does it stay around for so long simply because of its accuracy (which, at any rate, isn't great). Instead of postulating that technology speaks to us through Moore's law, why not study who else—perhaps Intel?—might be doing the talking. That this "what technology wants" kind of discourse allows technology companies to present their business strategies as a natural unfolding of history is not something we should treat lightly. Technology wants nothing— and neither does "the Internet."

Of Norms and Noises

Technological defeatism downplays the utility of resistance and conceals the avenues for seeking reform and change. Its model of the world is that encapsulated in the motto of Chicago's 1933 World's Fair: "Science Finds–Industry Applies–Man Conforms." As a result, too many people have been tricked into thinking that we can only change our norms, for there's literally nothing we can do about the autonomous march of technology. Concerns and anxieties about various technologies are recast as reactive fears and phobias, as irrelevant moral panics that will quickly fade away once users develop the appropriate coping strategies and upgrade their norms.

Such conflation of anxiety and technophobia has a long history. Historian Berhard Rieger has studied ambivalent reactions to new technologies in early twentieth-century Britain and found that such ambivalence was rarely an obstacle to innovation. Instead, he argues, "ambivalence should be understood as an integral element of British public debates, and one that supported a culture conducive to innovation." In fact, ambivalence about technology was probably a fully rational and healthy reaction, because the actual functioning of the new devices was beyond the grasp of most laypeople. Thus, Rieger writes of a certain tension that "existed between demands for rational conduct in the face of innovations and the fact that many contemporaries could only very partially found this conduct on an informed, or scientifically grounded, knowledge of new technologies." It's an attitude that we would do well to rediscover today.

As for the perennial reassurance that we just need to wait until our norms adapt to the new technological environment, here too the situation is far more complex. One example beloved by technology pundits is the story of how the spread of cameras at the end of the nineteenth century begot a generation of amateur paparazzi—also known as Kodakers—and triggered the first big debate about the death of privacy. A few decades later, the argument goes, such fears had mostly receded into the background as the public learned to live with the new device. Here, the logic is straight out of Kevin Kelly: the public noticed the ordained trajectory of the camera technology and modified all of its assumptions accordingly. And if we did it with the camera, why can't we do it with "the Internet"?

But how representative is this story of smart public responses to technology? Why should it be the template for future action? Adapting our norms is just one of the many possible responses; in some cases, such adaptations may not actually be the result of a conscious choice but only the outcome of failed collective action. History also has many examples of effective collective action, combined with smart policy and an assortment of technological fixes, making it unnecessary to change our norms in the face of technology.

Compare the story of Kodakers with the noise-abatement campaigns of the early twentieth century. As the cities industrialized, noise appeared to be everywhere: trams were beginning to screech, factories were beginning to buzz, and drivers were beginning to sound the horn (not to mention that the decadent middle classes were beginning to beat their rugs outside and play the piano at night). Various social movements—with names like the Anti-Noise League and the German Association for Protection from Noise—were formed to fight the noise menace. They tirelessly campaigned to institute laws that would prohibit the making of certain sounds while also introducing the public to numerous anti-noise innovations: noiseless typewriters, floating floors, quietly running electronic motors, silenced breakers, pneumatic railcars.

As Dutch historian Karin Bijsterveld points out, in the United Kingdom various campaigns by the Anti-Noise League led to the 1934 amendment of the Road Traffic Act, which prescribed a silencer to reduce exhaust noise, prohibited the sale of motor vehicles that caused excessive noise because of defects or lack of repair, and banned the sounding of motor horns between 11:30 P.M. and 7 A.M. in built-up areas. In New York, the Society for the Suppression of Unnecessary Noise ensured the creation of silence zones around hospitals and schools, successfully campaigned for a law against unnecessary horn signals in shipping, and even reduced fireworks on the Fourth of July.

Vienna is perhaps the most interesting example. Whenever the anti-din advocates—led by German intellectual Theodor Lessing—called for individual reforms, they were mostly unsuccessful. However, their struggle was not in vain, for through public debate they turned quietness into a leading indicator of urban life quality and firmly established it as a challenge for city councils. Or, as historian Peter Payer notes, "by changing public awareness of the acoustic environment, their endeavors influenced not only the way that urban space was to be restructured, but also how this space was to be perceived and used by the people living in the city." And even though many of Lessing's proposals sound eccentric—he wanted a professional, centralized rug-beating service to do all the work in some restricted area and for people to play musical instruments with their windows closed—many others sound quite reasonable even today, such as "the use of rubber tyres and quieter paving materials to dampen the cacophony of vehicular traffic, the careful packaging of freight shipped through cities to cushion it from rattling and banging, and the construction of schools in public gardens and forest preserves to ensure the tranquil atmosphere needed for learning." Lessing may have failed in advocating for particular measures, but he did feed and sustain the reformist imagination (not least because his early anti-noise activism was also tied to his two other favorite causes, socialism and feminism).

This is not to suggest that there were no technological defeatists at the time; many, like today's Internet pundits, with their tales of inevitability, argued that noise was here to stay, and the Viennese simply had to live with it. If only the Viennese could listen to the voice of technology—not an easy thing to do, given all the noise—they would accept the situation with no qualms. As Peter Payer explains, "Opponents of the antinoise campaign criticized Lessing and his supporters as hypersensitive fanatics resisting progress. Their refusal to put up with noise was seen as a neurotic sign of weakness, an inability to adapt to modern life. It was claimed that people could get used to noise if only they tried." In other words, the new norms were missing.

Noise, of course, hasn't disappeared from our cities entirely, but one can only imagine what it would be like if none of the measures advocated by the anti-noise campaigners had actually passed. Of course, some norms may have changed—being surrounded by noise has also made people more tolerant of it—but a combination of collective action and smart policy was far more effective. Why can't this be the template for our debates about "the Internet"?

We will only succeed in challenging technological defeatism if we refrain from using big words like "technology" and "the Internet." Instead, we need to uncover and set aside whatever cultural, intellectual, and political biases—cue Kevin Kelly—they introduce into our debates. We'd be far better off examining individual technologies on their own terms, liberated from the macroscopic fetishes of Silicon Valley.

Consider a sophisticated biometric technology like automated facial recognition. If you are stuck in the autonomous-technology/macroscopic view, you are likely to give up and simply accept it as is. This is what Slate's technology columnist Farhad Manjoo proposes when he writes that "technology marches forward and ordinary people—people who will be stalked, thrown in jail, or otherwise harassed on the basis of a facial identifi[cation]—will be collateral damage." So this is the pessimistic adaptation of the autonomy thesis: there will be blood, but resistance is futile. But suddenly Manjoo becomes an optimist again and promises us that norms will once again adapt: "Soon, though, we'll all learn to live with it. Etiquette and even regulations will develop around when it's OK to point your camera at someone and get her name." And just to make sure we don't actually do anything political about this technology, Manjoo reminds us yet again about the futility of our resistance: "It's too late to turn back now: If your face and your name are online today, you've already made yourself searchable. . . . Don't want yourself searchable, period? You can always get off the Internet, or always leave the house wearing a funny hat and a fake nose."

As social criticism, this is toothless; macroscopism has no way to talk about politics—all we can do is get offline or wear a fake noise—and even the heavy dose of snark does not help. As a prescription for social reform, Manjoo's fatalism is outright reactive. One can only wonder what his analysis would have been like if it were decoupled from the usual tropes—autonomy, macroscopism, norm adaptation—of technology talk.

To find out, compare Manjoo's sweeping proclamations with the careful work on facial recognition done by scholars like Kelly Gates and Shoshana Amielle Magnet. Gates, in her historical study of automated facial recognition, points out that such technologies rarely work as flawlessly as their proprietors claim. The entrepreneurs regularly misrepresent what their technologies can do in order to secure more government funding, which they use to improve the technologies. Gates investigates how the facial-recognition industry used the panic that followed 9/11 to pitch its solutions even more aggressively. She traces strategies by which companies try to enroll ordinary users in the project of helping them hone their technologies, sometimes by designing online games in which users are asked to identify pictures. Nobody reading Gates's book would conclude that the trends she describes can be summed up as "technology marches forward." Instead, through Gates's work, we can uncover novel avenues for critique and resistance. Perhaps the media should pay more attention to the ubiquitous failures of such technologies, not just to their deployment. Perhaps consumers in America and Europe need to be aware that their decision to seek better software to manage their photos could also complicate the lives of dissidents in China or Iran.

Shoshana Magnet, in her equally illuminating study of how biometric technologies fail, notices that one trope regularly used by industry representatives in promoting their innovations is that these technologies can root out discrimination, for unlike humans algorithms are neutral and blind to race or color (a story we've heard before). At the same time, she finds that these technologies often do the very opposite in that they "regularly overtarget, fail to identify, and exclude particular communities." Thus, biometric fingerprint scanners have difficulty scanning the hands of Asian women. Iris scanners exclude wheelchair users and those with visual impairments. The UK Biometrics Working Group found that it's particularly difficult to fingerprint those with "clerical, manual, [and] maintenance" occupations; thus, it might be a bit premature to claim that biometric fingerprint scanners are free of class biases. This is also another reason why some independent auditing of the algorithms would be a good thing.

One doesn't have to reject biometric technologies outright to argue that we need better, more empirical ways of talking about them; to present them as inevitable and developing in accordance with the logic of technology—or, in Kelly's case, of the entire universe—is to foreclose many fruitful interventions. They are anything but ordained. Just consider how facial-recognition technology might affect techniques like situational crime prevention and bolster the popularity of exclusionary strategies like the bouncer's right. When you can identify people's names by simply looking at their faces—without even asking them for any identification—you can fine-tune your access strategies in even more sophisticated ways. Or you can analyze faces to detect people's emotions and, if it looks like they are lying, simply deny them access.

Finding such connections between individual technologies and their possible roles in larger systems of control requires that we go beyond the technology talk and think on a much smaller—but firmer and more empirical—level. Once we leave the confines of the grandiose debates about "Technology" and "the Internet," another way of talking and thinking becomes possible, one that is technologically literate, attentive to details, mindful of legal and economic circumstances, and historically informed. It doesn't reject technological solutions per se; it just wants to question their appropriateness in each and every situation and perhaps to design a way for the community to continue debating such appropriateness even once a seemingly tiny and inconsequential technology engenders a giant sociotechnological system to support itself.

CHAPTER SEVEN

Galton's iPhone

"Neither information nor a drug fix ever gives any happiness when you have it, but will make you miserable when you don't."
—Michel Serres

"The day-by-day experience of a managed existence leads us all to take a world of fictitious substances for granted. . . . The verbal amoebas by which we designate the management-bred phantoms thus connote self-important enlightenment, social concern and rationality without however denoting anything which we could ourselves taste, smell or experience. In this semantic desert full of muddled echoes we need a Linus blanket, some prestigious fetish that we can drag around to feel like decent defenders of sacred values."
—Ivan Illich

The future belongs to datasexuals. As BigThink, a website promoting intellectual debate, explained in a brief but provocative essay posted in April 2012, "The same cultural zeitgeist that gave us the metrosexual—the urban male obsessive about grooming and personal appearance—is also creating its digital equivalent: the datasexual." BigThink didn't mean this as satire; the datasexual, it argued, is a real—and increasingly ubiquitous—archetype, a subtle hint that New York is losing the cultural battle to Silicon Valley. "The datasexual looks a lot like you and me," continued the essay, "but what's different is their preoccupation with personal data. They are relentlessly digital, they obsessively record everything about their personal lives, and they think that data is sexy. . . . Their lives—from a data perspective, at least—are perfectly groomed."

Datasexuals are to Silicon Valley what hipsters are to Brooklyn: both are ubiquitous and, after a certain point, annoying. These days, one has to search really hard to find daily activities that are not being tracked and recorded; now that everyone carries a smartphone, all walks of human existence are subject to measurement, analysis, and sharing. A bunch of inventive entrepreneurs have even developed smart toothbrushes that can record—and share—everything about our teeth-brushing habits; they come equipped with clever sensors that not only keep track of our brushing behavior but also share this data—thanks to a matching smartphone app—with dentists or care providers for treatment planning. Let's face it, who wouldn't relish a moment to reminisce over those graphs, especially if they can be displayed over our bathroom mirror? Besides, they're far more entertaining than those wonky charts about African poverty you saw on television.

Once you embrace the datasexual mind-set, there is no rest from self-monitoring, even at bedtime. In addition to a panoply of gadgets that already allow you to monitor your sleep cycle—well, as long as you are willing to attach their sensors to your head during sleep—a new generation of devices will enable us to relate the quality of our sleep to our environment. Thus, researchers at Intel are working on a system—reassuringly called Lullaby—that incorporates and processes data inputs from an infrared camera, two passive infrared motion detectors, and light, air-quality, sound, and temperature sensors. All these sensors collect data about what's happening around you and map it—with graphs, statistics, and all—on a touchscreen device on your bedside table.

Why would you want to turn your bedroom into a temple of surveillance and place a chart-spewing monitor next to your bed (after all, nothing beats enjoying some odd visualization porn while you sleep)? Well, the idea is, the researchers say, that Lullaby could "provide concrete recommendations for addressing the identified sleep disruptors." How did our prescientific selves even think of shutting windows and drawing blinds before? A complete mystery.

Now your sleep will be disturbed by anxiety, even if nothing in your environment has actually bothered you before. Now that the sensors say your sleep is full of "disruptors," who are you to argue with them? Solutionism would be funny if it weren't so tragic.

Alexandra Carmichael, a health entrepreneur and one keen devotee of the datasexual lifestyle, used to record forty things about her daily life, from sleep and morning weight to caloric intake and mood, not to mention sex, exercise, and day of menstrual cycle. The *Wall Street Journal* has profiled another datasexual—New York graphic designer Nicholas Felton—who, year in and year out, publishes his own personal annual report (the unassumingly titled Feltron Annual Report). What a blessing it must be to know that in 2007 he received thirteen postcards, lost six games of pool, and read 4,736 book pages; the lucky chap, we are told, also "tracked every New York street he walked and sorted the 632 beers he consumed by country of origin." In 2011, he logged forty-five visits to the gym and just nine visits to the liquor store. Felton's offspring won't have much to hold against him. His other statistics for that year must have been equally convincing: Facebook hired Felton in 2011 (it's probably safe to assume that no other candidate had a longer resume). What's not to like about this "Taylorism within"?

In *Financial Times*, we read of another self-tracker—a certain Joe Betts-LaCroix, who for three years in a row has been meticulously graphing not just his own weight but also that of his wife and two kids. We also learn that Joe has been tracking his wife's menstrual cycle for ten years—and yet it seems that she doesn't appreciate all the effort. "I was giving birth to our son, and instead of holding my hand and supporting me and hugging me, he was sitting in the corner entering the time between my contractions into a spreadsheet," she told *Financial Times* (let's hope that Joe was using open-source software).

The most impressive feat of self-measurement comes from Larry Smarr, a computer scientist recently profiled in the *Atlantic*. Smarr is in a different league from most self-trackers; he tracks everything they track—and more. For example, he collects and analyzes his poop. As the *Atlantic* puts it, "He is deep into the biochemistry of his feces, keeping detailed charts of their microbial contents. Larry has even been known to haul carefully boxed samples out of his kitchen refrigerator to show incautious visitors." Datasexuals, it seems, are not afraid to get their hands dirty.

But don't let Internet-centrism trick you into thinking that the digital revolution has taken some kind of unprecedented fecal turn. In fact, Smarr's quest to grasp the inner truth of his feces may be abetted by the latest technologies, but as self-improvement projects go, it's an old one. Meet Horace Fletcher (1849–1919), a health-food maniac on par with Larry Smarr, who earned the nickname "the Great Masticator" for urging his followers to chew their food thirty-two times. Fletcher didn't have Smarr's panoply of devices, but he still took to weighing his own feces and analyzing them under a microscope. The man was convinced that, if humans followed a proper mastication regime, their excreta would be quite dry, having only "the odor of moist clay or a hot biscuit" (that sounded convincing enough to Henry James, who was a big Fletcher fan and promoter). Fletcher's 1912 book *Fletcherism, What It Is: Or, How I Became Young at Sixty* contains charts bragging about the lightness of the author's stools; Fletcher was a datasexual par excellence (never mind that, having become young at sixty, he died at sixty-eight). His rhetorical question—"Is there anything more sacred than serving faithfully at the altar of our Holy Efficiency?"— is an apt slogan for contemporary datasexuals like Smarr.

Feces aside, there have been many similar experimenters before Fletcher. Some might point to Benjamin Franklin, who, obsessed with his quest to achieve "moral perfection," kept a diary ledger where he tracked his progress along thirteen virtues, like frugality and temperance. In 1880 Francis Galton, a pioneer of statistics and the godfather of eugenics, exhibited what he called a "pocket registrator," a clever invention that allowed him to record individuals of different types in a crowd without drawing attention.

According to his biographer, Michael Bulmer, Galton also "drew attention to the ease with which registers may be kept by pricking holes in paper in different compartments with a fine needle." What did Galton do with this clever method? According to Bulmer, Galton used it "to construct a 'Beauty-Map' of the British Isles, classifying the girls he passed in the street or elsewhere as attractive, indifferent, or repellent." London ranked highest for beauty and Aberdeen, lowest. Likewise, he counted the number of fidgets at meetings of the Royal Geographical Society as an indication of just how bored the audience was. Of course, we know where this obsession with measurements got Galton: it ended up in eugenics. Now, if only he'd had an iPhone! Although one can find many similar examples throughout history, most such attempts were either quasi-academic, small in scale, or pursued by wildly eccentric individuals like Fletcher or Galton. Today, such efforts are pursued on a much wider, global scale. It's true that many geeks who opt to participate in such schemes do qualify as eccentric. But they still look acceptable enough to attract the attention of venture capitalists and other uptight corporate investors, who have been pouring money into self-tracking start-ups.

Seeing Like a Self

It's hard to imagine the previous generations of self-trackers forming a social movement of some kind—one with its own proselytizers, regular conferences, and a set of shared goals and aspirations. The existence of such a movement would indicate that there was something cool, even laudable, about the very activity of tracking, a tracking aesthetics of sorts. As far as social movements go, this one would be all about celebrating a common means, not a common end.

Such a movement—widely known as the Quantified Self—has in fact emerged over the last five years under the leadership of its two cofounders, Kevin Kelly—the same Kelly who wrote *What Technology Wants*—and Gary Wolf, a technology journalist, formerly of *Wired*. In 2010 Wolf penned something of a manifesto for this nascent movement, which was published—not bad for a manifesto—in the *New York Times Magazine*, launching the Quantified Self movement not just nationally but globally.

In his article, Wolf identifies four factors that explain the meteoric rise of self-tracking over the last few years. First, electronic sensors shrank in size and became more powerful. Second, once they entered our smartphones, they became ubiquitous. Third, social media—from Facebook to Twitter—made sharing seem normal. Fourth, the idea of cloud computing made it possible (and acceptable) to offload one's data onto distant servers, where, merged with the data of other users, it can be expected to yield better results.

(Wolf, of course, doesn't put it this way; in the tradition of *Wired* mysticism, he invokes a spiritual dimension, writing of "the rise of a global superintelligence known as the cloud.") The sharing and cloud aspects are particularly important: revealing one's own measurements can provide additional motivation (e.g., many geeks desperate to lose weight are now buying electronic scales that automatically tweet their weight to their Twitter followers—yet another example of a solutionist intervention not available just ten years ago) while also fostering the same sense of community that propels well-established programs like Weight Watchers or Alcoholics Anonymous.

However, Wolf's four-factor list, although useful (even if a bit epochalist), explains only the technological infrastructure that has made mass-scale self-tracking possible. But has it become more desirable? Or did we want it all along, but the right gadgets and clouds were missing? Wolf, in true geek fashion, emphasizes the unique ways in which self-tracking—and quantification more broadly— can help shield us from subjectivity and emotion, supposedly a benefit. "We tolerate the pathologies of quantification—a dry, abstract, mechanical type of knowledge—because the results are so powerful," he notes. "Numbering things allows tests, comparisons, experiments. Numbers make problems less resonant emotionally but more tractable intellectually."

The idea that some comparisons or factoids probably should be left uninvestigated doesn't naturally occur to proponents of self-tracking. After all, they do fashion themselves as defenders of the Enlightenment who are fighting the dark forces of superstition and ignorance. Asked by the *Atlantic* if he'd rather not know something about his future diseases, poop aficionado Smarr frowns and says that he doesn't understand why anyone would ever want that. As the *Atlantic* puts it, "To him, not wanting to know something— even bad news—just doesn't compute. His whole life is about finding out. He's a scientist to his core." Scientism is the greatest enabler of innovation known to mankind.

Perhaps it's the hoarding urge that drives so many of the Quantified Self initiatives. Of all the things to be hoarded, data— especially data stored in the cloud rather than on hard drives in one's bedroom—has all the right attributes. It doesn't take much space, it's easy to move, and if you play your cards right, you can even make some money off it. Small, mobile, lucrative: it's a perfect hoarding target for our hypercapitalist age. It is a perfect response to the riddles and anxieties of our complex times, with every idea believed to be connected to every other idea and with the government and corporations hiding the truth from the rest of us.

In this world, the real causes are hidden and can only be uncovered through hard, diligent analysis—and the more quantitative it is, the better. Only if everything is recorded and quantified, can one discover what the Masons, the Vatican, the Ivy League, and the Man himself desperately want to hide. As one card-carrying member of the Quantified Self movement told the *Wall Street Journal*, "I want to create connections where I didn't know that they existed. I'm a natural annotator." What a great slogan for a Thomas Pynchon reading group!

Other proponents of self-tracking stress its potential to improve our decision making. British scientist turned entrepreneur Stephen Wolfram—among other accomplishments, he built Wolfram Alpha, a "computational knowledge engine" once touted as a competitor to Google—promotes what he calls "personal analytics" (which is just a synonym for self-tracking). According to the *New York Times*, Wolfram has scanned 230,000 pages of paper documents; his medical test data, complete genome, GPS location tracks, and room-by-room motion sensor data are all ready to be analyzed. Wolfram believes that one possible application of "personal analytics" would be to track the combination of factors that make people creative in their everyday lives (he's also on the record saying that soon "people will watch their health in a way that's a little closer to the way that they watch their financial portfolios").

Members of the Quantified Self movement may not always state this explicitly, but one hidden hope behind self-tracking is that numbers might eventually reveal some deeper inner truth about who we really are, what we really want, and where we really ought to be. The movement's fundamental assumption is that the numbers can reveal a core and stable self—if only we get the technology right. Thus, Wolf can write that "many of our problems come from simply lacking the instruments to understand who we are. . . . We lack both the physical and the mental apparatus to take stock of ourselves. We need help from machines." That the instruments and machines might also be pushing us in directions that we would normally avoid is conveniently omitted.

Wolf's is a double-click model of the self: you click the mouse or press the iPad screen, and a complete digital visualization of your real self pops up without any meditation. For Wolf, this fixed, coherent, and transcendental self is very much like what technology is for his partner in crime, Kevin Kelly: our true self has a voice, and it's trying to tell us a story; we just need to find the right set of apparatuses to hear it. Thus, only by attending to every single noise, by recording and visualizing all our wants, fears, and desires, can we aspire to rational action. Moreover, it would probably be irresponsible to act out in the world without first taking "stock of ourselves." In his last major book, philosopher Bernard Williams, a vocal critic of utilitarianism and an admirer of Nietzsche, proposed that such seemingly rational demands for a comprehensive listing of all our thoughts, dreams, and aspirations are driven by the unhealthy goal of "total explicitness" that rests "on a misunderstanding of rationality, both personal and political." Demands that "all my projects, purposes, and needs should be made, discursively and at once, considerations for me" must be resisted; instead, wrote Williams, "I must deliberate from what I am." For Wolf, though, knowing "what I am" is an impossibility unless spreadsheets are involved.

The recent appeal of self-tracking can only be understood when viewed against the modern narcissistic quest for uniqueness and exceptionalism. Self-tracking—especially when done in public—is often just a by-product of attempts to show off and secure one's uniqueness in a world where suddenly everyone has a voice and is expected to say things that matter. In addition to all the practical benefits—both real and imaginary—self-tracking offers, it also allows adherents to identify—and cement by means of sharing—the most unique aspects of their individuality. Thus, the logic goes, if you are not unique, you are simply not measuring enough indicators; we might all be thinking the same thoughts and watching the same viral videos, but surely at least our feces are not identical.

If not words, then at least numbers will reassure us—and, more importantly, the world at large—that we are who we (or, rather, our profiles) say we are. Wolf hints at this very motivation when he writes that "personal data are ideally suited to a social life of sharing. You might not always have something to say, but you always have a number to report." Self-tracking, then, is like blogging—only for shy people. In 2009, technology writer Bill Wasik published a *New York Times* op-ed where he argued that the Internet—well, "the Internet" really—is much like a hypercharged New York: it's full of creative energy; everyone sees what everyone else is doing and tries to keep up. "The Internet," for Wasik, is just one big city. He might be right, but in one important way, our new digital big city, looks more welcoming than New York: even if you've got nothing to say on arrival, you can still share your data and bask in your own exceptionalism.

The Ryanairation of Privacy

One can easily think of more tangible benefits of self-tracking, especially in the digital context. In fact, just drop "self-" from "self-tracking" and consider the many benefits of tracking. The main thing to remember here is that self-knowledge is never the ultimate goal. Nobody—not even Horace Fletcher or Larry Smarr—studies poop for aesthetic reasons; it's usually done to generate better data for decision making about one's health. Thus, with both tracking and self-tracking, the promise is that the data generated will yield some real benefits.

For example, many are persuaded by Google's arguments that by monitoring our e-mail and searches, the company can serve us better—more personalized—ads. Or that by studying what we type in its browser's search box, it can finish our queries for us. Thus, writes Slate's Farhad Manjoo, "I'm not just tickled by Instant Pages as a feature. I also like the philosophy behind it—the idea that my software is analyzing what I do and adjusting its behavior accordingly. . . . Why doesn't every other app [do that]?"

In a way, the rise of self-tracking might reverse the debate on privacy: instead of worrying about companies tracking what we do online, why not do the very opposite and lament that so much of what we do online is not yet recorded—thus not being used to improve our lives or at least traded on the market, earning us some cash? After all, once users can self-track, they can decide what to do with their data—so concerns about privacy become concerns about finding the right market and charging the right price. It's not particularly surprising, then, that the World Economic Forum in Davos is already hosting discussions to explore how personal data can be made into a new "asset class" on a par with wheat or widgets. As a high-placed Bain & Company executive who led the Davos discussion put it, "We are trying to shift the focus from purely privacy to what we call property rights."

A recent column in the *Observer* illustrates how market logic can easily invade discussions of privacy. "The parasitism of corporations snooping on us could become a symbiosis, in which information is freely surrendered in exchange for something concrete: say a garden gnome. Or, you know, adverts that are actually useful because they offer things we want to buy and ways of doing so more cheaply," writes British actor David Mitchell (and even though he's a comedian, he's not joking around). But notice how quickly the column—and, mind you, this is the left-leaning *Observer*—recasts questions of rights (such as privacy) in purely market terms. "This is the difference between a market and a war. In a war, if the other side wants something you've got, you definitely want to withhold it. If that happens in a market, and if you can strike the right deal, it's an opportunity to make everyone better off." By this logic, of course, even torture is okay—provided the prisoners "strike the right deal" and are well compensated.

But if one rhetorical goal of the Quantified Self movement is to spell out all the losses that accrue once our personal data is locked up, its other rhetorical goal is to show that, in principle, privacy is possible too—as long we are willing to pay for it. This idea already informs the operations of many self-tracking communities. Daytum.com allows its more than 80,000 users to track all sorts of personal data—from how many miles they run to how many beers they drink—but everyone's data is automatically shared publicly—unless, of course, you want to shell out $4 a month for a premium account and keep it private.

As Daytum's founder Nick Felton—he of the Feltron Annual Report—told *Forbes*, "If you want privacy, you have to pay for it. It's interesting to see what people choose to share publicly. Bathroom visits, sexual activity, drug use." Kevin Kelly, the cofounder of the Quantified Self movement, is convinced that this is what technology has wanted all along. "Privacy is mostly an illusion, but you'll have as much of it as you want to pay for," he told NPR. To borrow a term from political philosopher Glen Newey, this new ability to monetize privacy is yet another manifestation of the growing "ryanairation of social life"—named in honor of the infamous low-cost air carrier, which, in 2010, proposed charging customers even for bathroom visits (a fee that, to the relief of many, has yet to be charged in practice)—whereby once cash-free practices are broken down into severally billable units of account.

Under this new regime, it won't be enough to shell out for processing our data in private; we'll have to pay for proactively defending our online reputations as well. Defend from what exactly? Well, it might be something silly we did in the past—smoked pot at a college party where everyone had a smartphone—but it may also be something that lies beyond our control entirely: imagine a social-networking site leaking our private information, or Anonymous publicizing our membership on a hacked porn site, or a data-mining company drawing accurate inferences from disparate sources of data. This is where start-ups like Reputation.com come into picture; they promise to help clean up your online reputation—sometimes by cleverly manipulating search results and sometimes by asking site owners to take down damaging information by threatening litigation—but, of course, they charge hefty fees for their best work.

Those who can afford it probably do get wonderful service. In April 2011 the *New York Times* reported on how, during the economic collapse of 2008, investment bankers began using the services of such online specialists to protect their reputations. According to one New York–based image manager, "Some of these bankers were paying upwards of $10,000 a month to try to hide their names online as they began appearing in the press." Good for the bankers; bad for the rest of us. But what about those who have done nothing wrong but can't pay? Will a data-rich economy create new forms of digital divide, where only the rich can afford to defend their online reputations? It's also hard to overlook the fact that most reputation consultants have a direct interest in making everyone anxious about his or her reputation, for this is the only way to ensure stable business growth.

Silicon Valley visionaries like to imagine citizens as start-ups; thus, being constantly stressed out about one's reputation is seen as the normal cost of doing business. The goal is to get all of us off information welfare and into the information workforce, whereby we need to actively care for our online profiles and, if necessary, pay start-ups like Reputation.com for extra protection. That this might distract us from pursuing other important personal projects does not much matter. The benefit of transitioning to some kind of information welfare state, which will allow citizens to experiment and grow without risking their reputations, doesn't occur to our digital luminaries either.

Reid Hoffman, the founder of LinkedIn who fashions himself a digital philosopher, offers the best encapsulation of this ideology in his book with the telling title *The Start-Up of You: Adapt to the Future, Invest in Yourself, and Transform Your Career.* According to Hoffman, "You can think like a start-up, whoever you are and whatever you do." Thus, you need to live as if you were in permanent beta—"beta" is tech speak for software that is not yet ready—and "acknowledge that you have bugs, that there's new development to do on yourself, that you will need to adapt and evolve. . . . Permanent beta is essentially a lifelong commitment to continuous personal growth. Get busy livin', or get busy dyin'."

That our "bugs" might stem from lax or nonexistent laws, too much lobbying by the likes of LinkedIn, or various acts of mischief by Anonymous is not even alluded to; everything happens solely as a result of your own actions, never because of the environment. Hence, we must work diligently to fix all our bugs; self-tracking is just one step toward identifying them. Of course, permanent anxiety has always been one of Silicon Valley's favorite assets, but something more sinister is happening here: macro-level, reform-based solutions to problems are discarded in favor of carefully delineated action by atomized individuals.

The idea that our personal data—whether it's self-tracked or recorded by some other digital intermediary—can be profitably sold has also inspired several start-ups, known as "digital lockers," that want to quell public fears over data loss or accidental disclosures and enable full consumer participation in the reputation marketplace. Thus, a start-up called Personal.com has raised $7.6 million in venture funding based on the idea that consumers who are allowed to "curate" what data about themselves are made available to select marketers might end up with both more relevant ads and better discounts.

In a 2011 interview with the *San Jose Mercury News*, Personal's chief executive Shane Green invoked a hypothetical consumer who chooses to make specific data, such as favorite brands, available to advertisers. In return, the consumer gets 5 to 15 percent of a purchase price back, with Personal taking a cut of that rebate. Everybody wins. Jason Cavnar, cofounder of Singly, another digital locker start-up, promises many nonfinancial benefits as well. "Imagine," he says, "being able to combine all of your check-in data from Facebook and Foursquare with restaurants you have used a credit card at, and combining that with a list of reviews from Yelp to see what highly rated restaurants near you that you have not yet tried." If consumers can collect this data themselves—or authorize companies to collect it on their behalf—all the better.

The Great Unraveling

Silicon Valley is not making empty promises here: "digital lockers" will most likely ensure that we get better discounts. This rhetoric of empowerment is not disingenuous, at least not all of it. But to think of these changes solely in terms of how they empower individual consumers would be to miss some broader unintended consequences of creating more incentives for self-disclosure. Once we put on our technostructuralist hat, look beyond the individual consumer, and investigate how self-tracking and data lockers might transform the very sociopolitical environments in which such consumers go about their business, we are likely to see a very different picture.

Disclosure decisions are tricky because my decision to track and release some information about myself has implications for many other people who may not even know about data lockers or self-tracking. How so? If I choose to track and publicize my health, and you choose not to, then sooner or later your decision to do nothing might be seen as tacit acknowledgment that you have something to hide. Thus, when some members of society choose to self-track and self-disclose—and presumably those who do choose to self-disclose have little to fear from disclosure—it becomes much harder, if not outright impossible, for everyone (including those who'd rather keep their data to themselves) not to self-disclose.

Think of it this way: all of us have a right not to have a cell phone or a Facebook profile. But that right means little in a society where almost everyone has both those things, for people without cell phones or Facebook profiles are presumed to be weird outliers with their own reasons for staying low—and those reasons can't be good, can they? Law enforcement agencies already view those without cell phones as potential terrorists or drug dealers—this, if anything, turns your "right" to keep away from certain technologies into a joke. A similar set of interpretations has already emerged around the digital refuseniks who stubbornly resist opening a Facebook account.

If just a few years ago, they were seen as Luddites or, at best, as deeply spiritual individuals who didn't want to bother with the hassle of social networking, today such people are portrayed as suspicious creeps who either have no social life to report or are hiding some dark past from public view. This suspicion of Facebook holdouts permeates our public culture deeply. Thus, following the Aurora shootings in June 2012, the German newspaper *Der Tagesspiegel* pointed out that neither James Holmes, the Aurora gunman, nor the Norwegian mass murderer Anders Behring Breivik had Facebook accounts, implying that the absence of any Facebook activity might itself indicate that a person has problems. The same sentiment was echoed by Slate's columnist Farhad Manjoo, who suggested, "If you are going out with someone and they don't have a Facebook profile, you should be suspicious."

We'll see similar trends when it comes to the sharing of information generated through self-tracking. All this sharing will in turn lead to the unraveling of privacy. No amount of privacy-enhancing technologies or tighter laws—the hallmarks of traditional privacy activism—will be of much help here precisely because there will be good reasons to share rather than protect our data. Perfectly secure browsers and smartphones will mean little if their users suspect that maintaining their privacy is a major liability. Once the motivation for keeping one's data private goes away, all the conventional responses to the privacy crisis become inadequate.

Scott Peppet, a legal scholar at the University of Colorado Law School, argues that the proliferation of self-tracking will force us to create our own "personal prospectus," an assortment of various digital lockers populated by our self-tracked and verified information. Our digital prospectus will then mediate all our interactions with fellow citizens, firms, and public institutions, which, armed with access to all this data, will continue their transition from exclusionary vibes to the bouncer's right as their preferred discrimination strategy. Peppet musters a number of realistic examples to show just how empowering the idea of the personal prospectus might feel to consumers: "Want to price my health insurance premium? Let me share with you my FitBit data. Want to price my car rental or car insurance? Let me share with you my regular car's 'black box' data to prove I am a safe driver. Want me to prove I will be a diligent, responsible employee? Let me share with you my real time blood alcohol content, how carefully I manage my diabetes, or my lifelong productivity records."

In other words, there are very good reasons why those with excellent health, impressive driving habits, and Stakhanovite productivity will be excited to track and share their data. But what about the poor and the sick? What about those who don't have the time or the stamina—which those who work three daily jobs to stay afloat might lack—to engage in self-tracking? And what if the poor and the sick do embrace self-monitoring? What are they likely to discover? That they eat food high in calories and saturated fat and that they never "check in" at their local gym because the membership fees are too high or because they never have the time with all the odd jobs they are working? The danger here is quite obvious: if you are well and well-off, self-monitoring will only make things better for you. If you are none of those things, the personal prospectus could make your life much more difficult, with higher insurance premiums, fewer discounts, and limited employment prospects.

Several recent efforts to make the personal prospectus even more comprehensive hint at what we can expect in the near future; Peppet's concerns seem fully justified. Smartphones already offer a panoply of applications for self-diagnosis, which, if only indirectly, also create a trove of health data that can be put to good use (and it's not just smartphones: a recent study found that consumer-grade devices monitoring one's health will account for more than 80 percent of wireless devices in 2016). As Christopher Steiner notes in *Automate This*, an iPhone app from the Dutch technology company Philips already knows how to take vital measurements for whoever happens to be looking at its camera. The app can then figure out—with a high degree of accuracy—users' heart and breathing rates by examining tiny color changes in their faces and closely examining their chest movements, respectively. As Steiner notes, "Upcoming apps from Philips and other tech companies will allow for instant measurement of blood pressure, temperature, blood oxygenation levels, and signs of concussion." The next step will be to get insurance companies to see this data and reward the healthy self-trackers and punish everyone else.

Car insurers are already exploring ways to profit from the self-tracking craze. Thus, Aviva, the world's sixth-largest insurance company, has been testing a smartphone app called RateMyDrive, which monitors how well motorists deal with acceleration, braking, and cornering. After driving for two hundred miles, drivers get an individual score that, in turn, determines their insurance premiums; "safe" drivers can expect to shed as much as 20 percent off their premiums. There is no need to install a "black box" in your car—your iPhone takes care of everything. Another novel solution is to turn your car into a moving surveillance castle, outfit it with cameras and other sensors, and use all this data to achieve better fuel efficiency and lower accident rates. A San Diego start-up called SmartDrive Systems Inc. does just that. When sudden braking or swerving triggers its sensors, the system starts recording video and other data. Having used this technology to assess more than 44 million unsafe-driving incidents, the company claims it can improve fuel efficiency by 20 percent and reduce collisions by up to 80 percent.

Most interestingly, SmartDrive claims that the recordings allow many drivers to prove their innocence and avoid blame for accidents they didn't cause. In a world where you can record everything—if only to preempt complaints or false accusations—you will record everything just to be on the safe side. Our digital visionaries constantly celebrate the virtues of such proactive tracking and sharing—with constant releases of data becoming a potent form of reputation defense. Cue Jeff Jarvis, who, true to form, declares that "the way to affect your reputation is often to share more, not less. The best solution is to be yourself. If that makes you uneasy, talk with your shrink. Better yet, blog about it." But will you be able to afford a shrink once your insurance company starts reading your tell-all blog? Jarvis doesn't say.

As more people embrace this track-and-share mentality, those who refuse to participate in this great party will bear the brunt of the social costs. This is why we need a debate about the ethics of self-tracking; a decision to track and publicize a certain aspect of our daily lives cannot arise solely from our preoccupation with improving our own well-being—just as a decision about how much electricity or water to consume in our households cannot arise solely from our ability to pay for them or our material needs. As long as privacy is viewed as an arch-important enabler of human flourishing—an idea that many in Silicon Valley would surely contest—my decision to self-track, whatever great benefits it might confer on me personally, ought to be subjected to a much more complex moral evaluation than the Quantified Self evangelists have acknowledged so far. Scott Peppet puts his finger on the problem when he writes, "Your choice to quantify yourself (for personal preference or profit) thus has deep implications if it necessitates my 'choice' to quantify myself under the pressure of unraveling. What if I just wasn't the sort of person who wanted to know all of this real-time data about myself, but we evolve an economy that requires such measurement? What if quantification is anathema to my aesthetic or psychological makeup; what if it conflicts with the internal architecture around which I have constructed my identity and way of knowing?"

As Peppet also points out, it's important to ask "what sorts of people—artists? academics? writers?—will be most denuded or excluded by such a metric-based world," for it seems there will be many such metrics. For example, rare is the writer with a perfect credit score; find ten more such indicators—willingly embraced by the majority—and no sane human being will ever risk dabbling in writing. Up till now, the imperfections of our socioeconomic system—caused by, among other factors, the lack of adequate data—have led to a lot of barely justifiable risk taking, which has in turn fuelled cultural and social innovation. It would be a genuine loss if the advent of the personal prospectus made such risk taking less likely. The potential unraveling of privacy is not the only reason to worry about self-tracking, however. In fact, to worry about the phenomenon's secondary effects might very well already concede too much to the Quantified Self enthusiasts. Understanding the structural limitations of quantification schemes—especially zooming in on what they don't reveal in their quest to reveal everything— might provide another fruitful avenue for critique.

Between Nietzsche and Condorcet

Friedrich Nietzsche was one of the first to rebel against the quantification fetish that he saw present in the then popular utilitarian philosophy advocated by the likes of Francis Galton and Herbert Spencer (whom Nietzsche charmingly caricatures in his writings). In *The Gay Science*, Nietzsche bemoaned "the faith in a world that is supposed to have its equivalent and its measure in human thought and human valuations—a 'world of truth' that can be mastered completely and forever with the aid of our square little reason." Nietzsche was having none of it: "What? Do we really want to permit existence to be degraded for us like this—reduced to a mere exercise for a calculator and an indoor diversion for mathematicians? Above all, one should not wish to divest existence of its rich ambiguity that is a dictate of good taste, gentlemen, the taste of reverence for everything that lies beyond your horizon."

In his idiosyncratic way, Nietzsche offered a piercing critique of information reductionism, the naïve belief so popular with the Silicon Valley crowd that more information is always better. That one can collect and muster more measurements of a given phenomenon, Nietzsche reasoned, does not imply progress, for there may be other, better ways of talking about that phenomenon that do not easily lend themselves to quantitative measurements. "That the only justifiable interpretation of the world should be one in which *you* are justified because one can continue to work and do research scientifically in *your* sense (you really mean, mechanistically?)—an interpretation that permits counting, calculating, weighing, seeing, and touching, and nothing more—that is a crudity and naïveté, assuming that it is not a mental illness, an idiocy."

Most perceptively, Nietzsche understood that quantifiable information might be nothing but low-hanging fruit that is easy to pick but often thwarts more ambitious, more sustained efforts at understanding. "Would it not be rather probable that, conversely, precisely the most superficial and external aspect of existence— what is most apparent, its skin and sensualization—would be grasped first—and might even be the only thing that allowed itself to be grasped?" he wondered.

As if responding to Leibniz—who once wrote that music is an "occult exercise in mathematics performed by a mind unconscious of the fact that it is counting"—Nietzsche pointed out that in areas like art, quantitative measures are simply inappropriate. "Assuming that one estimated the value of a piece of music according to how much of it could be counted, calculated, and expressed in formulas: how absurd would such a 'scientific' estimation of music be! What would one have comprehended, understood, grasped of it? Nothing, really nothing of what is 'music' in it!" he wrote.

What would Nietzsche make of Google's Eric Schmidt, who actually seems to entertain the idea that one day Google might excel at algorithmic aesthetics? "Our mission is to get the best answer," said Schmidt in response to an interview question about why Google increasingly provides answers and not just search results. "So if you say, 'I want the best music from Lady Gaga,' and if we could algorithmically compute that answer, I would want to give it to you right then and there, subject to rules and copyright and all of that." Sure, there are some "ifs" involved here, but it doesn't sound as if Schmidt believes this job to be categorically impossible; it's all a matter of the right algorithms and enough computing power. "Best music from Lady Gaga" is just something objective that is out there, to be discovered by Google.

Nietzsche's conclusion about calculations and measurements was bitter but powerful: "An essentially mechanical world would be an essentially meaningless world." Now, compare this with Kevin Kelly's rhetorical attempt to exclude questions of meaning as something that the Quantified Self crowd ought even worry about:

"[Our critics say that] only intangibles like meaningful happiness count. Meaningfulness is very hard to measure, which makes it very hard to optimize. So far anything we can quantify has been getting better over the long term."

The last part, of course, is typical Silicon Valley nonsense: what about income inequality, or carbon emissions, or obesity rates in America? Kelly's positivism would shock even Auguste Comte. But proclamations like Kelly's also tap into the long-running scientific tradition—so astutely documented by historian Theodore Porter in his *Trust in Numbers*—that celebrates measurement as seemingly objective and consensus boosting. Alas, as with almost everything else they say, our digital boosters are often blind to this history. Kelly's logic rests on Lord Kelvin's famous dictum postulated in the nineteenth century: "If you can not measure it, you can not improve it." A century before Kelvin, the Marquis de Condorcet was already touting the benefits of measurement: "If this evidence cannot be weighted and measured, and if these effects cannot be subjected to precise measurement, then we cannot know exactly how much good or evil they contain." In this sense, the Quantified Self does continue in a formidable intellectual tradition, but it also suffers from the numerous weaknesses that bothered Nietzsche and many of his followers: Kelly, like Kelvin and Condorcet, has disturbingly little to say about the "intangibles"—both the ethics and aesthetics—and this, if anything, is a good reason to worry about this new movement.

Even when it comes to tangibles, however, the situation is much murkier than our philosophers of tracking let on. Gary Wolf once wrote that one of his main inspirations for the Quantified Self was the idea of the "macroscope," which, following entrepreneur Gilman Tolle, he defines as "a technological system that radically increases our ability to gather data in nature, and to analyze it for meaning." The naïve idea that data exists "in nature" and can simply be gathered or discovered without our having to account for our data-gathering tools, the knowledge systems that underpin them, and multiple layers of human interpretation is one of the defining features of information reductionism. For data to be gathered, someone first needs to decide—or defer to someone else's judgment about—what is being measured, in what manner, with what devices, and to what purpose. How we choose to slice up reality, what elements we highlight, and what elements we shade will greatly influence what kinds of measurements we generate.

One of the great dangers of the Quantified Self movement is that, in their belief in the natural origins of data, adherents will not question—or even reflect upon—the appropriateness of the measurement schemes that underwrite their data-gathering efforts. For Wolf, the world is black and white: there are the good guys who measure things, the heirs of Condorcet and Kelvin, and the bad, backward guys who don't. Which camp do you want to be in? In its simplicity, such rhetoric is similar to Kevin Kelly's musings on technology: you can either be a technophile like him or you can be the Unabomber (Kelly dedicates a chapter of his book to an imaginary dialogue with him). No other way of thinking about technology is possible.

So, just as Kelly defends technology, Wolf also passionately defends quantification. Both do it at such a level of generality that they lose sight of the sheer diversity of practices and approaches within each of these categories. Instead we need to draw out cases in which we must make highly consequential, painful choices over multiple ways to measure and quantify a certain phenomenon—including possibly refusing to quantify it altogether. In other words, we need a rich account of the very ethics of quantification. As sociologists Wendy Nelson Espeland and Mitchell L. Stevens observe, "An ethics of quantification should investigate how the world is made by measures but should strongly reject any conceit, scientific or otherwise, that measurement provides privileged or exclusive access to the real." Attempts at quantification are quite often attempts at simplification—and simplification is anything but apolitical, especially when competing interpretations of a problem are discarded in favor of something measurable and manageable.

Compare this concern with ethics of quantification to the highly unreflective approach that Wolf pursues in his manifesto. He writes, "It is normal to seek data. A fetish for numbers is the defining trait of the modern manager. Corporate executives facing down hostile shareholders load their pockets full of numbers. So do politicians on the hustings, doctors counseling patients and fans abusing their local sports franchise on talk radio." Well, yes, all these entities seek data, but then, there are different ways to go about seeking data, some of them better than others—and, in a few cases, it may be better not to surround oneself with numbers at all. After all, Enron, Arthur Andersen, and Lehman Brothers all had managers and shareholders; the much-hated Bush-era No Child Left Behind Act—which tied school funding to students' performance on tests—is suffused with a fetish for numbers; and doctors counseling patients regularly have different opinions even when they look at the same data.

From Nutritionism to Educationism

Celebrating quantification in the abstract, away from the context of its use, is a pointless exercise. Do we really want people to self-track just because "quantification" is cool or because a handful of Enlightenment thinkers said we should? It is like asking people—following Kevin Kelly's lead—to always celebrate technology in the abstract, regardless of how destructive its individual applications, if only to defy the Unabomber. Instead, we need to establish when quantification schemes are inappropriate. When do they suppress conflicting interpretations of reality? What do they conceal and make invisible, and is this something we can afford to lose sight of? How might they be invoked in the name of seemingly unrelated political projects? This exercise will be hard to complete without posing the thorny questions of meaning—which the Quantified Self movement has mostly avoided so far.

Robert Crease, author of *World in the Balance: The Historic Quest for an Absolute System of Measurement*, laments that "we tend to look away too much from what we are measuring, and why we are measuring, to the measuring itself." To make up for this deficiency, Crease urges us to focus on dissatisfactions, on what measuring does not deliver. "And we have to address these dissatisfactions," he notes, "not by discarding the measures we have and seeking to find newer and better ones, for these, too, will also eventually turn out not to do what we want and eventually need to be renounced, nor by assuming that what we are after lies 'beyond' measuring." Instead, argues Crease, "we . . . need to keep reminding ourselves of the human purposes that led us to create [the measurement] in the first place—and where, if at all, it interferes with any of these purposes." How can we acknowledge that the No Child Left Behind Act, while technically inspired by the same quantification measures that would have excited Condorcet, might actually be bad for education, even if it's marginally good—a big if, it seems—for test scores? We must first ask what we value about education—and this is primarily a question about the appropriateness of its ends, not the efficiency of its means.

Alas, education is one domain where it's easy to fall for the shallow, celebratory accounts of the benefits offered by quantification. Take a site like Rate My Professors, where students can opine about their classes and the instructors teaching them and rank them on a number of criteria. Even if we leave aside the obvious concern about introducing the consumerist mentality into education, it's worth asking just how the very process of ranking according to a number of set categories might convince students that those are the right criteria for assessing their learning experience. These are not just neutral, objective ways to measure teaching; they also shape and create norms according to which all future teaching will be assessed.

Rate My Professors offers four criteria: helpfulness, clarity, easiness, and hotness. The last is there mostly for humorous reasons, but what about others? Why should "easiness" be of concern in evaluating how we learn? The world out there is a complex place, and those who want "easiness" can always gorge themselves on TED talks. But even "clarity" has attracted the ire of many critics, primarily for creating the wrong impression that all complex ideas can and should be crammed into PowerPoint presentations. As writer Matthew Crawford points out, "Certainly clarity is desirable in a lecture, and the absence of it is often nothing but the professor's own confusion or his failure to extricate himself from the tertiary quarrels and jargon of his discipline. Yet the demand for clarity is often the demand for getting to the point, and this presumes that there is a bottom line. Busy executives demand clarity from those who submit reports. Undergraduates are busy too." Any learning enterprise that begins with the assumption that ideas have a bottom line will succeed in churning out the next generation of Bain consultants, but will it produce any talented essayists?

Or consider the kinds of quantification enabled by academic sites like Google Scholar and Mendeley. The latter draws on a global community of 1.8 million academics to keep track of 250 million research documents and has recently moved to provide additional information about who quotes whom, with what frequency, on what subjects, and so forth. On the whole, this looks like a good thing: Why not learn more about how ideas circulate, especially when universities already use other metrics, like the impact factor? Better data, the hope is, will ultimately improve efficiency. Cue Mendeley's cofounder and CEO, who believes that his company's "data is now helping some of the world's best universities work more efficiently and get to life-changing discoveries faster."

Viewed in the abstract, there is much to admire about this new layer of knowledge. But viewed in the context of other trends in today's academia, its effects no longer look unambiguously positive. First, such data feeds the ongoing efforts (e.g., by the British government) to tie funding for academic work to specific, easily measurable outputs—making it quite hard to receive funding if you teach and research classics. Second, whether one climbs up the academic ladder is already heavily determined by the ability to get published and quoted by others (and thus boost one's "impact-factor ranking"); this too has had rather mixed effects on the quality of scholarship produced. A recent *Wall Street Journal* investigation of how obsession with the impact factor has transformed scholarship reveals that some editors of academic journals might even be rejecting solid articles only because they do not quote enough papers already published in the editors' own journals. Or consider an even more outrageous episode. In an April 2012 post—provocatively titled "The Emergence of a Citation Cartel"—The Scholarly Kitchen blog called attention to a 2010 review article that recently appeared in a journal called *Medical Science Monitor*. The article cited 490 articles; 445 of those appeared in another journal, *Cell Transportation*. Partly as a result of this article, *Cell Transportation*'s impact factor rose by 21 percent between 2009 and 2010. This wouldn't look very suspicious if the two journals didn't have so much in common: of the four editors who worked on the *Medical Science Monitor* article, three also served on the editorial board of *Cell Transportation*. It's a win-win for everyone but scholarship.

Once we start factoring in such considerations—working in the technostructuralist mode, keenly aware of the trends and practices transforming our chosen field—we are likely to think twice about the virtues of "efficiency" that would accompany Mendeley's new tracking system. It's quite possible that it seeks to offer a great solution to a minor problem while exacerbating many grander problems along the way.

Quantification schemes get even trickier once they are based on seemingly universal and timeless scientific findings. Systems of knowledge guiding public policy tend to be unstable or incomplete; their conclusions—especially when expressed in the quantified form—usually imply hundreds of footnotes and qualifications, which can be studied in order to restore the kinds of complexity lost in the process of producing formulas and numbers. In our daily lives, we somehow get by, even if we disregard many of these footnotes. Simply knowing the temperature outside is often enough to decide what to wear, even if we know nothing about how the system of measuring temperature came about and what simplifications it rests on. Such a heuristic is possible only because the input-output relationship in this particular case is so straightforward: if the temperature is too low, we get cold; if it's too high, we get hot. Rocket science it isn't.

But the new frontiers of solutionism inspired by self-tracking are anything but straightforward. Dieting, for example, might seem relatively simple. Eat foods rich in calories and get fat; eat low-calorie foods and get slim. The simplicity of this theory explains the popularity of various sites and apps that measure the calorie count of the foods we eat. A smartphone app called Meal Snap allows you to take a photo of the food on your plate and see an estimate of its calorie count. FoodScanner, another smartphone app, allows you snap a photo of the barcode on the food's package, recognize the food, and see its calorie count along with some other nutritional information. Restaurant Calorie Counter contains information about more than 15,000 food items from over one hundred top restaurant chains, allowing us to easily generate a calorie count when eating out.

All of these sound like great apps—in the right hands. Focusing on calories—just because they are the easiest to count—is a somewhat defective way to think about nutrition and might even lead to dieting disorders. There is little agreement in the dieting community as to what exactly causes obesity. If it's the quantity of the food we eat, then calorie count might be a good approximation. However, if it's the quality, then we also need to look at the composition of the food we eat and perhaps police our consumption of foods that contain carbohydrates and sugar. For example, the *New York Times* recently reported on a high-profile study in the *Journal of the American Medical Association* that found that "the nutrient composition of the diet can trigger the predisposition to get fat, independent of the calories consumed." Now carbohydrates can be measured as well—through something called the glycemic index—but this shouldn't much bother us here.

Whether they track calories or carbohydrates, the apps of the Quantified Self do not, strictly speaking, measure nutrition; they measure, well, calories and carbohydrates. How each of those indicators translates into weight gain and weight loss—not to mention the enjoyment one derives from eating—is a far more circuitous process than deciding whether to wear a sweater based on what the thermometer tells us about the weather outside. Of course, it's possible that obsession with self-tracking and dieting might nudge some enthusiasts to read up on nutrition and develop better insights into how nutrition relates to health. But it's unrealistic to expect that of all self-trackers. In fact, the majority might feel too comfortable with their tools and stop investigating altogether.

In other words, when people start with confused ideas about nutrients, minerals, and vitamins, the ability to count within these seemingly unproblematic categories is not an unmitigated blessing. Some critics even proclaim that the world of dietary education suffers from its own ideology of information reductionism. Sociologist of science Gyorgy Scrinis calls such a tendency to think of food primarily in terms of the nutrients it contains "nutritionism"; anyone obsessed with eating foods that are only "low fat" or "reduced fat" is very likely under the sway of this ideology.

For Scrinis, there's nothing wrong with generating extensive knowledge about individual nutrients and using that knowledge in conjunction with other modes of encountering food, whereby we simply add what we know about individual nutrients to what we know about the quality of the food in question, how it was produced, how many additives it contains, how individual nutrients tie together in producing the overall nutrient profile of the food, and so on. But such complementarity is only rarely achieved; in most cases, the ease of measuring, say, fat tends to establish it as the indicator to watch for. The food industry, not surprisingly, is all too happy to oblige: it's not uncommon to see companies peddling nonfat milk that supplements what the product lacks in fat with an extra dose of corn syrup. But, of course, "no fat, high sugar" doesn't make for a very sexy food label.

There is no reason why the food industry would feel threatened by self-trackers: as long as such schemes are tied to just one popular indicator, both the manufacturing and the marketing processes can be reconfigured accordingly. Scrinis even suggests that the "shift to nutrient-level language and dietary advice arguably favored the interests of the food industry over the dietary advice of nutrition experts." Thus the industry easily exploited the reductive focus on fat, as it started substituting fat with highly processed and reconstituted ingredients of rather dubious nutritional value. Scrinis further notes that this "enabled the lay public to interpret their consumption patterns in these nutricentric terms and to seek out nutritionally engineered versions of what they were already eating. Rather than consuming less meat or dairy products, individuals could select 'lean' meats and low-fat milk or switch from red meat to white meat." Likewise, it allowed the public to continue consuming processed and fast foods—albeit now in a somewhat modified, fat-unfriendly form—rather than consuming less of these products.

In his critique of nutritionism, Scrinis too links its rise to the ease and appeal of quantification. Thus, he notes, one can discern a trend arising in the late nineteenth century whereby "nutrients, food components, or biomarkers—such as saturated fats, kilojoules, the glycemic index, and the body mass index—are abstracted out of the context of foods, diets, and bodily processes. Removed from their broader cultural and ecological ambits, they come to represent the definitive truth about the relationship between food and bodily health." Scrinis's critique of nutritionism is not unlike Nietzsche's critique of scientists who naïvely believed they could rank music via mathematics. Nutrition literacy cannot be reduced to a simple formula; it requires exercising critical thinking—and various self-tracking schemes, in a very perverse way, seek to free us from thinking about food altogether. This flight from thinking and the urge to replace human judgments with timeless truths produced by algorithms is the underlying driving force of solutionism. Bruno Latour distinguishes between "matters of facts," the old unrealistic way of presenting all knowledge claims as stable, natural, and apolitical, and "matters of concern," a more realistic mode that recognizes that knowledge claims are usually partial and reflect a particular set of problems, interests, and agendas. For Latour, one way to reform our political system is to acknowledge that knowledge is made of matters of concern and to identify all those affected by such matters; the proliferation of self-tracking—and the displacement of thinking by numbers—risks forever grounding us in the matters-of-fact paradigm.

Once we abandon thinking for optimizing, it becomes much more difficult not only to enact but to actually imagine possible reforms of the system being "measured" and "tracked." One potential problem with quantification is that it encourages the government not to bother with painful structural changes and simply to delegate all problem solving to citizens. Why bother with regulating highly processed foods or improving access to farmers markets and prohibiting fast-food chains from advertising to youngsters? After all, we can simply empower individual citizens to monitor how many calories they consume and not bother with any of these initiatives, pretending that obesity is just the result of weak-willed individuals ignorant of what they are eating. Once it becomes complicit in lending support to simplistic political ideologies of individual responsibility, self-tracking blocks the kind of ongoing self-reflective inquiry that John Dewey held as central to democratic life.

It's this imperialistic streak of quantification—its propensity to displace other meaningful and possibly intangible ways of talking about a phenomenon—that is so troubling. In the hands of enthusiastic and possibly well-meaning self-trackers, food becomes just another way of minimizing the risks of getting sick rather than a way of enjoying our limited time on this planet. Will the excessive emphasis on information that nutritionism traffics in eventually displace other criteria by which we might want to judge food? Of course, self-trackers would assure us that this new information will only complement what we already know; in reality, however, it will most likely displace—rather than complement—other criteria.

Why this would be the case is not so hard to grasp. One of the advantages gained through quantification is to make the problem at hand easier to handle; once it's expressed in numbers, we can discuss how it changes over time, measure how other factors might be influencing it, and so forth. Solutionism and quantification are thus inherently linked. In his great work *Seeking like a State*, political scientist James Scott writes that "certain forms of knowledge and control require a narrowing of vision . . . [which] brings into sharp focus certain limited aspects of an otherwise far more complex and unwieldy reality. This very simplification, in turn, makes the phenomenon at the center of the field of vision more legible and hence more susceptible to careful measurement and calculation." To limit the damage that solutionism can cause, then, one must find ways to restore some of the alternative perspectives effaced by this "narrowing of vision."

The Imperialism of Numbers

Ivan Illich, writing before the advent of smartphones but after the ideas from cybernetics and systems theory had already penetrated the public debate, noticed a fundamental shift in how his contemporaries thought about needs, desires, and necessities. For Illich, necessities and desires are fixed: we have to make tough moral decisions to abstain. Needs, however, are an entirely modern creation; we treat them as flexible—perhaps the influence of Madison Avenue?—and believe that they can be identified (either through quantification or greater self-introspection). Thus, the very project of "meeting our needs" doesn't strike us as moral in the least. This is how Illich put it in a 1987 interview with the Canadian broadcaster CBC, foreshadowing some of the pathologies of self-tracking:

A student was here last week. I wanted to offer her a second glass of the cider that you buy from the Amish around here, and I said, "This is good cider, have some." "Oh, no," she said, "my sugar requirements are met for today. I don't want to get into a sugar high." The idea that all people have specifiable needs which can be identified and classified and then ought to be satisfied represents a break with a very different perception of the human condition, a traditional perception of the human condition which took for granted that some things are necessary and can't be changed but must be accepted. In this traditional view the cultivation of desire and the regulation of desire in the context of necessity was the principal personal ethical and moral task for everyone, and for the community. Needs, therefore, are neither necessities that cannot be changed, nor desires that can't ever be satisfied. . . . Needs . . . result when technique is accepted as a means to change, to abolish, the necessities which the human condition imposes.

That last line—about abolishing the necessities imposed by the human condition—might sound gloomy and pessimistic, but it fits quite nicely with the broader critique of solutionism offered in this book: limits—and what are "necessities" if not limits?—can be productive and even conducive to human flourishing. Obstacles and barriers create the conditions in which our very humanity can come into existence. As literary critic Terry Eagleton once put it, "Being human . . . is something you have to get good at, like playing the tuba or tolerating bores at sherry parties." Remove the bores and replace the tuba with a self-tracking app, and you shrink the space in which our humanity can emerge. But, more broadly, the problem with the needs discourse is that the young lady who refuses the cider seems to believe that her moral compass is exhausted by her easily measurable and quantifiable needs—that is, how much sugar she consumes on a daily basis. That she might have a moral obligation— for example, to be polite to her professor and simply accept the drink—or that she might actually derive great sensual pleasure from drinking the cider doesn't naturally occur to her.

Illich probably wouldn't be surprised by the quantification predicaments we face today. Will we all end up eating liquid paste that meets all of the demands of nutritionism but lacks the texture, beauty, and aroma of a well-prepared meal? Technology journalist Greg Beato, writing in the libertarian magazine *Reason*, hints at what this heavily quantified future might entail—and not just in the context of nutrition but in other pursuits as well. He writes, "Soon, we'll know if the sea urchin panna cotta at the French Laundry inspires a greater leap in heart rate than the quail egg with caviar and cedar smoke at The Ritz-Carlton. We'll know which yoga teacher's students sleep most soundly at night. We'll know which activity is most likely to lead to sex on a first date—an art gallery opening or a night at the bowling alley. Suddenly, all the old measures that have been used to determine value and satisfaction will no longer be quite as relevant."

Perhaps this is how aesthetics was meant to end, with a bunch of enthusiastic devotees of the Quantified Self movement comparing notes on whether the nudes of Picasso or Degas generate longer erections. Human experience, run through the quantification mill, is reduced to little more than a stream of silent and mind-numbing bytes, a running digital commentary on our never-ending quest for a perfect genetic makeup, a perfect credit score, a perfect mating partner. Just as some clever investment bankers succumb to the functionalist temptation and buy thousands of never-to-be-read books to make their homes look "literary"—but what exactly is "literary" about homes where nothing is ever read?—we'll be making our selves look healthy or even artistically inclined through some rough combination of quick technological fixes that pay little heed to the ideals of health or art that we purportedly aspire to cultivate.

Steven Talbott, a technology critic in the deeply spiritual tradition of Jacques Ellul, correctly observes that "we have invested only certain automatic, mechanical, and computational aspects of our intelligence in the equipment of the digital age, and it is these aspects of ourselves that are in turn reinforced by the external apparatus. In other words, you see here what engineers will insist on calling a 'positive feedback loop,' a loop almost guaranteeing one-sidedness in our intelligent functioning." We ought not to be as pessimistic—the last chapter of this book will show that digital technologies can help awaken us from the ethical and aesthetic slumber we've been enjoying for far too long—but the gist of Talbott's assertion is right: we have to watch out for positive feedback loops.

Why do so many people find the vision of a fully quantified world so appealing, even liberating? To *Reason*'s Greg Beato, all the terrifying trends he identifies still point to some kind of happy end: once we know everything there is to know about the quail egg on offer at the Ritz-Carlton, marketing will be dead and objectivity will triumph. "Branding, marketing, and even qualitative customer reviews will give way to reports based on blood pressure rates, galvanic skin response, and quantified self-esteem. Instead of thinking with our flighty, emotional, easy-to-manipulate brains, we'll be feeling with our rational, measurable, hard-to-manipulate guts, crowning victors and condemning also-rans to failure based on what truly satisfies us most." This seems like geek think at its worst, blind to how power operates. Even if this utopia happens, all the marketing budgets will simply be spent on arguing which way of measuring things is more objective or natural or true. Instead of brands telling us that they all foster creativity, companies will compete to prove that their own brand of creativity—the one on which they get top marks—matters the most. This will only fuel the already pervasive feelings of anxiety and distrust that animate modern society.

Suppose for a minute that quantification won't destroy marketing but will instead allow corporations to push their products even more aggressively while also enjoying the anonymity defense that self-tracking gives them. Marissa Mayer, Yahoo!'s CEO and a former Google executive, talks of "contextual discovery," where search engines can, by studying what kind of information users seek online, supply this information proactively, before users even ask. Likewise, Mayer's former boss, Eric Schmidt, likes to talk about the idea of autonomous search—where our smartphones, by closely monitoring what we do, can also quietly perform related searches in the background. Schmidt gives an interesting example: "When I walk down the streets of Berlin . . . I want . . . my smartphone to be doing searches constantly. 'Did you know? Did you know? Did you know? Did you know? This occurred here. This occurred there.' Because it knows who I am. It knows what I care about. It knows roughly where I am. So this notion of autonomous search—this ability to tell me things I didn't know but am probably very interested in is the next great stage . . . of search."

Well, this sounds great for tourism, even though it would probably destroy the tourism industry, as Google would become the ultimate tour guide for everything. But consider other applications of autonomous search. Suppose Google—say, through its magic glasses—knows that you are feeling down and that, in order to keep your mood intact (perhaps to compensate for the sad phone call you've just had from your ex), you need to see a painting by Renoir. Well, Google doesn't exactly "know" it; it knows only that you are currently missing 124 units of "art" and that, according to Google's own measurement system, Renoir's paintings happen to average in the 120s. You see the picture and—boom!—your mood stays intact. Does it turn you into an art lover? Does it expand your horizons? Or would such utilitarian attempts to feed art, as if it were self-help literature, demean art as such?

Such deference to autonomous systems—and make no mistake, where there is autonomous search, there will be autonomous advertising—can transform many other areas of life. Bianca Bosker, a technology journalist, hints at this digital and highly automated future when she complains that she no longer finds places to eat; rather, they find her. Or, in the parlance of Silicon Valley, "search" is displaced by "discovery." She writes,

> My web searches for new neighborhood joints—"best brunch Flatiron NYC," "cafe East Village"—have given way to Foursquare insta-alerts that pop up on my phone to tell me there's a nice place nearby. Thanks to the app's "List" feature, which allows me to subscribe to lists of must-try destinations compiled by friends and city guides, Foursquare lets me know whenever I'm close to a restaurant that has scored an endorsement. Hunting and gathering online for ideas about where to get my next meal—or outfit, or book, or playlist, for that matter—has given way to sitting back and being served up snack-sized morsels of information. I'm not seeking. I'm ab-

sorbing. Our process for finding new information looks a lot less like a home-cooked casserole we've whipped up from ingredients cobbled together from the deli, Farmer's Market and back of the fridge, and a whole lot more like a drive-through meal. Quick, easy and slick, with just a hint of industrial perfection.

As Bosker correctly points out, this shift from manual search to "autonomous search" or "contextual discovery" results in technological systems that now deliver "a personalized selection of anything from songs to soulmates without an explicit request by the seeker." And the technology gurus concur. As Stefan Weitz, director of Bing, Microsoft's search engine, told Bosker, "The implicit searching on your behalf—without you initiating it via a query—is absolutely where we're going. Today the trigger is 'keyword' plus 'enter.' But tomorrow the trigger event could be you woke up and it's 8 AM and the train [you were supposed to take] is not functioning." This may all be revolutionary innovation, but it also sounds like the ultimate triumph of consumerism. And yet, thanks to our pro-innovation bias, consumerism—even Bosker doesn't mention the word—is not usually mentioned in the context of debates on "autonomous search" (she does point out, though, that if the current trends continue, "we'll be told what we want before we know we need it"; Illich wouldn't approve). To evaluate the Quantified Self and its impact on public life, then, it's not enough to simply hope that the tracking devices will help us solve a carefully delineated social problem. Such problems rarely exist—and the schemes to fix them would do much more than their promoters expect, as they would overlap with other systems, technologies, and agendas.

When Facts Are Made of Water

But, some might counter, surely some activities that have little to do with aesthetics might be more amenable to quantification? Measuring how much water or electricity we consume seems relatively unproblematic; should we really be concerned, following James Scott, that some "narrowing of vision" is taking place? When it comes to metering, it seems, relating inputs and outputs resembles our reading the thermometer and deciding whether to wear a sweater: if we save water, it's good for nature; if we don't, then it isn't. What could be more straightforward?

One could probably make a good case that the Quantified Self movement began in earnest once it became common—perhaps even fashionable—to install meters in our homes to monitor household consumption of water and electricity. Now, some might argue, the same logic is spreading to our smartphones and our browsers, which just happen to be more powerful. And even meters are now being supplanted by devices like the Wattcher, popular in the Netherlands, which shows not only current or daily energy consumption but also how well it compares with daily targets. Yet, even here not everything is what it seems at first sight. In her discussion of capabilities important for human flourishing, philosopher Martha Nussbaum notes that "citizens cannot relate well to the complex world around them by factual knowledge." Thus, she points to the importance of what she calls "narrative imagination." Even though Nussbaum defines this as "the ability to think what it might be like to be in the shoes of a person different from oneself [and] to be an intelligent reader of that person's story," we don't need to limit narrative imagination to person-to-person interaction only. Narrative imagination, thus, might also involve one's interaction with complex sociotechnological and political systems and the ability to see one's own role in them.

We can further contrast "narrative imagination" with the somewhat oxymoronic "numeric imagination," which can be defined as the predisposition to seek out quantitative and linear casual explanations that have little respect for the complexity of the actual human world. Where narrative imagination is self-reflexive—it's painfully aware that in order to account for the world, it also needs to account for the observer—numeric imagination believes in objective, firm accounts of reality out there; these accounts are timeless and never expire. The world just reveals itself before the observer much like electricity use reveals itself on the observer's metering system: there's not much to debate.

The problem with numeric imagination is that it's very bad at describing complex systems, let alone imagining how those systems can be rearranged. Facts are seen as eternal, so numeric imagination, by and large, lives in the present and eschews any kind of contingency and historicism. Narrative imagination, by contrast, knows that most present practices, norms, and commitments are not timeless and that, by claiming to be the only way of doing things, they usually conceal many other alternatives. It acknowledges that even facts can be revised; one day we might think that being overweight is very bad for your health, and just a few years later we might discover that the extra weight could actually protect you from many serious diseases.

The Quantified Self movement, in its current form, is madly devoted to articulating facts—that's what numbers are good for—but it still has no way of generating narratives out of them. In fact, it might even block the formation of narratives, as self-trackers gain too much respect for the numbers and forget that other ways of telling the story—and generating action out of it—are possible.

So, to return to the practice of metering water and electricity, it's easy to mistake one's decision to monitor resources for a genuine reform of how water and electricity get into our homes. Ideally, the decision to monitor should be just a tiny complement to other practices and attempts to generate narratives about water and electricity use and convert those narratives into action. The problem is that it's impossible to generate those narratives without first getting a good picture of how water, gas, and electricity get into our homes—and the metering practice does not provide those narratives.

As anthropologist Maria Kaika writes in *The City of Flows*, "In the advanced capitalist world, the supply of water, electricity, gas, and information now appears to enter miraculously the domestic sphere, coming from nowhere in particular and from everywhere. Even garbage disposal has become a matter of throwing things in a hole in the wall, where both trash and smell miraculously disappear. For the urban dweller, the end of the process of garbage disposal is the moment when the bag is thrown into the hole." To know what's inside our smart trash bins—which is what projects like BinCam seek to tell us—is not the same as to know what happens to our garbage once it leaves them. The latter is much more important to environmental reform than the former.

We know as little about garbage disposal as we do about cloud computing; only rarely do we ask what exactly it entails, why we do it the way we do, and how we can do it differently. Monitoring how much garbage we throw away, how much water we consume, and how much information we upload and download from "the cloud" doesn't get us any closer to understanding how these complex systems function. "Numeric imagination" enables us to think in numbers—that is, to ponder how much we can consume and, in the best of all cases, what we can unplug—but it never challenges us to think of how a different set of numbers might be generated. It seems naïve to believe that the problem of climate change can be solved if each of us spends a minute less in the shower; the solution might require both more substantial sacrifices and perhaps even stepping out of the shower and fighting that fight somewhere else.

As Veronica Strang, another anthropologist, observes in *The Meaning of Water*, metering—at least when promoted by water companies—is also embedded in a complex economic system that itself is based on certain assumptions about resource ownership and what constitutes ideal means of resource management. According to Strang, "Meters concretise private ownership and empower managers, rather than the population as a whole, to decide what constitutes 'profligate' water use, or, as government agencies put it more diplomatically, 'discretionary' or 'non-essential' purposes." Thus, she writes, meters "also express perfectly the social individuation that has led people to feel that their resource use takes place within the fortress of the family home, detached from the wider social and physical environment." One might think that the Quantified Self movement, decentralized as it is, would not be subject to similar pressures, but this too seems unlikely, as corporations both manufacture the gadgets used for self-tracking and own the online platforms and message boards where data is shared.

Devices like the Wattcher, which can simply be plugged into a socket, are not yet pushed by the utility providers as aggressively as were meters. But this day will soon arrive, even if the task of agitating for such devices falls to Kevin Kelly and Gary Wolf. Based on the evidence we have so far, however, it's not clear if such feedback devices merely lock users into their existing patterns of consumption or challenge them to think about their water and energy use—and how to cut it—with a little bit more creativity and imagination.

Yolande Strengers, an Australian sociologist who has studied how various energy-use feedback systems inform consumption practices in Australian homes, notes that participants in her experiments "did not, for the most part, pause to reflect on or change those activities they considered normal and necessary."

At the same time, as Strengers argues, what counts as normal and nonnegotiable is itself always in flux and, moreover, informed by the consumption system and its infrastructure. Washing one's clothes after every use may seem normal today, but it certainly was not fifty years ago, as sociologist Elizabeth Shove notes in *Comfort, Cleanliness and Convenience*, her exposé on how norms and expectations about comfort and cleanliness have changed over time. Likewise, using a dryer or leaving the air-conditioning on in relatively mild weather is also a recent development, not a timeless norm. Self-tracking can tell us how much energy our air-conditioning system consumes and might even tell us how well its demands match our own goals, but it cannot comment on the desirability of leaving the air-conditioning on. Numeric imagination might tell us how to use the air conditioner more efficiently, but narrative imagination can tell us whether we should use it at all.

In fact, feedback systems trigger what psychologists call a licensing effect in that, seeing that our energy consumption is lower than we predicted, we might stop worrying about it altogether. Yolande Strengers reports on how some Australian households responded to a feedback system called EcoPioneer that uses a traffic-light system to indicate whether a household is consuming too much electricity. One participant, for example, noted of the yellow signal she kept getting, "I was always worried about using the dryer so much, but I figure it doesn't make it scream red so it's OK." But if one were to examine the EcoPioneer system more closely, it's not even obvious if the green light means what we think it does. As Strengers notes, the system is meant to measure energy consumption in real time, not cumulative consumption over, say, twenty-four hours. Thus, to maintain a green or orange light, households just have to distribute their energy consumption across the day. Although this is good for electricity distributors (as it creates load shifting and results in more efficient distribution), it does not necessarily reduce demand. But it does look good on paper: the households are doing their "citizenship" bit, and the distributors are getting more efficient distribution. Without some kind of narrative imagination, though, this system may actually only lock in current energy habits.

Hunches and Fractured Pelvises

So what do attempts at self-tracking tell us? Well, all too often it's hard to say. Kashmir Hill, a *Forbes* journalist who has written about the Quantified Self and its numerous applications, expresses a sense of befuddlement over what to do with the results of one such self-tracking experiment. Thanks to some clever software, she finds out, "I'm happiest when drinking at bars (duh); least happy on planes and at work (ahem); Sunday is my happiest day of the week followed by Wednesday; I'm just as happy alone as with other people, and I'm happier interacting with my ex than with my current boyfriend." What to do now, though, Hill doesn't know. "I'm at a slight loss for what to do with these results. Does this mean I should spend more time in bars and less time at work to optimize my happiness? And should I rethink my relationship?"

The problem is that, as firm, scientific data, these results have no standing. As moral prompts to action or conclusions drawn from months of self-reflection, they hold no standing either, for clearly Hill did not deliberate much about her drinking or working habits in the process of using the software. At best, these are correlations. But what use do such correlations have? For some members of the Quantified Self movement, correlation is all that matters. Meet Seth Roberts, who claims that eating butter makes him faster—well, this is what his data says anyway ("Two years ago I discovered that butter—more precisely, substitution of butter for pork fat—made me faster," begins his blog post)—or Sanjiv Shah, who thinks that wearing yellow glasses before going to bed improves his sleeping patterns (it's all in the data, stupid!). Of course, some self-trackers are aware that their conclusions may not be, well, scientifically valid; as one such enthusiast told the *Economist*, "With self-tracking you never really know whether it is your experiment that is affecting the outcome, or your expectations of the experiment." In science, this is widely known as the placebo effect, and in academic experiments every effort is made to minimize its influence. With the Quantified Self, however, what matters is not knowledge per se but, rather, the utility of various knowledge claims in helping improve one's health or sex life.

Most curiously, one doesn't need to know how such knowledge will be used; much of it is generated and stored preemptively. As Wolf points out about his fellow Quantified Self members, "Although they may take up tracking with a specific question in mind, they continue because they believe their numbers hold secrets that they can't afford to ignore, including answers to questions they have not yet thought to ask." So do self-trackers collect data, information, or knowledge—to invoke the famous pyramid that dominated much of information-management literature for decades? Information scholar Martin Frické, writing of data-mining initiatives, observes that they promote a tendency to confuse data with information and encourage "the mindless and meaningless collection of data in the hope that one day it will . . . ascend to information—pre-emptive acquisition."

To make fun of such preemptive attempts, Peter Austin data-mined the health records of 10 million Ontario patients to draw some fascinating conclusions about them. One heart-wrenching, revolutionary finding was that "Virgos vomit more, Libras fracture pelvises." Alas, the results didn't hold when Austin and his colleagues tried this hypothesis on a second population. Austin notes that you only need to "replace astrological signs with another characteristic such as gender or age, and immediately your mind starts to form explanations for the observed associations. Then we leap to conclusions, constructing reasons for why we saw the results we did." However, he argues, "the more we look for patterns, the more likely we are to find them, particularly when we don't begin with a particular question." In other words, what Austin takes to be the mark of bad research has somehow become a defining, beloved feature of the Quantified Self movement. To be fair, the aversion to theories and absolute belief in the superiority of big data also form one foundation of solutionism; it's not unique to self-trackers as such. Kevin Kelly, in his typical celebratory mode, tells us that "exhaustive data, the Google way of doing science, is better than having a hypothesis." Harvard's David Weinberger writes a multi-page love letter to Hunch.com—a site (now owned by eBay) that asks users hundreds of questions to predict what movies or books they will like—calling it "a serious shift in our image of what knowledge looks like."

As is common with revolutionary rhetoric, the claims of revolutionary activity are everywhere—but where's the revolution? Hunch.com simply uses the techniques of statistics, data mining, and machine learning—all well-established disciplines that predate "the Internet"—to turn correlations into recommendations. For Weinberger, the claim that "75 percent of people who liked *Mad Men* also liked *Breaking Bad*" is revolutionary because, unlike Darwin's theory of evolution, it is "theory-free." However, such "theory-free knowledge"—think of census reports, surveys, and marketing questionnaires—has a very long history. Yes, people fill in these forms online now, but is this revolutionary? Rupture talk rears its ugly head again.

Is this the kind of knowledge that will help us cure cancer? Weinberger might be right in that "it doesn't have a hypothesis and it doesn't have a guess. It just has statistical correlations," but we also know what such utilitarian consumption mapping is good for fueling endless shopping sprees on Amazon. In the future, it will also be great for fueling conspiracy theories, as Glenn Beck, the Tea Party, Alex Jones, and anyone else with a lot of free time and cheap computing power will be running correlations between, say, race and educational performance or levels of happiness and social welfare. There might even be lots of volunteers eager to supply the data by tracking themselves. As per Weinberger's advice, this crowd won't need a hypothesis or a guess; it will just be mapping statistical correlations.

Of course, if critics like Austin have their way, such correlations will be dismissed as puerile nonsense. If, however, the likes of Weinberger, with their perennial revolutionary claims, get the upper hand, our institutions will need to spend even more of their cognitive resources on fighting off the challenges brought by various conspiracy theorists. As the never-ending arguments over climate change show, we are already living through a period when trust in expertise is all but gone. Supplying those who want to challenge it further with odd theories of knowledge will only make things worse.

The fact that the Quantified Self movement or data miners like Hunch.com can churn out "insights" doesn't—and shouldn't—elevate those insights to the status of knowledge, not if the word "knowledge" is to retain any meaning at all. Google's way of doing science is actually no way of doing science at all—it's something else entirely, and we shouldn't be treating it as on a par with authoritative, expertise-driven research. Sometimes perhaps a marketplace of ideas needs tighter regulation. As philosopher Philip Kitcher points out, "We lack institutions on which people can rely for facts that matter to their decisions." Kitcher is skeptical that "trust can be restored by untrammeled public discussion, for . . . once trust in expertise has broken down, 'free expression of ideas' often erodes further the credibility of those who know." Likewise, legal scholar Robert Post argues, "If a marketplace of ideas model were to be imposed upon *Nature* or the *American Economic Review* or *The Lancet*, we would very rapidly lose track of whatever expertise we possess about the nature of the world."

The problem, of course, is that the idea of "the Internet" that our pundits operate with, combined with the tremendous success of Wikipedia and Google, has all but prevented them from standing up to defend expertise and the practices that create and sustain it. Rather, in their populist mode, they prefer to celebrate movements like the Quantified Self and start-ups like Hunch.com as revolutionary and suitable, even if completely different, ways of replicating previous knowledge structures. They are not—and the sooner we acknowledge this, the healthier our public debate will be.

CHAPTER EIGHT

The Superhuman Condition

"From the microscopic to the heavens, all will be sensed, networked, and stored. This is not a forty-year-out wild guess. This is a decade-out sure bet. And I don't lose many bets."
—GORDON BELL

"The mistake is to think that communications will solve the problems of communication, that better wiring will eliminate the ghosts."
—JOHN DURHAM PETERS

Long before the Quantified Self movement, Gordon Bell, a high-level Microsoft engineer, was already recording every single detail of his time on Earth. He started doing it in the late 1990s and has been at it ever since. Bell achieved some considerable notoriety for eagerly wearing a device called a SenseCam around his neck; it's a small black camera, the size of a cigarette packet, that snaps a picture every twenty seconds, which, assuming he spends at least sixteen hours awake, adds up to almost 3,000 photos a day. But Bell's collection consists of more than just pictures. All of his handwritten notes—quite an archive given he was born in 1934—have been scanned, all his e-mails sorted, and all his GPS coordinates duly reported. His Microsoft Web page boasts of his having recorded "a lifetime's worth of articles, books, CDs, letters, memos, papers, photos, presentations, music, home movies, videotaped lectures . . . recordings of phone calls, IM transcripts, years of email, web browsing, and daily activities."

Is there a project more emblematic of solutionism than Bell's quest to transcend the limitations of human memory? To the solutionist, forgetting cannot be allowed to serve any productive purpose; it's a bug—never a feature—and the sooner it's fixed, the better. For Bell, forgetting is painful, perhaps even dirty and sinful, whereas wearing a SenseCam is extremely liberating and empowering. "It gives you kind of a feeling of cleanliness. . . . I feel much freer about remembering something now. I've got this machine, this slave, that does it," Bell told an interviewer in 2006. He doesn't take hourly snapshots of his brain, but this seems like a mere matter of time; Google's smart glasses might allow him to peer inside as well.

Gordon Bell has become a human-powered museum of all the bits, memes, and pixels that have ever entered the life of a single individual. Touting the benefits of a Gordon Bell existence, the real Gordon Bell enthuses, "You become the librarian, archivist, cartographer, and curator of your life." A tad narcissistic? Perhaps. But when storage is cheap and the fear of human frailty is as great as ever, distinguishing narcissism from pragmatism is no easy feat.

Some might object that calling Gordon Bell's digital archives "a museum" is a bit of a stretch. Museums, after all, operate on the premise that some things are more important than others; those things tend to be curated, promoted, and exhibited, while the less important things are set aside or discarded. Presumably, even if they had infinite shelf space, museums would not abandon the idea of curation. The latter is a deliberate commitment, not a technological constraint stemming from a lack of resources.

But Gordon Bell's one-man museum, while nominally promising to turn its heroes into curators, rejects the very selectionist spirit of curatorial work; like the self-trackers and data miners we met in the previous chapter, Gordon Bell opts for preemptive data acquisition, hoping that one day it will provide him not just with the right answers but also with the right questions. Or perhaps it will just tell him where his car keys are—and who among us relishes the time spent crawling under the table searching for them? But wearing a gadget like a SenseCam around your neck may also help you find the greatest keys of all: those to your inner self. Thus, in *Your Life, Uploaded*, his book-length manifesto on the benefits of lifelogging, Bell assures us that it will yield "enhanced self-insight, the ability to relive one's own life story in Proustian detail, the freedom to memorize less and think creatively more, and even a measure of earthly immortality by being cyberized." Armed with a SenseCam, Proust would be a sure viral hit on Instagram.

Bell has little use for terms like "self-tracking" and "quantified self"; instead, he describes his hobby as "lifelogging." Numbers play a minor role in his quest; it's not so much about generating statistics as about taming the inefficiency and unfaithfulness of human memory. Still, Bell wouldn't miss a chance to draw an inference or two from all the data he's accumulated. His rhetoric repeatedly emphasizes various lifesaving opportunities offered by lifelogging— even if they come at the cost of turning us into perpetually anxious individuals with little choice but to track the previously invisible and inconsequential aspects of our existence.

Suddenly, lifelogging turns from a quirky geek pursuit into a moral obligation that we have toward ourselves and, perhaps, even others; if you do not lifelog, you are harming humanity. Just pay close attention to a passage that Bell, along with a Microsoft co-author, penned for *Scientific American* in February 2007: "Portable sensors can take readings of things that are not even perceived by humans, such as oxygen levels in the blood or the amount of carbon dioxide in the air. Computers can then scan these data to identify patterns: for instance, they might determine which environmental conditions worsen a child's asthma. Sensors can also log the three billion or so heartbeats in a person's lifetime, along with other physiological indicators, and warn of a possible heart attack."

Even though Bell doesn't quite put it this way, he is essentially saying that what can be logged must be logged. And if it can't be logged, then it must be ethically and aesthetically deficient. Thus, the Fast Company profile of Bell notes that he is "annoyed by experiences that [can't] be stuffed into a hard drive," which already makes him unhappy with physical books. "I virtually refuse to own any books at this point. . . . I mean, I get them, I look at them, I occasionally read them. But then I give them away, because they're not in my memory. To me they're almost gone," laments Bell, without even noticing that his appreciation of literature has suddenly become hostage to his totalizing fetish for documenting that appreciation.

It's tempting to dismiss Bell's project as exotic and lump it with other contemporary forms of weird data-hoarding practices. He does seem like an odd duck in many other respects. A 2007 profile of him in the *New Yorker* noted, for example, that Bell "believes that one day houses will have no windows, so it won't matter where they are—screens on the walls will display whatever we want to look at." This man can make the horrors of *The Matrix* sound like a spring break in Cancun.

But if Bell is indeed a crank, he is a crank with influence. Widely known as "the Frank Lloyd Wright of computers," he's a distinguished and well-respected engineer and manager—in the 1970s he was one of the top executives at the then high-flying Digital Equipment Corporation, and in the 1980s he helped oversee the National Science Foundation's forays into "the Internet." And he clearly knows his way around Microsoft (Bill Gates wrote a gushing foreword to *Total Recall*; his own 1995 book, *The Road Ahead*, is peppered with Bell-like proclamations, such as "Someday we'll be able to record everything we see and hear"). The idea of lifelogging informs several of Microsoft's products—MyLifeBits is a software project that helps lifeloggers keep track of all the information they collect—and traces of this idea can be seen in some seemingly unrelated online innovations (Facebook's idea of frictionless sharing, whereby the site tracks and automatically publishes our online activity, is a case in point; it's lifelogging in public).

Bell's thought neatly encapsulates all the shortcomings and biases of the technological mentality. There is the pervasive talk of the autonomy of technology and the inevitability of its social effects—there is no point resisting the trends ("society at large is on an inexorable path toward Total Recall technology and it is going to transform the world around you"). Any political and social intervention in the trajectory of this technology is dismissed as simply part of—Bell's actual phrase—"catastrophic counterrevolution." Thus, writes Bell, "only a vast legal or political effort of social engineering can prevent [lifelogging] from effecting far-reaching changes in the way modern life is lived. That sort of catastrophic counterrevolution sounds far-fetched." Perhaps "vast legal and political effort"—the bedrock of democratic decision making—is simply not his thing. Predictably, Bell is also a big believer in the objectivity and neutrality of lifelogging technology; for him, "digital memory is objective, dispassionate, prosaic, and unforgivingly accurate."

Total Recall is also peppered with ubiquitous promises that everything will be okay as long as we wait long enough ("we'll invent social norms to navigate the times when lifelogging recording is appropriate or not") and assurances of empowerment and individual control over this technology ("you will be in total control, able to retrieve as much or as little as you want at any given time"). Bell's individuals enjoy perfect autonomy and independence from their fellow citizens and the technological mediators that enable them to lifelog everything. He poses not a single question about the political economy of information. No wonder, then, that Bell sees everything in a rosy light; his thinking is not attuned to the trends driving our information-sharing habits.

Thus, with his usual unabashed enthusiasm, he writes, "If the world follows my lead, Total Recall will be a very private matter. Encryption will be universal, e-memories will reside in Swiss data banks, and sharing will be careful and limited."

What are the odds, however, that the world will follow his lead? Perhaps Bell hasn't yet skimmed through Davos's "privacy as an asset class" paper (and those Davos people, I hear, know a thing or two about Swiss banks). Who, one might ask, will be building these data banks he is so enthusiastic about? So far, it seems that they will be built by the likes of Personal.com and Singly, which have structural incentives to get people to share all their data, even if the process of sharing is secure. If Bell thinks that Swiss banks just take their clients' money and generate outstanding returns by keeping it behind tight locks, he's badly mistaken about the banking enterprise.

Yet, Bell is most confused about the human condition. For someone in his seventies, he writes like an inexperienced teenager who's not had his fair share of diverse social interactions, with all the obligatory dissembling, innuendo, and pretending that they entail. What Michael Oakeshott wrote of the rationalist—"like a man whose only language is Esperanto, he has no means of knowing that the world did not begin in the twentieth century"—applies to solutionists like Bell as well, although their only language is C++. For Bell, all these deceptive practices are evils to be extirpated from social life in an effort to subject us to total transparency and honesty.

Retelling how his digital archives now enable him to compose better toasts for his friends' birthday celebrations, Bell enthuses, "My biological memory had reduced my relationship with Ivan down to the humdrum, but my e-memory stepped in to restore the significance of our history, making it possible for me to compose a fitting toast for his birthday." This sounds great—until one realizes that, once universalized, lifelogging will also rob us of any excuses that our frail and imperfect human memories now provide. In Bell's future, if you don't compose an elaborate, ten-page toast to your friend—peppered with obscure anecdotes and jokes that both of you have long forgotten—you are simply not working hard enough. Average time saved by finding your car keys through lifelogging: five minutes. Average time lost to the tyranny of unnecessary niceties entailed by lifelogging: a lifetime.

At times, Bell's preoccupation with the truth seems pathological. He wants to remember everything and forget nothing, no matter how dark, violent, and destructive. "It's up to you: You can tackle as much or as little truth about yourself as you have the stomach for. In court, we ask for the truth, the whole truth, and nothing but the truth. It might be painful, but I believe better memory really is better," notes Bell. We might very well ask for the truth in court—but why assume that the entire field of social interactions is like our legal system? Is there really no space for deception in our dealings with others or ourselves? Could deception, like forgetting, be productive in sustaining—perhaps even enabling—a more moral life? As philosopher David Nyberg points out, "Deception is not merely to be tolerated as an occasionally prudent aberration in a world of truth telling; it is rather an essential component of our ability to organize and shape the world, to resolve problems of coordination among individuals who differ, to cope with uncertainty and pain, to be civil and to achieve privacy as needed, to survive as a species and to flourish as persons." The striving for perfection, so typical of grandiose solutionist schemes, has no way to account for such tricky subtleties of the human condition.

And does our legal system function the way Bell describes? As information scholar Jean-François Blanchette points out in an incisive review of *Total Recall*, Bell seems to get that wrong too. "Court proceedings are ruled by elaborate rules governing the admissibility and evaluation of evidence, and the most cursory examination of these rules cannot fail to point to the fact that courts have, thanks to the adversarial process, a sophisticated understanding of the technological mediation of evidence," writes Blanchette. Evidence might be "true"—whatever that means—but it may still be disregarded.

"The question may well be: How much truth can you take?" asks Bell in a rare philosophical moment. To which, he provides a typically glib answer: "Successful people don't shy away from the honest record." Elsewhere, he complains that "some people have shared with me a worry that they may learn things about themselves that they don't really want to know—the depressing truth may get out." How does Bell the shrink console those poor saps? "They go further than the Soviets, who erased what they didn't like from their history; these folks would erase everything just in case there might be something they don't like."

It goes on like this *ad infinitum*. This, for example, is how lifelogging is supposed to turn us into better people: "Imagine being confronted with the actual amount of time you spend with your daughter rather than your rosy account of it. Or having your eyes opened to how truly abrasive you were in a conversation." Bell's is a world where no one needs to make trade-offs and compromises and do something ugly to avoid an even uglier outcome; the tyranny of self-introspection that he advocates all but strips human existence of its complexity and occasional irrationality, reducing it to a set of algorithms that can be derived from just a handful of moral rules.

That we may inhabit several moral and ethical worlds simultaneously, that those worlds might be governed by different commitments and principles, that it would be naïve to expect us to be high achievers in all those worlds—none of this occurs to Bell, who thinks that there can be some universal standard, a common benchmark of sorts, to measure and compare your behavior as a parent with your behavior as a friend or a colleague. As philosopher Michael Walzer notes in his much celebrated account of what he calls "complex equality,"

> Unjust societies make for simplified projects, since they hold forth the promise that success in winning one social good can be converted into general success. . . . A just society, by contrast, makes for complicated life plans, [where one figures] simultaneously as a loving parent, a qualified worker, a committed citizen, an apt student, a discerning critic, a faithful member of the church, a helpful neighbor. No doubt, it is easy to imagine people distributing themselves in this way and earning, as it were, less complementary adjectives. . . . We are more likely to aim at these different qualities if we are sure that intrinsic or at least different rewards are available for each of them—and no single convertible reward available for any one of them.

Bell's is a good example of a simplified project that prizes only one social good—Truth—above everything else. His preferred solution—perfect and comprehensive digital memory—would help promote that good and usher in a better society in the process. Walzer's admonition—that "a just society . . . makes for complicated life plans"—reveals one of the key problems with Bell's solutionism: if we imagine the self as inhabiting many different spheres and milieus—and always being in the process of pursuing multiple, irreconcilable, and perhaps even contradictory objectives, then a technology of "perfect truth" is of limited help, for we can't help but settle on a suboptimal outcome, and deluding ourselves may not be a bad coping strategy.

The goals of being a loving parent, a qualified worker, and a committed citizen are often at odds with each other—children of famous people do not end up in therapy for nothing—so to suggest that we can reconcile them simply by counting how much time we spend with kids versus how much time we spend working on that groundbreaking history of ancient Greece or volunteering to save the whales is rather naïve. Of course, in Silicon Valley—where the competing life projects often consist of finding the perfect yoghurt, surviving an exhausting yoga course, and founding yet another start-up—this might be less of a problem in that synergy is everywhere, and friction is nonexistent. This, alas, is not how the rest of the world lives—and Gordon Bell would be well advised to take note of such differences.

Madeleine: There's an App for That!

Bell's lack of appreciation for the complexity of the human condition is only part of the problem. He is equally confused over the roles—and even over the very definitions—of human memory and forgetting. Only by drawing nearly perfect equivalence between computer and human memory can he make a powerful solutionist argument in favor of lifelogging. But let's be honest: computers don't, strictly speaking, "remember" information; rather, they "store" it. Bell is hardly alone in his confused beliefs about memory—Kevin Kelly, in a similar vein, argues that "when the camera is fully ubiquitous, everything is recorded for all time. We have a communal awareness and memory"—which is one more reason to get to the heart of why this misunderstanding persists.

First of all, Bell's claim to a Proustian heritage is laughable. "Relieving one's own life story in Proustian detail," as Bell puts it, is not the same as knowing what the exact temperature was on a given day or being able to replay all the sounds—perhaps even reproduce all the smells—related to the events in question. Proust wrote (rather disparagingly) of a "simple cinematical vision" that by "professing to confine itself to truth in fact departs widely from it." The data fetish propelling lifelogging would horrify Proust. Here is how he put it in *In Search of Lost Time*:

> If reality were indeed a sort of waste product of experience, more or less identical for each one of us, since when we speak of bad weather, a war, a taxi rank, a brightly lit restaurant, a garden full of flowers, everybody knows what we mean, if reality were no more than this, no doubt a sort of cinematograph film of these things would be sufficient and the "style," the "literature" that departed from the simple data that they

provide would be superfluous and artificial. But was it true that reality was no more than this?

For Proust, the key to describing reality, both past and present, was not seeking more data but putting our imaginations to good use by connecting our senses with our memories (this, in part, explains why Proust thought that the novel was much better positioned to do this job than cinema or photography). Proust was not preoccupied with the proverbial madeleine because he needed a cooking recipe and "the Internet" was down at the time. Closer to nostalgia, his longing was much more about the inability to return to a mythical past than about remembering the factual detail; in fact, one can argue that only by filling in the gaps in the narrative—and doing it anew every time—can Proust's narrator make sense of the madeleine. Proust was a champion of the narrative (not numerical!) imagination, and for that imagination to flourish, gaps and inconsistencies are essential.

Svetlana Boym, a Russian American scholar who's written on the future of nostalgia, gets it right when she writes that "nostalgia tantalizes us with its fundamental ambivalence; it is about the repetition of the unrepeatable, materialization of the immaterial." Remove that ambivalence, make the unrepeatable repeatable—through lifelogging, self-tracking, or some other modern technology—and the whole nostalgia-making enterprise will crumble. Boym sees fundamental tension between the save-everything mentality of digital technologies and the state of mind predisposed to nostalgia. Gordon Bell perhaps knows this too—hence he posits that lifelogging "will surely make the truth of what we did and what happened around us more available, clearer, and less obscured by nostalgic make-believe." That the Proustian detail he celebrates is impossible without "nostalgic make-believe" does not occur to him; the detail will surely remain, but it's anti-Proustian in spirit.

The writings of French-Bulgarian philosopher Tzvetan Todorov can shed some more light on what geeks like Bell and Kelly don't get about memory. As Todorov notes, memory is not the opposite of oblivion. Rather, it is the result of a complex interaction between effacement (or forgetfulness) and conservation—two forces that constantly pull our minds in different directions. Thus, memory is unthinkable without selection; when we "remember" an event, it means that we conserve only some of its traits, while setting aside many others. Some of this we do immediately, some of it, over time and not very consciously. Thus, notes Todorov, "it is baffling that the ability computers have to save information is termed memory, since they lack a basic feature of memory, the ability to select." In other words, retention or storage of information without selection is not memory—at least not as we use the term when we speak of the human condition. Or, in the memorable phrase of French anthropologist Marc Augé, "Memories are crafted by oblivion as the outlines of the shore are created by the sea."

Once the difference between preserving and remembering has been established, one can trace how the former could undermine the latter. It might be that as more is preserved, less is remembered. This probably won't come as a surprise to anyone who has ever videotaped every single minute of a summer holiday in Spain; sometimes three photos can evoke stronger memories than two hundred hours of footage. As philosopher Björn Krondorfer points out, "In an age of memory inflation, the archiving and memorializing itself can be seen as permission to forget." Falling storage costs and the ability to snap photos and shoot videos with one's phone only contribute to that inflation.

Where there is no reflection about what ought to be preserved, the records—no matter how comprehensive—might trigger fewer challenging questions about the relative significance of recorded events; the enormity of the archive might actually conceal that significance. To some extent, organizations in the Holocaust remembrance community are already confronting this issue as they begin to deal with vast archives of survivor testimonies. Krondorfer estimates that the six main institutions dedicated to collecting such testimonies have accumulated around 177,500 hours of them. This is roughly twenty years of continuous watching—eight years longer than the duration of Hitler's rule. This might be a treasure trove for researchers, but turning it into an effective way to remember the Holocaust remains a great challenge.

Just as retention does not mean remembering, so deleting does not mean forgetting. It's easy to make computers erase things: just hit the delete button and be done with it. But there is no such thing as willful forgetting when it comes to human minds; you cannot forget something just by telling yourself not to think about it. You might delete the file from your hard drive, but the memory of it—and of the fact that you've deleted the file—might stay with you forever. When Bell complains of individuals who tell him they'd rather not live with "the truth" of certain events, they are not asking him for a lobotomy or mechanically induced amnesia. They have just reached a conscious decision that they'd rather not think about certain events in their pasts. Can they be confident that their mission will succeed? Of course not. But what exactly is wrong with people choosing to limit their exposure to facts and events that will bring up horrible memories of, say, child abuse or rape or some dreadful breakup with their significant other?

The idea that we somehow have a duty to always remember the wrongdoing and the suffering we have endured rests on dubious moral foundations. Theologian Miroslav Volf attacks it head-on in *The End of Memory*. Volf argues that we need not presume that remembering will always yield morally superior results than forgetting. He writes, "Instead of simply protecting a person, memory may wound another. Instead of generating solidarity with victims, it may breed indifference and reinforce cycles of violence. Instead of truthfully acknowledging wrongdoing, it may bolster a victim's false self-perceptions and unjust demands. Instead of healing wounds, it may simply reinjure." Or it may do none of those things—a possibility of which Volf is acutely aware. The point is that, *pace* Bell, we should not presume that remembering is the right thing to do in each and every case. Solutionism cannot replace moral reasoning; we should not let it dictate solutions presumed to be right only by virtue of being easy.

But neither should we fall for easy fixes and solutions when it comes to forgetting. If geeks like Bell and Kelly celebrate technological fixes that might rid us of the option to forget, some geeks want quick technological fixes to enable forgetting. Cyberlaw professor Viktor Mayer-Schoenberger, for example, argues that we need to build technologies that will allow us to attach expiration dates to private and public files, ensuring that embarrassing pictures or any other documents that might make us feel uncomfortable or lead to social conflict will self-destroy.

This might be an elegant solution, but here too there is little awareness of when forgetting is appropriate and when it isn't. Leaving aside the already mentioned concern that deleting files does not equal forgetting, it's important to remember that perhaps in some circumstances, forgiveness is morally preferable to forgetting. Once expressed in technological form, solutionism robs us of important conversations and deliberations about what is appropriate in each and every case; it imposes morality from above without giving us an outlet to question and, if necessary, revise the simplistic moral truths built into its accompanying technologies.

Philosopher Avishai Margalit draws a useful distinction between forgiveness as the process of deleting, which he calls "blotting out," and forgiveness as the process of covering up, which he calls "crossing-out." If you want to erase something you've written, there are two ways to go about it. You can delete it completely and make it invisible—blot it out, in Margalit's parlance—or you can cross it out, leaving traces of the original scribbles—that is, you can cover it up. For Margalit, the image of covering up is "conceptually, psychologically, and morally preferable to the picture of blotting out, [for] it is better to cross out than to delete the memories of an offense." Margalit's is a complex argument that builds on political philosophy and history to show that true forgiveness is based on disregarding a sin, not forgetting it.

While technology can—if only marginally, by tampering with factual evidence—help us with forgetting, it is not much help when it comes to forgiving. But even forgiving may not be desirable in each and every case; this too needs to be investigated, not assumed. Solutionism will not relieve us of the messiness of decision making for one simple reason: technology cannot provide an easy answer to morally intractable dilemmas about what we ought to remember and what we ought to forget, for there are no such easy answers—not when questions are posed in the abstract. We shouldn't mistake the easy availability of quick technological fixes for their moral desirability; the latter is anything but assured, and the seemingly uncontroversial moral truths that underpin both lifelogging and file-expiration technologies cannot be taken for granted. The cheap and artificial models of human memory peddled by technologists like Bell ought to be recognized for what they are: cheaper and faster ways of storing data.

The Nutritional Aspects of Jerry Springer

Where lifeloggers like Gordon Bell try to recruit new converts by invoking our civic duty to remember, another nascent geek movement reminds us that we have a responsibility to consume information conscientiously and think about its nutritional value. This is an outgrowth of the Quantified Self movement, but with an unusual civic streak. The hope here is that self-tracking and lifelogging will make us more aware of what we read on a daily basis and that we will readjust our consumption habits accordingly, with or without active participation from the technology companies that increasingly stand between us and published materials.

At first, the idea seems quite appealing and noncontroversial. If you spend too much time browsing FoxNews.com, why not check the website of the *New York Times*? If you only read about Justin Bieber, why not get the latest update about opera singer Anna Netrebko? If you are obsessed with the latest iPhone, why not explore the latest case argued in front of the Supreme Court? In the past, when we all used paper, it was hard to measure what each of us was reading; sure, there were some marketing surveys, and some of us had library cards, but by and large, the only way to monitor our reading habits was to note each item read in a diary.

The lack of reading statistics is no longer a problem, thanks to the proliferation of digital intermediaries. Our iPhones, iPads, Kindles, and soon Google's Project Glass: all of these can track what we read and even how much attention we give each article. In the near future, as our screens incorporate front-facing cameras, it will be easy to study our eye movements and perhaps even adjust content accordingly. Apple has already filed a patent application for a three-dimensional, eye-tracking user interface. Eye-tracking software from The Eye Tribe, a Danish company, is also about to hit tablets and smartphones, allowing us to manage them by eyesight alone;

a prototype video on the company's website showcases just how easy it will be to play popular games like Fruit Ninja in hands-free mode.

But the more interesting application lies not in better management of a gadget but, rather, in the collection of new information about the user. According to John Villasenor, a professor of engineering at the University of California, Los Angeles, eye tracking will allow marketing and publishing companies to ask a whole slew of interesting questions: "Did our eyes linger for a few seconds on an advertisement that, in the end, we decided not to click on? How do our eyes move as they take in the contents of a page? Are there certain words, phrases, or topics that we appear to prefer or avoid?"

In this context, the solutionist urge seems quiet natural: now that technology allows us to monitor both what we read it and how we read it, it's very tempting to come up with a metric that can quantify whether the information we consume is nutritious or not and reengineer our information habits accordingly. Clay Johnson, formerly of the Sunlight Foundation, makes the most forceful case for such an approach in *The Information Diet*, establishing a direct connection between the world of dieting and the world of information consumption. Johnson's thesis, thus, is relatively straightforward: "Much as a poor diet gives us a variety of diseases, poor information diets give us new forms of ignorance—ignorance that comes not from a lack of information, but from overconsumption of it, and sicknesses and delusions that don't affect the under-informed but the hyperinformed and the well-educated."

Once we have ascertained that we are indeed suffering from information obesity, Johnson wants us to take the situation into our own hands and start monitoring our daily information habits. As with food, we need to start by paying closer attention to what we consume. "The first step is realizing that there is a choice involved," writes Johnson. "In order for us to live healthy lives, we must move our information consumption habits from the passive background of channel surfing into the foreground of conscious selection." Monitoring and self-tracking thus become useful tools in this endeavor.

As previously observed, our diseases usually stem from a combination of factors, of which nutrition is just one. Many studies have documented that being physically active and overweight reduces the risk of disease far more than being thin and physically passive. But even if one were to focus on nutrition alone, it's hard to miss the fact that if traveling to the nearest farmers market requires a car and a lot of petrol, not everyone will be able to afford it—despite a desire to be healthy.

As writer Greg Critser shows in *Fat Land: How Americans Became the Fattest People in the World*, class and income often define just how easy it is to eat healthy food. He notes, "The poor . . . lead lives that are more episodic than those of the more affluent. They are more likely to experience disruptions in health care, interruptions in income. Food, and the ability to buy it, comes in similar episodes—periods of feeling flush, periods of being on the brink of an empty pantry. The impulse is to eat for today, tomorrow being a tentative proposition at best." Once we start factoring in structural factors like poverty and income inequality, then obesity lends itself to a very different set of solutions than when it's defined simply as a lack of individual responsibility or lack of knowledge about nutrition.

Likewise, adopting a light but nutritious information diet might seem easy, but it's not an option available to everyone. What would such a diet entail? Perhaps you'll need to spend a few weeks tracking the most interesting people on Twitter and subscribing to their feeds on your tablet using a panoply of clever apps like Flipboard or Zite. Perhaps you'll need to purchase subscriptions to the Kindle editions of the *New York Times*, the *Wall Street Journal*, the *Financial Times*, the *Economist*, and a dozen other publications. It may also help to invest in proprietary software that will show you links you may not have discovered, while removing links to stories you have already seen. Most of the measures on this hardly exhaustive list require one of two things: time or money. If you have neither, you are likely to end up on a high-fat information diet glued to aggregators like Gawker, TMZ, or The Huffington Post. Simply knowing that the *Wall Street Journal* is more nutritious than TMZ won't magically put $21.62 in your pocket to cover the cost of a monthly subscription via Kindle. If you can't afford an iPad, you won't start using Flipboard, useful as it is.

Just as with nutrition, recasting the problem of information obesity in richer, structural terms will probably make us prioritize a very different set of solutions. Perhaps we'd want to spend more resources on media reform and ensuring access to digital-only resources via public libraries rather than getting people to monitor what they read. In an ideal world, of course, we should do all of the above, but in the real world, our resources are constrained, and we need to make choices and trade-offs.

For Johnson, it seems that the project of pursuing media reform through collective action happily coexists with the project of seeking better understanding of our consumption practices via self-tracking; those two seem to run on two separate tracks without much overlap. "Should corporations building personalization algorithms include mutations to break a reader's filter bubble? . . . Absolutely. But readers should also accept responsibility for their actions and make efforts to consume a responsible, nonhomogenous [*sic*] diet, too," argues Johnson. Perhaps this pervasive emphasis on personal responsibility and individual salvation is the outcome of the Protestant streak in geek mentality documented by Chris Kelty.

The problem with "information diet" rhetoric is that it recasts the citizen as a passive consumer who cannot be expected to dabble in complex matters of media reform and government policy. Thus, instead of pushing for more robust public broadcasting or campaigning to ban negative ads, the consumer is asked to pursue the more logical option: if the current website is too low on nutrition, perhaps it's time to move on to a different one. If Clay Johnson were some right-wing automaton who hated big government, such sentiment could perhaps be understood, if not entirely forgiven. Johnson, though, has stellar left-wing credentials, being one of the founders of Blue State Digital, the new media-consulting juggernaut that helped elect Obama in 2008.

Of course, Johnson would counter that such diet monitoring would not be a replacement for policy and public engagement, just an add-on. Perhaps this would indeed be the case, but as is typical of geek theorists, Johnson makes no effort to situate us in the current media environment, among its existing power structures and political economy. What kinds of media and technology companies will embrace the idea of assessing the media environment from a dietary perspective? Which ones won't? Will Facebook and Google love this scheme because it will give them yet another argument to justify their already excessive monitoring of users? Or will they hate it because "social media" will earn fewer nutritional points than newspapers? Will the opinion page of the *Wall Street Journal* get the same "information calories" as its news pages? Will Glenn Beck's followers gain fewer information calories when they consume him on television rather than online?

Ideas are not like vegetables. Anyone who's ever eaten cucumbers can reasonably expect that eating another cucumber won't be a health menace; there's no need to taste a second cucumber to reach this conclusion. The fact that an idea is wrapped inside a TED talk—presumably, Johnson would put TED talks under nutritious, low-calorie sources—doesn't make it a good idea; one cannot assess its nutritional value before one has heard the talk (or read the transcript) and situated this idea in the broader intellectual context consisting of many other ideas. Approximating the calorie count of information based on where it comes from might preclude important, contrarian ideas—from small or fringe sources—from entering the public debate as forcefully as they deserve.

Ideas, unlike cucumbers, only have meaning in relation to other ideas, and that meaning itself is always in flux; one can't capture it—or even glimpse it—from afar. Presumably, if one views ideas as memes—as many geeks are wont to do—it might be possible to trace their genealogy and see who else has liked them before even knowing the content of the meme. But such endorsement hardly indicates anything: Martin Heidegger, arguably the greatest philosopher of the twentieth century, produced many brilliant ideas, but he was also a committed Nazi.

As already noted, introducing quantitative indicators like the calorie count or the glycemic index into dieting can easily lead to the ideology of nutritionism, especially if one loses sight of what makes the underlying food experience rich and tasty. But it's not at all certain that information consumption is amenable to any such indicators. People whom Johnson takes to be consuming the information equivalent of junk food probably believe the same thing about whatever it is that Johnson himself is consuming. *Jerry Springer* might be junk food; cat videos might be junk food; Alex Jones's conspiratorial radio broadcasts might be junk food—but their audiences rarely see them as such, and Johnson's camp cannot make easy rhetorical appeals to the authority of science and medicine. No science would show that *Jerry Springer* is somehow "intellectually less nutritional" than *60 Minutes*.

What makes *Jerry Springer* and Alex Jones junk food for the likes of Johnson is not the fact that they are being consumed at all but that their consumption crowds out the consumption of "things that truly matter," be it news about the Supreme Court or the warlord Joseph Kony. For all its presumed radicalism, this is a fairly traditional critique of how the public allocates attention to news. In its simplest form, this critique posits that citizens ought to aspire to omniscience and try to stay informed about everything under the sun. Alas, the criteria by which citizens ought to prioritize what really matters to them are never specified; the expectation is that they will somehow stay vigilant and keep an eye on everything.

This, of course, is not the only possible model of citizen engagement—there are other ways to think about responsible citizenship without assuming omniscience—but wrapped in the language of quantification, self-tracking, and individual responsibility, it's presented as the one and only objective, absolute truth. Once again, we run into one of the most serious civic dangers posed by solutionism: social engineers, enamored of the possibilities of "the Internet," no longer view their problems as amenable to a multiplicity of competing and controversial solutions and reforms. Blinded as they are by Internet-centrism, they just settle on whatever solution seems to correspond to the ill-defined spirit of "the Internet."

Phantoms and Backpacks

Walter Lippmann, in his landmark *The Phantom Public*, outlined a very different, more realistic model of public engagement—a model that, despite numerous subsequent efforts to discredit Lippmann as an authoritarian technocrat, still holds a lot of promise today. The premise of Lippmann's theory is simple: citizens cannot—and will not—be omniscient, let alone omnicompetent. No technology or government policy—not in a democracy anyway—could change that fact. "[The citizen] cannot know all about everything all the time, and while he is watching one thing a thousand others undergo great changes," argued Lippmann. "Unless he can discover some rational ground for fixing his attention where it will do the most good, and in a way that suits his inherently amateurish equipment, [the citizen] will be as bewildered as a puppy trying to lick three bones at once." In Lippmann's account, few theorists have offered good criteria for preferring one cause over another—and, in the absence of such criteria, it's not obvious why, for ordinary citizens, North Korea should matter more than Iran or deforestation should matter more than water depletion. Of course, there are issues on which citizens do raise their voices and come together; this is when a public is formed. Lippmann thought it futile to speak of "the public" as a monolithic, eternal entity with fixed and clearly demarcated interests. But when a controversy flares up and a group of citizens coalesce around a certain issue, this is the right time to think about the best ways to profit from citizen involvement—if only because the old, institutional ways of settling the problem no longer suffice (if they did, there would be no tension and no reason for the public to emerge in the first place).

One benefit of Lippmann's focus on publics in the making—as opposed to some fixed and given public that already exists—is that it allows us to attend to the material (and, today, also virtual) conditions in which they are formed. To use an example from an earlier chapter, Twitter can give rise to very different publics depending on how it goes about choosing which subjects make it to its "Trends" tab. That is, whether the company defines popularity through volume only, through the number of diverse clusters participating in the debate, or through the intensity of debate within each cluster will influence what kinds of publics emerge, how they sustain themselves, and what they have in common. In short, Lippmann's goal is to show that publics are fluid, dynamic, and potentially fragile entities that don't just discover issues of concern out "in nature" but negotiate how such issues are to be defined and articulated; issues create publics as much as publics create issues (which is only one more reason to pay closer attention to the communications infrastructure they use).

Most importantly, though, Lippmann believes that this way of thinking about publics will result in more effective action, as it "economizes the attention of men as members of the public, and asks them to do as little as possible in matters where they can do nothing very well. It confines the effort of men, when they are a public, to . . . a part which corresponds to their own greatest interest in any social disturbance; that is, to an intervention which may help to allay the disturbance, and thus allow them to return to their own affairs." In short, he'd rather have citizens do something well than do everything badly.

It's very easy—indeed, some have found it irresistible—to dismiss Lippmann as advocating some kind of parochial political defeatism; surely, even if few people care about climate change, there may be good reasons to cultivate their interest. But, on closer reading, such complaints are off target: the projects of public formation and citizen education can run in parallel. Thus, citizens can gradually come to appreciate the challenges posed by, say, climate change, while at the same time forming publics seeking to reform the current system of how education about climate change proceeds; other publics will form to argue that climate change is less important than the financial crisis, and so on. On this reading, Lippmann emerges as anything but a technocrat: yes, he does recognize the importance of delegating expertise, but he thinks that the exact terms on which such delegation happens could and should be up for constant reevaluation.

Media sociologist Michael Schudson, in reviving some of Lippmann's themes in the contemporary media context, has offered an interesting critique of what he calls "political backpacking." Many of us enjoy camping in the mountains and taking care of our own needs for a few days. But, once the holiday is over, we happily return home, turn on the stove, buy a packaged chicken, and drink pasteurized milk. We don't purify our own water but trust the metropolitan water supply system to do that for us. We delegate tasks to technologies. "Why, then, in public life, do we expect people to be political backpackers?" wonders Schudson. Why do we expect citizens to care about every single issue under the sun, as if the very idea of delegation would ruin our democracy?

For Schudson, these are unrealistic demands. "People may find pleasure in knowing the ropes of political information just as they may enjoy developing wilderness survival skills," writes Schudson. "There can be pleasure in this, there can be social advantage, one can gain in social esteem by knowing more than others in the same circles. . . . But most people will not be so inclined. . . . We cannot be and should not be political backpackers," he concludes and calls for "some distribution across people and across issues of the cognitive demands of self-government."

But Schudson's account does not do full justice to Lippmann and his old sparring partner John Dewey (who actually agreed with Lippmann on many issues). Both would pay far more attention to the constraints and opportunities of the material world—the stove, the chicken grill, the milk container—and argue that this material infrastructure of everyday living should be amenable to revision, deliberation, and what Dewey would call "inquiry." Climate change might be the cost we have to pay for taking the stove for granted for so long; backpacking is okay—as long as we still have options to reverse it. "No delegation without deliberation"—this would be the rallying cry of Dewey and Lippmann. In the political context, citizens should indeed delegate most issues to elected representatives and media gatekeepers, but the digital infrastructure that is so crucial to turning citizens into a public once a problem cannot be handled by existing institutions should never be taken for granted. As we have already seen, a set of design decisions might give us a very different Twitter—and a very different set of publics as a result.

This may seem like an arcane and highly theoretical debate that has little to do with today's digital culture. This is isn't so. Almost a century after Lippmann wrote *The Phantom Public*, his thought is still ignored by our technology gurus (not to mention democratic theorists), who imagine citizens to be omniscient and in need of learning about everything under the sun. This is an intellectual tragedy, of course, but there is another reason to worry, and it has to do with the resurgence of solutionism, which offers the tempting option to fix citizens once and forever. As already mentioned, a new set of digital intermediaries makes it possible to intervene in how we consume information in order to promote a better, healthier, more diverse information diet. Such tinkering was hard to pull off with newspapers and television, because they were targeting a mass audience; with Google's glasses and the latest e-readers, with their highly individualized approach, it finally becomes possible. By relying on nudges and other similar tricks, it might suddenly become possible to get people to pay attention to Africa or North Korea.

At first, such proposals flourished in the context of increasing "serendipity"—which is believed to be under perpetual assault by digital technologies. Thus, Eli Pariser in his *Filter Bubble* writes that "engineers . . . can solve for serendipity by designing filtering systems . . . to expose people to topics outside their normal experience." How exactly would it work? Pariser wants Internet companies to actively serve content that they know you haven't consumed—but think you should. "If Amazon harbors a hunch that you're a crime novel reader," he writes, "it could actively present you with choices from other genres."

Note what this technological fix actually implies. Doing this badly is easy—just pick random items and suggest them to customers. No one would do this though; it would likely be seen as yet another form of spam. Doing it well, however, would require companies to collect even more data about customers than they already do, so the quest for engineered serendipity can become just another excuse for Facebook and Amazon to collect more information and hone their algorithms. More disturbingly, it also means giving technology companies an even greater role in civic life at a time when they haven't shown any respect for the responsibilities they have already. To expect Silicon Valley to embrace such high levels of cultural paternalism in a responsible manner seems premature.

False and Imaginary Cosmopolitanisms

This solutionism-driven yearning for technological intervention is even more pronounced when it comes to international news, where the goal is not so much to promote serendipity as to turn every citizen into an exact copy of Nicholas Kristof, with his diverse wardrobe of global concerns. Ethan Zuckerman, founder of the blogging site Global Voices, argues that we are living in an age of "imaginary cosmopolitanism"—when "the Internet," despite popular belief, is not really bringing nations and peoples closer to each other—and that "the architects of Internet tools [ought to take] up the cause of helping to broaden worldviews."

How would this work? Zuckerman offers a few examples in a provocative essay that came out in the *Wilson Quarterly* in April 2012. "Facebook already notices that you've failed to 'friend' a high school classmate and tries to connect you. It could look for strangers in Africa or India who share your interests and broker an introduction." Search engines can play a role too. Zuckerman notes, "Google tracks every search you undertake so it can more effectively target ads to you. It could also use that information to help you discover compelling content about topics you've never explored, adding a serendipity engine to its formidable search function." Wondering why engineers are not building such tools, Zuckerman posits that "they may be waiting for indicators that we want them and are ready to use them." On this reading, Lippmann was wrong: we have always been budding omniscient cosmopolitans; we just never had the tools to fully develop those inclinations. Now that we have the tools, we can count on Silicon Valley to help us unleash our own inner Nicholas Kristof.

Zuckerman, alas, offers little evidence that we do indeed aspire to discuss shared interests with strangers in Africa or India. Now, enough claptrap has certainly been written about "the Internet" and its ability to build bridges and establish connections across nations. In that sense, Zuckerman is right: there is too much "imaginary cosmopolitanism" floating around. But Zuckerman himself is operating under a bunch of myths when he thinks that the reason people from Idaho have not yet talked to people from India—except when on hold with a call center in Bangalore—is that technology somehow has stood in the way. Whereas other technology pundits harbor illusions about the cosmopolitan nature of "the Internet," Zuckerman harbors illusions about the cosmopolitan nature—both its feasibility and desirability—of human beings as such. His is actually a more damaging kind of imaginary cosmopolitanism, for it assumes that "the Internet" is not turning all of us into xenophiles fast enough. Thus, only by tinkering with how "the Internet" works can this process of forced xenophilication be sped up.

Are Internet companies on board with such xenophilication? Google's Eric Schmidt believes that we already live in a post-cosmopolitan world. One key thing he learned at Google is that "people are the same everywhere." Thus, continues Schmidt, "it would be the simplest way to run the world, to recognize that the other people, other races, other cultures, people who don't speak the same language have roughly the same things that they care about as you do. We know this because we can prove it." And prove it they will, never bothering to ask if Google itself is responsible for much of the global homogenization that Schmidt attributes to natural causes or whether there may be other ways of expressing cultural diversity that are not easily captured via a Google search. Still, if we are all the same—and why wouldn't we be, when the world is flat?—perhaps there is no need for any cosmopolitan intervention at all. Eric Schmidt, it seems, would not be swayed by Zuckerman's arguments.

Facebook's Mark Zuckerberg, however, might be more open to such suggestions. In one of his most extraordinary public statements, Zuckerberg once proclaimed that the animosities in the Middle East do not "come from a deep hatred of anyone" but rather "from the lack of connectedness and lack of communication, lack of empathy and understanding." Zuckerberg believes that if only we were all connected, if only Facebook were available everywhere and everyone had an account, all misunderstanding would cease, and all wars would stop. Facebook's press releases are full of such pseudo-humanitarianism: "By enabling people from diverse backgrounds to easily connect and share their ideas, we can decrease world conflict in the short and long term." Israel and Palestine, according to this logic, will end up striking a peace agreement on Facebook—and the company is not averse to hosting "cyberpeace" initiatives between the two.

Zuckerman and Zuckerberg, despite their apparent differences over methods, both believe that better technology could—and should—root out human misunderstanding, removing costly imperfections from human communication. This view is not new and has an impressive pedigree. Media historian John Durham Peters has offered its most persuasive critique in his history of the very idea of communication, *Speaking into the Air*. As Peters and many other historians have pointed out, almost every new invention is met with great expectations that it will promote human understanding. Here are just a few: In 1852, essayist Michael Angelo Garvey predicted that, thanks to road transport, divisions across nations would disappear, and all peoples would soon speak one language. In 1889 Lord Salisbury argued that the telegraph had "combined together almost at one moment . . . the opinions of the whole intelligent world with respect to everything that is passing at that time upon the face of the globe." On founding the International Telegraph Union in 1865, the French foreign minister riffed on very Zuckerbergian themes: "If it is true that war . . . is born out of misunderstanding, are we not removing one of its causes by facilitating the exchange of ideas between people and by placing at their disposal this amazing transmission system . . . which permits swift and uninterrupted dialogue between the scattered members of the human family?"

The twentieth century produced even more such proclamations about the latest technologies. A 1913 letter to the editor of *Scientific American* proclaimed that Marconi's discoveries might allow "communication . . . at will, at any time, between human beings separated by great distances" without any technical apparatus. Less than a decade later, an article in *Collier's* hailed radio as a "tremendous civilizer" that would "spread culture everywhere," bringing "mutual understanding to all sections of the country, unifying our thoughts, ideals, and purposes, making us a strong and well-knit people." And if it could do all this within one country, imagine what it could have done for the world. Writing about the "era of images" in 1915, Jack London proclaimed that "time and distance have been annihilated by the magic film to bring together the peoples of the world."

The account goes on like this—with radical proclamations about the immense cosmopolitan potential of television, nuclear energy, the fax machine—all the way to today. So the excitement about the potential of "the Internet" to turn us all into cosmopolitans is easy to understand. But our debate here should not be exhausted by questions of feasibility; we should discuss desirability as well.

As Peters points out, it might be a mistake to think that better, faster, cheaper communications will solve the problem of communication, if only because misunderstanding might be a permanent feature of the human condition—and perhaps for good reasons.

"Sending clear messages," writes Peters, "might not make for better relations; we might like each other less the more we understood about one another. . . . 'Communication' presents itself as an easy solution to intractable human troubles: language, finitude, plurality." But these are false hopes; there are no quick fixes to such problems, for their roots lie not in a faulty transmission system but in diverging goals, values, and interests. Sometimes, those can't be bridged by dialogue alone; some political action is required. To return to the Peters epigram at the beginning of this chapter, a solutionist does think that better communications will solve the problem of communication; an antisolutionist, in contrast, recognizes that what we believe to be "the problem of communication" may not be a problem at all.

Modern technology can certainly facilitate intercontinental meetings of strangers. Self-tracking combined with subtle and not so subtle nudges built into search engines and social-networking sites would do the job—even assuming that popular sites were dumb enough to insert links to obscure articles on the AIDS situation in South Africa when traffic-boosting photos of Justin Bieber would bring in much more cash. But even if we set such monetary considerations aside, it's not obvious how sites like Google and Facebook should go about deciding on what issues they should expose users to. Why introduce you to strangers in Africa and India but not in Latin America or China? Why push you to learn more about South Sudan and not South Ossetia? Why send you to a site about Costa Rica and not Costa Brava? More broadly, why should the choice be about countries and geographies? Who said that the political situation in Madagascar is more important than the ethics of cloning or that the future of Hungary's government is more important than the growing use of steroids in sports?

Zuckerman believes that technology companies can, in the memorable phrase of Walter Lippmann, take citizens "on a sightseeing tour of the problems of the world," but he never spells out how the exact itinerary will be decided upon. But Lippmann is relevant here for yet another reason, for, in essence, Zuckerman wants digital platforms—previously relegated to the role of infrastructure—not just to shape, Twitter style, how publics are made but to actively create them by drawing attention to issues that those platforms believe to be important.

In a way, such attempts at nudging—and not just in the context of international news—represent the defeat of persuasion and deliberation as a way of inciting reform and activism. While one might follow Lippmann and argue that citizens ought to be left alone until they themselves identify an issue they care about, such an approach does not deny the important contributions that journalists, activists, and intellectuals can make on behalf of various causes. There is nothing wrong with a cohort of citizens spending thirty minutes a day following some remote crisis in Africa—only to read a *New York Times* editorial and suddenly switch their attention to Southeast Asia instead. We do want citizens who are aware of both their own limitations and of the power of collective action—and, more importantly, who think for themselves and allocate their attention judiciously, after some deliberation.

Issues that give rise to publics need to be backed by reason giving, not by some invisible ultimatum—eventually encoded in algorithms—from above. For all its other faults, the op-ed page of a major national newspaper does allow multiple stakeholders to articulate their reasons and try to enlist more supporters to their causes; the very infrastructure of our public sphere recognizes that a given issue might lend itself to different interpretations and have different publics behind it. Why would anyone want to scrap the system we have now, however imperfect, and replace it with Zuckerman's system, where Google and Facebook unilaterally decide what counts both as issues of importance and as the right ways to campaign on them? The only explanation I see has to do with Internet-centrism and solutionism: "the Internet" means we are living through unique times, we have the tools to do all of the above, and if a problem can be solved, then it must be solved.

Do we really want to move to a system that hijacks citizens' attention through nudges and other digital tricks that Google and Facebook might pull off without our even realizing it? Of course, some might argue that this is how Madison Avenue and much of corporate America operate anyway; to some observers, this is how the most visible and successful NGOs operate as well. Perhaps. But we don't have to pretend that this triumph of marketing and manipulation in the context of caring is a good thing. We want citizens who care about the war in Syria because they care about peace in the Middle East or the fate of humanity or some other such cause—not because Google and Facebook have manipulated them into embracing such causes.

Of course, if citizens willingly approach Internet companies, ask them to inject some serendipity and global caring into their algorithms, and then willingly use these services precisely because they want serendipity and caring, then it might be possible to think of ways to justify such interventions. In Lippmann's account, this is not likely to happen. But if citizens come to care about Bosnia or Rwanda or Syria not because they believe in the importance of humanitarian intervention or deliberately seek out news about those lands but because some combination of nudges and algorithms has made such caring all but inevitable, this seems like a tacit acknowledgment that deliberation and morality no longer command any respect in our political life and that now it all boils down to Skinnerian experimentation as to what combination of incentives—not arguments!—yields the desired action.

Gamify or Die

To see how the toolbox of nudges and incentives could be tapped in order to transform political participation, consider one of the features recently introduced by Google News, Google's flagship news aggregator. Beginning in mid-July 2011, Google News began rewarding its most dedicated users with badges based on how many stories they had read about a particular subject. Thus, if you care about basketball or Harry Potter, you can earn a badge for each—and there are multiple types of badges within each category. You can move from a bronze to a silver to a gold to a platinum and, finally, to an ultimate basketball badge, depending on how actively you follow basketball stories in the news.

The badges are private by default, but users can choose to make them public. As the company put it in a blog post accompanying the launch of this new system, you can tell your friends "about your news interests, display your expertise, start a conversation or just plain brag about how well-read you are." Google's logic, on introducing the feature, was that turning news reading into a game would make it more fun, perhaps even enticing people to read more news stories and, ultimately, to give the company more data about themselves.

As Google acknowledged, "This is just the first step—the bronze release, if you will—of Google News badges. Once we see how badges are used and shared, we look forward to taking this feature to the next level." What will that next level be? Well, one can imagine how the news badges system can be used to promote the kinds of goals favored by Zuckerman: if you read more stories about, say, Africa—an area traditionally overlooked by the mainstream media—you'll get more points than if you read about, say, Washington, DC. Once the virtual points and rewards are tied to tangible benefits—more free space on Google's servers, for example—they can be a powerful motivator.

Google's embrace of badges is not accidental but part of a broader trend. The proliferation of smartphones, with their ability to record one's GPS coordinates and easily share them with other people, combined with the popularity of social networks, which allow solutionists to build a social layer involving one's friends on top of almost any activity, has given social engineers the exciting option of solving important problems by turning them into games. Thanks to smartphones, games can be tied to the physical environment; thanks to social networks, they can be played with friends. This is not your average Tetris.

This trend toward introducing so-called game mechanics—the use of badges, points, levels, rewards, and virtual currencies—into diverse social practices is known as "gamification." A game like ChoreWars—where players, who could be flatmates or members of a family, do household tasks in the real world to accumulate points and discover treasures—is a good example of its logic in action. Recyclebank, a company that uses points and rewards to nudge consumers to perform eco-friendly activities, is another one. Once you accumulate enough points for your green behavior, Recyclebank allows you to convert them into discounts, free offers, and gift cards. Its very first offer? A discount on Hellmann's mayonnaise. Apparently, the company will use game incentives to make you greener and eat more mayonnaise. It makes perfect sense: someone else will then step in and gamify your eating experience by giving your points for not eating mayonnaise.

As ugly as it sounds, marketers have eagerly embraced the gamification trend—a recent survey shows that while two-thirds of them don't understand what "gamification" means, 78 percent believe customers are more likely to respond to game incentives. A survey by Gartner echoes these findings and predicts that by 2015, more than 50 percent of organizations that manage innovation processes will gamify them, rewarding customers and employees for suggestions. Some believers think that gamification can even solve problems like global warming, which is what Seth Priebatsch of the gamification startup SCVNG predicted at the South by Southwest Conference in 2011.

What is the connection between gamification and games? Some critics of gamification point out that the best video games are not exhausted by their reward systems. Virtual points do not produce experiences "of interest, enlightenment, terror, fascination, hope, or any number of other sensations," as game theorist Ian Bogost puts it; rather, those are produced by the content of the game and various narrative strategies adopted by game designers. In other words, one doesn't have to hate games to hate gamification; that process doesn't, strictly speaking, turn everything into a game—it turns everything into limited (and often completely unimportant) factors that we sometimes associate with games. Canadian media theorist Alan Chorney offers a very useful distinction between the two: "The use of game mechanics does not necessarily make the product a video game. To help make this distinction clear it may help to use the analogy of film. A director can use different shots, cuts, and special effects to affect the viewer, but the end result is not always a movie. It may, in fact, be an advertisement. The identity of the film is directly tied to the content of the film, not the mechanics of the film."

Not surprisingly, gamification has already become a favorite trick in the solutionist tool kit. That everything can be gamified does not mean that everything ought to be. *Wired* reports on how game theorist Jesse Schell, attempting to show that gamification has its limits, gave a conference talk describing "a world in which a person's every action—brushing their teeth, showing up to work on time, tattooing an advertisement for Pop-Tarts onto their forearm— earned points." Alas, Schell's attempt to encourage more critical thinking by gamification apologists backfired. As Schell told *Wired*, "I've had dozens of people come to me saying, 'Your talk was so in- fluential to me that I started a company. . . . All I can think is, oh God, don't blame me for that."

It all looks extremely appealing—especially to the bored and tired citizenry. To quote Mark Pincus, CEO of Zynga, the com- pany that has given us such world-saving Facebook hits as Far- mVille and Words with Friends, "Games should do good. We want to help the world while doing our day jobs." Gamification taps into the same do-gooder mentality that Slovenian philosopher- cum-entertainer Slavoj Žižek identifies in various charity programs that encourage citizens to support a fight against hunger in Africa by buying fancier coffee at Starbucks. If we can keep our day jobs and continue with our Frappuccino-powered soul-searching, why not help the world, after all? As for Zynga, its own forays into gam- ification seem rather ominous. For instance, it struck a deal with 7-Eleven by which, through some ingenious marketing, customers pay real money for FarmVille credits by buying a Slurpee. Don't miss the irony here: you buy a real sugary drink in order to win virtual points in a game where you play a farmer. As one gamifi- cation enthusiast explained the tie-up, "It's all money in and no money out!" Indeed. Helping the world by buying Slurpee—who'd have thought of that?

Of course, gamification enthusiasts would counter that games like Wii Sports allow us to exercise and hopefully lose weight by playing computer games; these are frequently mentioned in the context of gamification as well. These games are certainly fun— the only problem is that the expected weight loss is more myth than reality, as several recent studies suggest. One study published in *Pediatrics* has found that kids who play Wii Sports, convinced that they are losing weight, simply end up doing less physical ex- ercise, which all but restores any lost calories.

Occasionally, it's difficult to draw sharp distinctions between adherents of the Quantified Self and proponents of gamification. Both are funded by the same people, who serve as bridges between different communities, with self-trackers providing the quantitative cover without which gamification would be far less meaningful (after all, someone needs to count all those virtual points). For example, Tim Chang, managing director of Mayfield Fund, a respectable venture capital firm, has backed many of the early experiments in self-tracking and is now exploring gamification, with a particular focus on health care.

As Chang said in a recent interview, "The only way we'll fix our horribly broken healthcare system is by getting consumers to think about health and not healthcare. [Being healthy] could be made more engaging and actionable if it's gamified . . . [by] measuring daily actions and decisions, providing instant feedback and data back to users, and adding interactivity and game-like mechanics around this data to make health 'playable' by users." It's as if the twin problems of overdiagnosis and the continued invention and marketing of new diseases—rarely linked to actual symptoms—by the pharmaceutical industry never plagued the US healthcare system.

What can possibly go wrong with giving users virtual points for running even more checks on themselves and coming up with even more possible diagnoses? What's next, rewarding patients for trying out new drugs? No wonder venture capitalists love gamification: it's the kind of solution that aggravates some existing healthcare problems—but does so in an extremely profitable way. Well, at least Chang is not hiding the fact that gamification is something akin to hypnosis and allows us to get the "right" outcomes by circumventing the usual deliberative and policy channels. As he put it in the same interview, "You almost need to 'trick' the masses into being healthy, and gamification is a great way to do this."

It won't be surprising if politicians start jumping on the gamification bandwagon the way they jumped on the nudging bandwagon a few years ago: when all other instruments of policy have been tried, gamification, whatever its ethical problems, offers the prospect of easy—even pleasant—fixes. And, as the proponents of gamification argue, politicians may not even have a choice, as citizens are recast as consumers and players who expect everything to be fun and based on reward schemes. Note how Gabe Zichermann, a gamification entrepreneur, paints this future: "In a gamified future, I don't think many companies, including the government, will be able to avoid becoming part of this trend. . . . I think consumers will increasingly expect and demand that experiences become more fun and engaging. We can never ever go backward. People's expectations have been reset. This will be the new normal." The consideration that governments are not companies and citizens are not consumers doesn't figure prominently in the gamification agenda. People's expectations may well have been reset, but in politics people have more than expectations—they also have duties and obligations, which occasionally spoil all the fun.

B. F. Skinner Among the Unfinished Animals

Google's decision to introduce badges did attract a lot of criticism online, and in retrospect, it's not so hard to see why. A 2010 survey done by the Pew Research Center's Internet & American Life Project found that 69 percent of respondents followed news because they felt a "civic obligation to stay informed." Why reward people for reading news when they perceive it to be their civic obligation? Most of us would still balk at the idea of getting citizens to show up at the voting booth using an online game that required them to "check in" and collect points by casting a ballot. Can such schemes help boost turnout? Sure they do, but we do feel that, applied to civic duties, gaming incentives strip the idea of citizenship of much meaning. Such schemes send very misleading messages about politics and disappoint citizens whenever they are asked to do something that is not fun. As political scientists John Hibbing and Elizabeth Theiss-Morse argue, "The route to enhancing meaningful civic life is not badgering people to become engaged because politics is fun and easy; it is asking people to become engaged because politics is dreary and difficult."

Encouraging engaged citizenship is not just about getting people to do the right thing; it's also about having them do it for the right reasons. Well, not for Richard Thaler—he of the nudge thesis—who, in a February 2012 *New York Times* op-ed, argued that "if governments want to encourage good citizenship, they should try making the desired behavior more fun." (In this, the nudgers are very close to the gamifiers; the game entrepreneur

Gabe Zichermann is also on the record stating that "anything can be fun . . . we can make government fun.") Thaler, the doyen of solutionism, notes that "governments typically use two tools to encourage citizens to engage in civic behavior like paying their taxes, driving safely or recycling their garbage: exhortation and fines." Various fun-boosting tricks—like Google's news badges or the ability to earn frequenter flier miles for participating in recycling schemes—add a third incentive.

Thaler, however, does not spell out what exactly he means by "civic behavior." His use of that term in relation to exhortation— to various appeals to the common good—suggests that he uses the word "civic" in the conventional sense of "relating to the duties or activities of people in relation to their town, city, or local area." But if citizens engage in the "desired behavior" because it's more fun, then their actions have nothing to do with duty. Thus, "civic" here can only take on its other meaning: "pertaining to a city or town, especially its administration; municipal." To lump schemes that rely on exhortation with those that rely on various fun and game incentives is to overlook the fact that, because they are based on two different kinds of motivation, they might end up giving us two very different sets of citizens.

Psychologists and philosophers alike usually break down all human motivation into two categories: extrinsic (you do something because you are offered money, badges, or frequent flier miles) and intrinsic (you do something because you genuinely want to do it, perhaps because you think it's the right thing to do). The former rightly evoke images of B. F. Skinner or Frederic Taylor tinkering with rats and workers—showing them more food or promising a bonus—to elicit maximum performance on the treadmill or the factory floor. Do this, get that; input *a*, output *b*.

If you think that humans are like rats, or if you are a narrow-minded economist who believes that we are all utility-maximizing automatons, you might be tempted to employ extrinsic motivators everywhere. (If one believes in the laws of supply and demand, paying people—in cash or symbolic tokens—usually works.) Likewise, forcing people to pay for something—in the form of fines— provides strong extrinsic motivation as well. Hence, some recent social experiments: school children were paid for good grades, poor mothers were paid to send their kids to school or get them vaccinated, and San Francisco drivers who didn't violate traffic rules were entered in a draw to win prizes.

The problem is that the laws of economics are not always good at accounting for the complexities of human behavior. Thus, once intrinsic motivation is replaced by extrinsic incentives, humans respond in odd ways. Decades' worth of well-known research in social science attests to that. When citizens are offered cash for blood donations, fewer people donate blood. When citizens are offered cash to make up for the building of a nuclear waste storage facility next door, they tend to be much more disapproving of the project than if appeals are made to their sense of civic duty. When old people living in asylums are forced to subject their human relations to market relations—so that they can have someone else make their bed in exchange for vouchers—they soon become reluctant to do anything for their peers without first demanding compensation. When fines are imposed on parents who arrive late to pick up their children from the daycare center, it leads to more—not fewer—late pickups; apparently angry looks from center staff and the belief that they have an obligation not to be late work much better than fines.

Of course, one might counter that parents are late to pick up their kids because the fines are not high enough or that citizens who suddenly no longer want a waste dump nearby should be offered more money. Thus, the logic goes, the desired behavior can be ensured if only the right combination of incentives—of sticks and carrots, of tokens and badges—is found. But to start searching for the most effective set of incentives would be to miss the point that few of them were required previously.

There's an element of self-fulfilling prophecy at work here: if policymakers believe that self-interest is the only option available, they will shape social and legal institutions accordingly. Perhaps they might even solicit the desired behavior—thus getting the much-needed confirmation that the world does indeed work the way they think. As psychologist Barry Schwartz puts it, "Western society's enthusiastic embrace of the view that self-interest simply is what motivates human behavior has led us to create social structures that cater to self-interest." But it does not necessarily reflect any deep, timeless truth about human nature; it just reflects the popularity of utilitarian and Skinnerian thinking in the last hundred years or so. "Someone growing up in a post-Skinnerian world in which rewards were routinely manipulated by parents, teachers, clergy, physicians, and law-enforcement agents would surely believe that the control of human behavior by such rewards was universal and inevitable," notes Schwartz. "Such a person would be right about the universality but not about the inevitability."

Schwartz marshals a panoply of examples to show how the cult of self-interest results in what psychologists call the "overjustification effect," whereby the introduction of rewards for tasks normally undertaken without them changes how and why people pursue them. In one study cited by Schwartz, researchers prompted participants to think about money in unconventional ways; for example, they showed them a computer screen saver with various denominations of paper money floating underwater. This alone was enough to induce participants to be less helpful to others and to prefer working alone to working in groups.

A different study tested how participants would go about distributing compensation for work they'd done as a group. It turns out that when participants are paid with goods that have clear monetary value but are not mediums of exchange—like candy—they favor equal distribution, and everyone gets the same share. When participants are compensated with money, they favor a compensation scheme in which everyone gets a share proportional to the work he or she accomplished. As Schwartz notes, "Human beings are 'unfinished animals'; what we can reasonably expect of people depends on how our social institutions 'finish' them." If we opt for incentives, some such schemes might work—but their supposed effectiveness shouldn't blind us to their costs. Incentives are not the only way of getting people to do the right thing.

Political theorist Ruth Grant has offered perhaps the sharpest critique of the modern turn toward incentives in her recent book *Strings Attached*. Grant echoes some of Schwartz's conclusions in that incentives tend to lead people to construe their responsibilities too narrowly; in responding to various carrots and sticks, citizens lose sight of the lofty goals and values of their common enterprise. Grant's problems with incentives are threefold. First, seemingly clever incentive schemes often backfire and produce the opposite of the intended effects. Second, incentives—especially of the monetary kind—tend to crowd out motivations of the less mercenary kind, thus having a detrimental effect on character. Finally, incentive schemes like to perpetuate themselves, for as people get used to being paid for good driving or separating their trash, they may no longer do so once incentives are removed. Thus, writes Grant, "incentives are a tool with inherent limitations. . . . Once they are removed, their effectiveness ends. Incentives treat symptoms and not causes; they are a superficial fix. Since they do not address causes, they will be needed indefinitely if nothing else is done."

To understand the limits of incentives, we need to abandon the dry language of economics, with its simplistic assumptions about *homo economicus*, and develop a more complex view of human behavior. Only then, argues Grant, will we recognize "that incentives are not necessarily preferable to all forms of coercion; that incentives sometimes substitute for persuasive processes, which is a real cost in a democracy; and that the fact that incentives are voluntary transactions does not settle the ethical questions raised by their use." Incentive schemes are similar to technological systems in that once both become entrenched, it gets very hard to rethink and overthrow them; they do not easily lend themselves to the Deweyan process of inquiry, and efficient as they are, they easily survive even very devastating criticisms.

Monkeys, Sex, and Predictable Duress

Alas, our leading proponents of gamification operate solely in utilitarian territory, never raising any concerns about how building game incentives into social and political activities might affect citizens. Perhaps they just don't think that earning points and rewards in a game is the same as being offered a check to observe traffic rules or separate their garbage. But is there really much difference? Although it's true that no cash changes hands, it's quite clear that the motivation has changed: whereas before you tried to observe the rules because you cared about your own safety and that of other drivers, and you separated your garbage because you cared about the environment, now you do it because it's fun. Most of the critiques of incentive schemes hold: once the game incentives are removed, it's not obvious that you will go back to your old habits. Likewise, the point about the potentially corrosive impact such schemes have on character holds as well: sometimes we want citizens to do the right thing for the right reason, not just because it's more fun than playing Angry Birds.

Skimming through gamification literature can be both frustrating and instructive, for it shows the rhetorical tricks deployed by game enthusiasts to promote their schemes and the inherent limitations of their mind-set. Take *Gamification by Design* by game designers Gabe Zichermann and Christopher Cunningham. One has to praise the book—something of a primer on gamification—for being completely transparent about its Skinnerian philosophy: the cover features five playful monkeys, who presumably are on their way to being gamified.

Like most gamification literature, this book, from the very outset, blurs any distinction between games and play and posits that both are natural and inevitable. "Play and games are enshrined in our cultural record, emerging with civilizations, always intertwined. We are also now coming to understand that we are hardwired to play, with researchers increasingly discovering the complex relationships between our brains, neural systems, and game play," the authors proclaim. This may be true, but isn't there a great difference between games as play and games as incentives? Are we really expected to believe that accumulating frequent flier miles or even earning points for green behavior is the same as playing chess?

Besides, the fact that something is natural or advantageous doesn't automatically justify its use in every situation. Law too is ancient and enshrined in our cultural record, but there is a reason why no one is advocating sending people to jail for not calling their grandmothers on Sunday; to rely on law in this situation would be ridiculous. Although theorists of situational crime prevention might believe otherwise, technology too is ancient, and it surely affects our brain, but this is no reason to embed digital-preemption schemes into our everyday existence. The fact that many of us enjoy playing soccer, often forgetting ourselves in the game, does not automatically license social engineers to build game incentives into everything.

Gamification by Design suffers from all the common sins of geek think. Zichermann and Cunningham don't even try to hide the

Skinnerian underpinnings of their work. "Games," they write, "marry the desire-drive of sex with the predictability of duress—except without force and, when successful, driven entirely by enjoyment." Predictable duress that is as enjoyable as sex but involves no coercion: how can exhortation ever compete with this? B. F. Skinner, not Marshall McLuhan, is the real patron saint of "the Internet."

Zichermann and Cunningham are mostly interested in the business applications of gamification—getting people to click things—so they don't say much about its political and social implications (well, except for the curt remark that "fun is the new 'responsible'"; Richard Thaler would approve). For that, we need to turn to the true bible of the gamification movement, Jane McGonigal's *Reality Is Broken*. A Silicon Valley guru and popular game designer, McGonigal is also a fellow at the Institute for the Future—Palo Alto's premier facility for producing sound-bite-friendly futurism.

McGonigal has emerged as the leading cheerleader for applying the logic of gamification to solve the world's greatest problems; if solutionism has a goodwill ambassador, she's it. She argues that games can "help ordinary people achieve the world's most urgent goals: curing cancer, stopping climate change, spreading peace, ending poverty." Arm UN diplomats with Wii consoles, and all of the world's problems will go away. As writer and game aesthete Steven Poole argued in his review of *Reality Is Broken*, "You know that a new fad herbal supplement or therapy technique is bullshit when it promises to cure absolutely everything, from shyness to baldness to cancer."

McGonigal also has a personal story to tell: a few years ago she accidentally hit her head on a cabinet door and got a concussion, which grounded her for a long and very lonely month. But thanks to a clever game she designed, McGonigal managed to get her relatives to regularly call her and check on how she was doing. Progress has never smelled so sweet. Before the advent gamification, who would have ever thought to call to check up on a sick sister, child, or partner? How did we ever manage without badges and feedback loops? And what exactly did the badge say: "50 Points of Awesomeness: I called my sick child today"?

McGonigal's case for gamification rests on the assumption that the real world is inferior to the virtual one precisely because it lacks game mechanisms. Her laments about reality run over several hundred pages, but here are a few representative samples: "The real world just doesn't offer up as easily the carefully designed pleasures. . . . Reality doesn't motivate us as effectively. Reality isn't engineered to maximize our potential. Reality wasn't designed from the bottom up to make us happy." Games, in contrast, are everything that reality is not: "Computer and video games are fulfilling genuine human needs that the real world is currently unable to satisfy. Games are providing rewards that reality is not. They are teaching and inspiring and engaging us in ways that reality is not. They are bringing us together in ways that reality is not." Thus, the only possible conclusion that McGonigal can draw from all of this is that reality ought to be more like games: "What if we decided to use everything we know about game design to fix what's wrong with reality? What if we started to live our real lives like gamers, lead our real businesses and communities like game designers, and think about solving real-world problems like computer and video game theorists?" Well, replace "game designers and theorists" with "B. F. Skinner," and the answer to all these what-ifs might be very different.

What to make of McGonigal's project and her "personal mission to see a game developer win a Nobel Peace Prize in the next twenty-five years"? She seems so utterly confused about human experience—this probably comes with a Palo Alto zip code—that it's tempting to read the whole book as a cynical satire of the whole gamification enterprise, if not the complacency of Western consumerism as such. How exactly to react to proclamations like this one: "Compared with games, reality is too easy. Games challenge us with voluntary obstacles and help us put our personal strengths to better use"?

Reality might be too easy for a designated fellow of the Institute for the Future, but one just needs to leave University Avenue in Palo Alto and drive a few miles to East Palo Alto or Oakland, and a different picture of an all-too-easy reality will emerge. Tetris and golf do have built-in obstacles that make these games more fun, but to complain that reality is missing such challenges is ridiculous. From discriminatory laws to structural income inequality to deeply entrenched racist and sexist attitudes, our lives are full of obstacles, even if these may not be visible in Silicon Valley. And some of them are completely voluntary: the game of life would be too easy if we could steal and kill as we pleased.

The more of McGonigal one reads, the harder it is to avoid the impression that she has never worked a day in her life. It's like a bad parody of Mitt Romney. "Compared with games, reality is unproductive. Games give us clearer missions and more satisfying, hands-on work. Satisfying work always starts with two things: a clear goal and actionable next steps toward achieving that goal. Having a clear goal motivates us to act: we know what we're supposed to do. And actionable next steps ensure that we can make progress toward the goal immediately." This might seem like "satisfying work" to Frederic Taylor, but it sounds like the very opposite, at least for workers who are not just cogs in some factory assembly line. What's so bad about not having clear goals and actionable next steps? Can't the workers gain some autonomy and chart their own paths or perhaps even challenge the suitability of the paths they are on right now?

McGonigal's overall method slowly becomes clear: start with some shallow and deficient definition of reality, stripped of any complexity of human interaction, present gamification as the ultimate savior, and never mention the fact that games are not neutral tools for getting things done but incentive schemes that might be transforming the gamers, by manipulating their motivations and attitudes, into social and political communities. Like most geeks, McGonigal falls for macroscopism; she has no respect for local communities and prefers to think of planets, galaxies, and centuries instead. "The great challenge for us today and for the remainder of the century," she concludes her book, "is to integrate games more closely into our everyday lives, and to embrace them as a platform for collaborating on our most important planetary efforts." That the pursuit of interplanetary happiness might also produce communities where citizens refuse to lift their fingers unless they are provided with a cash incentive or a badge does not much bother her.

Don't Fold It at Home

There is clearly space for games with a humanitarian bent. The Folding@home application for PlayStation—which McGonigal discusses—allows gamers to log in, accept a mission to investigate how particular proteins fold and misfold (more on this in a second), and donate the power of their console to get the mission done. Proteins have a final structure—what biochemists call their "native state"—but scientists don't yet fully understand the mechanisms through which it's reached and how it's affected through interaction with other molecules. Understanding this can help shed more light on the causes of Alzheimer's disease, Huntington's disease, and many forms of cancer. Researchers at Stanford have found a way through which gamers can donate their spare computing time to help analyze protein folding, which explains media headlines like "PS3 Gamers Trying to Save the World."

Or consider a simple game called FreeRice that allows players to learn fancy English words while being exposed to online ads that help raise money to buy rice for the UN World Food Programme. Still, it's a bit disingenuous to invoke such games to justify other gamification interventions (it's telling that McGonigal herself never mentions the ugly word "gamification" in her book). Folding @home is not actually replacing anything; it just offers a new way to use computer power to process protein folding. It did give rise to a game called FoldIt, in which the gamers are asked to solve puzzles—it's like Tetris for brainiacs—that might help scientists predict the shape of a protein they haven't folded yet. This is truly great—but it has very little in common with the kinds of "gamification" excesses discussed earlier, as the game creates entirely new behaviors rather than provides new motivations for engaging in them. Had an army of geeks been doing all those calculations manually, pen in hand, a game like FoldIt may have posed a problem, but even here, given that new and faster scientific discoveries might save lives, it seems appropriate to outsource this task to the computer.

Likewise, FreeRice seems to do what many other sites already do (i.e., allow you to learn a foreign language), only instead of pocketing the money from advertising, the creator of the site has committed to donating the profits to a good cause. The crowding-out effect might still happen—for example, some language learners might no longer give money to charity if they think that they raise their share via online ads. However, this might be a risk worth taking, for it seems that most people who use FreeRice don't do it to raise money for charity but, rather, to study a foreign language. Simply put, people don't use the FreeRice game because they like playing games; FreeRice actually has few game mechanics. And as far as language-learning alternatives go, FreeRice might even be the ethically correct choice, for in theory it does everything that other sites do—and more.

But most gamification projects are not like Folding@home or FreeRice, so, again, it's a bit disingenuous for the gamification gurus to invoke these projects to prove their civic credentials. Gamifiers don't create novel ways of doing things or simply add a humanitarian layer onto the old ways. Instead, they get you to do what you ought to do by using a combination of feedback loops, badges, and rewards that substitute pleasure for duty. There is a very important difference between folding proteins because you want to help science and folding proteins because you earn points for doing so; the world-saving rhetoric of McGonigal blurs that difference.

Few gamification enthusiasts emphasize this parallel, but the way in which game mechanics have invaded and colonized our lives closely mirrors the spread of market logic into our social, cultural, and political institutions. Using games to get people to take their medications or quite smoking or go to school is not all that different from paying them to do so: in both cases, the effects go far beyond considerations of efficiency. Is it so unreasonable to assume that a kid who is paid to read books will think about reading differently than a kid who comes to enjoy reading for its own sake? As philosopher Michael Sandel points out in *What Money Can't Buy*, his critique of market fundamentalism, "What begins as a market mechanism becomes a market norm," transforming our attitudes to the good in question—whether it's education or health—and such transformations are not always for the better.

Gamification is no different; a project that enlists citizens into helping science by relying on game mechanics rather than by appealing to higher values will eventually come to transform how citizens relate to science. Thus, game mechanics carry far more significant normative implications than their proponents publicly acknowledge; if game mechanics unwittingly transform what is being gamified, we'd better decide whether we actually want such transformations—regardless of considerations of utility and efficiency.

What Sandel writes of markets is equally true of games: "To decide where the market belongs, and where it should be kept at a distance, we have to decide how to value the goods in question—health, education, family life, nature, art, civic duties, and so on. These are moral and political questions, not merely economic ones. To resolve them, we have to debate, case by case, the moral meaning of these goods and the proper way of valuing them."

Gamification, like self-tracking, can easily desensitize citizens to the messy reality around them. Just like quantifying the output of complex sociotechnical systems to make our own practices more effective and less wasteful might preclude us from imagining how such systems might be supplanted and replaced, so can gamification, with its promise of making every activity more enjoyable, make us perpetually content with the current way of doing things.

Chromaroma is a game for London commuters that taps into the journey data saved on their travel cards. It features fancy visualizations of routes and stops; players can join teams and earn bonuses for discovering new routes and even plant traps at stations for the opposition. The *Guardian* even called the game "the makeover London commuting has been waiting for." Well, as writer Steven Poole points out, "actually, the makeover London commuting has been waiting for is a more reliable service, with Tube lines that don't close every weekend and trains that can hold more than 17 people. Overlaying a game onto the current state of the system is not a makeover; it's a spangly sticking plaster on a festering wound."

Now, it may be that everyone playing Chromaroma will learn so much about the troubles of the London transportation system that they will create an activist organization demanding better service. This is the optimistic scenario. But it's as likely that the opposite will happen: instead of finally getting frustrated with the service and taking collective action, the atomized players of Chromaroma will find a better way to enjoy the bad service. That, with some tinkering, people can find satisfaction, even enjoyment, in the most degrading environments is no reason to celebrate gamification as an unalloyed good.

After all, the Soviet planners were also great gamification enthusiasts, even if they never used the term; their preferred label was "socialist competition," and it meant pitting workers, collectives, and entire factories against each other to compete for that greatest reward of all: a medal of the Order of the Red Banner of Labor. As games researcher Mark Nelson notes of the Soviet experience with gamification, "Factory competitions could blend fuzzily into sports competitions: factories would not only compete against each other in production, but also as field teams in soccer leagues. This attempted to leverage genuine game competition, together with cultural aspects such as local city pride and sports fandom, in an ambitious strategy of comprehensively gamifying industrial production." Sure, the workers may have enjoyed the competitive aspect, but we shouldn't be blind to the fact that such enjoyment might have distracted them from realizing just how awful and grueling their working conditions were.

Gaming theorist Ian Bogost, who is perhaps the most vehement critic of gamification, makes this point forcefully in a provocative essay—with the self-explanatory title of "Shit Crayons"—in which he notes that imprisoned Nigerian poet Wole Soyinka managed to compose beautiful poems with whatever writing material was available. For Bogost, games like FarmVille give players few choices to exercise their autonomy and creativity and are not much better than the Nigerian prison; all you can do is click and, if you are lucky, move things around (Bogost was writing this in response to the phenomenal online success of his own game—initially developed as satire—in which players can do little else but click on an ugly cow). That the digital prisoners, much like Soyinka, come up with ways to circumvent control and remain creative is no reason to forget that they are still in a prison cell. To quote Bogost, "A despot in a sorcerer's hat does not deserve praise for inciting desperate resilience." The London Underground is still just as awful—even if the journey has become more tolerable.

Mad Men, Faded Denims, and Real Phonies

All these attempts to fix the human condition—to reduce our biases by quantifying everything, to circumvent the frailties of our memory by recording everything, to rid us of our lowly, provincial interests by getting technology companies to serve us a more nutritious information diet, to get us to do the right thing by turning everything in life into a game—are indicative of Silicon Valley's unease with imperfection as well as its glorification of the powerful tools at its disposal. Our geek kings do not realize that inefficiency is precisely what shelters us from the inhumanity of Taylorism and market fundamentalism. When inefficiency is the result of a deliberative commitment by a democratically run community, there is no need to eliminate it, even if the latest technologies can accomplish that in no time.

Silicon Valley's greatest ambition, though, is to ensure that all our social interactions—and even ourselves—exist under the yoke of authenticity. The fear of appearing inauthentic, of being a fake, has propelled nearly as much technological innovation as pornography. As already noted, the quantifying urge of self-trackers, especially their desire to publish these numbers, should be seen as part of this quest to ensure—once and for all—that they are not just authentic but also original. We might all be thinking the same thoughts, using the same apps, and wearing the same T-shirts, but it's quite reassuring to know that at least our DNA, daily caloric intake, sleeping patterns are different.

But—and this is the implicit promise of self-tracking—perhaps if you track all those physical things long enough, you'll uncover some deeper numerical pattern, something that will allow you to discover who you really are. As Gary Wolf notes, "Behind the allure of the quantified self is a guess that many of our problems come from simply lacking the instruments to understand who we are. Our memories are poor; we are subject to a range of biases; we can focus our attention on only one or two things at a time." And what will it take to discover "who we are"? Well, says Wolf, a bunch of self-tracking gadgets—reporting to the health-care industry or marketers on Madison Avenue—would do the job. "We don't have a pedometer in our feet, or a breathalyzer in our lungs, or a glucose monitor installed into our veins. We lack both the physical and the mental apparatus to take stock of ourselves. We need help from machines." Had Sigmund Freud lived long enough, he would have probably been replaced by a pedometer: in this brave new world, who needs psychoanalysis—the obsolete practice of narrative imagination—to "take stock of ourselves," when the algorithmic option looks so tempting?

If the Quantified Self movement allows us to establish our authenticity with numbers, social networking allows us to accomplish that in subtler, seemingly more creative ways: by curating the timeline of our life, by uploading our favorite photos, by using the coolest apps on the block, by maintaining a unique social graph (Facebook speak for a set of human connections that each user has). If only one looks closely enough, one can discern how the themes of fakeness and authenticity shape Facebook's own self-presentation. So Mark Zuckerberg claims that "the social web can't exist until you are your real self online." Peter Thiel, the first private investor in Facebook, contrasts the authenticity offered by Facebook—where no pseudonyms are allowed—with that of its former rival, MySpace, where everything goes. "MySpace is about being someone fake on the internet; everyone could be a movie star. [It is] very healthy that the real people have won out over the fake people," he notes.

Sheryl Sandberg, Facebook board member and chief operating officer, goes even further in emphasizing how central the idea of authenticity is to the company's activities. "Expressing our authentic identity will become even more pervasive in the coming year," she notes in an essay she wrote for the *Economist* about 2012. "Profiles will no longer be outlines, but detailed self-portraits of who we really are, including the books we read, the music we listen to, the distances we run, the places we travel, the causes we support, the video of cats we laugh at, our likes and our links. And yes, this shift to authenticity will take getting used to and will elicit cries of lost privacy."

There's certainly something ironic about a company that makes all its money from advertising—one industry in which fakes like *Mad Men*'s Don Draper feel truly at home—waging a modern-day crusade for authenticity. This crusade is anything but new, as Lionel Trilling showed in *Sincerity and Authenticity*, tracing it back to the time of Shakespeare. But, as Trilling correctly noted, while sincerity and authenticity may have their uses, there's little to admire about a deliberate quest to establish oneself as a truly authentic person. This simplistic impulse to authenticity—toward "proving ourselves not merely good, but true, true to ourselves, true to our nature, true perhaps even to some notion that we have of what human beings ought to be"—is itself anything but authentic.

As Trilling warned, we shouldn't confuse authenticity "with a kind of dress, with faded denims, perhaps, with a look that's down to earth," for "as soon as you begin attaching moral meanings to a fashion, to a symbol of that kind, and as soon as those meanings . . . become the mark of a certain kind of person who asks for a certain kind of respect," then authenticity loses its value. Of course, our denunciations needn't go as far as those of Theodor Adorno, who, in his *Jargon of Authenticity*, complained that "in the name of contemporary authenticity even a torturer could put in all sorts of claims for compensation, to the extent that he was simply a true torturer." But Adorno does have a point: authentic things are not necessarily morally good, and morally good things are not necessarily authentic. What we are authentic about matters as well. As philosopher Charles Guignon puts it, "What is crucial about authenticity is not just the intensity of the commitment and fervor of the expression it carries with it, but the nature of the content of the commitment as well."

Furthermore, in the hands of Facebook, authenticity becomes just a rhetorical weapon that fuels user anxieties and results in even more data being uploaded to the site. When Sheryl Sandberg writes that Facebook profiles are now "detailed self-portraits" that "express our authenticity identity," she is also stating the obvious: the only way to make such portraits even more authentic is by uploading and sharing even more details. But Facebook wouldn't be Facebook if it didn't stack the cards against users. Thus, its embrace of the ideology of "frictionless sharing," in which everything we do is automatically shared by default and we need to choose what not to share—not only exposes our "self-portrait" for everyone to see but also results in other users discovering and perhaps even liking our favorite songs and books. But if there are other users who like the very same things that you do, then perhaps you are just a fake—so you need to discover and upload and share something unique. This is a vicious circle, for no one ever achieves true authenticity on Facebook. Sandberg's dream of an authentic identity is just a clever marketing slogan.

In this, the authenticity rhetoric of Facebook is strikingly similar to the public debates in 1950s America over whether uniformity (everyone living in mass society is essentially the same) was a greater sin than conformity (some people adopt ideas, habits, and beliefs only to get along). The latter, the conformists, were seen as phonies who chose to be someone else; the former, those who were uniform by design, were seen as real phonies—as people who thought they were making choices and being their unique selves, when in fact they were anything but. Literary scholar Abigail Cheever argues that this fear of uniformity—the possibility, as she puts it, that "the unique American individual was not just hiding beneath a phony mask, but rather no longer existed at all"—was much greater than the fear of conformity and pervaded the work of writers as diverse as J. D. Salinger and David Riesman.

While Cheever believes that such fears may have abated by the end of the last century, it's unlikely that they have gone away altogether. Both Facebook and the Quantified Self promise to give us concrete, even numerical, proof that we have a deep and authentic identity waiting to be discovered, that we need to carry that identity with us when we log into Facebook, and that there will be something tangible and unique after, in Wolf's words, we "have taken stock of ourselves." It's an appealing, even irresistible, proposition that taps into long-running fears. It's unlikely that either social networking or self-tracking will reassure us about our own uniqueness, if only because neither Facebook nor the manufacturers of self-tracking tools would want to undermine their own businesses. But it may also be that we need to temper our appetite for authenticity and accept that inauthentic doesn't always mean bad and that, without a little deception and phoniness, no social relations would be possible.

CHAPTER NINE

Smart Gadgets, Dumb Humans

"The moral law is in our hearts,
but it is also in our apparatuses."
—Bruno Latour

O n May 8, 2012, the website of the City of Santa Monica in California published an innocuous looking press release. Titled "City Expands Parking Meter Sensors," it looked as mundane, uncontroversial, and inconsequential as millions of other documents churned out by American officialdom that day.

The City of Santa Monica was both announcing the expansion of its smart parking program and bragging about its own innovation credentials. Why "smart"? New meters would come with embedded sensors, allowing authorities to track the duration of the average parking stay (regardless of whether the fare was paid or not). Armed with this new data, the city hoped to adjust both the number of parking spots and the time limits to find the balance that suited everyone.

The whole scheme would seem perfectly acceptable, but the press release also announced two more "innovations." First, the sensors would allow the meters to reset automatically when a car left the spot—regardless of how much prepaid time remained on the meter. Second, a driver would have no way to overstay the posted time limit by paying several times: the sensors would identify each car and, once the permitted time was up, tell the meter not to accept further payments.

Many would welcome even these two changes. Why not block those who want to trick the system and overstay the limit? After all, free parking is anything but free. As Donald Shoup, professor of urban planning at the University of California, Los Angeles, shows in his *The High Cost of Free Parking*, if people paid the fair market price for parking, they might drive less, and the perpetually cash-deprived cities might raise more money too. Seems like a win-win.

But ought we to consider other aspects of the Santa Monica initiative? To return to Albert Hirschman's futility-perversity-jeopardy triad, the first of those concerns doesn't seem to be a problem. Unless they find a way to easily circumvent it, drivers will likely comply with the smart metering system; there's no good reason to deem the scheme futile—at least not yet. A charge of perversity, too, is hard to substantiate: it's not obvious how smart sensor-based metering could worsen the parking situation.

What about jeopardy? Is there a "previous, precious accomplishment," to use Hirschman's language, that smart metering endangers? There is, of course, the standard set of criticisms associated with situational crime prevention discussed at length in Chapter 6. Perhaps, if we universalize this scheme and prohibit citizens from breaking the law everywhere, we'll end up with morally deficient citizens who won't do the right thing unless the technological infrastructure explicitly robs them of the opportunity to do the wrong thing.

Might automatically resetting meters somehow undermine the bonds of solidarity between drivers, depriving some of opportunities to engage in virtuous behavior while convincing others that the world is a fully atomized space where no acts of altruism are permitted? Such concerns might initially seem convincing, but they seem to rest on faulty logic, as the seemingly "virtuous" behavior in question (leaving prepaid time on meters for use by the next person who parks) is most probably self-serving, particularly if the departing drivers initially thought they would be staying longer. That some other people benefit from the drivers' largess is mostly the consequence of an imperfectly designed system—not the result of a deliberate commitment to benefit random strangers using the same meter.

But before we accept the Santa Monica parking system as an unmitigated good, let's consider an alternative system. What if, instead of automatically renewing the meter once the sensors figured out that the car was leaving, the driver were offered the option to either keep the money in the meter—to be used by some future driver in need of parking—or to reset the meter, preventing a potential parking subsidy and boosting the city budget. And, to make this "smart" system truly earn that description, suppose it could also inform the driver of statistics about cars that usually park in the area. Are they fancy new cars that only rich people can afford? Or are they mostly old, decrepit cars used by grad students or illegal immigrants?

Under this new scheme, the driver would be compelled to weigh the pros and cons and decide what was more important: fighting congestion and helping the city or being a good fellow citizen and helping those in need with their parking bill. Suddenly, the driver must think about the severity of the parking problem and confront the factors creating it—perhaps enough so to order a copy of Donald Shoup's book. Whereas it was previously impossible to get the driver to show virtuous behavior—"virtue" was just an accident of the system's design—now the driver is forced to deliberate about which course of action would be more virtuous. By comparison, the actual scheme—where the decision is made on the driver's behalf—now looks too restraining and paternalistic.

Thus, even a minor tweak to the inner workings of something as mundane as a parking system could produce very different citizens. In the first, fully automated scenario, we get a perfectly efficient system and citizens who are not likely to spend much time thinking about, well, the philosophy of parking: why it's run the way it's run, what social problems may have created congestion, whether there are better ways to fix it, and so on. Under the second scenario—where drivers are forced to make choices and decide which values are more important to them—there is a much better chance that at least some drivers will confront the big, meaty issues involved in how parking works.

The first scheme seeks to maximize the economic efficiency of the parking system; the second seeks to maximize the deliberative efficiency of our democracy as a whole. The first scheme doesn't scale well: to maximize efficiency in other settings would require a new set of sensors and smart technologies. The second scheme scales beautifully: citizens who are prodded to think critically about the hidden costs of the invisible infrastructure that surrounds them are likely to approach many other aspects of life with the same critical mind-set. The second scheme may not raise as much money as the first, but what it does raise—citizens' awareness—is arguably far more important in the long term, even if less tangible.

If we start from the assumption that the reform, rather than the preservation, of the current parking system should be the goal of public policy, then it's important to have eager citizens who are capable of reflecting on how that reform ought to proceed and what values should matter in the process. So perhaps Hirschman's first two categories—futility and perversity—do apply to the Santa Monica scheme after all.

If the goal of our policymakers is to maintain the current system as it is and to find a more effective enforcement mechanism, then the Santa Monica system works fine. But if the goal is to come up with better, more sustainable, and ecologically friendlier ways of parking, and even of managing transportation as a whole, then the Santa Monica scheme fails, for it optimizes the efficiency of only the local—not the global—system. That is, if it gives us citizens who don't normally reflect on their parking and driving habits, then the scheme might still be considered a failure, even if it leads to more efficient billing of parked cars. Such unreflective attitudes toward transportation have given us both urban decay and climate change. We can postpone thinking about seemingly trivial everyday issues for only so long—eventually, they will come back to haunt us.

Victorian Trains and Montana Huts

In a way, various smart systems like the one in Santa Monica suffer from the same problem as self-tracking: if quantification gives us an opportunity to save three gallons of water without questioning how this water gets into our bathrooms to begin with, then perhaps the savings are not as significant as we believe and maybe they even detract from our seeking more innovative ways of reforming the water system. In this sense, the Santa Monica scheme is futile (in Hirschman's sense) in that it doesn't really alter how drivers and citizens relate to the problems of parking and congestion. Potentially, the scheme is also perverse, especially if it gives us citizens who no longer feel the need to show concern for other drivers, the city, or the environment whenever smart meters and other forms of policing are missing.

Such schemes thwart the development of what we earlier called "narrative imagination" and what some design theorists call "system thinking"—an intellectual approach that grants complexity to both the causes and effects of a problem and, instead of reducing the roots of that problem to a handful of easily identifiable and controllable factors, seeks to redescribe them in the language of relations, structures, and processes. In fact, studies show that design students primed to think in terms of systems who receive additional training in nondesign disciplines, such as psychology, anthropology, development, or ecology, tend to come up with more innovative and sustainable solutions than design students only primed to think like efficiency-maximizing engineers.

Properly designed, technological schemes can expand—rather than shrink, as the technophobes would argue—both the deliberative spaces where we think through our shared problems and the number of concrete avenues through which virtue and citizenship can be exercised. The real problem with the Santa Monica scheme is not that it's smart but that's it's not smart enough: a truly smart system would find a way to turn us into more reflective, caring, and humane creatures. Technology can certainly assist in that mission, but both the technologists and the social engineers guiding them would have to acquire a very different mind-set.

Spanish writer José Ortega y Gasset once wrote that "to be an engineer . . . is not enough to be an engineer." This is a more profound insight than it seems at first. An engineer familiar with the immense challenges of living in a moral community, of mingling and struggling with other human beings, is not likely to be driven by considerations of efficiency alone. As the Santa Monica example illustrates, there is no need to abandon technological solutions altogether; rather, an alternative, more open-ended design can help achieve similar results while allowing human agents to continue exercising the tough, challenging choices that distinguish them from machines, which act on their own agendas with mindless and emotionless brutality.

One of the greatest misconceptions of the last few decades has been the idea that technology ought not to intrude on questions of morality, that it ought to tread its own carefully delineated path, separate from that of humans and their political projects, like liberalism. Morality here, technology there: the two should never overlap. In this view—most eloquently expressed by French theologian Jacques Ellul and eagerly promoted by his numerous American and Canadian followers in the 1970s and 1980s—technology, acting in its usually sly and autonomous fashion, can only compromise morality. Left unchecked, technology ushers in what Neil Postman called "technopoly"—a society in which "the culture seeks its authorisation in technology, finds its satisfactions in technology, and takes its orders from technology."

Such grand rhetoric, for all the quasi-religious fervor it used to generate, is long past its expiration date. It's time to give up this talk of "Technology" with a big *T* and instead figure out how different technologies can boost or compromise the human condition. As far as analytical categories go, "Technology" holds as much promise as "the Internet": it's very hard to reach precision as the cultural biases implied and produced by such terms are too many. Once we move to a lower—that is, more detailed, empirical, and analytically precise—level of analysis, we are likely to notice things that may have escaped the attention of French theologians.

For example, we might discover that something like liberalism is unthinkable without an array of technologies to support it. Most liberal reformers have never shied away from the technological toolbox. Oscar Wilde was right: mechanical slavery is the enabler of human liberation. Or, as he himself put it, "unless there are slaves to do the ugly, horrible, uninteresting work, culture and contemplation become almost impossible. Human slavery is wrong, insecure, and demoralizing. On mechanical slavery, on the slavery of the machine, the future of the world depends."

Chris Otter, a historian specializing in technology and science in Victorian Britain, convincingly argues that Victorian values like punctuality, cleanliness, and attentiveness presuppose the existence of reliable watches, running water, and eyeglasses and would not have emerged without them. Otter goes even further to propose that "many of the characteristics of liberal subjectivity were simply impossible without their corresponding technologies. The mobile subject was nothing without his trains; the attentive subject lost without her spectacles and gas flame; the punctual subject was late without her watch; the clean subject filthy unless hooked up to his bathtub and toilet; the industrialist financially ruined without his steam-engines and telegraphic connection to the stock exchange."

Of course, not every problem is amenable to a technological fix—and as we saw in Chapter 6 on situational crime prevention, we should probably keep it that way. In some situations, politics will be preferable to technology or law will do a better job as it creates more opportunities for public debate on a given issue to emerge.

But, obviously, not all problems are like this: politics and law won't get you from New York to Los Angeles or clean your apartment—unless you become a dictator and force somebody else to do it for you. Short of that, get a vacuum cleaner! So, in many a situation, technological fixes may be unavoidable, and this is hardly a reason to cry, "Technopoly!" and retreat to a hut in Montana.

But to grant that technological fixes are unavoidable is not the same as to grant that they are all equally good or equally bad, even if they get the job done. That they are "technological" means little, as "technology" says little about their moral import; if we do grant that "technological" does not automatically mean "amoral" or "in-humane" or "antidemocratic," we'll have to investigate each and every technological system on its own terms and imagine how a different technological system might achieve the same objectives in a manner more conductive to debate, reform, and deliberation. In other words, we need to develop a better way of evaluating, comparing, and discriminating across technological fixes—rather than repeating the same tiring message that social fixes are always better. It's when we need to decide on the best technological fix that Ortega's admonition that, to be an engineer, it's not enough to be an engineer: there is no "right" way to design the Santa Monica parking system, and we should stop pretending otherwise.

Radios, Caterpillars, and Lamps

We humans do not live elegantly engineered lives, well modeled and adjusted after technical trials to remove imperfections. Instead, we have competing obligations and complicated life plans. We often do things that are not in our best interest because of pride or altruism or patriotism. We fail to respond to incentives—or we get to love incentives so much that we no longer respond to anything else. We live in a world that seems firm and permanent only to find out that it isn't—and that many of the practices we take for granted are harming the planet, or our neighbors, or teenage factory workers in Cambodia, or squirrels in Tajikistan, or some as-yet-unnamed community that is only now beginning to articulate its opposition to our way of life.

Our world is ridden with conflict and antagonism—often a good thing, for it does not allow one particular group to enjoy near-universal hegemony for too long—and our laws are imperfect by design and in need of constant revision and reinterpretation. All our actions have unpredictable consequences, but instead of shying away from this predicament, we should try to rebuild our social and political structures accordingly. We are suckers for various technologies—even the most inconsequential—but we rarely recognize that their use is only made possible by vast sociotechnological systems, like water supply and now cloud computing, that mostly remain invisible to us but have consequences much more significant than our own use of the technologies these systems make possible.

This understanding of the human condition lends itself to a very different set of technological fixes. Contrast our usual suspect, metered electricity, with an approach pioneered by Swedish designers from the Interactive Institute under the name of "erratic appliances." Instead of starting from the conventional assumption that our gadgets ought to work flawlessly and recede into the background, never threatening our confidence in the abundance of the resources they produce and consume, the Swedish designers decided to build home appliances that start to behave strangely as energy consumption increases. The strangeness is deliberate: it seeks to introduce aspects of risk and indeterminacy into the use of such devices. Thus, the behavior of, say, a toaster will depend on the overall electricity consumption in the apartment; users are thus deliberately forced to make choices, as leaving the kettle on might interfere with the toaster or the blender or the coffee machine. The purpose of the project, as the Swedes acknowledge, is somewhat humorous. But the humor raises important questions.

Another prototype of an erratic appliance is a radio set that tunes to a different frequency once the energy consumption in the household rises above a certain threshold. To make this happen, the Swedish designers hacked an ordinary radio set and installed a sensor—not all sensors enslave us!—that could measure the electrical fields around the radio. Imagine hungry radio listeners bringing the radio set into the kitchen to grab some food without missing their favorite show. As they move around the kitchen, the show gets increasingly difficult to hear, as the sound reflects the strength of the electrical magnetic field in the current location. As the designers note, "It is like walking around some contaminated area with a Geiger-counter."

Is it the most functional radio on earth? Certainly not—but this is not what the designers were after; their goal was to show how the radio depends on energy, something that conventional designers have done their best to hide. The shift away from ease of use is intentional, write the Swedes, "we have tried to complicate typical conceptions of energy and technology as belonging in the background." But, as they also note, usability does not have to go altogether; a better balance between making the user more aware of energy consumption and not disrupting the favorite show can probably be found. However, by encouraging what they call "user-unfriendliness" and "para-functionality," the Swedish designers seek to "discourage unthinking ideological assimilation and promote skepticism by increasing the poetic distance between people [and] products." Their project of "increasing the poetic distance" fits rather nicely with the goal of expanding our narrative imaginations discussed earlier.

In a similar vein, a trio of German designers at the Folkwang University of the Arts set out to build what they call "transformational products," which aspire to engage their owners in "dialogues without words." One is the Caterpillar, which is an extension cord (shaped like a caterpillar) that seeks to make its owner think about the energy wasted by devices in standby mode. The Caterpillar has three modes: when the plugged-in device—say, a TV set—is on, then the caterpillar breathes slowly and unobtrusively; if it's off, it does nothing; but if it's in standby mode, then the Caterpillar starts twisting and turning, as if in pain. Will owners attend to its needs as they would for a living thing? Perhaps not—but as long as it adds depth and substance to their experience of using extension cords, the mission is accomplished.

The designers deliberately want users to engage, even though they could have easily done the job for them: the Caterpillar could simply detect connected devices in standby and switch them off automatically. Like Santa Monica's smart parking system, this would maximize local and economic efficiency—but only at the cost of decreasing global and deliberative efficiency. Automating virtue in one instance, as we have already seen, might require automating it everywhere—not to mention that, in the context of energy, it might result in more reckless consumption overall.

The Caterpillar's designers see friction—not efficiency or ease of use—as a productive resource that, properly deployed, can highlight complex issues that are very hard to see in a frictionless world.

Another of their transformational products is a Forget Me Not reading lamp. Once switched on, Forget Me Not starts closing like a flower, as its light gradually gets dimmer and more obscure. For the lamp to reopen and shine again, the user needs to touch one of its petals. Thus, the user is in a constant dialogue with the lamp, hopefully aware of the responsibility to use energy appropriately.

Do the Caterpillar and Forget Me Not even qualify as technological fixes? Or are they more like technological unfixes, forcing us to question what we normally take for granted? Most likely, it's the latter—and the designers want it that way. As they note, "The *Caterpillar* or *Forget Me Not* . . . are not problem-solvers, but troublemakers. Technology is typically seen as problem-solver, and well-designed technology is supposed to follow an according aesthetic of efficiency, ease and—ultimately—automation. Transformational Products attempt to break up rather than to fit into established routines. They intentionally cause friction." In other words, whereas most modern technologies offer us a trouble-free existence—cue Apple's promise of "automatic, effortless, and seamless" experience in one of its ad slogans—"these troublemakers need to be tamed and they can only be tamed by thinking through how they work and how they fit together."

All these projects have in common their aspiration to sensitize us to our shared "technological unconscious," to uncover the infrastructures that make our techno-binges possible, to transcend the reductionism of numbers, the paternalism of nudges, and the simplicity of gamification, and to engage users as citizens—rather than as consumers who only understand the language of prices and percentage points, or children who can't be trusted to do the right thing, or Skinnerian rats who can't do the right thing unless the matching incentive is present. All these projects assume that users are capable of thinking, deliberating, and articulating their own needs and concerns; the users are imagined as complex human beings who, in using these devices, will not only make inevitable and painful trade-offs based on the values they hold dear but may even come to revise those values as they enter into a dialogue with the devices. These users are anything but the automatons of rational-choice theory or classical economics who approach every issue with fixed and well-articulated principles and a perfect understanding of their utility curves.

The Natural Fuse and Its Adversaries

Without a thorough theoretical scaffolding, all these "erratic appliances" and "technological troublemakers" can be easily dismissed as quirks of fancy postmodern design. The pull of functionalism—broadly speaking, the idea that the technologies we use have clearly predefined functions and purposes and that designers should put all their effort into building devices that express them most cogently—makes it all but impossible to argue that designers have a responsibility to use the artifacts they build as conversation starters.

But this argument holds only if we reject the idea that deliberation about technologies we use—and the broader sociotechnical systems that make them possible—is not itself an important function. What if we change the initial assumption guiding functionalism—that there's broad agreement over what a device should do and how—and opt for a more Deweyan approach that would view such agreements as temporary and contingent and always liable to revision through debate and deliberation?

Under this new system, the goal of design is not just to build an artifact to fulfill some genuine social need "out there" but also to make us reflect on how that need has emerged, how it has become a project worth pursuing, and how, all things considered, it may actually not be worth pursuing at all. Designers shouldn't force these answers on users, but they should make it easier for users to ask questions that may or may not lead to such answers. The Caterpillar and the Forget Me Not lamp do just that; their ordinary equivalents do not.

Both these projects fall under the rubric of "adversarial design," a novel approach to thinking about technology and politics articulated by media and design theorist Carl DiSalvo. DiSalvo's thought is worth surveying in depth, if only because it provides the much-needed theoretical scaffolding that turns the disjointed insights of "erratic appliances" and "technological troublemakers" into a paradigmatic program and philosophy of design.

Drawing on the work of political theorists like Carl Schmitt and Chantal Mouffe, DiSalvo articulates a new way of designing things that, instead of promoting consensus and efficiency, is inspired by the idea of endless antagonism and contestation of social and political norms and arrangements. "If we abandon the notion that any one design will completely or even adequately address our social concerns or resolve our social issues," he writes, "then adversarial design can provide those spaces of confrontation—in the form of products, services, events, and processes—through which political concerns and issues can [be] expressed and engaged."

DiSalvo marshals up numerous examples to show what adversarial design looks like in practice: crime maps that, instead of showing the distribution of crimes on a city map, show which city blocks have the most former residents incarcerated; browser extensions that add information about military funding to the websites of universities or convert all prices on sites like Amazon into their equivalent in barrels of oil based on current prices; and umbrellas with electric lights that defeat the recognition algorithms of surveillance cameras. Two of DiSalvo's examples, however, are particularly worth discussing at length. One is the Spore 1.1 project designed by Matt Kenyon and Doug Easterly, which is built around a rubber tree plant bought from the Home Depot retailer with the unconditional guarantee that it can be exchanged for a new plant if it dies in the first year. The plant is connected to an automated watering system that works on a somewhat bizarre principle: Every Friday it checks how the Home Depot's stock is performing on the New York Stock Exchange. If the stock performs too poorly, no water is administered to the plant; if it does well, water is administered. If the plant dies, it's exchanged for a new one, and the process starts again. In a brief paper that Kenyon and Easterly wrote about their project, they note that the plant had already died five times—due to overwatering. The art project was meant to get observers to reflect on the potentially high but invisible costs of unchecked economic growth: it's somewhat odd that the rubber tree plant, indigenous to Southeast Asia and "a symbol of life and ecology," has become "trapped inside a synthetic ecosystem, awaiting the arcane results of the NYSE."

DiSalvo's other memorable example of adversarial design is the Natural Fuse, an art project designed by London-based architect Usman Haque. To understand Haque's creative intervention, it's helpful to know something about strategies to fight climate change. Many such contemporary efforts revolve around the idea of carbon offsets, whereby nations or corporations are allocated a certain number of allowances, which determine how much carbon they can emit into the atmosphere. Once such allowances are exceeded, additional allowances must be purchased, with the proceeds usually going to create and bolster so-called carbon sinks, carbon-sequestering natural or artificial reservoirs that absorb carbon.

The logic of carbon offsetting—and the idea that sustainability can be bought through market relations—has now trickled down from nations and corporations to individuals. Thus, we are now asked to monitor—yet another instance of self-tracking—our carbon footprint and to minimize our own carbon emissions by buying more efficient products or using greener transportation methods. But even as we gain the ability to monitor our own carbon footprint, do we really know what those numbers actually mean? Or is taking such measurements yet another way to make us feel good about our own sacrifices without making any fundamental changes to the system? Do we know the relative importance of our tiny contribution? If everyone makes the same small efforts, will they be enough to reverse the troubling trends? Or will some other drastic measures still be required? Most of us don't know—and probably would rather not know, as long we can make up for our own indulgences by shopping in carbon-friendly online stores (which are probably powered by servers that eat up far more carbon than what we save by shopping for "sustainable products").

The Natural Fuse aims to go beyond the reductionism of numbers and give citizens a better understanding of the logic and the ethics of carbon offsets. In other words, it seeks to promote narrative imagination and make us think of carbon in terms of structures, relations, and systems—and not just numbers. Here is how it works: Imagine a suite of household plants hooked up to sensors, connected to a computer network, and plugged into a home electric outlet, thus functioning as a gateway to all electricity from that outlet. Thus, if you want to use a lamp, you have to plug it into the outlet connected to the plants. The plants function as a carbon sink; your lamp will stay on as long as the plants can absorb all the carbon it emits; normally, this time varies from a few seconds to a few minutes. Similar plants are distributed to your neighbors or to anyone connected to the computer network.

Each plant also carries a switch marked "off/selfless/selfish." Once your lamp goes dark, you face a dilemma: you can turn on the selfish mode and borrow energy allotments from other plants— provided they are in the selfless mode—on the network. A complex system of sensors embedded in all the plants communicates with the central server, which makes allocations based on the energy levels and carbon offsets of individual plants. If your selfish desire to power your own plant draws too much power from another plant, then this other plant dies—in which case all participants get an e-mail informing them of the plant's death. Once the plant reaches its three-death limit, a jar of vinegar is automatically poured into its soil—and it dies for real.

With the Natural Fuse, carbon sinking no longer happens in some distant land, far away from users; it happens right at their desks—and the painful decisions that we, as consumers, thought we would never have to make suddenly become visible to us as citizens. We can either continue indulging our individual desires—to the detriment of everyone else—or we can start investigating how we can contribute to the common welfare.

The design of the Natural Fuse is most interesting, and most adversarial, in that it shuns the assurances of equilibrium and consensus—usually of the Oprahesque "everything will be fine if only we work hard" variety—that invariably accompany admonitions to engage in energy-saving behavior. As DiSalvo points out, strife is built into the operation of the Natural Fuse's very system. "By design, the system enables and almost requires users to engage in contests with one another. In fact, it is not clear whether the counterbalance sought by most carbon sink and carbon offset programs is even achievable with *Natural Fuse*."

The fact that the Natural Fuse makes no normative or prescriptive claims—there is no "right" way to use it—is its feature, not a bug. While it does not punish those who overconsume or reward those who share with others, it reveals the material relations that define our consumption habits and highlights the ethical issues involved. It aims not to maximize energy efficiency but rather to maximize deliberative efficiency, to force users into confronting issues they'd rather ignore. Just like the transformational products that sought to start a dialogue instead of providing a straightforward solution, the Natural Fuse, according to DiSalvo, "instead of using design as a means of providing a solution . . . uses design to problematize the situation."

The Natural Fuse makes the problem of carbon offsetting more visible—but the visibility it affords is very different from that provided by numerous carbon-offset calculators available online. It provides a second-order, superior visibility: not only do we know how much carbon we need to sink to offset the electricity we use, but we actually know how much sacrifice—by us and by other people—is needed to sink that carbon. Sociologist Anthony Giddens distinguishes between "practical" and "discursive" consciousness. The former, characterized by routine and habitual interaction, refers to the everyday knowledge we have about how to do things; the latter, characterized by greater reflexivity about our own actions, refers to the social conditions in which we do things.

Thus, practical consciousness helps us locate the light switch as we leave a building; discursive consciousness explains why we turn off the lights. While most of our energy-consumption habits operate on the level of practical consciousness—which partly explains the problem of climate change—projects like the Natural Fuse allow us to shift them to the level of discursive consciousness. Thus, while self-tracking and lifelogging of the conventional variety provide us with the kind of visibility that doesn't extend beyond practical consciousness, the self-reflexivity triggered by projects like the Natural Fuse introduce visibility not just to our own actions but to the social relations in which they occur, allowing us to exercise our narrative imagination.

Notice that the Natural Fuse is anything but antitechnology. In fact, it would have been impossible without modern sensors and the ability to link users to each other via a computer network. It doesn't look down on numbers; quite the opposite—the quantification of our energy use and the carbon-offsetting capacity of each plant is at its very core. But instead of using all of these tools, networks, and techniques to give us a false impression of control and ultimate mastery of the world around us, it seeks to show us that the systems we rely on may need to be overturned rather than optimized. It promises us another way to think of our current predicaments, not just the ability to apply quick fixes within them. Sensors, networks, and numbers are not enemies; they become enemies only once they are merged with ill-considered, one-dimensional, and naïve ideologies.

Games can be remade with adversarial design in mind. It's not that they cannot be used to articulate political concerns or force citizens to see and confront issues they would rather leave unseen and unconfronted; it's just that the way various game elements— the game mechanics, as the gamification industry calls them—have been put to use is likely to produce fun-seeking but docile citizens who will never question anything unless promised a golden badge. As game theorist Ian Bogost has shown in *Persuasive Games,* games that seek to persuade without allowing players to deliberate are just another form of coercion—perhaps of the soft variety—not persuasion.

"But who cares about deliberation if we get the results we want? If achievement-like structures can get kids to brush their teeth or adults to exercise more, why does one's original motivation matter?" ponders Bogost. It's hard to disagree with his answer: "Because to thrive, culture requires deliberation and rationale." If, after extensive deliberation, we cannot find a rationale, then perhaps we shouldn't be pursuing that activity in the first place. The worst instances of gamification, however, leave no space for deliberation and put many social and political processes on a kind of autopilot, where citizens engage in them not because it is the right thing to do but because it gives them the best combination of badges.

Compare two games that claim to have a social edge in that they try to make players more aware of a problem like obesity. Zamzee is a game developed by a nonprofit called HopeLab started by the spouse of eBay's founder, Pierre Omidyar. The idea behind the game is simple: kids get to wear real monitors that track their physical activity and earn points depending on how much they move. CNN recently reported on a fourteen-year-old who got two hundred points for walking his dog and five hundred points for running a mile. After he had amassed a total of 47,074 such points, he redeemed them for Legos and $150 worth of Best Buy gift cards. Who funds this conversion of points into real goods? His parents, of course: thanks to the monitor, they can see the amount of exercise and set targets that, once met, will lead them to reward their kids with gift cards and the like.

There are good reasons to doubt whether Zamzee will be very effective; past studies show that many teenagers soon lose interest, and parents quickly discover that their kids want to be paid for literally everything. But this shouldn't much preoccupy us here. More interesting is the kind of thinking about obesity and health that a game like Zamzee triggers in players. Most likely, the dominant narrative goes something like this: if I work hard enough, I'll succeed. Being slim and being healthy are thus just the natural consequences of good individual behavior; they have little to do with structural factors like family income, access to healthy food, or the risks of jogging around the neighborhood.

Now, contrast Zamzee with a game like Fatworld developed by Ian Bogost. Unlike Zamzee, which takes place entirely in the real world, Fatworld is a more conventional effort that takes place entirely in a virtual world of cartoonish characters. But it is much better than Zamzee at conveying the complexity of the obesity problem. In Fatworld you start by choosing weight and health conditions—predispositions toward ailments like diabetes, heart disease, or overeating—for your character. Then you decide what you want to eat and how much you want to exercise—and make sure to balance your budget. You are also invited to see what it's like to make nutritional choices for others—by designing menus in your own restaurant. The realism is impeccable: you can influence public policy by paying bribes to officials at the Govern-o-Mat and check on your own health—if you can afford to—at the Health-o-Mat. As Bogost puts it, "The game's goal is not to tell people what to eat or how to exercise, but to demonstrate the complex, interwoven relationships between nutrition and factors like budgets, the physical world, subsidies, and regulations."

Fatworld, an apt example of adversarial design, portrays obesity as a highly complex and multidimensional problem that cannot be solved through personal responsibility alone; this game induces its players to think about reform, not just individual sacrifice. Does it encourage players to exercise? No, but it makes them think. A game like Zamzee, with its obsessive self-tracking, parental surveillance, and monetary rewards, may help users shed a few pounds, but it's unlikely to move us anywhere closer to addressing the various problems and challenges posed by obesity.

Can Content Farms Be Organic?

How can we apply the lessons of adversarial design to how we consume information? After all, it's a very different form of consumption from energy consumption—the focus of most such projects to date. For one, the relationship between energy use and climate change seems direct: the less you consume, the better it is for everyone else. (In reality, of course, it's not so straightforward. Do you really know if it's better for the environment for you to be a driving vegetarian or a cycling carnivore?) It is not like this with information: more pictures of cats, just like more poems, don't necessarily make you into a better or worse person. But once we abandon our fixation with the specific content of information and instead pay attention to how it is produced, once we understand what kinds of political, social, and cultural relations are implicated in its distribution and consumption, we can make more informed decisions and trade-offs. Or, at the very minimum, we can have a debate about those relations.

A picture of a cat may be as good as a poem—but a picture of a cat "borrowed" from another website is probably worse than a picture of a cat snapped personally or bought from its publisher. Or perhaps it isn't, and our copyright laws are outdated and in need of revision. An article about a local town hall meeting might be worse than an article about the peace process in the Middle East. But it might also be better, if one is more likely to read the town hall article and actually do something with it rather than merely express desperation at the Middle East situation and do nothing. Google's personalization algorithms might be worse than a nonpersonalized search. But they may also be better if the algorithms produce more interesting links.

All of these are open-ended questions that do not easily lend themselves to straightforward nudging, self-tracking, and gamification. Why should we be measuring the calorie counts of our articles when we are not even sure that stories about the Middle East are more important than stories about the town hall meeting? Why should we be pushing Google and Facebook to broker introductions to strangers in Africa rather than strangers living next door? Why presume that we have the right answer when we don't? Why, instead of getting users to do what designers and social architects believe to be the right thing, not pursue a different strategy and let users arrive at their own conclusions as to what that "right" thing really is?

We need more erratic appliances that can disrupt our information-consumption habits and jolt us out of our well-established and habitual practices. Why can't our browsers temporarily shut down or fade to black when we open too many windows? (Well, they often do shut down on their own, but only because someone at Microsoft or Firefox didn't foresee our information glut.) Why not tie the availability or presentation of articles on the *New York Times* website to the stock price of the parent company? So, as the stock performs poorly, every fifth word of an article gets deleted or some of the pictures become blurred—at least for those not paying for the online subscription? Why not create a striking visualization of the kinds of information that allow Google to personalize our search results, so that we are more aware of the actual privacy costs of personalization? If we can design the Natural Fuse, can't we design the Natural Filter, where, to get better search results, users are forced to reveal something intimate about themselves or even their friends—perhaps their favorite color or cocktail?

Of course, some might counter that these suggestions are impractical and seem more like art projects than consumer utilities. But there is little reason to believe that the erratic radio set or the Caterpillar extension cord cannot be put into mass production if users decide that they would rather act like grown-ups and not hide from the actual consequences of their actions. As Bruno Latour once wrote, "The unpredictable consequences are the most expected thing on Earth." In this sense, our information habits are not very different from our energy habits: spend too much time getting all your information from various news aggregators and content farms who merely repackage expensive content produced by someone else, and you might be killing the news industry in a way not dissimilar from how leaving gadgets in the standby mode might be quietly and unnecessarily killing someone's carbon offsets.

It's possible that some news aggregators have tremendous value as well—The Huffington Post, to name just one, also provides jobs for many professional reporters—so the "right thing to do" cannot be determined in advance. But this doesn't mean that we cannot better represent and make more visible in our browser windows the economics of news consumption, if only to let us decide what the right thing is. We should not, however, reduce the pursuit of this "right thing" to a mere information calorie count, or allow ourselves to be lured to quality sites through "game mechanics," or task technology companies with steering us toward particular courses of action. Projects that pursue the "right thing" should always have a way through which the very definition of what counts as the "right thing" can be challenged and subverted. Some of this happens anyway as users find a way to hack into their own devices. But this is not enough; designers and technologists should embrace the idea that their goal is not limited to making people use their devices; it's also to make people think with their devices.

The Perils of Willpower

At great risk of oversimplifying things, we can say that one way to make design more self-conscious and more sensitive to critiques of solutionism is to replace its fetish for psychology (and, increasingly, neuroscience) with a fetish for philosophy—both moral and political. Worrying about usability—the chief concern of many designers today—is like counting calories on the sinking *Titanic*. This obsession with usability, with making technology invisible and unobtrusive, has created a world where we are hardly aware of how much energy our households consume. It won't take long until we discover that our smartphones, in their quest for usability, also hide an equally disturbing reality: that massive toxic dumps of electronic waste usually find their way to cash-strapped developing countries.

The triumph of psychology over philosophy is not limited to industrial design; policy designers and social engineers have succumbed to this trend as well—all in the name of science, for psychology and neuroscience are presumed to be more scientific than philosophy simply because they run experiments and tests. But the fact that matters of morality do not lend themselves to easy measurement does not mean we should disregard such concerns and recast them in neuroscientific and psychological terms. Nowhere is this tendency more evident than in discussions of willpower, in which once highly complex and painful decisions about right and wrong are now recast as instances of strong or weak will—which we can address by managing our willpower reserves carefully, much as we do our bank accounts.

The very idea of willpower is enjoying a renaissance in psychology departments and partially explains the recent fascination with nudges and gamification. The basic idea is this: we have a fixed amount of willpower to spend on our decisions, so using it to pursue one course of action might make it harder for us to pursue another. Thus, if we convince ourselves not to have this delicious but high-fat cookie now, we won't be strong enough to choose walking over driving an hour later. We can't decline the cookie and the car simultaneously.

John Tierney and Roy Baumeister assert in their recent book about willpower that "decision making depletes your willpower, and once your willpower is depleted, you're less able to make decisions." A typical experiment takes two groups of hungry students. One is offered some food—radish, cookies, and candy—but told to resist the last two and stick with the radish. The other group is offered no food whatsoever. The two groups are then told to work on puzzles for about twenty minutes. Those who had been tempted with cookies and candies gave up in just eight minutes—much sooner than the other group. Willpower is thus more like "a muscle that could be fatigued through use."

Contrast this with how a philosopher like Peter Singer writes about altruism. Singer, writing in the 1970s, attacks economists who think that altruism is a resource like oil, "the more of which we use the less we have." Singer, in contrast, asks, "Why should we not assume that altruism is more like sexual potency—much used, it constantly renews itself, but if rarely called upon, it will be begin to atrophy and will not be available when needed?" Likewise, philosopher Michael Sandel, echoing Singer, writes that "altruism, generosity, solidarity, and civic spirit are not like commodities that are depleted with use. They are more like muscles that develop and grow stronger with exercise."

Granted, the cookie example above does not involve sacrifice in the name of others, but it's easy to imagine how it might: after all, a failure to cooperate with others—in sharing cookies, for example—might be blamed on low reserves of willpower as well. To use the language of Ivan Illich, willpower is a need that feels entirely natural and can be explained physiologically; altruism and all those other virtues Sandel lumps under "civic spirit" are more like moral requirements that we must come to appreciate and practice. The same act can probably be explained through both paradigms with one key distinction: willpower talk has no way to talk about right and wrong; it has no sophisticated way of differentiating between worthy and unworthy actions that goes beyond the individual. But surely, in deciding whether to pursue a course of action, we need to know much more than just how it will affect our willpower reserves. What do we need all this willpower for? On that, the psychologists are silent.

Tierney and Baumeister are big fans of self-tracking, writing that "now that computers are getting smarter, now that more and more of them are watching us, they're not becoming self-aware (at least not yet) and they're not seizing power from us. Instead, they're enhancing our powers by making us more self-aware." For willpower proponents, self-awareness is key to changing behavior. But notice that they advocate the self-awareness of the individualist consumer, not that of the citizen concerned with common welfare and the broader social, legal, and technological infrastructure in which that welfare is pursued. The self-awareness they want differs greatly from the kind of poetic self-awareness fostered by the Natural Fuse, the Caterpillar extension cord, or the Fatworld computer game.

Tierney and Baumeister's promises do sound very sweet: "Instead of paying doctors and hospitals to repair your body, you can monitor yourself to avoid illness. Instead of heeding marketers' offerings of fast foods and instant pleasures, you can set up your life so that you're bombarded with messages promoting health and conscientiousness." Here is the mind-set of an atomized consumer who couldn't care less about health-care reform but is only preoccupied with maximizing his or her own well-being. Presumably, those who cannot afford self-tracking devices or don't want to self-track due to privacy concerns will be dismissed as unsophisticated technophobes. This is reminiscent of Bogost's shit-crayons metaphor: yes, some of us might find ingenious engineering solutions to resist insidious marketing, but in all this celebration of modern technology, shouldn't we also do something about the marketing itself? Why force consumers to monitor themselves and hone their willpower techniques if we can make it harder for food companies to sell unhealthy food or target children? Instead, political action all but disappears; rather than reforming the system, we just tinker with ourselves and tend to our reservoirs of willpower the way Swiss bankers tend to their vaults.

Another recent book on willpower, *The Willpower Instinct* by Kate McGonigal, takes this individualistic logic even further. McGonigal (whose twin sister, Jane, of *Reality Is Broken* fame, we met in the previous chapter) notes that since we have only limited supplies of willpower and self-control, we might as well not waste them on big and important national projects; rather, we should save them for individual pursuits like dieting. "Rather than hope that we as a nation develop more willpower in order to meet our biggest challenges, our best bet might be to take self-control out of the equation whenever possible—or at least reduce the self-control demands of doing the right thing," she writes. Thus, she endorses the nudges of Cass Sunstein and Richard Thaler, for they "make it easier for people to make good decisions consistent with their values and goals."

In practice this means that instead of confronting open-ended devices like the Caterpillar cord or the Forget Me Not lamp that force us to recognize our own consumption habits, McGonigal would rather have us switch to fully automated systems that simply turn off the standby devices and reading lamps without any human intervention. These new systems will just do the "right" thing even if humans never get a chance to recognize it as such. Here it's important to note the difference between, say, cars that won't allow drunk driving and extension cords that won't tolerate the standby mode. As already discussed, it might seem that as long as users knowingly decide to outsource some of their own decision making to machines, this act might still count as virtuous—at least as long as users are well aware of their own cognitive biases.

However, the technology to fight drunk driving is not implicated in a system of social relations as complex as that of using consumer electronics. It's possible that having such technology in your car might make you less concerned about the very problem of drunk driving, but, arguably, once all cars have such technology, this problem will probably go away. Yet, even if all extension cords turn off devices whenever they enter standby mode, this probably will not solve the energy problem. In fact, it may only give users false feelings of control and self-importance, sanctioning even heavier energy use. That we have cognitive biases should not give us an excuse not to think about complex systems that mediate our behavior;

to outsource all decision making to a smart extension cord may correct for one particular cognitive bias but amplify many others. Not all psychology is useless.

In her analysis of willpower, McGonigal, much like her twin sister in her analysis of gamification, completely sidesteps all moral questions and simply treats them as irrelevant. She argues that we need to stop talking about behavior in moral terms, using words like "virtue," and instead focus on how our individual actions make us feel. "We idealize our own desire to be virtuous, and many people believe that they are most motivated by guilt and shame. But who are we kidding? We are most motivated by getting what we want and avoiding what we don't want. Moralizing a behavior makes us more, not less, likely to feel ambivalent about it." Now, this is a very odd statement: it assumes that citizens do nothing but gorge on chocolate bars and drive SUVs; no other types of behavior are possible. Were the Swiss citizens whom we met in the previous chapter—those who agreed to host a waste dump near their village—motivated by self-interest? If this were the case, then they would have taken the cash. Do people who pick up and throw away someone else's litter in a public park only have their own self-interest in mind?

McGonigal's only argument as to why we should no longer operate in moral terms is the frequent occurrence of the licensing effect, whereby individuals think that they are already doing enough good things—say, by shopping at Whole Foods—so they don't need to worry about climate change. "When you feel like a saint, the idea of self-indulgence doesn't feel wrong. It feels right. . . . And if the only thing motivating your self-control is the desire to be a good enough person, you're going to give in whenever you're already feeling good about yourself," writes McGonigal. But here, once again, we can see that McGonigal's citizens have plenty of rights and virtually no responsibilities. They merely choose between various brands of soap and sushi, resisting those that are unhealthy or too expensive. But she has little to say about those instances in which doing the right thing requires some sacrifice for the common good or where what counts as the "right thing" is not even obvious. And it's not hard to explain her silence: she'd rather have Sunstein and Thaler deal with all those sacrifices by means of nudges, so that no willpower is wasted on them at all.

The growing appeal of self-tracking, nudges, gamification, and even situational crime prevention and digital preemption can only be understood in the broader intellectual context of the last few decades. As already noted, the sad reality is that philosophy, with its preoccupation with virtue and the good life, has been all but defeated by psychology, neuroscience, economics (of the rational-choice variety), and their various combinations, like behavioral economics. Hence, instead of investigating and scrutinizing the motivations for our actions, trying to separate the good ones from the bad, policymakers fixate on giving us the right incentives or removing the option to do the wrong thing altogether. Better safe than sorry, as the saying goes.

Of course, even within philosophy it's no longer fashionable to talk about virtue and the good life; those who do are viewed as die-hard conservatives. Rare exceptions like Michael Sandel and Martha Nussbaum do exist, but they only prove the rule: the politically correct liberal ideology that dominates both our public and our academic debates holds that the individual alone is to decide questions of the good life. As a result, our philosophers have come up with numerous theories about the best way to distribute goods, but they have very little to say about how to value them. Yet, what Michael Sandel has written of markets fully applies to technology as well: "Our reluctance to bring competing conceptions of the good life into political debate has not only impoverished our public discourse; it has also left us ill equipped to contend with the growing role and reach of markets in our lives."

It's not that self-tracking and gamification make our lives less pleasant—for all we know, we might be enjoying the games we play; it's that they make our lives less meaningful, less compatible with the quirks and demands of the human condition. Such schemes might still be stunting our personal and political growth, even if they do allow food companies to launch new nutritional supplements with the help of our bodies and technology companies to test their new apps with our fingers. Is it naïve to suppose that there's more to life than tracking the efficiency of nutritional supplements and testing the performance of gaming apps?

On Frictionless Traps

Solutionism will rule supreme until designers, architects, and engineers (of both social and technological varieties) abandon simplistic models of what it's like to be human. Despite what Facebook's Sheryl Sandberg believes, we do not bring our stable, authentic self to technologies we use, only to recover it in the same mint condition ten years later. Technologies actively shape our notion of the self; they even define how and what we think about it. They shape the contours of what we believe to be negotiable and nonnegotiable; they define the structure and tempo of our self-experimentation. If our entire life is optimized in accordance with situational crime prevention schemes, if all temptation is eliminated, if we have no choice but to do the right thing always, then the spiritual pasture where our self is to be cultivated shrinks considerably.

If we adopt a dynamic view of selfhood as something that emerges only slowly and gradually—both in the context of individual self-development and across generations in the broader historical context—then we are likely to pay more attention not just to what we do and don't do but also to how we do and don't do it. In other words, if the self itself is taken to be contingent and always in flux, then the process through which it emerges is as important as the actions that it produces. Under this approach, the processes and procedures through which we act are as important as the outcomes of our actions, for only through a mutual appreciation and tension between the two do we become who we are.

A scheme that wants to get children to help senior citizens by awarding them badges and game points is likely to produce very different children than a scheme that appeals to their civic duty, even if both schemes yield the same results. The problem with simplistic models imported from economics and rational-choice theory is that, whenever they tackle a novel case, they start with a new set of abstract, independent, and ahistorical citizens. Thus, children who were just helping senior citizens by playing games are forgotten and swept away, and a new set of children—like so many widgets and coconuts—is mustered up to engage in some different task, perhaps to solve math puzzles after resisting the cookies. But, of course, children can't reboot the way computers can; we have the same children doing both—and their experiences accumulate rather than cancel each other out. Constructing a world preoccupied only with the most efficient outcomes—rather than with the processes through which those outcomes are achieved—is not likely to make them aware of the depth of human passion, dignity, and respect. We don't earn our dignity by collecting badges; we do it by behaving in a dignified manner, often in situations in which we have other options. Tinker with this spiritual pasture, and those options might go away—along with the very possibility of dignity.

Other thinkers have also recognized the importance of processes, frameworks, and procedures in enabling human flourishing and democratic debate. Ian Bogost, writing on video games, notes that rather than their content, what he calls their "procedural logic" is most conducive to deliberation. "Procedural media like videogames get to the heart of things by mounting arguments about the processes inherent in them," writes Bogost. "When we create videogames, we are making claims about these processes, which ones we celebrate, which ones we ignore, which ones we want to question. When we play these games, we interrogate those claims, we consider them, incorporate them into our lives, and carry them forward into our future experiences."

Bogost gives the example of the Howard Dean for Iowa Game—a game produced by the Howard Dean campaign during the 2004 presidential election. The goal is to recruit as many volunteers to the Dean camp as possible; this recruitment is its key process. As you play the game, you are likely to conclude that politics is just a numbers game, regardless of the issues that candidates campaign on: the more volunteers you recruit and the more money you raise, the higher the odds of winning. Was this game a success? Well, it didn't result in more real-world money or support for Dean's campaign, then perhaps it wasn't. But Bogost argues that this might be the wrong benchmark. "Rather than producing assent, which can be measured with a yea or nay, the game produces deliberation, which implies neither immediate assent nor dissent." This game lends itself to a critique of politics and democratic debate. A game that has you clicking a news headline only to receive a badge does not.

Likewise, legal theorist Julie Cohen has highlighted the importance of processes and structures in the context of copyright policing and privacy. Some of those structures will be barriers and boundaries, which, despite what many geeks believe, are also important for the self to emerge. "Computer scientists and technology designers are inclined to view technical barriers to interoperability as artificial constraints to be overcome," writes Cohen. She thinks that this conviction partly derives from geeks' "commitment to seamless, interoperable design that is both intellectual and aesthetic, and that is deeply internalized in the technoculture of computer science and engineering." Given Facebook's fixation on frictionless sharing (and Microsoft's fixation on frictionless capitalism almost two decades earlier), as well as Apple's promise of "seamless" computing, Cohen might well be right. But, as she is also quick to point out, "the question is not whether constraints should exist at all, but how to locate them in a way that most effectively promotes all aspects of human flourishing. Wherever they are located, they will be challenged, but that does not necessarily make all constraints illegitimate."

We gain the ability to erect and maintain such constraints around the spaces where our self can emerge with the help of privacy, which, thanks to the proliferation of self-tracking, lifelogging, and ubiquitous computing, is now under constant assault. It's these constraints that mark the zone of our spiritual pasture and allow our individuality to emerge—without them, we'll be just part of the herd. The goal of privacy is not to protect some stable self from erosion but to create boundaries where this self can emerge, mutate, and stabilize. What matters here is the framework—or the procedure—rather than the outcome or the substance. Limits and constraints, in other words, can be productive—even if the entire conceit of "the Internet" suggests otherwise.

Something similar can be said about authenticity: we achieve it not by trying to express some inner truth about ourselves (Rousseau debunked this account of authenticity back in the eighteenth century) but by trying to behave autonomously and consistently within the constraints—of norms and tradition—erected by other members of the group we belong to. As philosopher Bernard Williams argues in *Truth and Truthfulness*, authenticity as a project only makes sense when viewed against such social constraints; without them, that project loses all its meaning. For all the freedom that such an option provides, one can't be authentic if born and raised alone on a desert island.

Thus, contra Sheryl Sandberg, instead of assuming that Facebook simply allows us to express our authentic selves, we should inquire into how Facebook mediates the very conditions of authenticity, sometimes by erecting new barriers and constraints but, much more often, by destroying them.

Digital technology has greatly expanded the windows and doors in our own little rooms for self-experimentation—but we are now at a point where these rooms are on the verge of turning into glass houses. Historian of science Peter Galison and legal scholar Martha Minow even warn of a technologically and legally driven "downward spiral" that "could affect the very sense of self people have—the sense of room for self-expression and experimentation, the sense of dignity and composure, the sense of ease and relief from public presentation."

That all these concepts have their own histories and, thus, should not be treated as immutable should not distract us from the urgent task of recognizing the enabling roles they play in our lives and trying to defend them. Perhaps it's time to entertain the possibility that when people surrender their privacy—in exchange for coupons or more personalized and effective searching—they are giving up far more than they realize, giving away not just something they own but something that should not be for sale. We need some kind of Natural Fuse project for privacy and dignity: so many of us are happy to trade our privacy for better search because the consequences of doing so are not fully visible to us. We don't know how our decision to release our health information into the wild will affect someone else with an illness, and unless such considerations about that person are brought to bear on us, we are not likely to factor in them into our decision making.

This is hardly surprising, for the process through which our own self emerges remains barely traceable, and many of us probably still believe that we have a stable, fully autonomous self that never changes anyway. But while we are waiting for such a project to emerge, perhaps it's wise to heed Galison and Minow's advice, ditch simplistic utilitarian theories, and preserve some space where the self can emerge and flourish. As they write, "Given the complexity of the self, trying to reduce the privacy concept to a purely utilitarian framework is like steamrolling a statue to capture its essence in the simpler space of the two-dimensional plane. Such flattening may make security and privacy look like a simple balancing act—twelve ounces of each on the two sides of the scale—but it does nothing to acknowledge the space people need to deliberate, to try out new ways of acting or different ways of speaking."

A deeper appreciation of the dynamic and emergent nature of the self can also help us better evaluate many emerging technologies. Consider, for example, automated profiling, which relies on data-mining techniques to predict certain things about us and perhaps use such knowledge to better customize the websites we browse or the online ads we receive. In his celebrated book *Oneself as Another*, French philosopher Paul Ricoeur, argues that our sense of self is partly constructed by looking at ourselves from a distance by taking on someone else's perspective. To act, we need to anticipate how others anticipate us and try to predict what meanings they attribute to our behavior. Our identity emerges as we reject or self-consciously embrace what we believe others believe about us. But, as Belgian legal philosopher Mireille Hildebrandt, following Ricoeur, points out, when our profiles are built by computer systems rather than real people, "we have no access to these profiles. We cannot question them, contest their application, or amend their content as one can remonstrate with a human person who profiles us."

Of course, we do our best to project the best portrait of ourselves via Facebook—which, ironically, may simply be the consequence of the fear that others will misread us if we post no profile at all—but we may no longer have the capacity to anticipate how others will anticipate us, for we have little idea about not just what kinds of data about us are floating around the Web but what kinds of insights can be gleaned from such data with different algorithms. This seems like a major shift in how our identity is constructed—and there's little reason to believe that such uncertainty will make for better humans.

Likewise, if we start with the premise that being in command of your own ship is constitutive of being human, then online profiling may be problematic for another reason. Hildebrandt offers an excellent example. Suppose you are contemplating becoming vegetarian and visit a few websites on the subject. The profiling software—which may belong to Facebook or Google or any other online intermediary—correctly infers your aspirations and estimates that there's an 83 percent chance that you will stop eating meat within the coming month.

Whoever operates the software then sells this information to the industry association of meat producers. All of a sudden, you start receiving free samples of excellent meat while ads about the benefits of eating beef follow you everywhere on "the Internet." This happens because the profiling software has calculated that sustained exposure to thoughts about meat will reduce the chance that you will stop eating meat by 23 percent, which—magic!—you decide not to do in the end.

You, of course, remain unaware of the connection between your vegetarian aspirations and the free meat samples in your fridge. You seem to be exercising autonomy while, in reality, you aren't: while you believe you are making conscious choices, parties you are not even aware of are actually influencing them invisibly. And the Internet companies are not ashamed to acknowledge their own role in all of this. FetchBack, a company that seeks to bombard consumers with ads for products they once exhibited an online interest in, puts it this way: "When prospects leave [a company's] site and browse the Internet, [the site's] ads will display on other sites they visit, keeping [the original] website in their peripheral vision and top of mind." When something is deliberately kept in your peripheral vision without you realizing it, it's perhaps a good time to question your own autonomy.

If all that matters is getting you to behave in a manner desired by the social engineer—whether it's to stop wasting energy or eat healthy food or care for the elderly—then there's no need to worry about any such loss of autonomy. As long as the right response is solicited, the intervention counts as a success. But there's something

profoundly disgusting about this approach, for it not only tricks—
rather than talks—us into doing the right thing but also gives us
a fake feeling of mastery over our own actions. This illusion, in
turn, precludes us from questioning the ends that the social engineer
is pursuing, no matter how benign they may be.

None of this is to deny that technology—from sensors to
games—can be used to improve the human condition; as we have
seen, it can provoke debate and lead us to question dominant social
and political norms. But this can happen only if our geeks, designers,
and social engineers take the time to study what makes us human
in the first place. Trying to improve the human condition by first
assuming that humans are like robots is not going to get us very far.

Technologies and Truths

Designers and policy engineers get even weirder ideas once they
fall for Internet-centrism and the technological defeatism that it
generates. Note how Google's privacy counsel, Peter Fleischer, dis-
misses concerns about the longevity of data posted online, which,
according to some critics, does not reflect how humans usually remember. "Should the Internet be re-wired to be more like the human brain? . . . I guess this means the Internet should have
gradations between memory, and sort of hazy memories, and forgetting. Well, computers don't work that way. This part of the debate is sociological and psychological, but I don't see a place for it
in the world of computers," writes Fleischer.

But who said that computers don't work that way? It might
be true that they don't work that way now, but this needn't be the
case forever. An interesting project, Last Great Thing, asked people,
for twenty days only, to share something interesting they found
online. Each link lasted for a day and then disappeared completely;
there was no archive, so it was important to pay attention to the
site every day (after the experiment ended, the team behind it did
put together an archive). There was also no way to link to anything. Yes, it was a project built on a different logic from the save-
everything mentality of Google. But Last Great Thing is not
necessarily inferior, especially if it helps to bring attention to important articles that might otherwise go unnoticed.

How our digital technologies unfold in the future will be a factor not of how "the Internet" works or how computers work but of how we choose to make them work. Some will need to rely on an ethic of openness and transparency; others, on an ethic of secrecy and opacity. Some will foster collaboration; others will foster individuality and solitude. There's no great logic to "the Internet"; contrary to what Kevin Kelly and others like him believe, "the Internet" tells us nothing. The important transformations that we are living through—self-tracking, lifelogging, nudges, gamification, and digital preemption—would not have been possible on such a grand scale fifty or even twenty years ago. But the institutional and political logics—and the plural here is deliberate, for it would be incorrect to blame them on capitalism or neoliberalism or globalization—that are quietly inserting these approaches into the policymaking tool kit are hardly novel and don't have all that much to do with "the Internet."

If, like some of the most prominent adherents of Internet-centrism, we believe that Steve Jobs was the greatest enemy of freedom or creativity, we risk misunderstanding—and even understating—the enemy. To talk about gamification without also discussing B. F. Skinner's behaviorism or to talk about digital preemption without bring up rational-choice theory and the Chicago school of economics seems misguided; the nearly universal excitement about "the Internet," mobile phones, and Wikipedia distracts us from noticing that many of the underlying phenomena are anything but new. As someone who grew up in the final years of the Soviet Union, even I remember the penchant that Soviet managers had for gamification: students were shipped to the fields to harvest wheat or potatoes, and since the motivation was lacking, they too were assigned points and badges. That today points are assigned via the mobile phone and no one has to go to the fields doesn't fundamentally alter the nature of the practice. We shouldn't let the fake novelty of these phenomena mislead us into thinking that we ought to wait and see how they will play out: we have done all the waiting already—and the picture that has emerged is anything but pretty.

There is a tendency to think of geeks and engineers as conservative or, at least, as resistant to change: they just follow orders and build on demand. This is an extremely wrongheaded view, for engineers are anything but. Engineering always entails a revolutionary dimension as it refuses to accept the current state of affairs as the only one possible. As historian Ken Alder once put it, "Engineering operates on a simple, but radical assumption: that the present is nothing more than the raw material from which to construct a better future. In this process, no existing arrangement is to be considered sacrosanct, everything is to be examined in the light of present aspirations, and all practices refashioned according to the dictates of reason." The problem with engineers is not that they are conservative; it's that they are not conservative enough. For them, everything is negotiable—dignity and autonomy included.

To quote Bernard Crick once again, "Boredom with established truths is a great enemy of free men." Perhaps it wouldn't be such a bad thing for our newly empowered geeks and engineers to recognize that there are good reasons not to run our politics as a startup; that our politicians face competing demands and that the quest to eradicate lies and hypocrisy may do more harm than good; that there are good reasons to value subjective but high-quality criticism, even if it doesn't stem from the "wisdom of crowds"; that the dream of flawless communication across nations may not only be unachievable but also undesirable; that humans are complex and occasionally irrational creatures who care about why they do certain things as much as they care about what it is they are doing; that numbers often tell us less than we think and quantification as such might actually thwart reforms.

But even established truths do get overturned eventually. Ideally, this happens after extensive debate and deliberation. Designers and social engineers don't have to become unambitious bureaucrats scared of innovating, but perhaps they could practice innovation in a different key. The goal of their interventions—in both products and policies—should be not just to provide answers but also to make it easier to pose new questions. If technological fixes are inevitable, and if some forms of solutionism cannot be avoided, let us at least make sure that this solutionism is of the self-reflexive, perhaps even neurotic, kind. Only through radical self-doubt can solutionism transcend its inherent limitations.

Postscript

As I was setting out to write this book, I held two truths to be self-evident. First, I believed that a good, critical account of "the Internet" could be—nay, should be—provided without ever using it as an explanans, only as an explanandum. In simpler terms, "the Internet" cannot be invoked to explain other things, if only because it itself needs explanation. Second, I suspected that the readability of a book is inversely proportional to the number of obscure "isms" that it coins. As I survey the final product, I do feel a certain disappointment. While I did stay faithful to the spirit of the first dictum, I failed in the second one miserably. Well, perhaps there is an ism to describe that?

While most trade books these days desperately seek to feature One Big Idea, I've bucked the trend and pursued a study of two middle-sized ideas—Internet-centrism and solutionism—that feed on each other in complex and often unpredictable ways. I wish I could say that I have a magic formula—or at least a glitzy Power-Point slide—to accurately describe their relationship. Alas, I haven't found it yet; nor do I believe it exists. These concepts play very different roles in different contexts, be it preventing crime, improving politics, fighting obesity, or saving the planet. To observe them in action, I tried to peer into as many areas as I could, but I know that my study is far from thorough; entire books could be written on the interplay between solutionism and Internet-centrism in the contexts of online education or economic development or even within each of the fields I did look at.

I concluded my previous book, *The Net Delusion*, with a lengthy discussion of so-called "wicked problems" that don't have neat and precise solutions. (Just how bad are "wicked" problems? We don't even know how to define them; forget about recognizing when they have been solved.) It seemed to me that modern authoritarianism—the target of so many "Internet freedom" campaigns—was one such genuinely hard and barely tractable problem. To expect that a vague concept like "Internet freedom" could help unseat highly sophisticated authoritarian regimes seemed extremely naïve, if not outright dangerous.

Back when I was finishing that first book in 2010, I was awed both by the immensity of the challenge of unseating dictators—it probably helped that I hail from Belarus, that oasis of tolerance in the middle of Europe—and the sheer callousness and utopianism with which this project was pursued in Washington and some European capitals. In retrospect, I realize just how lucky I was to address a problem that no one—not even Eastern European curmudgeons like me—would dare deny; left, right, or center, we all seem to agree that there are plenty of awful dictators out there, and the world would surely be better off without them. How we get to recognize all these truths is subject for debate—of course, it would be nice if it's 99 percent blogs and 1 percent bombs, not vice versa—but few disagree with the basic premise of that project: authoritarianism is real and not particularly enjoyable for anyone involved.

I don't have the luxury of tackling a clear-cut issue in the current book in that I argue that many circumstances that solutionists and Internet-centrists see as problems may not be problems at all; gone is the moral simplicity of fighting authoritarianism. In this book, what's truly wicked are not the problems—those may not even exist—but the solutions proposed to address them. That so much of our cultural life is inefficient or that our politicians are hypocrites or that bipartisanship slows down the political process or that crime rates are not yet zero—all of these issues might be problematic in some limited sense, but they do not necessarily add up to a problem worth solving—any more than having a soccer match that lasts for ninety minutes rather than an eternity and features twenty-two people instead of everyone at the stadium is a problem to be solved. We see them as problems, I have argued, more because of the sheer awesomeness of our digital tools than due to the genuine need to rid our public life of these incoherencies and imperfections. At its most simple, this book argues that perfect is the enemy of good, that sometimes good is good enough, and that no matter what tool we are holding in our hands, both these statements still hold.

I have little doubt that the solutionist impulse, in its various mutations, will survive the current excitement over "the Internet" and latch on to some later ideology or political project. As confident as I am in my ability to take down unworthy ideas, I don't think I can do much about solutionism—at least, no more than I can do something about utopianism or romanticism. Occasionally, they might have their uses, but all three also have a long history of abuse.

While we can't rid the world of people who want to "fix" politics, we can at least ridicule those who want to do so by subjecting politics to "lessons learned" from Wikipedia or even "the Internet" as a whole. While we can't rid ourselves of solutionism, we can try to rid ourselves of Internet-centrism, thereby making certain solutionist schemes harder to advocate and, hopefully, impossible to implement.

On the odd chance that this book succeeds, its greatest contribution to the public debate might lie in redrawing the front lines of the intellectual battles about digital technologies. Those front lines will separate a host of Internet thinkers who are convinced that "the Internet" is a useful analytical category that tells us something important about how the world really works from a group of post-Internet thinkers who see "the Internet," despite its undeniable physicality, as a socially constructed concept that could perhaps be studied by sociologists, historians, and anthropologists—much as they study the public life of ideas such as "science," "class" or "Darwinism"—but that tells us nothing about how the world works and even less about how it should work. The former group thinks that "the Internet" is the key to solving some of the greatest policy puzzles of the day; the latter thinks that "the Internet" is only confusing policymakers more and that the sooner digital activists learn how to make their arguments without appealing to "the Internet," the better.

Since my own theoretical sympathies should be quite clear by now—I'm with the second camp, in case you fell asleep at the wheel—I won't bore you with the details of how I think the first camp will come down in flames. Instead, I'd rather use this opportunity to articulate a very broad outline of what this second, post-Internet approach to technology might look like and what its preoccupations might be.

First, it would abstain from the highly emotional and polemical discussions over what "the Net" or even "social media" do to our brains, freedom, and dictators. This post-Internet approach is much more interested in the world of trash bins and parking meters in our mundane everyday lives than in the role of Twitter in the Arab Spring—and not because it's parochial in outlook but because it doesn't believe in the power of such ambitious and ambiguous questions. The role of Twitter's algorithms in highlighting the #Jan25 hash tag, which brought some global attention to the cause of the protesters in Tahrir Square, on the other hand, is fair game. Will a viral TED talk emerge out of this second approach? Probably not; its findings won't be very sexy, and it won't default to some banal abstract truth about "democracy" or the "Middle East." On the whole, though, this highly empirical but small-scale approach will probably tell us more about the opportunities and limitations of digital technologies than the entire "Does social media cause revolutions?" debate that wasted so much of everyone's time— including mine—in early 2011.

Those pursuing this post-Internet approach will be extremely cautious—even skeptical—about any causality claims made with respect to digital technologies. They will recognize that, more often than not, these technologies are not the causes of the world we live in but rather its consequences. The post-Internet approach will not treat these digital technologies as if they fell from the sky and we should therefore not—God forbid—question their origins and only study their impact. Instead, those relying on a post-Internet approach will trace how these technologies are produced, what voices and ideologies are silenced in their production and dissemination, and how the marketing literature surrounding these technologies taps into the zeitgeist to make them look inevitable.

Internet theorists looking at, say, MP3 technology will think "Napster"—that quintessential "Internet technology"—and start their account from the mid-1990s; post-Internet theorists looking at MP3 technology will think of the history of sound compression and start their account in the 1910s (as Jonathan Sterne has done in his recent *MP3: The Meaning of a Format*). Internet theorists studying search engines will begin with Stanford and Google perhaps, with a cursory mention of Vannevar Bush's memex; post-Internet theorists will look much further back than that, unearthing such obscure figures as Albert Kahn (and his effort to create "The Archives of the Planet" through photographs), as well as Paul Otlet and Henri La Fontaine with their Mundaneum, an attempt to gather all the world's knowledge. This list can go on indefinitely, but the trend is clear: one unexpected benefit of a post-Internet approach is that it deflates the shallow and historically illiterate accounts that dominate so much of our technology debate and opens them to much more varied, rich, and historically important experiences.

Once we realize that for the last hundred years or so virtually every generation has felt like it was on the edge of a technological revolution—be it the telegraph age, the radio age, the plastic age, the nuclear age, or the television age—maintaining the myth that our own period is unique and exceptional will hopefully become much harder. Perhaps, this will make it all but impossible for solutionists to mobilize revolutionary rhetoric to justify their radical plans to the public. Once we move to a post-Internet world, there is a small chance that our technology pundits (and perhaps even some academics) will no longer get away with proclaiming something a revolution and then walking away without supplying good, empirical evidence—as if that revolution were so self-evident and no further proof was needed.

I too used to be one of those people—albeit very briefly—sometime between 2005 and 2007. I remember perfectly the thrill that comes from thinking that the lessons of Wikipedia or peer-to-peer networking or Friendster or Skype could and should be applied absolutely everywhere. It's a very powerful set of hammers, and plenty of people—many of them in Silicon Valley—are dying to hear you cry, "Nail!" regardless of what you are looking at. Thinking that you are living through a revolution and hold the key to how it will unfold is, I confess, rather intoxicating. So I can relate to those Internet thinkers who feel extremely comfortable with the current state of debate, even though I can probably not forgive them.

This book, I hope, has shown that most Internet theorists venerate an imaginary god of their own creation and live in denial.

Secularizing our technology debate and cleansing it of the pernicious influence of Internet-centrism is by far the most important
task that technology intellectuals face today. Everything else—
especially particular policies—hinges on how such secularization
proceeds, if it does so at all. Consider one example from what used
to be my own favorite field: what exactly is the point of operating
with a term like "Internet freedom" if the very idea of "the Internet"
is contested and full of ambiguity? Discussing the particulars of
the "Internet freedom agenda" without resolving the many con-
tradictions in its initial formulation seems counterproductive to
me, as it might only legitimize that concept further.

Once our debate moves into post-Internet territory, many of
the technophobic, ahistorical accounts will hopefully become harder
to pull off as well. If "the Internet" is no longer seen as a unified
force that acts on our brains or our culture, any account of what
digital technologies do to our neurons or books will need to get
empirical and start talking about individual technologies and individual practices, perhaps with a nod to how such practices evolved
and coped in the past. So far, we get none of that: we are told that
"the Net" is rewiring our brains, which is not at all a good starting
point for debate. After all, so what if it's rewiring our brains? And
what should we do about "the Net" anyway? It stirs fears alright,
but we quickly get mired in cheap populism.

If technophobic accounts do become harder to produce, then
there's also a small chance we will be able to have a meaningful debate about not just the appropriateness of technological fixes to a
given problem but also about the desirability of *particular* technological fixes. Once we can't reject technology outright, we'll need
to explain why some fixes are better than others. If it makes us
think and ask questions, it is a worthy enterprise all by itself.

Technology is not the enemy; our enemy is the romantic and
revolutionary problem solver who resides within. We can do nothing to tame that little creature, but we can do a lot to tame its favorite weapon: "the Internet." Let's do that while we can—it would
be deeply ironic if humanity were to die in the crossfire as its
problem solvers attempted to transport that very humanity to a
trouble-free world.

Notes

Introduction

vii **"In an age of advanced technology"**: quoted in Aldous Huxley, *Brave New World* (Cutchogue, NY: Buccaneer Books, 1995), xii.

vii **"Complexity is a solvable problem"**: quoted in Jeff Jarvis, "Rewired Youth?," Buzz Machine, February 29, 2012, http://buzzmachine.com/2012/02/29/rewired-youth.

vii **"Technology is not really about hardware"**: quoted in Zach Church, "Google's Schmidt: 'Global Mind' Offers New Opportunities," MIT News Office, November 15, 2011, http://web.mit.edu/newsoffice/2011/schmidt-event-1115.html.

vii **"make the world more open and connected"**: United States Securities and Exchange Commission, Form S-1, Registration Statement, SEC, February 1, 2012, http://www.sec.gov/Archives/edgar/data/1326801/000119312512034517/d287954ds1.htm, 70.

vii **"We don't wake up in the morning"**: ibid., 69.

vii **"There are a lot of really big issues"**: see Mark Zuckerman interview with Sarah Lacy at SXSW 2008. Video is available at http://allfacebook.com/mark-zuckerberg-sarah-lacy-interview-video_b1063.

ix **those who've never bothered to vote:** While I initially wrote this sentence in jest, the gamification of voting has, in fact, already been proposed. See Gabe Zicherman, "Rethinking Elections with Gamification," The Huffington Post, November 22, 2012, http://www.huffingtonpost.com/gabe-zicherman/improve-voter-turn-out_b_2127459.html.

Chapter One: Solutionism and Its Discontents

1 **"In the future, people will spend"**: Eric Schmidt, "The World Around Us," speech delivered at Zeitgeist 2012 conference, October 15, 2012, available at http://www.youtube.com/watch?v=kUHF43xjMJM.

1 **"'Solutionism' . . . is indeed the name of the game"**: quoted in Gilles Paquet, *The New Geo-Governance: A Baroque Approach* (Ottawa: University of Ottawa Press, 2005), 315.

1 **"The overriding question"**: Paul Dourish and Scott D. Mainwaring, "UbiComp's Colonial Impulse," in *Proceedings of the 2012 ACM Conference on Ubiquitous Computing*, UbiComp '12 (New York: ACM, 2012), 133–142. http://doi.acm.org/10.1145/2370216.2370238, 6.

1 **While Mark Zuckerberg insists:** see, e.g., Zuckerberg's interview with Charlie Rose: "Exclusive Interview with Facebook Leadership: Mark Zuckerberg, CEO/Co-Founder and Sheryl Sandberg, COO," *Charlie Rose*, November 7, 2011, http://www.charlierose.com/view/interview/11981.

2 **BinCam, a new project from researchers in Britain and Germany:** my account of Bin-Cam is based on a paper written by its designers. See Anja Thieme et al., "'We've Bin Watching You': Designing for Reflection and Social Persuasion to Promote Sustainable Lifestyles," in *Proceedings of the SIGCHI Conference on Human Factors in Computing Systems* (New York: ACM, 2012), 2337–2346. Also available at http://doi.acm.org/10.1145/2207676.2208394.

3 **Today we already have smart mirrors**: Daisuke Wakabayashi, "Mirrors That Double as Computers," *Wall Street Journal*, September 25, 2012, http://online.wsj.com/article/SB10000872396390444358804578016562948686482.html.

4   **British designer-cum-activist Chris Adams:** my discussion of Adams's work owes much to two papers by Noortje Marres, in which I first discovered it. See Noortje Marres, "The Costs of Public Involvement: Everyday Devices of Carbon Accounting and the Materialization of Participation," *Economy and Society* 40, no. 4 (2011): 510–533, and Noortje Marres, "The Environmental Teapot and Other Loaded Household Objects: Reconnecting the Politics of Technology, Issues and Things," forthcoming in *Objects and Materials: A Routledge Companion*, ed. Penelope Harvey et al. (London and New York: Routledge, 2013).

4   **smart carpets and smart bells that can detect when someone has fallen over:** on carpets, see Douglas Heaven, "Smart Carpet Detects Falls and Strange Footsteps," Newscientist.com, September 4, 2012, http://www.newscientist.com/blogs/onepercent /2012/09/smart-carpet-detects-falls-a.html; on bells, see Karin Slyker, "New Technology Could Detect a Fall Before It Happens," Texas Tech Today, August 22, 2012, http:// today.ttu.edu/2012/08/new-technology-could-detect-a-fall-before-it-happens.

4   **a start-up with the charming name of BigBelly Solar:** see Mike Wheatley, "Big Data Bins Hope to Revolutionize Waste Collection," Silicon Angle, October 11, 2012, http:// siliconangle.com/blog/2012/10/11/big-data-bins-hope-to-revolutionize-waste-collection.

4   **city officials in Boston have been testing Street Bump:** Rodrique Ngowi, "App Detects Potholes, Alerts Boston City Officials," Associated Press, July 12, 2012, http://big story.ap.org/article/app-detects-potholes-alerts-boston-city-officials.

5   **Google relies on GPS-enabled Android phones:** for more, see Chris Crum, "Google Maps Gives Live Traffic Updates to a Lot More Cities," WebProNews, August 7, 2012, http://www.webpronews.com/google-maps-gives-live-traffic-updates-to-a-lot-more-cities -2012–08.

5   **"the will to improve":** Tania Murray Li, *The Will to Improve: Governmentality, Development, and the Practice of Politics* (Durham, NC: Duke University Press Books, 2007).

6   **"for the answer before the questions have been fully asked":** Michael Dobbins, *Urban Design and People*, 1st ed. (New York: Wiley, 2009), 182.

6   **How problems are composed:** on the notion of "composition," see Bruno Latour, "An Attempt at a 'Compositionist Manifesto,'" *New Literary History* 41, no. 3 (2010): 471–490.

6   **a subject I address at length in *The Net Delusion*:** Evgeny Morozov, *The Net Delusion: The Dark Side of Internet Freedom* (New York: PublicAffairs, 2012), 308–311.

6   **In his influential book *The Rhetoric of Reaction*:** Albert O. Hirschman, *The Rhetoric of Reaction: Perversity, Futility, Jeopardy* (Cambridge, MA: Belknap Press of Harvard University Press, 1991).

8   **"when the utopian writers deal with work":** Thomas Steven Molnar, *Utopia: The Perennial Heresy* (London: Tom Stacey Ltd., 1972), 230.

8   **"Education is not the transmission of information or ideas":** Pamela Hieronymi, "Don't Confuse Technology with College Teaching," *Chronicle of Higher Education*, August 13, 2012, http://chronicle.com/article/Dont-Confuse-Technology-With/133551.

9   **"educational equivalent of a highly trained professor":** Adam F. Falk, "In Defense of the Living, Breathing Professor," *Wall Street Journal*, August 28, 2012, http://online.wsj .com/article/SB10000872396390444327204577615592746799900.html.

9   **"is to deny the most significant purposes of education":** ibid.

10   **"It might be supposed that an ignorant man":** Michael Oakeshott, "Political Education," in *Rationalism in Politics and Other Essays*, exp. ed. (Indianapolis: Liberty Fund, 1991), 52.

10   **"A cook . . . is not a man who first has a vision of a pie":** Michael Oakeshott, "The Idea of a University," *Academic Questions* 17, no. 1 (2004): 23.

10   **"the book speaks only to those who know already":** Oakeshott, "Political Education."

11   what's going on in our kitchens: this section draws considerably on an earlier article of mine: Evgeny Morozov, "Stay Out of My Kitchen, Robots," Slate, August 27, 2012,

http://www.slate.com/articles/technology/future_tense/2012/08/why_you_don_t_want_a
_robot_in_your_kitchen.html.

11 **British magazine *New Scientist* recently covered:** Jacob Aron, "Smart Kitchens Keep
Novice Chefs on Track," *New Scientist* 215, no. 2877 (August 11, 2012): 17, http://
www.newscientist.com/article/mg21528774.900-augmented-reality-kitchens-keep-novice
-chefs-on-track.html.

11 **"For example, if the system detects sugar pouring into a bowl":** ibid.

14 **"life, the universe and everything":** reference to Douglas Adams, *Life, the Universe and
Everything* (Los Angeles, CA: Del Rey, 1995).

14 **In the afterword to my first book, *The Net Delusion*:** Morozov, *The Net Delusion*, 337.

14 **French philosopher Bruno Latour:** Bruno Latour, *The Pasteurization of France* (Cambridge, MA: Harvard University Press, 1993), 15.

15 ***What Would Google Do?*:** Jeff Jarvis, *What Would Google Do?*, 1st ed. (New York: Harper-
Collins, 2009).

16 **Following the work of Latour and Thomas Kuhn:** see Bruno Latour, *Science in Action*
(Cambridge, MA: Harvard University Press, 1987), and Thomas Kuhn, *The Structure of
Scientific Revolutions*, 3rd ed. (Chicago: University of Chicago Press, 1996).

Chapter 2: The Nonsense of "the Internet"—and How to Stop It

17 **"The internet is not territory to be conquered":** Nicholas Mendoza, "Metal, Code,
Flesh: Why we Need a 'Rights of the Internet' Declaration," February 15, 2012, AlJazeera
.com, http://www.aljazeera.com/indepth/opinion/2012/02/201228715322807.html.

17 **"What made Blockbuster close?":** Eric Snider, "Cranky Chicagoan: 'The Internet Is Ruining Film Criticism!,'" Moviefone, April 15, 2010, http://blog.moviefone.com/2010/
04/15/cranky-chicagoan-the-internet-is-ruining-film-criticism.

17 **"The Next Battle for Internet Freedom":** Rick Kelly, "The Next Battle for Internet Freedom Could Be over 3D Printing," TechCrunch, August 26, 2012, http://techcrunch
.com/2012/08/26/the-next-battle-for-internet-freedom-could-be-over-3d-printing.

18 **"All too many U.S. lawmakers are barely":** Bill Snyder, "Facial Recognition Abuse Is
Bad, Government Regulation Even Worse," CIO, July 23, 2012, http://blogs.cio.com
/privacy/17254/facial-recognition-abuse-bad-government-regulation-even-worse.

18 **That facial-recognition technology developed:** see Kelly A. Gates, *Our Biometric Future:
Facial Recognition Technology and the Culture of Surveillance* (New York: New York University Press, 2011).

19 **a common modern dissonance:** see Bruno Latour, *We Have Never Been Modern* (Cambridge, MA: Harvard University Press, 1993).

19 **"to be fed the way the Net fed it":** Nicholas Carr, *The Shallows: What the Internet Is
Doing to Our Brains* (New York: W. W. Norton & Company, 2011), 16.

19 **"the Net . . . provides a high-speed system":** ibid., 117.

20 **McLuhan went as far as to calculate sense ratios:** see Marshall McLuhan, *The Gutenberg
Galaxy: The Making of Typographic Man* (Toronto: University of Toronto Press, 2011), 28.

20 **they can do so many other things in so many different ways:** see Ian Bogost, *How to
Do Things with Videogames* (Minneapolis: University of Minnesota Press, 2011).

20 **"My interest is description, not prescription":** Felix Gillette, "Feats of Clay," *New York
Observer*, June 9, 2010, http://observer.com/2010/06/feats-of-clay.

21 **"the network . . . is not going away":** Larry Lessig, "Against Transparency," *The New
Republic*, October 2009, http://www.tnr.com/article/books-and-arts/against-transparency.

22 **To paraphrase Frederic Jameson on capitalism:** for Jameson's original quote, "Someone
once said that . . . ," see Frederic Jameson, "Future City," *New Left Review* 21 (2003):
65–80.

22 **this experience of the "offline" is also profoundly affected:** Nathan Jurgenson, "The IRL
Fetish," *The New Inquiry*, June 28, 2012, http://thenewinquiry.com/essays/the-irl-fetish.

23   **the French finally pull the plug on Minitel:** Scott Sayare, "After 3 Decades in France, Minitel's Days Are Numbered," *New York Times*, June 27, 2012.

23   **Silicon Valley's own version of the end of history:** see Francis Fukuyama, *The End of History and the Last Man,* reprint ed. (New York: Free Press, 2006).

23   **"policymakers should work with the grain of the Internet":** Eric Schmidt, "Let Luvvie Embrace Boffin in the Digital Future," *The Guardian*, August 26, 2011.

23   **"without a major upgrade":** Rebecca MacKinnon, "Why Doesn't Washington Understand the Internet?," *Washington Post*, January 22, 2012.

23   **"nagging fear Germans harbor":** Jeff Jarvis, *Public Parts: How Sharing in the Digital Age Improves the Way We Work and Live* (New York: Simon & Schuster, 2011).

24   **"Web 2.0 means using the Web":** Paul Graham, "Web 2.0," PaulGraham.com, November 2005, http://www.paulgraham.com/web20.html.

24   **"There are laws of Nature":** David Post, *In Search of Jefferson's Moose: Notes on the State of Cyberspace* (Oxford: Oxford University Press, 2009), 211.

25   **it's not "the solution to the problem":** Steven Johnson, *Future Perfect: The Case for Progress in a Networked Age* (New York: Penguin, 2012), xxxv.

25   **"one could use the Internet directly":** ibid., xxxv,

26   **"the creation of ARPANET and TCP/IP":** ibid., 16.

26   **"Slowly but steadily":** ibid., 18.

26   **"The question with Kickstarter":** ibid., 43.

27   **Kickstarter's most famous failed alumnus is Diaspora:** see Jenna Wortham, "Success of Crowdfunding Puts Pressure on Entrepreneurs," *New York Times,* September 17, 2012, http://www.nytimes.com/2012/09/18/technology/success-of-crowdfunding-puts-pressure-on-entrepreneurs.html.

28   **Inge Ejbye Sørensen has studied how crowdfunding:** see Inge Ejbye Sørensen, "Crowdsourcing and Outsourcing: The Impact of Online Funding and Distribution on the Documentary Film Industry in the UK," *Media, Culture & Society* 34 no. 6 (September 2012): 726–743; I've written about Sørensen's research in my Slate column, from which the following few paragraphs are drawn: see Evgeny Morozov, "Kickstarter Will Not Save Artists from the Entertainment Industry's Shackles," Slate, September 25, 2012http://www.slate.com/articles/technology/future_tense/2012/09/kickstarter_s_crowdfunding_won_t_save_indie_filmmaking_.single.html.

29   *What Would Google Do?*: Jeff Jarvis, *What Would Google Do?*, 1st ed. (New York: HarperCollins, 2009).

29   **struck a deal with Verizon:** Todd Shields, "Google, Verizon Said to Strike Deal on Web Traffic Rules," *Bloomberg News*, August 5, 2010, http://www.bloomberg.com/news/2010-08-04/google-verizon-are-said-to-have-reached-deal-on-how-to-handle-web-traffic.html.

30   **books with titles like *Wikinomics* and *Wiki Government*:** Don Tapscott and Anthony D. Williams, *Wikinomics: How Mass Collaboration Changes Everything*, exp. ed. (New York: Portfolio Hardcover, 2008), 46; and Beth Simone Noveck, *Wiki Government: How Technology Can Make Government Better, Democracy Stronger, and Citizens More Powerful* (Washington, DC: Brookings Institution Press, 2009), 44.

30   **"The bureaucracy of Wikipedia":** Kevin Kelly, "The Collaborative Community," in *What Have You Changed Your Mind About?: Today's Leading Minds Rethink Everything*, ed. John Brockman (New York: HarperCollins, 2009), 177.

30   **"everything I knew about the structure of information":** ibid., 176.

30   **"the Republic of Macedonia and the Province of Macedonia, Greece":** see http://en.wikipedia.org/wiki/Wikipedia:MOSMAC.

30   **Its bureaucracy is anything but small:** I discuss the issue of Wikipedia bureaucracy in more detail in "The Battle for Wikipedia's Soul," *The Economist*, March 6, 2008.

31   **Zittrain's is a very elegant and pithy theory:** Zittrain's theory is laid out in Jonathan Zittrain, *The Future of the Internet—and How to Stop It* (New Haven, CT: Yale University Press, 2009).

34 **"Theo . . . Mrs. Sol Schwimmer is suing me":** Woody Allen, *The Complete Prose of Woody Allen* (New York: Wings Books, 1991), 105.

35 **"when we think of information technology":** David Edgerton, *Shock of the Old: Technology and Global History Since 1900* (London: Profile Books, 2011), xvi.

36 **"the most wrenching cultural transformation since the Industrial Revolution":** "'Antichrist of Silicon Valley,' Andrew Keen Wary of Online Content Sharing," *Economic Times*, May 29, 2012.

37 **they don't always capture the historical complexity:** on the longitude problem, see Dava Sobel's accessible history *Longitude: The True Story of a Lone Genius Who Solved the Greatest Scientific Problem of His Time*, reprint ed. (New York: Walker & Company, 2007). On early crowdsourcing efforts by the Smithsonian, see "Smithsonian Crowdsourcing since 1849!," Smithsonian Institution Archives, April 14, 2011, http://siarchives.si.edu/blog/smithsonian-crowdsourcing-1849. I learned of Toyota's efforts via this blog post on pre-Internet crowd-sourcing efforts: "Crowdsourcing Is Not New—the History of Crowdsourcing (1714 to 2010)," DesignCrowd, October 28, 2010, http://blog.designcrowd.com/article/202/crowdsourcing.

37 **"Knowledge is taking on the shape of the Net":** David Weinberger, *Too Big to Know: Rethinking Knowledge Now that the Facts Aren't the Facts, Experts Are Everywhere, and the Smartest Person in the Room Is the Room* (New York: Basic Books, 2012), 17. Also, this is my review of Weinberger's book: Evgeny Morozov, "What Lies Beneath," The Daily, January 1, 2012, http://www.thedaily.com/page/2012/01/01/010112-opinions-books-weinberger-morozov-1-3.

38 **"a shift in network architecture":** C. W. Anderson, "The Difference between Online Knowledge and Truly Open Knowledge," *The Atlantic*, February 3, 2012, http://www.theatlantic.com/technology/archive/2012/02/the-difference-between-online-knowledge-and-truly-open-knowledge/252516.

39 **"At the very same time [that "the Internet" is blamed]":** Weinberger, *Too Big to Know*, xii.

40 *Here Comes Everybody*: Clay Shirky, *Here Comes Everybody: The Power of Organizing without Organizations* (New York: Penguin, 2009).

40 **Susanne Lohmann's explanation of the 1989 protests in East Germany:** Susanne Lohmann, "The Dynamics of Informational Cascades: The Monday Demonstrations in Leipzig, East Germany, 1989–91," *World Politics* 47, no. 1 (October 1, 1994): 42–101.

40 **Ronald Coase's theory of the firm:** Ronald Coase, "The Nature of the Firm," *Economica*, 4 (1937): 386–405.

40 **in order to explain the 1989 protests:** Lohmann, "The Dynamics of Informational Cascades."

41 **"Generalizing about social movements":** Stephen Kotkin, *Uncivil Society: 1989 and the Implosion of the Communist Establishment* (New York: Random House Digital, Inc., 2009), 147.

41 **"behavior is motivation that has been filtered through opportunity":** Clay Shirky, *Cognitive Surplus: How Technology Makes Consumers into Collaborators*, reprint ed. (New York: Penguin Books, 2011), 195.

41 **"share a propensity to engage in method-driven research":** Ian Shapiro, *The Flight from Reality in the Human Sciences* (Princeton, NJ: Princeton University Press, 2007), 68.

41 **"it may be shaped by enthusiasm for the collective objectives":** ibid., 76.

42 **"a dispassionate search for the causes":** ibid., 88.

43 **Yochai Benkler also draws heavily on Coase:** Yochai Benkler, "Coase's Penguin, or, Linux and 'The Nature of the Firm,'" *Yale Law Journal* 112, no. 3 (December 1, 2002): 369–446.

43 **"the Internet not only drops transaction and collaboration costs in business":** "Don Tapscott: Four Principles for the Open World," TED, June 2012, http://www.ted.com/talks/don_tapscott_four_principles_for_the_open_world_1.html?quote=1723.

44 **"a historical break, the dawn of a new era":** Gabrielle Hecht, *The Radiance of France: Nuclear Power and National Identity after World War II* (Cambridge, MA: MIT Press, 2009), and Paul N. Edwards et al., "AHR Conversation: Historical Perspectives on the Circulation of Information," *American Historical Review* 116, no. 5 (December 1, 2011): 1393–1435.

44 **"we wouldn't really have a conference here":** Zittrain's remark is included in this video of highlights from the conference: "Cyber Dialogue 2011: Video Highlights," Cyber Dialogue, July 8, 2011, http://www.cyberdialogue.ca/2011/07/securing-the-cyber-commons-video-highlights.

45 **publication of a book . . . which promised "social harmony of humanity":** Michael Angelo Garvey, *The Silent Revolution, or, the Future Effects of Steam and Electricity upon the Condition of Mankind* (William and Frederick G. Cash, 1852).

45 **"town and country, work and leisure, brain and hand":** Armand Mattelart, *Networking the World, 1794–2000* (Minneapolis: University of Minnesota Press, 2000), 21.

45 **Or what to do with Nazi engineers like Franz Lawaczeck:** Lawaczeck's beliefs are discussed in T. Rohkrämer, "Antimodernism, Reactionary Modernism and National Socialism: Technocratic Tendencies in Germany, 1890–1945," *Contemporary European History* 8, no. 1 (1999): 29–50.

45 **"it's not a revolution if nobody loses":** Shirky, *Here Comes Everybody*, 209.

46 **"bringing a new ethic of openness":** Tapscott and Williams, *Wikinomics*, 46.

46 **"rather than being passive recipients":** ibid., 47.

46 **"a generation of scrutinizers":** ibid., 47.

46 **"today young people are authorities":** ibid., 47.

46 **"among all age groups, higher proportions":** quoted in Joseph Turow, *The Daily You: How the New Advertising Industry Is Defining Your Identity and Your Worth* (New Haven, CT: Yale University Press, 2012), 189.

46 **"the online savvy many attribute to younger individuals":** ibid., 189.

46 **These conclusions are echoed in a recent study from the European Commission:** Tom Espiner, "Young People Are Not 'Digitally Competent,' EC Warns," ZDNet, March 22, 2012, http://www.zdnet.com/young-people-are-not-digitally-competent-ec-warns-4010025719.

46 **A 2009 empirical study of students at five British universities:** Chris Jones et al., "Net Generation or Digital Natives: Is There a Distinct New Generation Entering University?," *Computers & Education* 54, no. 3 (April 2010): 722–732.

47 **"the past is not transformed into the 'modern world'":** Steven Shapin, *The Scientific Revolution* (Chicago: University of Chicago Press, 1998), 7.

48 **"historians have read into the 1880s":** Michael Worboys, "Was There a Bacteriological Revolution in Late Nineteenth-Century Medicine?," *Studies in History and Philosophy of Biological and Biomedical Sciences* 38, no. 1 (March 2007): 20–42.

48 **"When someone demands to know":** Clay Shirky, "Newspapers and Thinking the Unthinkable," Shirky.com, March 13, 2009, http://www.shirky.com/weblog/2009/03/newspapers-and-thinking-the-unthinkable.

48 **"the more serious you are about believing something is a revolution":** "Richard S. Salant Lecture on Freedom of the Press with Clay Shirky," John Shorenstein Center, October 14, 2011, http://shorensteincenter.org/wp-content/uploads/2012/03/salant_lecture_2011_shirky.pdf.

49 **"nothing will work, but everything might":** Shirky, "Newspapers and Thinking the Unthinkable."

49 **"There is never going to be a moment":** Shirky, *Here Comes Everybody*, 73.

49 **dedicates several pages of his *Cognitive Surplus*:** Clay Shirky, *Cognitive Surplus: How Technology Makes Consumers into Collaborators*, reprint ed. (New York: Penguin Books, 2011), 42–56.

49 **"we're collectively living through 1500":** Shirky, "Newspapers and Thinking the Unthinkable."

49 **"It is too early to tell":** Clay Shirky, "Tools and Transformations," Penguin Group, March 11, 2008, http://us.penguingroup.com/static/html/blogs/tools-and-transformations-clay-shirky.

49 **"It's not much of an exaggeration":** Marshall Poe, "The Internet Changes Nothing," History News Network, November 28, 2010, http://www.hnn.us/articles/133910.html.

50 **Gutenberg, we learn, "must have been an archetypal geek":** John Naughton, *From Gutenberg to Zuckerberg: What You Really Need to Know about the Internet*, Kindle ed. (London: Quercus, 2011).

50 **"by looking in more detail at the transformations":** ibid., Kindle location 195–196.

50 **"possibly the world's first technology entrepreneur":** Jeff Jarvis, "Gutenberg the Geek," Amazon Kindle Single, 2012.

50 **"Gutenberg—just like a modern-day startup":** ibid., Kindle location, 97–99.

50 **"the parallels between his enterprise":** ibid., Kindle location 9–11.

51 **"The democratizing impact of television":** Daniel Joseph Boorstin, *The Republic of Technology* (New York: HarperCollins, 1979), 7.

51 **"the era when television became a universal engrossing American experience":** ibid., 7.

51 *Two Bits: The Cultural Significance of Free Software*: Christopher M. Kelty, *Two Bits: The Cultural Significance of Free Software* (Durham, NC: Duke University Press, 2008).

52 **"the Protestant Reformation makes for good allegory":** ibid., 65.

52 **"explain a political, technical, legal situation":** ibid., 72.

52 *The Printing Press as an Agent of Change*: Elizabeth L. Eisenstein, *The Printing Press as an Agent of Change* (Cambridge: Cambridge University Press, 1980).

52 **Nicholas Carr draws on Eisenstein's work in** *The Shallows*: Nicholas Carr, *The Shallows (New York: W.W. Norton, 2011)*, 70, 75.

53 **"from her sources those facts and statements":** Anthony T. Grafton, "The Importance of Being Printed," *Journal of Interdisciplinary History* 11, no. 2 (October 1, 1980): 265–286.

53 **"the extent to which any text could circulate":** ibid., 273.

53 **"No hard fact of technology dictates":** Michael Warner, *The Letters of the Republic: Publication and the Public Sphere in Eighteenth-Century America* (Cambridge, MA: Harvard University Press, 1990).

53 **"we know what we mean":** ibid., 7.

54 **"Politics and human agency disappear":** ibid., 6.

54 **"[Eisenstein's] press is something 'sui generis'":** Adrian Johns, *The Nature of the Book: Print and Knowledge in the Making* (Chicago: University of Chicago Press, 2000), 19.

54 **"identifies as significant only the clearest instances of fixity":** ibid., 19.

55 **"there is no intellectually coherent conservative position":** Shirky, "Tools and Transformations."

56 **"How to Acknowledge a Revolution":** Adrian Johns, "How to Acknowledge a Revolution," *The American Historical Review* 107, no. 1 (2002): 106–125.

56 **"[Johns] accuses . . . Eisenstein":** Jeff Jarvis, "Gutenberg of Arabia," Buzz Machine, February 13, 2011, http://buzzmachine.com/2011/02/13/gutenberg-of-arabia.

58 *The Master Switch*: Tim Wu, *The Master Switch: The Rise and Fall of Information Empires*, reprint ed. (New York: Vintage, 2011).

59 **Wu himself seems to be enamored of Amazon:** see Ken Auletta, "Paper Trail," *The New Yorker*, June 25, 2012, http://www.newyorker.com/reporting/2012/06/25/120625fa_fact_auletta.

59 **the success of the French film industry in the 1960s:** see Peter Cowie, *Revolution!: The Explosion of World Cinema in the Sixties* (New York: Macmillan, 2005), 31.

60 **"the government didn't invite rival postal firms"**: Paul Starr, "The Manichean World of Timothy Wu," *American Prospect* (July–August 2011), http://prospect.org/article/manichean -world-tim-wu.

60 **"government's only proper role"**: ibid.

60 **"Government policy, in Wu's distorted recounting"**: ibid.

60 **"Why Politicians Should Never Make Laws about Technology"**: Paul Venezia, "Why Politicians Should Never Make Laws about Technology," InfoWorld, January 3, 2012, http://www.infoworld.com/d/data-center/why-politicians-should-never-make-laws-about -technology-182374.

62 **"a 'secularization' of communication"**: Philippe Breton, *The Culture of the Internet and the Internet as Cult: Social Fears and Religious Fantasies*, trans. David Bade (Los Angeles: Litwin Books, LLC, 2011), 9.

Chapter 3: So Open It Hurts

63 **"Owning pipelines, people, products"**: Jeff Jarvis, *What Would Google Do?*, 1st ed. (New York: HarperCollins, 2009), 4.

63 **"Radical transparency for firms and governments"**: see Tapscott's blurb for Andy Greenberg's book, available here: http://www.amazon.com/This-Machine-Kills -Secrets-WikiLeakers/dp/0525953205.

64 **Fast-forward to 2008:** see coverage of Eightmaps.com in Brad Stone, "Prop 8 Donor Web Site Shows Disclosure Law Is 2-Edged Sword," *New York Times*, Business Section, February 8, 2009, http://www.nytimes.com/2009/02/08/business/08stream.html.

64 **"would you give to the Council on American-Islamic Relations"**: Rod Dreher, "Eightmaps and the Strange Knock at Your Door," BeliefNet, January 4, 2011, http:// web.archive.org/web/20110104040839/http://blog.beliefnet.com/crunchycon/2009/01 /eightmaps-and-the-strange-knoc.html.

65 *Republic, Lost:* Lawrence Lessig, *Republic, Lost: How Money Corrupts Congress—and a Plan to Stop It* (New York: Hachette Digital, Inc., 2011).

66 **"These troubles with transparency point to a pattern"**: Lawrence Lessig, "Against Trans- parency," *The New Republic*, October 2009, http://www.tnr.com/article/books-and -arts/against-transparency.

67 **"the singular virtue of accepting the architecture"**: ibid.

67 **"But the network is not going away"**: ibid.

69 **used free, open-source tools:** I draw primarily on David Sasaki's account of the story in his blog post. See David Sasaki, "Democracy Building 2.0: The Open Government Part- nership, Game Changer or Symbolic Slogan?," DavidSasaki.name, July 11, 2011, http://davidsasaki.name/2011/07/democracy-building-2–0-the-open-government -partnership-game-changer-or-symbolic-slogan.

70 **"a major step backward for open government in Argentina"**: Sasaki, "Democracy Building 2.0."

72 **"Campaign Disclosure, Privacy and Transparency"**: Deborah G. Johnson, Priscilla M. Regan, and Kent Wayland, "Campaign Disclosure, Privacy and Transparency," *William & Mary Bill of Rights Journal* 19, no. 4 (2011): 959. A somewhat different version of this article was also published as Kent Wayland, Roberton Armengol, and Deborah Johnson, "When Transparency Isn't Transparent: Campaign Finance Disclosure and Internet Sur- veillance," in *Internet and Surveillance: The Challenges of Web 2.0 and Social Media*, ed. Christian Fuchs et al. (New York: Routledge, 2012), 239–255.

72 **that . . . Bruno Latour calls "double click":** Bruno Latour, "What If We Talked Politics a Little?," *Contemporary Political Theory* 2, no. 2 (July 2003): 143–164.

73 **"Instead of [allowing] others to see what is happening inside"**: Wayland, Armengol, and Johnson, "When Transparency Isn't Transparent," 239.

74 **"I take great pains in this course"**: James A. Gardner, "Anonymity and Democratic Cit- izenship," *William & Mary Bill of Rights Journal* 19 (2011): 927.

75 **the radical step of giving users the right to respond to search results**: see Frank Pasquale, "Asterisk Revisited: Debating a Right of Reply on Search Results," *Journal of Business & Technology Law* 3, no. 1 (2008).

76 **"When participants start getting burned"**: Peter Winn's remarks in D. J. Capra et al., "Panel One: General Discussion on Privacy and Public Access to Court Files," *Fordham Law Review* 79, no. 1 (2011): 8.

76 **"If information about individuals is extracted"**: ibid., 5.

76 **"In effect . . . by making all this information"**: ibid., 5.

77 **"a policy with a default to redact"**: A. Conley et al., "Sustaining Privacy and Open Justice in the Transition to Online Court Records: A Multidisciplinary Inquiry," *Maryland Law Review* 71 (2012): 844.

80 **"the 'right' varieties of transparency"**: David Heald, "Transparency as an Instrumental Value," in *Transparency: The Key to Better Governance?*, eds. Christopher Hood and David Heald (Oxford: Oxford University Press, 2006), 68.

80 **Vladimir Putin orders workers to install Web cams:** Richard Boudreaux and Olga Razumovskaya, "Putin Deploys Election-Cams," *Wall Street Journal*, March 2, 2012, http://online.wsj.com/article/SB10001424052970204571404577253282324442446.html.

80 **In Germany, the Pirate Party:** "Sinking Ship: Voters Growing Disillusioned with Germany's Pirate Party," *Der Spiegel*, October 25, 2012, http://www.spiegel.de/international /germany/german-voters-grow-disillusioned-with-pirate-party-a-863234.html.

81 **"Fed policymakers appear to have responded"**: Ellen E. Meade and David Stasavage, "Publicity of Debate and the Incentive to Dissent: Evidence from the US Federal Reserve," *Economic Journal* 118, no. 528 (2008): 695–717.

81 **In a 1999 study, Jennifer Lerner and Philip Tetlock found:** Jennifer Lerner and Philip Tetlock, "Accounting for the Effects of Accountability," *Psychological Bulletin* 125 (1999): 255–275.

81 **consistent decision makers:** For a good overview, see Axel Gosseries, "Publicity," *Stanford Encyclopedia of Philosophy*, 2005, http://plato.stanford.edu/entries/publicity, and R. J. MacCoun, "Psychological Constraints on Transparency in Legal and Government Decision Making," in "Symposium on Publicity and Accountability in Governance," ed. Axel Gosseries, *Swiss Political Science Review* 12 (2006): 112–123.

81 **"had the members committed themselves publicly at first"**: Madison is quoted in MacCoun, "Psychological Constraints."

82 **"increasing transparency can produce a flood"**: Onora O'Neill, *A Question of Trust* (Cambridge: Cambridge University Press, 2002), 72–73.

83 ***Stealth Democracy: Americans' Beliefs about How Government Should Work***: John R. Hibbing and Elizabeth Theiss-Morse, *Stealth Democracy: Americans' Beliefs about How Government Should Work* (Cambridge: Cambridge University Press, 2002).

83 **"we should not look to new ways"**: ibid., 213.

84 **"the difference between a 100 percent attendance record"**: ibid., 212–213.

84 **"members would be doing something much more beneficial"**: ibid., 213.

84 **Michael Power, in his classic study:** Michael Power, *The Audit Society: Rituals of Verification* (Oxford: Oxford University Press, 1999).

85 **"books and auditing of accounts"**: Jean-Jacques Rousseau, *Discourse on Inequality* (Whitefish, MT: Kessinger Publishing, 2004), 71.

86 **"the information-processing imperative"**: Julie E. Cohen, *Configuring the Networked Self: Law, Code, and the Play of Everyday Practice* (New Haven, CT: Yale University Press, 2012), 117.

86 **"to organize the world's information and make it universally accessible and useful"**: Google, "Company Overview," http://www.google.com/about/company.

86 **"discursive shift . . . towards economics"**: Tony Judt and Timothy Snyder, *Thinking the Twentieth Century: Intellectuals and Politics in the Twentieth Century* (London: William Heinemann, 2012), 361.

86 **"Intellectuals don't ask if something is right or wrong":** ibid., 361.

87 **"The reason they do this is not necessarily":** ibid., 361.

87 **for assuming that "a set of indices":** Haridimos Tsoukas, "The Tyranny of Light: The Temptations and the Paradoxes of the Information Society," *Futures* 29, no. 9 (November 1997): 827–843.

87 **"at its core . . . transparency theory":** Mark Fenster, "The Opacity of Transparency," *Iowa Law Review* 91 (2005): 885–949.

88 **"the modern government's sprawling, often incoherent bureaucracy":** ibid., 915.

88 **"any 'message' that government information comprises":** ibid., 922.

88 **As linguist George Lakoff argued:** quoted in Tsoukas, "The Tyranny of Light," 830.

88 **"To reduce something to allegedly objective information":** ibid., 830.

89 **"open tends toward obfuscation":** Christopher M. Kelty, "Conceiving Open Systems," *Washington University Journal of Law & Policy* 30 (2009): 139.

89 **it is never quite clear:** ibid., 139.

89 **"Is openness good in itself":** ibid., 143.

90 **Take Tim Wu who celebrates Google:** Tim Wu, *The Master Switch: The Rise and Fall of Information Empires*, Kindle ed. (New York: Vintage, 2011).

90 **Google's birth was "audacious":** ibid., 287.

90 **its ideas are "vaguely messianic":** ibid., 272.

90 **"style themselves the challengers to the existing order":** ibid., 272.

90 **nothing less than the "utopia of openness":** ibid., 303.

91 **"plant the flag of openness deep in the heart":** ibid., 293.

91 **never dares to "resist or subdue the Internet's essential structure":** ibid., 283.

91 **"the greatest corporate champion of openness":** ibid., 318.

91 **leader of the "openness movement":** ibid., 296.

91 **"the incarnation of the Internet gospel of openness":** ibid., 270.

91 **one of the "apostles of openness":** ibid., 296.

91 **the "apostle of perfectibility":** ibid., 277.

91 **a "competition apostle":** ibid., 243.

91 **"an apostle par excellence of [the] control model":** ibid., 266.

91 **"Tim helped us catalyze a strategy":** Spencer E. Ante, "Tim Wu, Freedom Fighter," *Businessweek*, November 18, 2007, http://www.businessweek.com/stories/2007–11 –08/tim-wu-freedom-fighterbusinessweek-business-news-stock-market-and-financial -advice.

92 **"it is highly questionable whether Android":** K. Spreeuwenberg and T. Poell, "Android and the Political Economy of the Mobile Internet: A Renewal of Open Source Critique," *First Monday* 17, no. 7–2 (2012), http://www.firstmonday.org/htbin/cgiwrap/bin/ojs /index.php/fm/article/view/4050/3271.

92 **"while Android was publicly introduced":** ibid.

92 **"'openness' and 'connectedness' are not the principles":** James Curran, Natalie Fenton, and Des Freedman, *Misunderstanding the Internet* (London: Routledge, 2012), 87.

93 **information available online in open formats:** see Peter Orszag, Executive Office of the President, Memorandum No. M-10-06, Open Government Directive 1 (2009), http:// www.whitehouse.gov/sites/default/files/omb/assets/memoranda_2010/m10–06.pdf.

94 **"people all around the world":** "Open Government Declaration," Open Government Partnership, September 2011, http://www.opengovpartnership.org/open-government -declaration.

94 **the smartest analysis:** Harlan Yu and David G. Robinson, *The New Ambiguity of "Open Government,"* 59 UCLA L. Rev. Disc. 178 (2012).

94 **"A government can provide 'open data'":** ibid., 181.

95 **Just look at America:** see "Justice Department Wins Rosemary Award for Worst Open Government Performance in 2011," *The National Security Archive,* February 14, 2012, http://www.gwu.edu/~nsarchiv/news/20120214/index.htm.

95   **"improve public knowledge of the agency":** see Executive Office of the President, "Digital Government: Building a 21st Century Platform to Better Serve the American People," undated, http://www.whitehouse.gov/sites/default/files/omb/egov/digital-government/digital-government.html.

96   **"an electronic release of the propaganda statements":** Yu and Robinson, "The New Ambiguity of 'Open Government,'" 196.

96   **"it's much cooler":** Nathaniel Heller, "Is Open Data a Good Idea for the Open Government Partnership?," Global Integrity, September 15, 2011, http://globalintegrity.org/blog/open-data-for-ogp.

96   **David Cameron and his ministers have even commended:** "Cameron Announces New Plans on Transparency," Conservatives.com, February 10, 2010, http://www.conservatives.com/News/News_stories/2010/02/Cameron_announces_new_plans_on_transparency.aspx.

97   **"furring up the arteries of government":** Martin Beckford, "Data Watchdog Criticises David Cameron's 'Grudging' Stance on Freedom of Information," *Daily Telegraph*, March 14, 2012, http://www.telegraph.co.uk/news/politics/9143542/Data-watchdog-criticises-David-Camerons-grudging-stance-on-Freedom-of-Information.html.

97   **flirting with the idea of charging for any such requests:** see Juliette Jowit, "Mass of Government Data on Public Services to Be Published," *The Guardian*, June 27, 2012, http://www.guardian.co.uk/politics/2012/jun/27/public-services-data-published-price.

97   **rhetorical attempts in conservative circles to use the rise of "armchair auditors":** on the complicated relationship between transparency initiatives and traditional journalism, see Kevin Marsh, "The Illusion of Transparency," *The Political Quarterly* 82, no. 4 (October–December 2011).

97   **"support for more open data":** Justin Longo, "#Opendata: Digital-Era Governance Thoroughbred or New Public Management Trojan Horse?," *Public Policy & Governance Review* 2, no. 2 (spring 2011): 38.

98   **a 2011 survey by an insurance company:** quoted in David Hand, "Open Data Is a Force for Good, but Not without Risks," *The Guardian*, July 10, 2012, http://www.guardian.co.uk/society/2012/jul/10/open-data-force-for-good-risks.

98   **"the open data initiative ignores":** ibid.

98   **actually empowered the rich and powerful:** see, especially, Solomon Benjamin and Raman Bhuvaneswari, "Illegible Claims, Legal Titles, and the Worlding of Bangalore," *Tiers Monde* 206, no. 2 (2011): 37, and Raman Bhuvaneswari, "The Rhetoric of Transparency and Its Reality: Transparent Territories, Opaque Power and Empowerment," *Journal of Community Informatics* 8, no. 2 (2012).

Chapter 4: How to Break Politics by Fixing It

100   **"Wikipedia is just the beginning":** Steven Johnson, *Future Perfect: The Case for Progress in a Networked Age* (New York: Penguin, 2012), 213.

100   **"We are not politicians":** quoted in Bernard Crick, *In Defence of Politics* (New York: Continuum International Publishing Group, 2005), 2.

100   **"What we're offering is not a program":** quoted in "Sinking Ship: Voters Growing Disillusioned with Germany's Pirate Party," *Der Spiegel*, October 25, 2012, http://www.spiegel.de/international/germany/german-voters-grow-disillusioned-with-pirate-party-a-863234.html.

101   **strategically deploying the rhetoric of "freedom":** see, e.g., "Megaupload's Kim Dotcom Accuses Obama of Trampling Internet Freedom," Associated Press, July 24, 2012.

102   **the German Pirates use a panoply of tools:** for good journalistic overviews of the German Pirates, see David Meyer, "How the German Pirate Party's 'Liquid Democracy' Works," TechPresident.com, May 2012, http://techpresident.com/news/wegov/22154/how-german-pirate-partys-liquid-democracy-works; "Is the Pirate Party Its Own Worst Enemy?," Spiegel Online, March 28, 2012, http://www.spiegel.de/international/germany/pirate

-party-emerges-as-political-force-in-germany-a-823993.html; Eric Westervelt, "A Party on the Rise, Germany's Pirates Come Ashore," NPR, June 6, 2012, http://www.npr.org /2012/06/06/154388897/a-party-on-the-rise-germanys-pirates-come-ashore.; "Sinking Ship: Voters Growing Disillusioned with Germany's Pirate Party," *Der Spiegel*, October 25, 2012, http://www.spiegel.de/international/germany/german-voters-grow-disillusioned -with-pirate-party-a-863234.html.

102 **"What other party streams the meetings":** Annett Meiritz, "Support Wanes for Germany's Upstart Pirates," Spiegel Online, August 24, 2012, http://www.spiegel.de /international/germany/pirate-party-in-germany-loses-popularity-amid-growing -problems-a-851864.html.

102 **"the constant chatter of the crowd":** ibid.

103 **"the ridiculous truth about the Pirates":** Westervelt, "A Party on the Rise."

104 **"the Pirate phenomenon was so fascinating":** Annett Meiritz, "Suddenly out of Fashion: Support Wanes for Germany's Upstart Pirates," Spiegel Online, August 24, 2012, http:// www.spiegel.de/international/germany/pirate-party-in-germany-loses-popularity-amid -growing-problems-a-851864.html.

105 **paradoxes that . . . we should not even try to resolve:** Hanna F. Pitkin, *The Concept of Representation* (Berkeley: University of California Press, 1972).

106 **"If Mr. Obama had followed the Pirate method":** Steve Kettmann, "The Pirate Party Logs a New Politics," *New York Times*, May 1, 2012, http://www.nytimes.com/2012/ 05/02/opinion/the-pirate-party-logs-a-new-politics.html.

106 **2009 Open for Questions initiative:** Sheryl Gay Stolberg, "Obama Makes History in Live Internet Video Chat," *New York Times*, March 27, 2009, http://www.nytimes .com/2009/03/27/us/politics/27obama.html?_r=0.

107 **"in a liquid democracy, you can transfer your vote":** Johnson, *Future Perfect*, 170.

107 **"Proxy voters are like the influential bloggers":** ibid., 175.

108 **"by transferring your vote to your more knowledgeable friend":** ibid., 172.

108 **"you don't need to be an expert":** ibid., 172.

108 **"instead of choosing a candidate once every few years":** ibid.176.

108 **Lewis Carroll wrote:** Lewis Carroll, *The Principles of Parliamentary Representation* (London: Harrison and Sons, 1884).

108 **"we must face up to the fact that communication costs":** James C. Miller, "A Program for Direct and Proxy Voting in the Legislative Process," *Public Choice* 7, no. 1 (1969): 107–113.

108 **"the advancing technology of electronic computers":** ibid., 107.

108 **"Instead of electing representatives periodically":** ibid., 108.

109 **"The most concerned voter would vote":** ibid., 108.

109 **Neither of them mentions:** I'm thankful to Joshua Cohen for helping to crystallize my thinking on this issue.

109 **Such plebiscites exert a paralyzing effect on the state:** for an excellent discussion of plebiscite-driven politics, see Yannis Papadopoulos, "Analysis of Functions and Dysfunctions of Direct Democracy: Top-Down and Bottom-Up Perspectives," *Politics & Society* 23 (December 1995): 421–448.

110 **"what Amazon.com did to books":** Thomas L. Friedman, "Make Way for the Radical Center," *New York Times*, July 23, 2011, http://www.nytimes.com/2011/07/24/opinion /sunday/24friedman.html.

111 **"10,000 clicks from 10 states":** Lawrence Lessig, "The Last Best Chance for Campaign Finance Reform: Americans Elect," *The Atlantic*, April 25, 2012, http://www.the atlantic.com/politics/archive/2012/04/the-last-best-chance-for-campaign-finance-reform -americans-elect/256361.

111 **Cue the Shirky-esque tone of Mark Zuckerberg's remarks in 2008:** see his interview with Sarah Lacy at SXSW 2008. Video is available at http://allfacebook.com/mark -zuckerberg-sarah-lacy-interview-video_b1063.

111 **"outdated and antiquated":** Steven Overly, "Web Start-Up Ruck.us Aims to Engage the Politically Independent," *Washington Post*, March 12, 2012, http://www.washington post.com/business/capitalbusiness/web-start-up-ruckus-aims-to-engage-the-politically -independent/2012/03/09/gIQAKvU55R_story.html.

112 **"the word comes from rugby":** Ruck.us, "FAQs," http://blog.ruck.us/faqs.

112 **"Whereas 30 years ago we were blissfully ignorant":** Nathan Daschle, "How to Pick Your Presidential Candidate Online," CNN.com, April 19, 2012, http://www.cnn.com /2012/04/19/opinion/daschle-elect/index.html.

113 **"the Americans Elect innovation is so exciting":** ibid.

113 **"The trends are undeniable":** ibid.

113 **"Politics is the last sector":** Alex Fitzpatrick, "Ruck.Us Breaks Up Party Politics on the Social Web," Mashable, May 11, 2012, http://mashable.com/2012/05/11/ruckus.

114 **"Plots to disrupt the two-party system":** Steve Freiss, "Son of Democratic Party Royalty Creates a Ruck.us," Politico, June 26, 2012, http://www.politico.com/news/stories/0612 /77847.html.

114 **"our two-party system doesn't form":** ibid.

114 **"the creativity of party politics":** Nancy L. Rosenblum, *On the Side of the Angels: An Appreciation of Parties and Partisanship* (Princeton, NJ: Princeton University Press, 2010), 7.

115 **Partisanship . . . "does not see pluralism":** ibid., 7.

115 **"rescuing politics from the unreasonable":** ibid., 8.

115 **"the anti-party current is by definition":** Sean Wilentz, "The Mirage," *The New Republic*, October 26, 2011, http://www.tnr.com/article/books/magazine/96706/post-partisan -obama-progressives-washington.

115 **"boredom with established truths":** Crick, *In Defence of Politics*, 1.

116 **"eternal imperfection, a mixture of sinfulness":** quoted in Peters, *Courting the Abyss*, 281.

117 **"there is a cultural change":** quoted in "The Open Society," *The Economist*, February 25, 2010, http://www.economist.com/node/15557477.

117 **"What we despise as political 'mediocrity'":** Bruno Latour, *The Pasteurization of France* (Cambridge, MA: Harvard University Press, 1993), 210.

117 **"The fundamental danger is that consumerism":** quoted in Matthew Flinders, *Defending Politics* (Oxford: Oxford University Press, 2012), 83.

118 **"controlling, monitoring, and scrutinizing politicians":** ibid., 44.

118 **"my idea of a politician is a thief":** John Harris, "Local Democracy: The Future Looks Bleak for Political Activism," *The Guardian*, July 6, 2012, http://www.guardian.co.uk /politics/2012/jul/06/local-democracy-political-activism.

118 **"rejoices in the taking of political scalps":** Flinders, *Defending Politics*, 45.

118 **"standards of service that they would commonly expect":** ibid., 67.

119 **The Truth Goggles project:** for more on this project, see Andrew Phelps, "Are You Sure That's True? Truth Goggles Tackles Fishy Claims at the Moment of Consumption," Nieman Journalism Lab, July 12, 2012, http://www.niemanlab.org/2012/07/are-you-sure -thats-true-truth-goggles-tackles-fishy-claims-at-the-moment-of-consumption.

120 **Glenn Greenwald pointed out:** Glenn Greenwald, "PolitiFact and the Scam of Neutral Expertise," Salon, December 5, 2011, http://www.salon.com/2011/12/05/politifact _and_the_scam_of_neutral_expertise.

120 **PolitiFact labeled as "mostly false" a Ron Paul claim:** "Ron Paul says Defense Department budget changes definitions of al-Qaeda and Taliban, making Americans vulnerable," PolitiFact.com, November 22, 2011, http://www.politifact.com/texas/statements/2011 /dec/04/ron-paul/ron-paul-says-defense-department-budget-changes-de.

122 *Ordinary Vices*: Judith N. Shklar, *Ordinary Vices* (Cambridge, UK: Belknap Press of Harvard University Press, 1985).

122 **"The paradox of liberal democracy":** ibid., 48.

122 **"the blanket condemnation of hypocrisy":** Ruth W. Grant, *Hypocrisy and Integrity: Machiavelli, Rousseau, and the Ethics of Politics* (Chicago: University Of Chicago Press, 1999), 180.

122 **David Runciman advanced similar arguments:** David Runciman, *Political Hypocrisy: The Mask of Power, from Hobbes to Orwell and Beyond* (Princeton, NJ: Princeton University Press, 2010).

122 **"truth-telling can ... be a weapon":** Martin Jay, *The Virtues of Mendacity: On Lying in Politics*, reprint ed. (Charlottesville: University of Virginia Press, 2012), 180.

122 **"Politics, however we chose to define":** ibid., 180.

123 **"Ambiguity enables the transformation":** Deborah Stone, *Policy Paradox: The Art of Political Decision Making, Revised Edition*, 3rd ed. (New York: W. W. Norton & Company, 2001).

123 **"'Defending American interests' is an ambiguous idea":** ibid., 158.

123 **"legislators can satisfy demands to 'do something'":** ibid., 158–159.

123 **"Ambiguity facilitates negotiation and compromise":** ibid., 159.

124 **"organized political parties won't be needed":** Josh Quittner, "The Merry Pranksters Go to Washington," *Wired USA* 2 (1994), http://www.wired.com/wired/archive/2.06/eff_pr.html.

124 **"The Net is merely a means":** ibid.

124 **"instead of re-engineering the Internet":** Heather Brooke, *The Revolution Will Be Digitised* (New York: Windmill Books, 2012), 230.

125 **"if institutions don't work":** Beth Simone Noveck, *Wiki Government: How Technology Can Make Government Better, Democracy Stronger, and Citizens More Powerful* (Washington, DC: Brookings Institution Press, 2009), 44.

125 **"democratic theory and the design":** ibid., 16.

125 **"Newly capable groups are assembling":** Clay Shirky, *Here Comes Everybody: The Power of Organizing without Organizations* (New York: Penguin, 2009), 24.

126 **"there was no way the State Department":** Clay Shirky, "Richard S. Salant Lecture on Freedom of the Press with Clay Shirky," John Shorenstein Center, October 14, 2011, http://shorensteincenter.org/wp-content/uploads/2012/03/salant_lecture_2011_shirky.pdf.

126 **WikiLeaks did offer the State Department:** the account that follows is based on Andrew D. Murray, "Nodes and Gravity in Virtual Space," *Legisprudence* 5, no. 2 (2011): 195–221.

127 **"unfortunately ... the idea of hierarchy":** David Harvey, *Rebel Cities: From the Right to the City to the Urban Revolution*, 1st ed. (New York: Verso, 2012), 70.

127 **"If you think about revolutionary heroes":** "U.S. Innovation Adviser: 'Internet Freedom Is Not a Regime-Change Agenda,'" RadioFreeEurope/RadioLiberty, July 18, 2011, http://www.rferl.org/content/us_innovation_adviser_says_internet_freedom_is_not_a_regime_change_agenda/24269090.html.

127 **"the older style of revolution":** Mehdi Hasan, "The NS Interview: Wael Ghonim, Egyptian Democracy Activist," *New Statesman*, January 23, 2012, http://www.newstatesman.com/middle-east/2012/01/interview-arab-revolution.

127 **"It was the difference between Web 1.0":** ibid.

128 **"as long as revolutionaries cannot organize":** Hazem Kandil, "Soldiers Without Generals: Whither the Egyptian Revolution?," *Dissent* 59, no. 3 (2012): 11–17.

128 **"We are the spark":** David D. Kirkpatrick, "Egyptian Revolt's Leaders Count Their Mistakes," *New York Times*, June 14, 2012, http://www.nytimes.com/2012/06/15/world/middleeast/egyptian-revolts-leaders-count-their-mistakes.html?pagewanted=all.

129 **German-born investor Peter Thiel:** some of the best reporting on Thiel includes Brian Caulfield and Nicole Perlroth, "Life After Facebook," *Forbes*, February 14, 2011, http://www.forbes.com/forbes/2011/0214/features-peter-thiel-social-media-life-after-facebook.html; Jonathan Miles, "The Billionaire King of Techtopia," *Details*, September 2011, http://www.details.com/culture-trends/critical-eye/201109/peter-thiel-billionaire-paypal-facebook-internet-success; George Packer, "No Death, No Taxes," *The New Yorker*, November 28, 2011, http://www.newyorker.com/reporting/2011/11/28/111128fa_fact_packer; Ashlee Vance and Brad Stone, "Palantir, the War on Terror's Secret Weapon," *Businessweek*, November 22, 2011, http://www.businessweek.com/magazine/palantir-the-vanguard-of-cyberterror-security-11222011.html.

129 **a video on Palantir's YouTube channel:** see "Creating Transparency with Palantir," uploaded July 5, 2012; available at http://www.youtube.com/watch?v=8cbGChfagUA&feature=plcp.

130 **"because the first place most of us want to experiment":** Tabatha Southey, "A Billionaire's Waterworld Takes Libertarianism to New Depths," *Globe and Mail*, August 19, 2011, http://www.theglobeandmail.com/commentary/a-billionaires-waterworld-takes-libertarianism-to-new-depths/article548981.

130 **"In our time, the great task":** Peter Thiel, "The Education of a Libertarian," Cato Unbound, April 13, 2009, http://www.cato-unbound.org/2009/04/13/peter-thiel/the-education-of-a-libertarian.

130 **"the critical question then becomes":** ibid.

130 **"in the late 1990s, the founding vision":** ibid.

130 **PayPal revised how it deals:** Cyrus Farivar, "PayPal Sets Down Stricter Regulations for File-Sharing Sites," *Ars Technica*, July 11, 2012, http://arstechnica.com/business/2012/07/paypal-sets-down-stricter-regulations-for-file-sharing-sites.

131 **"when seen through the lens of technology":** Peter H. Diamandis and Steven Kotler, *Abundance: The Future Is Better than You Think*, 5th impression (New York: Free Press, 2012), 6.

131 **"The high-tech revolution created":** ibid., 10.

131 **"in today's hyperlinked world":** ibid., x.

132 **"because arresting its effects":** Jon Gertner, "'Abundance,' by Peter H. Diamandis and Steven Kotler," *New York Times*, March 30, 2012, http://www.nytimes.com/2012/04/01/books/review/abundance-by-peter-h-diamandis-and-steven-kotler.html?pagewanted=all.

133 **"if the geeks take over":** Jeff Jarvis, *What Would Google Do?*, 1st ed. (New York: HarperCollins, 2009), 48.

133 **"to the extent that . . . new media":** Anthony Ha, "Sean Parker: Defeating SOPA was the 'Nerd Spring,'" *TechCrunch*, March 12, 2012, http://techcrunch.com/2012/03/12/sean-parker-defeating-sopa-was-the-nerd-spring.

133 **"a vegetarian trapped inside the sausage factory":** quoted in Steven Levy, *In the Plex: How Google Thinks, Works, and Shapes Our Lives* (New York: Simon & Schuster, 2011), 327.

133 **"an incumbent protection machine":** Derek Thompson, "Google's CEO: 'The Laws Are Written by Lobbyists,'" *The Atlantic*, October 1, 2010, http://www.theatlantic.com/technology/archive/2010/10/googles-ceo-the-laws-are-written-by-lobbyists/63908.

133 **"it is overdue to rethink":** Noveck, *Wiki Government*, 16.

133 **"the digital environment offers":** ibid., 40.

133 **"most of the work":** ibid., 40.

134 **"a generative governance system can":** Parag Khanna and Ayesha Khanna, *Hybrid Reality: Thriving in the Emerging Human-Technology Civilization*, Kindle ed. (New York: TED Conferences, 2012).

134 **"positive change . . . using technology":** ibid., Kindle location 730–731.

134 **"we cannot be afraid of technocracy":** ibid., Kindle location 733–734.

134 **"To the extent that China provides":** ibid., Kindle location 736–737.

135 **"Thinking about government policy sends shivers":** David Ewing Duncan, "Why Do Our Best and Brightest End Up in Silicon Valley and Not D.C.?," *The Atlantic*, May 6, 2012, http://www.theatlantic.com/technology/archive/2012/05/why-do-our-best-and-brightest-end-up-in-silicon-valley-and-not-dc/256767.

135 **"nothing would be more fatal":** Theodore M. Porter, *Karl Pearson: The Scientific Life in a Statistical Age* (Princeton, NJ: Princeton University Press, 2005), 293.

136 **"in the new political order":** quoted in Crick, *In Defence of Politics*, 73.

136 **"Suppose the 'arbitrariness' which Saint-Simon":** ibid., 74.

136 **following Thomas Kuhn's work on scientific paradigms:** Thomas S. Kuhn, *The Structure of Scientific Revolutions*, 3rd ed. (Chicago: University of Chicago Press, 1996).

136 **much of the presumed unity is a myth:** see Peter Galison and David Stump, eds., *The Disunity of Science: Boundaries, Contexts, and Power,* 1st ed. (Palo Alto, CA: Stanford University Press, 1996).

137 **"rescue mankind from the lack of certainty":** Crick, *In Defense of Politics,* 70.

137 **"everything in society is . . . capable":** ibid., 71.

137 **"one of the most important components":** quoted in Robert D. Putnam, *Elite Transformation in Advanced Industrial Societies: An Empirical Assessment of the Theory of Technocracy* (Ann Arbor: Institute of Public Policy Studies, University of Michigan, 1976), 11.

137 **"For Larry [Page] and Sergey [Brin], truth was often self-evident":** Douglas Edwards, "Google Goes Electric," Xooglers, March 22, 2011, http://xooglers.blogspot.com /2011/03/google-goes-electric.html.

138 **fundamental assumption "is that disagreements occur":** F. Ridley and J. Blondel, *Public Administration in France* (London: Routledge and Kegan Paul, 1964).

138 **Jane Jacobs' attack on unimaginative urban planning, Isaiah Berlin's attack on "procrusteanism," Hayek's attack on central planning, Popper's attack on historicism, Michael Oakeshott's attack on rationalism:** see Jane Jacobs, *The Death and Life of Great American Cities* (New York: Vintage, 1992); on Berlin's "anti-procusteanism" see Jonathan Allen, "Isaiah Berlin's Anti-Procrustean Liberalism: Ideas, Circumstances, and the Protean Individual," paper presented at the annual meeting of the American Political Science Association (August 28–31, 2003, Philadelphia, PA). Available at http://berlin.wolf.ox.ac.uk /lists/onib/allen2003.pdf; Friedrich Hayek. "The Use of Knowledge in Society," *The American Economic Review* 35, no. 4 (September 1, 1945): 519–530; Karl Popper. "The Poverty of Historicism, I," *Economica* 11, no. 42 (May 1, 1944): 86–103; Michael Oakeshott, *Rationalism in Politics and Other Essays,* exp. ed. (Indianapolis: Liberty Fund, 1991).

139 **"while advanced degrees may help our modern Leviathans":** Miguel Angel Centeno, "The New Leviathan: The Dynamics and Limits of Technocracy," *Theory and Society* 22, no. 3 (1993): 330.

Chapter 5: The Perils of Algorithmic Gatekeeping

140 **"Yes, the internet is democratizing":** Inge Ejbye Sørensen, "Crowdsourcing and Outsourcing: The Impact of Online Funding and Distribution on the Documentary Film Industry in the UK," *Media, Culture & Society* 34 no. 6 (September 2012), 740.

140 **"Do you remember 'books'?":** Adrian Chen, "What Would You Buy for People Who Read Books?: A Gift Guide," *Gawker,* November 19, 2012.

140 **highbrow online magazine called *Guernica*:** *Guernica* account is based on personal e-mail communication with Joel Whitney.

141 **"even after consulting a friend":** ibid.

141 **a similar e-mail from Google:** while I learned of this case from a members-only mailing list, this post mentions Sahara Reporters' AdSense problem: "SaharaReporters Beats Attack by 'James Ibori' on Our Website," Sahara Reporters, February 2, 2012, http://sahara reporters.com/news-page/saharareporters-beats-attack-james-ibori-our-website.

143 **It's hard to say if Bettina Wulff:** Nicholas Kulish, "Keystrokes in Google Bare Shocking Rumors about Bettina Wulff," *New York Times,* September 18, 2012, http://www .nytimes.com/2012/09/19/world/europe/keystrokes-in-google-bare-shocking-rumors -about-bettina-wulff.html.

143 **In Japan, Google was ordered:** "Google Autocomplete Change Order," BBC, March 26, 2012, http://www.bbc.co.uk/news/technology-17510651.

143 **in France Google was ordered:** "Google Convicted Again in France over Google Suggest," Search Engine Land, September 26, 2010, http://searchengineland.com/google-convicted -again-in-france-over-google-suggest-51663.

143 **"We believe that Google should not be held liable":** Barry Schwartz, "Google Must Censor Google Instant in Italy for Derogatory Suggestions," Search Engine Land, April

5, 2011, http://searchengineland.com/google-must-censor-google-instant-in-italy-for-derogatory-suggestions-71661.

143 **a marketer named Brent Payne:** "How Google Instant's Autocomplete Suggestions Work," Search Engine Land, April 6, 2011, http://searchengineland.com/how-google-instant-autocomplete-suggestions-work-62592.

144 **links that come from, say, The Pirate Bay:** Dana Kerr, "Google Wipes Pirate Bay from Autocomplete Searches," CNET, September 10, 2012, http://news.cnet.com/8301-1023_3-57510052-93/google-wipes-pirate-bay-from-autocomplete-searches.

144 **with another, now-defunct Google service—Places:** David Segal, "Closed in Error on Google Places, Merchants Seek Fixes," *New York Times*, September 5, 2011, http://www.nytimes.com/2011/09/06/technology/closed-in-error-on-google-places-merchants-seek-fixes.html.

144 **"We're trying to build a virtual mirror":** M. G. Siegler, "Marissa Mayer's Next Big Thing: 'Contextual Discovery'—Google Results without Search," TechCrunch, December 8, 2010, http://techcrunch.com/2010/12/08/googles-next-big-thing.

144 **"It is a mistake to look into the mirror":** James Robinson, "Twitter and Facebook Riot Restrictions Would Be a Mistake, Says Google Chief," *The Guardian*, August 27, 2011, http://www.guardian.co.uk/media/2011/aug/27/twitter-facebook-riot-restrictions-eric-schmidt.

145 **"our role in the system":** Ian Paul, "Facebook CEO Challenges the Social Norm of Privacy," *PCWorld*, January 11, 2010, http://www.pcworld.com/article/186584/facebook_ceo_challenges_the_social_norm_of_privacy.html.

145 **What sociologist Donald MacKenzie wrote:** Donald MacKenzie, *An Engine, Not a Camera: How Financial Models Shape Markets* (Cambridge, MA: MIT Press, 2008).

146 **"Brin and Page both believed":** Steven Levy, *In the Plex: How Google Thinks, Works, and Shapes Our Lives* (New York: Simon & Schuster, 2011), 174.

147 **"democracy on the Web works":** "Ten Things We Know to Be True," Google, http://www.google.com/about/company/philosophy.

147 **"We're scientists":** quoted in Shawn Donnan, "Think Again," *Financial Times*, July 8, 2011, http://www.ft.com/intl/cms/s/2/b8e8b560-a84a-11e0-9f50-00144feabdc0.html.

148 **"It never occurred to me":** quoted in Levy, *In the Plex*, 171.

148 **"criticize the consumer for doing things":** Julie Moos, "Transcript of Google CEO Eric Schmidt's Q&A at NAA," Poynter.org, April 7, 2009, http://www.poynter.org/latest-news/top-stories/95079/transcript-of-google-ceo-eric-schmidts-qa-at-naa.

149 **"filters no longer filter out":** David Weinberger, *Too Big to Know: Rethinking Knowledge Now that the Facts Aren't the Facts, Experts Are Everywhere, and the Smartest Person in the Room Is the Room* (New York: Basic Books, 2012), 11.

149 **"instead of reducing information and hiding":** ibid., 13.

149 **Weinberger identifies five "most basic properties":** ibid., 50.

150 **This was the case with the Occupy Wall Street discussion:** Tarleton Gillespie, "Can an Algorithm Be Wrong?," *limn* 2, 2012, http://limn.it/can-an-algorithm-be-wrong.

151 **"(a) it is being deliberately censored":** ibid.

151 **"technocratic pose"—an attitude:** Ken Alder, *Engineering the Revolution* (Princeton, NJ: Princeton University Press, 1999), 20.

151 **"Trends promises a mathematical and an exhaustive analysis":** Gillespie, "Can an Algorithm Be Wrong?"

152 **"a term that has trended before":** ibid.

152 **this preference of breadth over depth:** ibid.

153 **Nathan Jurgenson has an apt term:** see, e.g., Nathan Jurgenson, "The IRL Fetish," *The New Inquiry*, June 28, 2012, http://thenewinquiry.com/essays/the-irl-fetish.

153 **advanced most persuasively by historians and sociologists of science:** see Bruno Latour, *We Have Never Been Modern* (Cambridge, MA: Harvard University Press, 1993), and Donna Haraway, *The Haraway Reader* (New York: Routledge, 2003).

153 **When advertisers use our social-networking data:** Jason Del Rey, "Web Ads Target Based on What You Watched on TV," *AdAge*, August 1, 2012, http://adage.com/article /digital/web-ads-target-based-watched-tv/236433.

154 **when Facebook has already developed a way to check:** Emily Steel, "Datalogix Leads Path in Online Tracking," *Financial Times*, September 23, 2012, http://www.ft.com/intl /cms/s/0/8b9faecc-0584–11e2–9ebd-00144feabdc0.html.

154 **"I really can't stand":** Niall Ferguson, "Niall Ferguson Defends Newsweek Cover: Correct This, Bloggers," Daily Beast, August 21, 2012, http://www.thedailybeast.com/articles /2012/08/21/niall-ferguson-defends-newsweek-cover-correct-this-bloggers.html.

155 **According to a report in *USA Today*:** Paul Singer, "Twitter Memes Go Viral with Help of Big Media Tweeters," *USA Today*, October 21, 2012, http://www.usatoday.com/story /news/politics/2012/10/21/twitter-media-invisibleobama-binders/1641967.

155 **"I don't think someone could have designed":** Ryan Holiday, *Trust Me, I'm Lying: Confessions of a Media Manipulator*, Kindle ed. (New York: Portfolio Hardcover, 2012), 21.

156 **"create the perception that the meme":** ibid., 23.

156 **"trading up the chain":** ibid., 18.

156 **"beachheads for manufacturing news":** ibid., 21.

156 **"I dashed off a fake internal memo":** ibid., 50.

157 *The Dialectic of Enlightenment*: Max Horkheimer and Theodor Adorno, *Dialectic of Enlightenment* (Palo Alto, CA: Stanford University Press, 2007).

157 **"No one knows exactly how":** B. J. Mendelson, *Social Media Is Bullshit* (New York: Macmillan, 2012), 46.

158 **Taina Bucher discovered on studying Facebook's EdgeRank algorithm:** see, especially, Taina Bucher, "Want to Be on the Top? Algorithmic Power and the Threat of Invisibility on Facebook," *New Media & Society* 14, no. 7 (2012), available at http:// nms.sagepub.com/content/14/7/1164; Bucher, "The Friendship Assemblage: Investigating Programmed Sociality on Facebook," *Television & New Media*, August 2012, http://tvn.sagepub.com/content/early/2012/08/14/1527476412452800.abstract; and Bucher, "A Technicity of Attention: How Software Makes Sense,'" *Culture Machine* 13 (2012), http://culturemachine.net/index.php/cm/article/viewArticle/470.

158 **"the algorithmic bias towards making those stories":** Bucher, "Algorithmic Power."

158 **Media scholar C. W. Anderson:** C. W. Anderson, "Deliberative, Agonistic, and Algorithmic Audiences: Journalism's Vision of Its Public in an Age of Audience Transparency," *International Journal of Communication* 5 (2011): 529–547.

159 **"If something is a total bummer":** quoted in Ryan Holiday, *Trust Me, I'm Lying*, 62.

159 **"The economics of the web":** ibid., 62.

159 **"efficiencies and the new breadth of artists":** Christopher Steiner, *Automate This: How Algorithms Came to Rule Our World* (New York: Portfolio Hardcover, 2012), 86.

160 **historians of science Peter Galison and Lorraine Daston:** Lorraine J. Daston and Peter Galison, *Objectivity* (New York: Zone Books, 2010), 115–191.

160 **"Algorithms may bring us new artists":** Steiner, *Automate This*, 88.

161 **As Joseph Turow points out:** Joseph Turow, *The Daily You: How the New Advertising Industry Is Defining Your Identity and Your Worth* (New Haven, CT: Yale University Press, 2012).

162 **"when an ad is served":** ibid., 126.

162 **"a basketball fan receiving an ad":** ibid., 126.

162 **"trying to figure out how":** ibid., 124.

162 **"lots of firms are beginning to create":** ibid., 124–125.

162 **"be nimble in the use of data":** ibid., 125.

162 **"We are entering a world":** ibid., 7.

163 **already employ algorithms to produce stories automatically:** for more on this, see my Slate column: Evgeny Morozov, "A Robot Stole My Pulitzer," Slate, March 19, 2012,

http://www.slate.com/articles/technology/future_tense/2012/03/narrative_science_robot
_journalists_customized_news_and_the_danger_to_civil_discourse_.html.

163 **"I often wonder how many people"**: Katy Waldman, "Popping the Myth of the Filter
Bubble," Slate, April 13, 2012, http://www.slate.com/articles/news_and_politics/intelli
gence_squared/2012/04/the_next_slate_intelligence_squared_debate_is_april_17_why_
jacob_weisberg_rejects_the_idea_that_the_internet_is_closing_our_minds_in_politics_
.single.html.

163 **"beneficial inefficiency" that accompanied:** David Karpf, *The MoveOn Effect: The Unexpected Transformation of American Political Advocacy*, 1st ed. (New York: Oxford University Press, 2012), 169.

164 **"advertisers can measure impressions and clickthroughs":** ibid., 44.

164 **"Better-targeted ads produce economic benefits":** Matthew Yglesias, "Me Want Cookies!," Slate, March 5, 2012, http://www.slate.com/articles/business/moneybox/2012/03
/apple_vs_google_the_war_over_third_party_cookies_.html.

164 **"in a world of user tracking":** ibid.

165 **easily one of the ugliest words in the English language:** I've discussed the myth of disintermediation in a Slate column, from which this section partly draws. See Evgeny Morozov, "Muzzled by the Bots," Slate, October 26, 2012, http://www.slate.com/articles
/technology/future_tense/2012/10/disintermediation_we_aren_t_seeing_fewer_gatekeepers
_we_re_seeing_more.html.

165 **The company claims to have developed a technology:** Mark Risher, "The Dark Side of
Social: Protect Your Brand from Abusive Social Spam," *The Allied Front* (Impermium's
corporate blog), October 10, 2012, http://www.impermium.com/blog/2012/10/10/the
-dark-side-of-social-protect-your-brand-from-abusive-social-spam.

166 **"is chock-full of books":** Jeff Bezos, "The Power of Invention," SEC.gov, April 2012,
http://sec.gov/Archives/edgar/data/1018724/000119312512161812/d329990dex991.htm.

167 *The Shock of the Old*: David Edgerton, *Shock of the Old: Technology and Global History
Since 1900* (London: Profile Books, 2011), 35.

167 **A study by a team of Scandinavian researchers:** Karl-Erik Sveiby, Pernilla Gripenberg, and
Beata Segercrantz, eds., "The Unintended and Undesirable Consequences: Neglected by Innovation Research," in *Challenging the Innovation Paradigm* (London: Routledge, 2012).

168 **"The innovator was a heretic":** Benoit Godin, "Καινοτομία: An Old Word for a New
World, or the De-Contestation of a Political and Contested Concept," in ibid., *Challenging
the Innovation Paradigm*, 37.

168 **"Innovation got a positive hearing":** ibid., 53.

169 **"Depending on what is created":** Allen Buchanan, Tony Cole, and Robert O. Keohane,
"Justice in the Diffusion of Innovation," *Journal of Political Philosophy* 19, no. 3 (2011):
307.

169 **technoneutrals "typically tend to be the consultants":** Majid Tehranian, *Technologies
of Power: Information Machines and Democratic Prospects* (New York: Ablex Publishing,
1990), 5.

169 **"Is it wise to ban a technology":** Jeff Jarvis, *Public Parts: How Sharing in the Digital Age
Improves the Way We Work and Live* (New York: Simon and Schuster, 2011), 61.

170 **technologies "[develop] out of institutional needs":** Tehranian, *Technologies of Power*, 5.

170 **"neither as technologies of freedom":** ibid., 20.

171 **To return to the late Tony Judt:** Tony Judt and Timothy Snyder, *Thinking the Twentieth
Century: Intellectuals and Politics in the Twentieth Century* (London: William Heinemann,
2012), 361.

173 **the infamous owner of a pizzeria in Florida:** John Tozzi, "Obama's Pizza Stop Creates
Least Helpful Yelp Profile Ever," *Bloomberg Businessweek*, September 11, 2012,
http://www.businessweek.com/articles/2012–09–11/obamas-pizza-stop-creates-least-help
ful-yelp-profile-ever.

173 **As the sociologist Grant Blank points out:** this section draws significantly on Grant Blank, *Critics, Ratings, and Society: The Sociology of Reviews* (Lanham, MD: Rowman & Littlefield Publishers, 2006).

174 **"include wearing hats, wigs, glasses":** ibid., 54.

174 **"French cuisine is complex":** ibid., 58.

174 **"results as close to scientific":** ibid., 106.

175 **even the "undatabased restaurants":** Joshua Cohen, *Four New Messages* (Minneapolis: Graywolf Press, 2012), 113.

176 **"What are your favorite New York restaurants?":** Steven A. Shaw, "The Zagat Effect," *Commentary* 110, no. 4 (2000). https://www.commentarymagazine.com/article/the-zagat-effect.

176 **"if you want to know how good a restaurant is":** ibid.

176 **"Union Square Café is, indeed":** ibid.

176 **"nowhere does Shaw spell out":** Clay Shirky, *Cognitive Surplus: How Technology Makes Consumers into Collaborators*, reprint ed. (New York: Penguin Books, 2011), 151.

177 **"unwilling to condemn Union Square":** ibid.

177 **"Back when professional reviews were":** ibid.

177 **"It is the vision of great chefs":** Shaw, "The Zagat Effect."

178 **"It cannot be denied that the erosion":** Nancy Weiss Hanrahan, "If the People Like It, It Must Be Good: Criticism, Democracy and the Culture of Consensus," *Cultural Sociology* 11 (July 2012), http://cus.sagepub.com/content/early/2012/05/15/1749975512453656.abstract.

179 **"without expertise, without a habitual knowledge":** quoted in ibid., 4.

179 **"the consumption mentality of reviews":** Ryan Gillespie, "The Art of Criticism in the Age of Interactive Technology: Critics, Participatory Culture, and the Avant-Garde," *International Journal of Communication* 6 (2012), 66. Available at http://ijoc.org/ojs/index.php/ijoc/article/viewDownloadInterstitial/936/683.

179 **"all criticism is based on that equation":** Daniel Mendelsohn, "A Critic's Manifesto," *The New Yorker*, August 28, 2012, http://www.newyorker.com/online/blogs/books/2012/08/a-critics-manifesto.html.

Chapter 6: Less Crime, More Punishment

181 **"Imagine what would have happened":** Ursula Franklin, *The Real World of Technology* (Toronto: House of Anansi, 1999), 18.

181 **"What the utopian denounces":** Thomas Molnar, *Utopia: The Perennial Heresy* (London: Tom Stacey Ltd., 1972), 6.

182 **ShotSpotter:** Ethan Watters, "Shot Spotter," *Wired*, March 2007, http://www.wired.com/wired/archive/15.04/shotspotter.html.

183 **PredPol:** on PredPol and predictive policing in general, see "Sci-fi Policing: Predicting Crime before It Occurs," Associated Press, July 1, 2012; Joel Rubin, "Stopping Crime before It Starts," *Los Angeles Times*, August 21, 2010, http://articles.latimes.com/2010/aug/21/local/la-me-predictcrime-20100427–1.

183 **Consider the New York Police Department's latest innovation:** "NYPD, Microsoft Push Big Data Policing into Spotlight," *Informationweek*, August 20, 2012, http://www.informationweek.com/security/privacy/nypd-microsoft-push-big-data-policing-in/240005838.

183 **"understand the unique groups in their customer base":** C. Beck and C. McCue, "Predictive Policing: What Can We Learn from Wal-Mart and Amazon About Fighting Crime in a Recession?," *Police Chief* 76, no. 11 (2009), http://www.policechiefmagazine.org/magazine/index.cfm?fuseaction=print_display&article_id=1942&issue_id=112009.

185 **"Predictive algorithms are not magic boxes":** Andrew Guthrie Ferguson, "Predictive Policing: The Future of Reasonable Suspicion," *Emory Law Journal*, May 2, 2012, http://ssrn.com/abstract=2050001.

185 **"the environmental vulnerability that encouraged"**: ibid.

185 **financial authorities in Hong Kong and Australia**: for more on this, see Jeremy Grant, "Australia Clamps Down on 'Algo' Trading," *Financial Times*, August 13, 2012, http://www.ft.com/intl/cms/s/0/ad11c4bc-e4f2–11e1–8e29–00144feab49a.html, and "Hong Kong Considers Annual Inspections of Algorithms," Automated Trader, July 26, 2012, http://www.automatedtrader.net/headlines/129847/hong-kong-considers-annual -inspections-of-algorithms.

186 **Facebook began using PhotoDNA**: Riva Richmond, "Facebook's New Way to Combat Child Pornography," *New York Times* Gadgetwise, May 19, 2011, http://gadgetwise .blogs.nytimes.com/2011/05/19/facebook-to-combat-child-porn-using-microsofts -technology.

186 **"We've never wanted to set up an environment"**: Joseph Menn, "Social Networks Scan for Sexual Predators, with Uneven Results," Reuters, July 12, 2012, http://www .reuters.com/article/2012/07/12/us-usa-internet-predators-idUSBRE86B05G20120712.

187 **A headline that appeared in the *Wall Street Journal***: "Can Data Mining Stop the Killing?," *Wall Street Journal*, July 24, 2012, http://online.wsj.com/article/SB100 00872396390443570904577546671693245302.html.

187 **In 2011 TomTom:** Maija Palmer, "TomTom Sorry for Selling Driver Data to Police," *Financial Times*, April 28, 2011, http://www.ft.com/cms/s/2/3f80e432–7199–11e0 –9b7a-00144feabdc0.html.

187 **Privacy advocate Chris Soghoian**: Christopher Soghoian, "The Law Enforcement Surveillance Reporting Gap," Social Science Research Network, April 10, 2011, http://ssrn .com/abstract=1806628 or http://dx.doi.org/10.2139/ssrn.1806628.

188 **"Tap the Power of Social Media to Drive Better Policing Outcomes"**: "Tap the Power of Social Media to Drive Better Policing Outcomes," Accenture, http://www.accenture .com/us-en/Pages/insight-tap-power-social-media-drive-better-policing-outcomes.aspx.

188 **"a social media surveillance solution"**: Becoming an Agile Digital Detective, ECM Universe, February 2012, http://www.ecmuniverse.com/products/ECM_Universe_Law _Enforcement_IBM_Solution_Profile.pdf.

188 **"The solution . . . employs text analytics"**: ibid.

188 **"kill people" and "burn [expletive] school"**: Dana Milbank, "From Tracking al-Qaeda to Tracking the Wayward Spouse," *Washington Post*, April 4, 2012, http://www.wash ingtonpost.com/opinions/from-tracking-al-qaeda-to-tracking-the-wayward -spouse/2012/04/03/gIQAF75ytS_story.html.

188 *The Silicon Jungle*: Shumeet Baluja, *The Silicon Jungle: A Novel of Deception, Power, and Internet Intrigue*, 1st printing (Princeton, NJ: Princeton University Press, 2011).

191 **"crime is an event"**: David Garland, *The Culture of Control: Crime and Social Order in Contemporary Society* (Chicago: University of Chicago Press, 2002).

191 **"Attention should centre not upon individuals"**: ibid., 16.

191 *Against Security*: Harvey Molotch, *Against Security: How We Go Wrong at Airports, Subways, and Other Sites of Ambiguous Danger* (Princeton, NJ: Princeton University Press, 2012).

191 **"It is ethically more defensible to arrange society"**: Graeme R. Newman, R. V. G. Clarke, and S. Giora Shoham, *Rational Choice and Situational Crime Prevention: Theoretical Foundations* (London: Ashgate Publishing Limited, 1997), 215.

192 **SCP has five policy levers**: D. B. Cornish and R. V. Clarke, "Opportunities, Precipitators and Criminal Decisions: A Reply to Wortley's Critique of Situational Crime Prevention," *Crime Prevention Studies* 16 (2003): 41–96.

195 **"the best policy is to regard most strangers"**: quoted in Andrew von Hirsch, David Garland, and Alison Wakefield, *Ethical and Social Perspectives on Situational Crime Prevention* (Oxford: Hart Publishing, 2000), 41.

195 **"flies in the face of traditionalist ideas"**: Garland, *The Culture of Control*, 183.

195 **dangers inherent in the quest to "automate human virtue"**: Ian R. Kerr, "Digital Locks and the Automation of Virtue," in *"Radical Extremism" to "Balanced Copyright": Canadian*

Copyright and the Digital Agenda, ed. Michael Geist (Toronto: Irwin Law, 2010), 247. Available at SSRN: http://ssrn.com/abstract=2115655.

195 **"digital locks would ensure particular outcomes":** ibid.

197 **"it is more important to understand why":** Tristan Gooley, *The Natural Navigator: The Rediscovered Art of Letting Nature Be Your Guide*, reprint ed. (New York: The Experiment, 2012), 10.

197 **Recent writings of legal theorist Roger Brownsword:** Roger Brownsword, "Whither the Law and the Law Books? From Prescription to Possibility," *Journal of Law and Society* 39, no. 2 (2012): 296–308; Brownsword, "Lost in Translation: Legality, Regulatory Margins, and Technological Management," *Berkeley Technology Law Journal* 26 (2011): 1321–1366; and Brownsword, *Rights, Regulation and the Technological Revolution* (New York: Oxford University Press, 2008).

198 **some casinos now rely:** "Smile! You're on Casino Camera," Associated Press, February 11, 2009, http://www.cbsnews.com/2100-205_162-274604.html.

198 **Canadian casinos have recently solved:** Ashlee Vance, "A Privacy-Friendly Way to Ban Gambling Addicts from Casinos," *Bloomberg Businessweek*, August 29, 2012, http://www.businessweek.com/articles/2012-08-29/a-privacy-friendly-way-to-ban-gambling-addicts-from-casinos.

198 **what Cass Sunstein and Richard Thaler call "nudges":** Richard H. Thaler and Cass R. Sunstein, *Nudge: Improving Decisions about Health, Wealth, and Happiness*, updated ed. (New York: Penguin Books, 2009).

199 **as some recent studies speculate:** F. Godlee, "Obesity and Climate Change," *British Medical Journal* 345 (2012), http://www.bmj.com/content/345/bmj.e6516.

200 **"Moral communities need to keep debating":** Brownsword, "Lost in Translation," 1356.

200 **John Dewey expressed almost a century earlier:** the best short introduction to Dewey's thought on technology and paternalism (from which most of the Dewey quotes in the book are taken) is Tan Sor Hoon, "Paternalism—a Deweyan Perspective," *Journal of Speculative Philosophy* 13, no. 1 (January 1, 1999): 56–70. For a longer treatment of Dewey and technology, see Larry A. Hickman, *Philosophical Tools for Technological Culture: Putting Pragmatism to Work* (Bloomington: Indiana University Press, 2001).

200 **"intellectual instruments to be tested and confirmed":** quoted in Tan Sor Hoon, "Paternalism," 63.

200 **"Just as physical life cannot exist":** quoted in ibid., 62.

201 **"To maintain the reversibility of foldings":** Bruno Latour, "Morality and Technology: The End of the Means," *Theory, Culture & Society* 19, no. 5–6 (December 1, 2002): 247–260.

203 **In an important article on digital preemption:** Daniel Rosenthal, "Assessing Digital Preemption (and the Future of Law Enforcement?)," *New Criminal Law Review* 14, no. 4 (October 2011): 576–610.

203 **"if making certain conduct impossible":** Michael Rich, "Should We Make Crime Impossible?," *Harvard Journal of Law and Public Policy* (March 26, 2012), http://ssrn.com/abstract=2029201.

204 **many philosophers and legal theorists have argued:** Kimberley Brownlee, "Civil Disobedience," *Stanford Encyclopedia of Philosophy*, ed. Edward N. Zalta, spring 2010, http://plato.stanford.edu/entries/civil-disobedience.

204 **Ronald Dworkin, for example, has argued:** Ronald Dworkin, *Taking Rights Seriously* (Cambridge, MA: Harvard University Press, 1978).

205 **"defection . . . an engine for innovation":** Bruce Schneier, *Liars and Outliers: Enabling the Trust that Society Needs to Thrive*, 1st ed. (New York: Wiley, 2012), 248.

205 **"Sometimes a whistle-blower needs":** ibid., 248.

206 **"[While] courts alter laws":** see Rosenthal, "Assessing Digital Preemption," 601.

206 **"Virginia's anti-miscegenation law was overturned":** see Rich, "Should We Make Crime Impossible?"

207 **"with only a minimal perceived intrusion":** ibid.

207 **"Academics have sometimes portrayed":** Rosenthal, "Assessing Digital Preemption," 584.

209 ***Information and Exclusion:*** Lior Jacob Strahilevitz, *Information and Exclusion* (New Haven, CT: Yale University Press, 2011).

210 **One study published in the *Journal of Law and Economics*:** H. J. Holzer, S. Raphael, and M. A. Stoll, "Perceived Criminality, Criminal Background Checks, and the Racial Hiring Practices of Employers," *Journal of Law and Economics* 49, no. 2 (2006): 451–480.

211 **Another recent study found:** Kwoh Leslie, "Facebook Profiles Found to Predict Job Performance," *Wall Street Journal*, February 21, 2012, http://online.wsj.com/article/SB10001424052970204909104577235474086304212.html.

211 **"social norms and traditions are strong":** Strahilevitz, *Information and Exclusion*, 51.

213 **"whatever the mix of good and bad":** Gordon Crovitz, "Is Technology Good or Bad? Yes," *Wall Street Journal*, August 23, 2010, http://online.wsj.com/article/SB10001424052748703579804575441461191438330.html.

213 **"whether it's good for society or bad":** Nick Bilton, *I Live in the Future and Here's How It Works: Why Your World, Work, and Brain Are Being Creatively Disrupted* (New York: Random House Digital, 2010), 216.

213 **"the flow of technology is at most slowed":** Parag Khanna and Ayesha Khanna, *Hybrid Reality: Thriving in the Emerging Human-Technology Civilization* (New York: TED Conferences, 2012).

214 ***Autonomous Technology: Technics-out-of-Control as a Theme in Political Thought:*** Langdon Winner, *Autonomous Technology: Technics-out-of-Control as a Theme in Political Thought* (Cambridge, MA: MIT Press, 1978).

214 ***What Technology Wants:*** Kevin Kelly, *What Technology Wants*, Kindle ed. (New York: Penguin Books, 2011).

214 **cite Kelly's *What Technology Wants* as an influence:** for Wu, see his Amazon review of the book: http://www.amazon.com/review/R3JVF5DQVTG1HU; for Johnson, see Steven Johnson, *Future Perfect: The Case for Progress in a Networked Age* (New York: Penguin, 2012), 224.

214 **"the technium wants what we design it to want":** ibid., 15.

214 **"But in addition to those drivers":** ibid., 15.

214 **"our concern should not be about whether to embrace":** ibid., 187.

215 **"with minor differences, the evolution of the technium":** ibid., 44.

215 **"only by listening to technology's story":** ibid., 6.

215 **"We can choose to modify":** ibid., 174.

215 **"The first response to a new idea":** ibid., 252.

216 **"By constraining the suite of acceptable occupations":** ibid., 237.

217 **"If we take a global view of technology":** ibid., 242.

217 **"In a global marketplace, nothing is eliminated":** ibid., 243.

217 **"Technology's dominance ultimately stems":** ibid., 70.

217 **"We tend to isolate manufactured technology":** ibid., 22.

217 **"It would be paradoxical if the works of technology":** quoted in John C. Guse, "Nazi Technical Thought Revisited," *History and Technology: An International Journal* 26, no. 1 (2010): 10.

218 **"a 'restricted' technology is the equivalent":** Ayn Rand, *The Return of the Primitive: The Anti-Industrial Revolution*, Kindle ed. (New York: Plume, 1999).

218 **"restrictions [on technology] mean":** ibid., Kindle location 4889–4890.

218 **"Who can predict when":** ibid., Kindle location 4887–4888.

218 **"computers programmed by a bunch of hippies":** ibid., Kindle location 4905.

218 **"the curve [behind Moore's Law] is one way":** Kelly, *What Technology Wants*, 170.

218 **"Strictly speaking there is no such Law":** Ilkka Tuomi, "The Lives and Death of Moore's Law," *First Monday* 7, no. 11 (2002), http://firstmonday.org/htbin/cgiwrap/bin/ojs/index.php/fm/article/view/1000/921.

218 **"sociologically Moore's Law is a fascinating case":** ibid.

219 **"I never said eighteen months":** quoted in ibid.

219 **"The industry has been continuously falling forward":** Tuomi, "The Lives and Death of Moore's Law."

219 **"Instead of filling a market need":** ibid.

220 **"Science finds–Industry applies–Man conforms":** quoted in Carroll W. Pursell, "Government and Technology in the Great Depression," *Technology and Culture* 20, no. 1 (January 1, 1979): 162.

220 **"ambivalence should be understood as an integral element":** Bernhard Rieger, "'Modern Wonders': Technological Innovation and Public Ambivalence in Britain and Germany, 1890s to 1933," *History Workshop Journal* 55, no. 1 (January 1, 2003): 171.

220 **"existed between demands for rational conduct":** ibid., 170.

221 **spread of cameras at the end of the nineteenth century:** Robert E. Mensel, "'Kodakers Lying in Wait': Amateur Photography and the Right of Privacy in New York, 1885–1915," *American Quarterly* 43, no. 1 (March 1, 1991): 24–45. Jeff Jarvis draws connections between Kodakers and social media in *Public Parts: How Sharing in the Digital Age Improves the Way We Work and Live* (New York: Simon and Schuster, 2011), 63.

221 **noise-abatement campaigns of the early twentieth century:** Karin Bijsterveld, "The Diabolical Symphony of the Mechanical Age: Technology and Symbolism of Sound in European and North American Noise Abatement Campaigns, 1900–40," *Social Studies of Science* 31, no. 1 (February 1, 2001): 37–70; Peter Payer, "The Age of Noise Early Reactions in Vienna, 1870–1914," *Journal of Urban History* 33, no. 5 (July 1, 2007): 773–793; Egbert Klautke, "Anarchy and Noise: New Perspectives on the History of Fin-de-Siecle Vienna," *Central Europe* 7, no. 2 (2009): 161–168.

222 **led by the German intellectual Theodor Lessing:** on Lessing, see Lawrence Baron, "Noise and Degeneration: Theodor Lessing's Crusade for Quiet," *Journal of Contemporary History* 17, no. 1 (1982): 165–178.

222 **"by changing public awareness of the acoustic environment":** Payer, "The Age of Noise," 790.

222 **"the use of rubber tyres and quieter paving materials":** Baron, "Noise and Degeneration," 168.

222 **"Opponents of the antinoise campaign":** Payer, "The Age of Noise," 782.

223 **"technology marches forward":** Farhad Manjoo, "Smile, You're on Everyone's Camera," Slate, July 13, 2011, http://www.slate.com/articles/technology/technology/2011/07/smile_youre_on_everyones_camera.single.html.

223 **"Soon, though, we'll all learn to live with it":** ibid.

223 **"It's too late to turn back now":** ibid.

224 **scholars like Kelly Gates and Shoshana Amielle Magnet:** Kelly A. Gates, *Our Biometric Future: Facial Recognition Technology and the Culture of Surveillance* (New York: New York University Press, 2011), and Shoshana Amielle Magnet, *When Biometrics Fail: Gender, Race, and the Technology of Identity,* Kindle ed. (Durham, NC: Duke University Press Books, 2011).

224 **"regularly overtarget, fail to identify, and exclude":** Magnet, *When Biometrics Fail,* Kindle location 145–146.

225 **those with "clerical, manual, [and] maintenance" occupations:** ibid., Kindle location 458–459.

Chapter 7: Galton's iPhone

226 **"Neither information nor a drug fix":** Michael Serres, *The Five Senses: A Philosophy of Mingled Bodies* (New York: Continuum International Publishing Group, 2008), 104.

226 **"The day-by-day experience of a managed existence":** Ivan Illich, *In the Mirror of the Past: Lectures and Addresses, 1978–1990* (New York: M. Boyars, 1992), 223.

226 **"The same cultural zeitgeist":** Dominic Basulto, "Meet the Urban Datasexual," The Big Think, April 16, 2012, http://bigthink.com/endless-innovation/meet-the-urban-datasexual.

226 **"The datasexual looks a lot":** ibid.

227 **A bunch of inventive entrepreneurs have even developed smart toothbrushes**: Ariel Schwartz, "The Beam Toothbrush Knows If You're Not Brushing Enough," Co.Exist, 08 October 2012, http://www.fastcoexist.com/1680659/the-beam-toothbrush-knows -if-youre-not-brushing-enough.

227 **"provide concrete recommendations for addressing":** M. Kay et al., "Lullaby: Environmental Sensing for Sleep Self-Improvement," Workshop on Personal Informatics, CHI 2011, May 7–12, 2011, Vancouver, British Columbia, Canada, http://personal informatics.org/docs/chi2011/kay.pdf.

228 **record forty things about her daily life:** Alexandra Carmichael, "Quantifying Myself," The Quantified Self, December 13, 2008, http://quantifiedself.com/2008/12/quantify ing-myself.

228 **"tracked every New York street he walked":** Jamin Brophy-Warren, "The New Examined Life," *Wall Street Journal*, December 6, 2008, http://online.wsj.com/article/SB122852 285532784401.html.

228 **Facebook hired Felton in 2011:** Suzanne Labarre, "Facebook Hires Infographic Gurus Nicholas Felton and Ryan Case," Co.Design, April 27, 2011, http://www.fastcodesign.com /1663718/facebook-hires-infographic-gurus-nicholas-felton-and-ryan-case.

228 **"I was giving birth to our son":** April Dembosky, "Invasion of the Body Hackers," *Financial Times*, June 10, 2011, http://www.ft.com/intl/cms/s/2/3ccb11a0–923b-11e0 –9e00–00144feab49a.html.

228 **"He is deep into the biochemistry of his feces":** Mark Bowden, "The Measured Man," *The Atlantic*, August 2012, http://www.theatlantic.com/magazine/archive/2012/07/the -measured-man/309018.

229 **Meet Horace Fletcher (1849–1919), a health food maniac:** on Fletcher, see T. A. Turley, "The Merchant of Venice: Horace Fletcher and 'Fletcherism,'" *Nutrition Today* 21, no. 6 (1986): 15–21; A. G. Christen and J. A. Christen. "Horace Fletcher (1849–1919): 'The Great Masticator,'" *Journal of the History of Dentistry* 45 (1997): 95–100; Horace Fletcher, *Fletcherism, What It Is: Or, How I Became Young at Sixty* (Carlisle, MA: Applewood Books, 2008). On Fletcher and Henry James, see Tim Armstrong, ed., "Disciplining the Corpus: Henry James and Fletcherism," in *American Bodies: Cultural Histories of the Physique* (New York: New York University Press, 1996).

229 **quite dry, having only the "odor of moist clay or of a hot biscuit":** Fletcher, *Fletcherism*, 58.

229 **"Is there anything more sacred":** ibid., 128.

229 **Some might point to Benjamin Franklin:** see his autobiography: Benjamin Franklin, *The Autobiography of Benjamin Franklin* (Mineola, NY: Dover Publications, 1996).

229 **In 1880 Francis Galton:** Michael Bulmer, *Francis Galton: Pioneer of Heredity and Biometry*, 1st ed. (Baltimore: Johns Hopkins University Press, 2003), 30.

229 **"drew attention to the ease":** ibid., 30.

229 **"to construct a 'Beauty-Map' of the British Isles":** ibid., 30.

230 **In 2010 Wolfe penned something of a manifesto**: Gary Wolf, "The Data-Driven Life," *New York Times*, April 28, 2010, http://www.nytimes.com/2010/05/02/magazine/02self -measurement-t.html?pagewanted=all&_r=0.

231 **"the rise of a global superintelligence":** ibid.

231 **"We tolerate the pathologies of quantification":** ibid.

231 **"To him, not wanting to know something":** Bowden, "The Measured Man."

232 **"I want to create connections":** Brophy-Warren, "The New Examined Life."

232 **Wolfram has scanned 230,000 pages:** Anne Eisenberg, "Mining Our Own Personal Data, for Self-Discovery," *New York Times*, April 7, 2012, http://www.nytimes.com/2012 /04/08/business/mining-our-personal-data-for-our-own-good.html.

232 **"people will watch their health in a way that's a little closer":** Ki Mae Heussner, "Will Monitoring Our Health Be Like Managing a Stock Portfolio?," *GigaOm*, October 16,

2012, http://gigaom.com/data/will-monitoring-our-health-be-like-managing-a-stock-portfolio-2.

232 **"many of our problems come from":** Wolf, "The Data-Driven Life."

233 **"total explicitness" that rests "on a misunderstanding":** Bernard Williams, *Truth and Truthfulness: An Essay in Genealogy* (Princeton, NJ: Princeton University Press, 2004).

234 **"personal data are ideally suited":** Wolf, "The Data-Driven Life."

234 **published a *New York Times* op-ed:** Bill Wasik, "Bright Lights, Big Internet," *New York Times*, July 30, 2009, http://www.nytimes.com/2009/07/30/opinion/30wasik.html.

234 **"I'm not just tickled by Instant Pages":** Farhad Manjoo, "My PC Needs ESP," *Slate*, August 3, 2011, http://www.slate.com/articles/technology/technology/2011/08/my_pc_needs_esp.html.

235 **World Economic Forum in Davos is already hosting discussions:** "Personal Data: The Emergence of a New Asset Class," World Economic Forum, January 2011, http://www.weforum.org/reports/personal-data-emergence-new-asset-class.

235 **"We are trying to shift the focus":** Julia Angwin and Emily Steel, "Web's Hot New Commodity: Privacy," *Wall Street Journal*, February 27, 2011, http://online.wsj.com/article/SB10001424052748703529004576160764037920274.html.

235 **"The parasitism of corporations snooping":** David Mitchell, "There's No Point Resisting Corporate Websites. It's Time to Sell Yourself," *The Observer*, June 17, 2012, http://www.guardian.co.uk/commentisfree/2012/jun/17/corporate-websites-david-mitchell.

235 **"This is the difference between a market and a war":** ibid.

235 **Daytum.com allows its more than 80,000 users:** see Daytum.com.

235 **"If you want privacy":** Kashmir Hill, "Taking My Measure," *Forbes*, April 25, 2011, http://www.forbes.com/forbes/2011/0425/features-health-personal-data-work-out-taking-my-measure.html.

236 **"Privacy is mostly an illusion":** quoted in "Privacy 2.0: The Garbo Economy," NPR, April 27, 2011 http://www.npr.org/2011/04/27/135623137/privacy-2-0-the-garbo-economy.

236 **the growing "ryanairation of social life":** Glen Newey, "You Have £2000, I Have a Kidney," *London Review of Books*, June 21, 2012, http://www.lrb.co.uk/v34/n12/glen-newey/you-have-pounds2000-i-have-a-kidney.

236 **"Some of these bankers were paying":** Nick Bilton, "Erasing Individual's Digital Past," *New York Times*, April 1, 2011, http://www.nytimes.com/2011/04/03/fashion/03reputation.html?pagewanted=all.

237 **"You can think like a start-up":** Reid Hoffman and Ben Casnocha, *The Start-up of You: Adapt to the Future, Invest in Yourself, and Transform Your Career* (New York: Crown Business, 2012), 19.

237 **"acknowledge that you have bugs":** ibid.

238 **In a 2011 interview with the *San Jose Mercury News*:** Mike Swift, "Battle Brewing over Control of Personal Data Online," *San Jose Mercury News*, June 29, 2011, http://phys.org/news/2011-06-brewing-personal-online.html.

238 **"Imagine . . . being able to combine":** ibid.

239 **the German newspaper *Der Tagesspiegel*:** Katrin Schulze, "Machen sich Facebook-Verweigerer verdächtig?," *Der Tagesspiegel*, July 24, 2012, http://www.tagesspiegel.de/weltspiegel/nach-dem-attentat-von-denver-kein-facebook-profil-kein-job-angebot/6911648-2.html.

239 **"if you are going out with someone":** quoted in Kashmir Hill, "You Don't Need a Facebook Account to Be Considered 'Normal' (but It Helps)," Forbes.com, August 13, 2012, http://www.forbes.com/sites/kashmirhill/2012/08/13/you-dont-need-a-facebook-account-to-be-considered-normal-but-it-helps.

240 **"Want to price my health insurance premium?":** Scott R. Peppet, "Unraveling Privacy: The Personal Prospectus & the Threat of a Full Disclosure Future (August 7, 2010)," *Northwestern University Law Review* (2011), http://ssrn.com/abstract=1678634.

241 **"Upcoming apps from Philips and other tech companies"**: Christopher Steiner, *Automate This: How Algorithms Came to Rule Our World* (New York: Portfolio Hardcover, 2012), 159.

241 **Aviva . . . has been testing a smartphone app:** Hillary Osborne, "Aviva to Trial Smartphone Car Insurance Technology," *Guardian*, August 13, 2012, http://www.guardian .co.uk/money/2012/aug/13/aviva-trial-smartphone-car-insurance-technology.

241 **A San Diego start-up called SmartDrive Systems Inc.:** "Start-Up Monitors Professional Drivers," *Wall Street Journal*, June 26, 2012, http://online.wsj.com/article/SB200014 24052702303640804577488911381529248.html.

242 **"the way to affect your reputation"**: Jeff Jarvis, *Public Parts: How Sharing in the Digital Age Improves the Way We Work and Live* (New York: Simon and Schuster, 2011), 131.

242 **"Your choice to quantify yourself"**: Peppet, "Unraveling Privacy."

242 **"what sorts of people"**: ibid.

243 **"the faith in a world"**: Friedrich Nietzsche, *The Gay Science* (Mineola, NY: Courier Dover Publications, 2006), 64.

243 **"What? Do we really want to permit"**: Caroline Molina Y. Vedia, *Philosophical Writings: Friedrich Nietzsche* (New York: Continuum International Publishing Group, 1995), 157.

243 **"That the only justifiable interpretation"**: ibid., 157.

244 **"Would it not be rather probable"**: ibid., 157.

244 **As if responding to Leibniz**: quoted in Rob Young, "The Ultimate Magical Synaesthesia Machine," *London Review of Books*, September 22, 2011, http://www.lrb.co.uk/v33 /n18/rob-young/the-ultimate-magical-synaesthesia-machine.

244 **"Assuming that one estimated the value"**: Vedia, *Philosophical Writings: Friedrich Nietzsche*, 158.

244 **"Our mission is to get the best answer"**: "We're Trying to Answer the Question," *Slate*, December 9, 2011, http://www.slate.com/articles/technology/technology/2011/12 /google_s_eric_schmidt_an_interview_with_the_search_giant_s_chairman_.html.

244 **"So if you say, 'I want the best music'"**: ibid.

244 **"An essentially mechanical world"**: Vedia, *Philosophical Writings: Friedrich Nietzsche*, 158.

245 **"[Our critics say that] only intangibles"**: Kevin Kelly, *What Technology Wants* (New York: Penguin Books, 2011), 100.

245 **so astutely documented by historian Theodore Porter**: Theodore M. Porter, *Trust in Numbers: The Pursuit of Objectivity in Science and Public Life* (Princeton, NJ: Princeton University Press, 1996).

245 **"if you can not measure it"**: quoted in Susan Rose-Ackerman, *International Handbook on the Economics of Corruption* (Northampton, MA: Edward Elgar Publishing, 2006), 52.

245 **"If this evidence cannot be weighted"**: Steven Lukes and Nadia Urbinati, *Condorcet: Political Writings* (Cambridge: Cambridge University Press, 2012).

245 **"a technological system that radically increases"**: Gary Wolf, "QS & The Macroscope," Aether Blog, http://aether.com/themacroscope.

246 **"An ethics of quantification should investigate"**: W. N. Espeland and M. L. Stevens, "A Sociology of Quantification," *European Journal of Sociology* 49, no. 3 (2008): 401–436.

246 **"It is normal to seek data"**: Wolf, "The Data-Driven Life."

247 **"we tend to look away too much"**: Robert P. Crease, *World in the Balance: The Historic Quest for an Absolute System of Measurement* (New York: W. W. Norton & Company, 2011), 275.

247 **"And we have to address these dissatisfactions"**: ibid., 275.

248 **"we . . . need to keep reminding ourselves"**: ibid., 275–276.

248 **"Certainly clarity is desirable"**: Matthew B. Crawford, "The Computerized Academy," *The New Atlantis* (summer 2005), http://www.thenewatlantis.com/publications/the -computerized-academy.

249 **"data is now helping some":** quoted in Bobbie Johnson, "Mendeley Injects Some Pace into Academia with Fast, Big Data," GigaOM, August 6, 2012, http://gigaom.com /europe/mendeley-injects-some-pace-into-academia-with-fast-big-data.

249 **A recent *Wall Street Journal* investigation:** Gautam Naik, "Journals' Ranking System Roils Research," *Wall Street Journal*, August 24, 2012, http://online.wsj.com/article /SB10000872396390444082904577609313125942378.html.

249 **In an April 2012 post:** Phil Davis, "The Emergence of a Citation Cartel," The Scholarly Kitchen, April 10, 2012, http://scholarlykitchen.sspnet.org/2012/04/10/emergence-of -a-citation-cartel.

251 **"the nutrient composition of the diet":** Gary Taubes, "What Really Makes Us Fat," *New York Times*, June 30, 2012, http://www.nytimes.com/2012/07/01/opinion /sunday/what-really-makes-us-fat.html.

251 **Sociologist of science Gyorgy Scrinis calls such a tendency:** Gyorgy Scrinis, "Nutritionism and Functional Foods," in *The Philosophy of Food*, ed. David Kaplan (Berkeley: University of California Press, 2012); and Scrinis, "On the Ideology of Nutritionism," *Gastronomica* 8, no.1 (February 2008): 39–48.

252 **"shift to nutrient-level language":** ibid.

252 **"enabled the lay public to interpret":** ibid.

252 **"nutrients, food components, or biomarkers":** ibid.

253 **Bruno Latour distinguishes between "matters of facts":** for a distinction between "matters of fact" and "matters of concern," see Bruno Latour, "Why Has Critique Run out of Steam? From Matters of Fact to Matters of Concern," *Critical Inquiry*, 30, no. 2 (winter 2004): 225–248.

254 **"certain forms of knowledge and control":** James C. Scott, *Seeing like a State: How Certain Schemes to Improve the Human Condition Have Failed* (New Haven, CT: Yale University Press, 1998), 11.

255 **"A student was here last week":** David Cayley, *Ivan Illich in Conversation* (Toronto: House of Anansi, 1992), 166.

255 **"Being human . . . is something you have to get good at":** Terry Eagleton, "So Bad It's Good: Why Do We Find Evil So Much More Fascinating Than Goodness?," *The Independent*, May 7, 2010, http://www.independent.co.uk/arts-entertainment/books/features /so-bad-its-good-why-do-we-find-evil-so-much-more-fascinating-than-goodness -1965587.html.

256 **"Soon, we'll know if the sea urchin":** Greg Beato, "The Quantified Self," *Reason*, January 2012, http://reason.com/archives/2011/12/16/the-quantified-self.

256 **"we have invested only certain automatic":** Steven Talbott, *Devices of the Soul: Battling for Our Selves in an Age of Machines* (Sebastopol, CA: O'Reilly Media, 2007), 14.

257 **"Branding, marketing, and even qualitative customer reviews":** Beato, "The Quantified Self."

257 **Marissa Mayer . . . talks of "contextual discovery":** M. G. Siegler, "Marissa Mayer's Next Big Thing: 'Contextual Discovery'—Google Results without Search," TechCrunch, December 8, 2010, http://techcrunch.com/2010/12/08/googles-next-big-thing.

257 **"When I walk down the streets of Berlin":** Matt McGee, "Google's Schmidt: 'Next Great Stage' of Search Is Autonomous, Personal," Search Engine Land, September 7, 2010, http://searchengineland.com/schmidt-great-stage-search-is-autonomous-personal -50014.

258 **"My web searches for new neighborhood joints":** Bianca Bosker, "Don't Search, Just Absorb: The Dawn of the Couch Potato Web," The Huffington Post, May 13, 2012, http://www.huffingtonpost.com/bianca-bosker/web-searching_b_1512741.html.

259 **"a personalized selection of anything":** ibid.

259 **"The implicit searching on your behalf":** ibid.

259 **"we'll be told what we want":** ibid.

260 **"citizens cannot relate well":** Martha C. Nussbaum, *Not for Profit: Why Democracy Needs the Humanities* (Princeton, NJ: Princeton University Press, 2012), 95.

260 **"the ability to think what it might be like":** ibid., 96.

261 **"In the advanced capitalist world":** Maria Kaika, *City of Flows: Modernity, Nature, and the City* (Oxford: Psychology Press, 2005), 46.

262 **"Meters concretise private ownership":** Veronica Strang, *The Meaning of Water* (London: Berg, 2004), 228.

262 **"also express perfectly the social individuation":** ibid., 230.

263 **"did not, for the most part, pause":** Yolande Strengers, "Negotiating Everyday Life: The Role of Energy and Water Consumption Feedback," *Journal of Consumer Culture* 11, no. 3 (November 1, 2011): 319–338.

263 **Elizabeth Shove notes in *Comfort, Cleanliness and Convenience*:** Elizabeth Shove, *Comfort, Cleanliness and Convenience: The Social Organization of Normality* (London: Berg Publishers, 2004).

263 **"I was always worried about using the dryer": Yolande** Strengers, "Negotiating Everyday Life," and "Designing Eco-Feedback Systems for Everyday Life," in *Proceedings of the 2011 Annual Conference on Human Factors in Computing Systems* (New York: ACM), 2135–2144, 2011.

264 **"I'm happiest when drinking":** Hill, "Taking My Measure."

264 **"I'm at a slight loss":** ibid.

264 **"Two years ago I discovered that butter":** Seth Roberts, "Butter and Arithmetic: How Much Butter?," Seth's Blog, November 25, 2011, http://blog.sethroberts.net/2011/11/25/butter-and-arithmetic-how-much-butter.

264 **Sanjiv Shah, who thinks that wearing yellow glasses:** Mathew Cornell, "Quantified Self Boston Meetup #5, the Science of Sleep: Recap," The Quantified Self, April 1, 2011, http://quantifiedself.com/2011/04/quantified-self-boston-meetup-5-the-science-of-sleep-recap.

264 **"With self-tracking you never really know":** "The Quantified Self: Counting Every Moment," *The Economist*, March 3, 2012, http://www.economist.com/node/21548493.

265 **"Although they may take up tracking":** Wolf, "The Data-Driven Life."

265 **"the mindless and meaningless collection of data":** Martin Frické, "The Knowledge Pyramid: a Critique of the DIKW Hierarchy," *Journal of Information Science* 35, no. 2 (April 1, 2009): 131–142.

265 **"Virgos vomit more":** Peter C. Austin et al., "Testing Multiple Statistical Hypotheses Resulted in Spurious Associations: A Study of Astrological Signs and Health," *Journal of Clinical Epidemiology* 59, no. 9 (September 2006): 964–969.

265 **"replace astrological signs with another characteristic":** see "Charting Our Health by the Stars?," ScienceDaily, February 28, 2007, http://www.sciencedaily.com/releases/2007/02/070218140157.htm.

265 **"the more we look for patterns":** ibid.

265 **"exhaustive data, the Google way of doing science":** quoted in Ethan Zuckmerman, "Kevin Kelly on Context for the Quantified Self," My Heart's in Accra, May 29, 2011, http://www.ethanzuckerman.com/blog/2011/05/29/kevin-kelly-on-context-for-the-quantified-self.

266 **"a serious shift in our image":** David Weinberger, *Too Big to Know: Rethinking Knowledge Now that the Facts Aren't the Facts, Experts Are Everywhere, and the Smartest Person in the Room Is the Room* (New York: Basic Books, 2012), 35. I've discussed Weinberger's claims about Hunch in my review of his book: Evgeny Morozov, "What Lies Beneath," The Daily, January 1, 2012, http://www.thedaily.com/page/2012/01/01/010112-opinions-books-weinberger-morozov-1–3.

266 **"it doesn't have a hypothesis":** ibid., 33.

267 **"We lack institutions on which people can rely":** Philip Kitcher, *Science in a Democratic Society* (Amherst, NY: Prometheus Books, 2011), 185.

267 **"trust can be restored by untrammeled public discussion":** ibid., 185.

267 **"If a marketplace of ideas model":** Robert C. Post, *Democracy, Expertise, and Academic Freedom: A First Amendment Jurisprudence for the Modern State* (New Haven, CT: Yale University Press, 2012), xii.

Chapter 8: The Superhuman Condition

268 **"From the microscopic to the heavens":** Gordon Bell and Jim Gemmell, *Your Life, Uploaded: The Digital Way to Better Memory, Health, and Productivity* (New York: Plume, 2010), 219.

268 **"The mistake is to think":** John Durham Peters, *Speaking into the Air: A History of the Idea of Communication* (Chicago: University of Chicago Press, 2001), 9.

268 **every single detail of his time on Earth:** in addition to his book (Bell and Gemmell, *Your Life, Uploaded*), I relied on several reported pieces about Bell. In particular, see Alec Wilkinson, "Remember This?," *The New Yorker*, May 28, 2007, http://www.newyorker .com/reporting/2007/05/28/070528fa_fact_wilkinson; Clive Thompson, "A Head for Detail," *Fast Company*, November 1, 2006, http://www.fastcompany.com/58044/head -detail; Scott Carlson, "On the Record, All the Time," *Chronicle of Higher Education* 53, no. 23 (February 9, 2007), http://chronicle.com/article/On-The-Record-All-the-Time/10891.

268 **"a lifetime's worth of articles":** "Gordon Bell," Microsoft Research, http://research .microsoft.com/en-us/people/gbell.

269 **"It gives you kind of a feeling of cleanliness":** quoted in Thompson, "A Head for Detail."

269 **"You become the librarian":** Bell and Gimmel, *Your Life, Uploaded*, 5.

270 **"enhanced self-insight, the ability to relive":** ibid., 8.

270 **"Portable sensors can take readings":** Gordon Bell and Jim Gremmel, "A Digital Life," *Scientific American*, February 18, 2007, http://www.scientificamerican.com/article .cfm?id=a-digital-life.

270 **"annoyed by experiences":** Thompson, "A Head for Detail."

270 **"I virtually refuse to own any books":** ibid.

271 **"believes that one day houses":** Wilkinson, "Remember This?"

271 **"the Frank Lloyd Wright of computers":** ibid.

271 **"someday we'll be able to record everything":** quoted in Bell and Gimmel, *Your Life, Uploaded*, 28.

271 **"society at large is on an inexorable path":** ibid., 7.

272 **"a vast legal or political effort":** ibid., 8.

272 **"we'll invent social norms to navigate":** ibid.

272 **"you will be in total control":** ibid., 3.

272 **"If the world follows my lead":** ibid., 213.

273 **"like a man whose only language is Esperanto":** Michael Oakeshott, *Rationalism in Politics and Other Essays*, expanded ed. (Indianapolis: Liberty Fund, 1991), 39–40.

273 **"My biological memory had reduced":** Bell and Gimmel, *Your Life, Uploaded*, 52.

273 **"It's up to you":** ibid., 167.

273 **"Deception is not merely to be tolerated":** David Nyberg, *The Varnished Truth* (Chicago: University of Chicago Press, 1995), 219.

274 **"Court proceedings are ruled":** Jean-François Blanchette, "The Noise in the Archive: Oblivion in the Age of Total Recall," in *Computers, Privacy and Data Protection: An Element of Choice*, ed. Serge Gutwirth et al. (Netherlands: Springer, 2011), 25–38.

274 **"The question may well be":** Bell and Gimmel, *Your Life, Uploaded*.

274 **"Successful people don't shy away":** ibid.

274 **"some people have shared with me":** ibid.

274 **"They go further than the Soviets":** ibid.

274 **"Imagine being confronted":** ibid.

275 **"Unjust societies make for simplified projects":** Michael Walzer, *Thick and Thin: Moral Argument at Home and Abroad* (Notre Dame, IN: University of Notre Dame Press, 1994), 38.

276 **"when the camera is fully ubiquitous":** Kevin Kelly, *What Technology Wants* (New York: Penguin Books, 2011), 299.

276 **"Relieving one's own life story":** Bell and Gimmel, *Your Life, Uploaded.*

276 **"professing to confine itself to truth":** Marcel Proust, *Time Regained*, vol. 6 of *In Search of Lost Time*, ed. D. J. Enright and Joanna Kilmartin, trans. Andreas Mayor and Terence Kilmartin, new ed. (New York: Modern Library, 1999), 289.

276 **"If reality were indeed a sort of waste product":** ibid., 290.

277 **"nostalgia tantalizes us with its fundamental ambivalence":** Svetlana Boym, *The Future of Nostalgia*, first trade paper ed. (New York: Basic Books, 2002), xvii.

277 **"will surely make the truth of what we did":** Bell and Gimmel, *Your Life, Uploaded,* 8.

278 **"it is baffling that the ability computers have":** Tzvetan Todorov, "The Abuses of Memory," *Common Knowledge* 5 (1996): 6–26.

278 **"Memories are crafted by oblivion":** Marc Auge, *Oblivion* (Minneapolis: University of Minnesota Press, 2004), 20.

278 **"In an age of memory inflation":** Björn Krondorfer, "Is Forgetting Reprehensible? Holocaust Remembrance and the Task of Oblivion," *Journal of Religious Ethics* 36, no. 2 (2008): 233–267.

279 **"Instead of simply protecting a person":** Miroslav Volf, *The End of Memory: Remembering Rightly in a Violent World*, 1st ed. (Grand Rapids, MI: William B. Eerdmans Publishing Company, 2006), 33.

279 **Cyberlaw professor Viktor Mayer-Schoenberger:** Viktor Mayer-Schoenberger, *Delete: The Virtue of Forgetting in the Digital Age* (Princeton, NJ: Princeton University Press, 2011).

280 **"conceptually, psychologically, and morally preferable":** Avishai Margalit, *The Ethics of Memory* (Cambridge, MA: Harvard University Press, 2004), 189.

281 **manage them by eyesight alone:** Jon Russell, "The Eye Tribe Raises $800,000 to Let You Control Your Phone with Your Eyes," The Next Web, August 16, 2012, http://then extweb.com/eu/2012/08/16/the-eye-tribe-raises-800000-let-control-phone-eyes.

282 **"Did our eyes linger":** John Villasenor, "Eye-Tracking Computers Will Read Your Thoughts," Slate, March 27, 2012, http://www.slate.com/articles/technology/future _tense/2012/03/eye_tracking_computer_programs_and_privacy_.html.

282 **"Much as a poor diet":** Clay A. Johnson, *The Information Diet: A Case for Conscious Consumption* (Sebastopol, CA: O'Reilly Media, 2012), 6.

282 **"The first step is realizing":** ibid., 6.

282 **"In order for us to live healthy lives":** ibid., 6.

283 **"The poor . . . lead lives":** Greg Critser, *Fat Land: How Americans Became the Fattest People in the World*, reprint (New York: Mariner Books, 2004), 111.

284 **"Should corporations building personalization algorithms":** Johnson, *The Information Diet*, 24.

286 **"[The citizen] cannot know all":** Walter Lippmann, *The Phantom Public*, reprint (Piscataway, NJ: Transaction Publishers, 1993), 15.

287 **One benefit of Lippmann's focus:** this point is very well made in Noortje Marres, *Material Participation: Technology, the Environment and Everyday Publics* (New York: Palgrave Macmillan, 2012).

287 **"economizes the attention of men as members of the public":** Lippman, *The Phantom Public*, 199.

288 **"Why, then, in public life":** Michael Schudson, *The Good Citizen: A History of American Civic Life* (Cambridge, MA: Harvard University Press, 1999), 309–310.

288 **"People may find pleasure in knowing the ropes":** ibid., 311.

288 **"There can be pleasure in this, there can be social advantage"**: ibid., 311.

288 **"some distribution across people"**: ibid., 310.

290 **"engineers . . . can solve for serendipity"**: Eli Pariser, *The Filter Bubble: What the Internet Is Hiding from You*, Kindle ed. (New York: Penguin Press, 2011), 235.

290 **"If Amazon harbors a hunch"**: ibid., 233.

290 **"the architects of Internet tools"**: Ethan Zuckerman, "A Small World After All?," *Wilson Quarterly* (spring 2012), http://www.wilsonquarterly.com/article.cfm?AID=2153.

290 **"Facebook already notices that you've failed"**: ibid.

291 **"Google tracks every search you undertake"**: ibid.

291 **"they may be waiting for indicators"**: ibid.

291 **"people are the same everywhere"**: see Eric Schmidt's remarks at the Princeton Colloquium on Public and International Affairs, "Prosperity or Peril? The Next Phase of Globalization," hosted by the Woodrow Wilson School of Public and International Affairs, on April 18, 2009, Video available at http://www.youtube.com/watch?feature=player_embedded&v=9nXmDxf7D_g#!.

291 **"it would be the simplest way to run the world"**: ibid.

292 **"come from a deep hatred of anyone"**: see his interview with Sarah Lacy at SXSW 2008. Video is available at http://allfacebook.com/mark-zuckerberg-sarah-lacy-interview-video_b1063.

292 **"By enabling people from diverse backgrounds"**: ibid.

292 **Facebook's press releases**: quote from here http://peace.facebook.com.

292 **Israel and Palestine**: Ethan Bronner, "Mideast Facebook Page Links Israelis to Palestinians," *New York Times*, July 9, 2011, http://www.nytimes.com/2011/07/10/world/middleeast/10mideast.html.

292 **Media historian John Durham Peters has offered**: Peters, *Speaking into the Air*.

292 **Michael Angelo Garvey predicted**: quoted in Jo Guldi, *Roads to Power: Britain Invents the Infrastructure State* (Cambridge, MA: Harvard University Press, 2012), 2.

293 **"combined together almost at one moment"**: Michael Freeman, *Railways and the Victorian Imagination* (New Haven, CT: Yale University Press, 1999), 59.

293 **"If it is true that war"**: Armand Mattelart, *Networking the World, 1794–2000* (Minneapolis: University of Minnesota Press, 2000), 20.

293 **"communication . . . at will, at any time"**: Peters, *Speaking into the Air*, 105.

293 **"tremendous civilizer" that would "spread culture"**: Michele Hilmes, *Radio Voices: American Broadcasting, 1922–1952* (Minneapolis: University of Minnesota Press, 1997), 13.

293 **"time and distance have been annihilated"**: Mattelart, *Networking the World*, 19.

293 **"Sending clear messages . . . might not make"**: Peters, *Speaking into the Air*, 30.

296 **Google News began rewarding**: Nathan Olivarez-Giles, "Google News Badges Track What You Read, Are Sharable and Social," *Los Angeles Times* Tech Now blog, July 15, 2011, http://latimesblogs.latimes.com/technology/2011/07/google-launches-sharable-news-badges-for-google-news-readers.html.

296 **"about your news interests"**: Natasha Mohanty, "Shareable Google News Badges for Your Favorite Topics," Google News, July 14, 2011, http://googlenewsblog.blogspot.com/2011/07/shareable-google-news-badges-for-your.html.

297 **"This is just the first step"**: ibid.

297 **A game like ChoreWars**: see http://www.chorewars.com.

297 **Recyclebank, a company that uses points**: "Rewards for Yourself and the Planet," Recyclebank, https://www.recyclebank.com/join/earnpoints.

298 **a recent survey shows**: Charlotte McEleny, "Two-Thirds of Marketers Do Not Understand the Term 'Gamification,'" NewMediaAge, October 10, 2011, http://www.nma.co.uk/news/two-thirds-of-marketers-do-not-understand-the-term-%E2%80%98gamification%E2%80%99/3030830.article.

298 **A survey by Gartner:** "Gartner Says By 2015, More Than 50 Percent of Organizations That Manage Innovation Processes Will Gamify Those Processes," press release, Gartner, April 12, 2011, http://www.gartner.com/it/page.jsp?id=1629214.

298 **Seth Priebatsch of the gamification startup SCVNG:** Jemima Kiss, "SXSW 2011: SCVNGR's Seth Priebatsch on How Gaming Will Change the World," *The Guardian*, March 14, 2011, http://www.guardian.co.uk/technology/pda/2011/mar/14/sxsw-2011 -scvngr-seth-priebatsch.

298 **"of interest, enlightenment, terror":** Ian Bogost, "Persuasive Games: Exploitationware," Gamasutra, May 3, 2011, http://www.gamasutra.com/view/feature/134735/persuasive _games_exploitationware.php?print=1.

298 **"The use of game mechanics":** Alan I. Chorney, "Taking the Game out of Gamification," *Dalhousie Journal of Interdisciplinary Management* 8, no. 1 (2012), http://ojs.library .dal.ca/djim/article/view/2012vol8Chorney.

298 **"a world in which a person's every action":** Jason Tanz, "The Curse of Cow Clicker: How a Cheeky Satire Became a Videogame Hit," *Wired*, December 20, 2011, http://www .wired.com/magazine/2011/12/ff_cowclicker.

299 **"I've had dozens of people":** ibid.

299 **"Games should do good":** quoted in Rob Cox, "The Ruthless Overlords of Silicon Valley," *Newsweek*, March 12, 2012, http://www.thedailybeast.com/newsweek/2012/03/11 /the-robber-barons-of-silicon-valley.html.

299 **Slovenian philosopher-cum-entertainer Slavoj Žižek identifies:** Slavoj Žižek, *First as Tragedy, Then as Farce* (New York: Verso, 2009), 54.

299 **it struck a deal with 7-Eleven:** Brian Morrisey, "Zynga, 7-Eleven Link Virtual, Real Goods," *AdWeek*, May 24, 2010, http://www.adweek.com/news/advertising-branding /zynga-7-eleven-link-virtual-real-goods-107403.

299 **"It's all money in":** quoted in Heather Chaplin, "I Don't Want to Be a Superhero," Slate, March 29, 2011, http://www.slate.com/articles/technology/gaming/2011/03 /i_dont_want_to_be_a_superhero.single.html.

299 **One study published in *Pediatrics*:** see the write-up of the study at Randall Stross, "'Active' Video Games Don't Make Youths More Active," *New York Times*, June 23, 2012, http://www.nytimes.com/2012/06/24/business/active-video-games-dont-make-youths -more-active.html?gwh=46C64CFF68C25F75639A71242B10117F.

300 **"The only way we'll fix":** "This VC Thinks Health Tracking Is About to Take Off— Like PCs in the 1970s," *Business Insider*, February 7, 2012, http://articles.businessinsider .com/2012–02–07/tech/31032948_1_credit-scores-healthcare-data.

300 **overdiagnosis and the continued invention and marketing of new diseases:** see Joseph Dumit, *Drugs for Life* (Durham, NC: Duke University Press, 2012) and Jeremy Greene, "Prescribing by Numbers: Drugs and the Definition of Disease" (Baltimore: The Johns Hopkins University Press, 2008).

300 **"You almost need to 'trick' the masses":** see "This VC Thinks Health Tracking."

300 **"In a gamified future":** quoted in Chris O'Brien, "Get Ready for the Decade of Gamification," *San Jose Mercury News*, October 24, 2010, http://chris-obrien.com/clips /Gamification.pdf.

301 **A 2010 survey done by the Pew Research Center's Internet & American Life Project:** Kristen Purcell et al., "Understanding the Participatory News Consumer," Pew Internet, March 1, 2010, http://www.pewinternet.org/Reports/2010/Online-News.aspx.

301 **"The route to enhancing meaningful civic life":** Elizabeth Theiss-Morse and John R. Hibbing, "Citizenship and Civic Engagement," *Annual Review of Political Science* 8, no. 1 (2005): 227–249.

301 **"if governments want to encourage good citizenship":** Richard H. Thaler, "Making Good Citizenship Fun," *New York Times*, February 13, 2012, http://www.nytimes .com/2012/02/14/opinion/making-good-citizenship-fun.html?_r=0.

302 **"anything can be fun":** quoted in Chorney, "Taking the Game out of Gamification," 8.

302 **"governments typically use two tools":** Thaler, "Making Good Citizenship Fun."

302 **"relating to the duties or activities":** "Civic," Oxford Dictionaries, http://oxford dictionaries.com/definition/english/civic.

302 **into two categories:** for some reviews of the motivation literature in psychology and economics, see Roland Bénabou and Jean Tirole, "Intrinsic and Extrinsic Motivation," *Review of Economic Studies* 70, no. 3 (July 1, 2003): 489–520, and Richard M. Ryan and Edward L. Deci, "Intrinsic and Extrinsic Motivations: Classic Definitions and New Directions," *Contemporary Educational Psychology* 25, no. 1 (January 2000): 54–67.

302 **Hence, some recent social experiments:** discussed in Gabe Zichermann and Christopher Cunningham, *Gamification by Design: Implementing Game Mechanics in Web and Mobile Apps*, 1st ed. (Sebastopol, CA: O'Reilly Media, 2011), 16.

303 **Decades' worth of well-known research:** the cases that follow are discussed in Ruth W. Grant, *Strings Attached: Untangling the Ethics of Incentives* (Princeton, NJ: Princeton University Press, 2011); Michael J. Sandel, *What Money Can't Buy: The Moral Limits of Markets*, 1st ed. (New York: Farrar, Straus and Giroux, 2012); B. S. Frey and R. Jegen, "Motivation Crowding Theory," *Journal of Economic Surveys* 15, no. 5 (2001); and B. S. Frey, "Morality and Rationality in Environmental Policy," *Journal of Consumer Policy* 22 (1999): 395–417.

303 **"Western society's enthusiastic embrace":** Barry Schwartz, "Crowding out Morality: How the Ideology of Self-Interest Can Be Self-Fulfilling," in *Ideology, Psychology, and Law*, ed. Jon Hanson and John Jost (Oxford: Oxford University Press, 2012), 160.

304 **"Someone growing up in a post-Skinnerian world":** ibid., 167.

304 **"Human beings are 'unfinished animals'":** ibid., 181. The notion of humans as "unfinished animals" comes from Clifford Geertz.

305 **"incentives are a tool with inherent limitations":** Grant, *Strings Attached*, 118.

305 **"that incentives are not necessarily preferable":** ibid., 8.

306 *Gamification by Design:* Gabe Zichermann and Christopher Cunningham, *Gamification by Design: Implementing Game Mechanics in Web and Mobile Apps*, 1st ed. (Sebastopol, CA: O'Reilly Media, 2011).

306 **"Play and games are enshrined":** ibid., ix.

307 **"Games . . . marry the desire-drive of sex":** ibid., 16.

307 **"fun is the new 'responsible'":** ibid., xiii.

307 *Reality Is Broken:* Jane McGonigal, *Reality Is Broken: Why Games Make Us Better and How They Can Change the World,* Kindle ed. (New York: Penguin, 2011).

307 **"help ordinary people achieve":** ibid., Kindle location 332–334.

307 **"You know that a new fad herbal supplement":** Steven Poole, "Opinion: Devastating Humanism," *EDGE*, March 12, 2012, http://www.edge-online.com/features/opinion -devastating-humanism.

308 **"The real world just doesn't offer":** McGonigal, *Reality Is Broken*, Kindle location 121–123.

308 **"Computer and video games are fulfilling":** ibid., Kindle location 146–147.

308 **"What if we decided to use everything":** ibid., Kindle location 199–201.

308 **"personal mission to see a game developer win a Nobel Peace Prize":** ibid., Kindle location 237–238.

308 **"Compared with games, reality is too easy":** ibid., Kindle location 400–401.

309 **"Compared with games, reality is unproductive":** ibid., Kindle location 951–952.

309 **"The great challenge for us today":** ibid., Kindle location 5777–5778.

310 **headlines like "PS3 Gamers Trying to Save the World":** ibid., Kindle location 3893–3894.

311 **"What begins as a market mechanism":** Sandel, *What Money Can't Buy*, 61.

312 **"To decide where the market belongs":** ibid., 10.

312 **"the makeover London commuting has been waiting for":** Jemima Kiss, "Chromaroma: The Makeover London Commuting Has Been Waiting For," *The Guardian*, November 30, 2010, http://www.guardian.co.uk/media/pda/2010/nov/30/chromaroma-oyster -transport-gaming.

312 **"actually, the makeover London commuting has been waiting for":** Steve Poole, "Nil Point," *Edge Magazine*, March 25, 2011, http://www.edge-online.com/features/nil-point.

313 **"Factory competitions could blend fuzzily":** Mark Nelson, "Soviet and American Pre-cursors to the Gamification of Work," Proceedings of the 16th International Academic MindTrek Conference, pp. 23–26. Available at SSRN: http://ssrn.com/abstract=2115483.

313 **"A despot in a sorcerer's hat":** Ian Bogost, "Shit Crayons," Ian Bogost's blog, undated, http://www.bogost.com/writing/shit_crayons.shtml.

314 **"Behind the allure of the quantified self":** Gary Wolf, "The Data-Driven Life," *New York Times*, April 28, 2010, http://www.nytimes.com/2010/05/02/magazine/02self -measurement-t.html.

314 **"We don't have a pedometer in our feet":** ibid.

315 **"the social web can't exist":** quoted in Julianne Pepitone, "Facebook Is Now Too Big to Buy," CNNMoney, November 8, 2011, http://money.cnn.com/2011/11/08/technology /zuckerberg_charlie_rose/index.htm.

315 **"MySpace is about being someone fake":** quoted in Holman Jenkins, "Technology = Salvation," *Wall Street Journal*, October 9, 2010, http://online.wsj.com/article /SB10001424052748704696304575537882643165738.html.

315 **"Expressing our authentic identity":** "United States: Sharing to the Power of 2012," *The Economist*, November 17, 2011, http://www.economist.com/node/21537000.

315 **"Profiles will no longer be outlines":** ibid.

315 **as Lionel Trilling showed:** Lionel Trilling, *Sincerity and Authenticity* (Cambridge, MA: Harvard University Press, 1972).

315 **as Trilling correctly noted:** Trilling et al., "Sincerity and Authenticity: A Symposium," *Salmagundi* 41 (1978): 87–110.

315 **"of proving ourselves not merely good":** ibid., 98.

316 **"with a kind of dress, with faded denims":** ibid., 96.

316 **"in the name of contemporary authenticity":** Theodor Adorno, *The Jargon of Authenticity* (Oxford: Psychology Press, 2006), 102.

316 **"What is crucial about authenticity":** Charles Guignon, *On Being Authentic* (Oxford: Psychology Press, 2004), 81.

317 **"the unique American individual":** Abigail Cheever, *Real Phonies: Cultures of Authenticity in Post–World War II America*. Athens: University of Georgia Press, 2010.

Chapter 9: Smart Gadgets, Dumb Humans

318 **"The moral law is in our hearts":** Bruno Latour, "Morality and Technology: The End of the Means," *Theory, Culture & Society* 19, no. 5–6 (December 1, 2002): 247–260.

318 **"City Expands Parking Meter Sensors":** "City Expands Parking Meter Sensors," May 8, 2012, http://www.smgov.net/Main/News_Tab/City_Expands_Parking_Meter _Sensors.aspx; also see Nate Berg, "Did Parking Meters Just Get Too Smart?," May 15, 2012, http://www.theatlanticcities.com/commute/2012/05/did-parking-meters-just -get-too-smart/2007.

319 **As Donald Shoup . . . shows:** Donald C. Shoup, *The High Cost of Free Parking* (Chicago: American Planning Association [Planners Press], 2005).

319 **To return to Albert Hirschman's futility-perversity-jeopardy triad:** Albert O. Hirschman, *The Rhetoric of Reaction: Perversity, Futility, Jeopardy* (Cambridge, MA: Belknap Press of Harvard University Press, 1991).

322 **"to be an engineer . . . is not enough":** quoted in Philip Brey, Adam Briggle, and Edward Spence, *The Good Life in a Technological Age* (London: Routledge, 2012), 330.

323 **what Neil Postman called "technopoly":** Neil Postman, *Technopoly: The Surrender of Culture to Technology*, 1st ed. (New York: Vintage, 1993), 91.

323 **"unless there are slaves":** Oscar Wilde, *Collected Works of Oscar Wilde* (Hertfordshire, UK: Wordsworth Editions, 2007), 1051.

324 **"many of the characteristics of liberal subjectivity":** Chris Otter, "Making Liberal Objects," *Cultural Studies* 21, nos. 4–5 (2007): 570–590; and Otter, *The Victorian Eye: A Political History of Light and Vision in Britain, 1800–1910* (Chicago: University of Chicago Press, 2008).

325 **under the name of "erratic appliances":** Anders Ernevi, Samuel Palm, and Johan Redström, "Erratic Appliances and Energy Awareness," *Knowledge, Technology & Policy* 20, no. 1 (2007): 71–78; Johan Redström, "Persuasive Design: Fringes and Foundations," in *Persuasive Technology*, edited by Wijnand I. Jsselsteijn et al., Lecture Notes in Computer Science 3962 (Heidelberg: Springer Berlin, 2006), 112–122, http://www.springer link.com/content/m38028676v3w3214/abstract; Ramia Mazé and Johan Redström, "Difficult Forms: Critical Practices of Design and Research," conference paper available at http://www.redstrom.se/johan/papers/difficult.pdf.

326 **"It is like walking around some contaminated area":** Ernevi, Palm, and Redström, "Erratic Appliances and Energy Awareness, 74.

326 **"we have tried to complicate":** ibid., 78.

326 **"discourage unthinking ideological assimilation":** Mazé and Redström, "Difficult Forms," 5.

326 **a trio of German designers:** M. Laschke, M. Hassenzahl, and S. Diefenbach, "Things with Attitude: Transformational Products," Create11 Symposium, June 2011, http://www .create-conference.org/storage/create11papersposters/Things%20with%20attitude.pdf.

327 **"The *Caterpillar* or *Forget Me Not . . .* are not problem-solvers":** ibid., 2.

328 **Apple's promise of "automatic, effortless, and seamless" experience:** "Guide for iCloud—iOS 6 Edition," itunes.apple.com, https://itunes.apple.com/ag/app/guide -for-icloud/id473525028?mt=8.

329 **under the rubric of "adversarial design":** Carl DiSalvo, *Adversarial Design*, Kindle ed. (Cambridge, MA: MIT Press, 2012).

329 **"If we abandon the notion":** ibid., Kindle location 2449–2452.

330 **One is the Spore 1.1 project:** see http://www.swamp.nu/projects/spore-1-1; Douglas Easterly and Matt Kenyon, "Spore 1.1," in *ACM SIGGRAPH 2005 Emerging Technologies*, SIGGRAPH '05 (New York: ACM, 2005), http://doi.acm.org/10.1145/1187297.1187316.

330 **"a symbol of life and ecology" has become "trapped inside a synthetic ecosystem":** ibid.

330 **DiSalvo's other memorable example of adversarial design is the Natural Fuse:** see http://www.haque.co.uk/naturalfuse.php.

332 **"By design, the system enables and almost requires users":** DiSalvo, *Adversarial Design*, Kindle location 1997–1998.

332 **"instead of using design as a means of providing a solution":** ibid., Kindle location 2018–2019.

333 **Sociologist Anthony Giddens distinguishes:** see chapter 2 of Anthony Giddens, *The Constitution of Society: Outline of the Theory of Structuration* (Berkeley: University of California Press, 1986).

334 **As game theorists Ian Bogost has shown:** Ian Bogost, *Persuasive Games: The Expressive Power of Videogames* (Cambridge, MA: MIT Press, 2007).

334 **"But who cares about deliberation":** Ian Bogost, "Persuasive Games: Shell Games," Gamasutra, March 3, 2010, http://www.gamasutra.com/view/feature/132682/persuasive _games_shell_games.php.

334 **Zamzee is a game:** see https://www.zamzee.com.

334 **a fourteen-year-old who got two hundred points for walking his dog:** Madison Park, "Gaming Reality," CNN.com, August 2012, http://www.cnn.com/interactive/2012 /08/tech/gaming.series/obesity.html.

335 **a game like Fatworld:** see http://www.persuasivegames.com/games/game.aspx?game=fatworld and http://fatworld.org.

335 **"The game's goal is not to tell people":** see the game's description on its site http://fatworld.org/game.php.

337 **"The unpredictable consequences are the most expected":** Bruno Latour, "'It's the Development, Stupid!' or How to Modernize Modernization?.," in *Postenvironmentalism*, ed. J. Proctor (Cambridge, MA: MIT Press, 2008).

339 **"decision making depletes your willpower":** Roy F. Baumeister and John Tierney, *Willpower: Rediscovering the Greatest Human Strength,* Kindle ed. (New York: Penguin, 2011), Kindle location 1448–1449.

339 **"a muscle that could be fatigued through use":** ibid., Kindle location 362–363.

339 **"Why should we not assume that altruism":** Peter Singer, "Altruism and Commerce: A Defense of Titmuss against Arrow," *Philosophy & Public Affairs* 2, no. 3 (April 1, 1973): 312–320.

339 **"altruism, generosity, solidarity, and civic spirit":** Michael J. Sandel, *What Money Can't Buy: The Moral Limits of Markets*, 1st ed. (New York: Farrar, Straus and Giroux, 2012), 130.

339 **To use the language of Ivan Illich:** on Illich's distinction between "needs" and "requirements," see David Cayley, *Ivan Illich in Conversation* (Toronto: House of Anansi, 1992), 166.

340 **"now that computers are getting smarter":** Baumeister and Tierney, *Willpower*, Kindle location 1616–1618.

340 **"Instead of paying doctors and hospitals":** ibid., Kindle location 1718–1720.

341 **"Rather than hope that we as a nation":** Kelly McGonigal, *The Willpower Instinct: How Self-Control Works, Why It Matters, and What You Can Do to Get More of It*, Kindle ed. (New York: Avery, 2011).

341 **"make it easier for people to make good decisions":** ibid., Kindle location 1207–1208.

342 **"We idealize our own desire to be virtuous":** ibid., Kindle location 1326–1328.

342 **"When you feel like a saint":** ibid., Kindle location 1321.

343 **"Our reluctance to bring competing conceptions":** Michael Sandel, "Response: Keeping Markets in Their Place," *Boston Review*, May/June 2012, http://www.bostonreview.net/BR37.3/ndf_michael_j_sandel_replies_markets_morals.php.

345 **"Procedural media like videogames":** Bogost, *Persuasive Games*, 25.

345 **"Rather than producing assent":** ibid., Kindle location 6119–6120.

346 **"Computer scientists and technology designers are inclined":** Julie E. Cohen, *Configuring the Networked Self: Law, Code, and the Play of Everyday Practice* (New Haven, CT: Yale University Press, 2012), 258.

346 **"commitment to seamless, interoperable design":** ibid., 258.

346 **"the question is not whether constraints should exist at all":** ibid., 262.

347 **As philosopher Bernard Williams argues:** Bernard Williams, *Truth and Truthfulness: An Essay in Genealogy* (Princeton, NJ: Princeton University Press, 2004).

347 **"downward spiral" that "could affect":** Peter Galison and Martha Minow, "Our Privacy, Ourselves in the Age of Technological Intrusions," *Human Rights in the War on Terror* (Cambridge: Cambridge University Press, 2005), 259.

348 **"Given the complexity of the self":** ibid., 286.

348 **Oneself as Another:** Paul Ricoeur, *Oneself as Another*, trans. Kathleen Blamey (Chicago: University of Chicago Press, 1995).

348 **"we have no access to these profiles":** Mireille Hildebrandt and Bert-Jaap Koops, "The Challenges of Ambient Law and Legal Protection in the Profiling Era," *Modern Law Review* 73, no. 3 (2010): 428–460.

349 **"When prospects leave [a company's] site and browse the Internet":** "FetchBackSite," FetchBack, http://fetchback.com/products/site-retargeting.

350 **"Should the Internet be re-wired":** Peter Fleischer, "Foggy Thinking about the Right to Oblivion," March 9, 2011, http://peterfleischer.blogspot.com/2011/03/foggy-thinking -about-right-to-oblivion.html.

350 **Last Great Thing:** see http://lastgreatthing.com.

352 **"Engineering operates on a simple, but radical assumption":** Ken Alder, *Engineering the Revolution* (Princeton, NJ: Princeton University Press, 1999), 15.

352 **"Boredom with established truths is a great enemy":** Bernard Crick, *In Defence of Politics* (New York: Continuum International Publishing Group, 2005), 1.

Postscript

356 **as Jonathan Sterne has done:** Jonathan Sterne, *MP3: The Meaning of a Format* (Durham, NC: Duke University Press Books, 2012).

357 **unearthing such obscure figures as Albert Kahn:** on Khan, see Paula Amad, *Counter-Archive: Film, the Everyday, and Albert Kahn's Archives de la Planète* (New York: Columbia University Press, 2010); David Okuefuna, *The Dawn of the Color Photograph: Albert Kahn's Archives of the Planet* (Princeton, NJ: Princeton University Press, 2008).

357 **Paul Otlet and Henri La Fontaine with their Mundaneum:** on Mundaneum, see Alistair Black, Dave Muddiman, and Helen Plant, *The Early Information Society* (London: Ashgate, 2007); W. Boyd Rayward, *European Modernism and the Information Society: Informing the Present, Understanding the Past* (London: Ashgate, 2008); Isabelle Rieusset-Lemarié, "P. Otlet's Mundaneum and the International Perspective in the History of Documentation and Information Science," *Journal of the American Society for Information Science* 48, no. 4 (1997): 301–309.

Acknowledgments

I started working on this book while I was a visiting scholar at Stanford University. Without Joshua Cohen, Larry Diamond, Terry Winograd, and their interdisciplinary Liberation Technology program, my stay at Stanford—most of it spent in the Bender Room of the Green Library—would not be possible. I was also lucky to be on a fellowship at the New America Foundation at the same time; many thanks to Andrés Martinez, who runs their fellowship program, for not demanding too much of me given that I was on a different coast.

I stumbled upon many of the texts that I quote in the book thanks to the research advisory work I've been doing for the Open Society Foundations (OSF); I'd like to thank Darius Cuplinskas for making that possible. Two other people at OSF—Lenny Benardo and Laura Silber—have always offered excellent advice, for which I also remain grateful.

I'd like to thank Alex Carp, Louise Loftus, Leafan Rosen, and Zach Wehrwein for research assistance. My agent, Max Brockman, has been a pleasure to work with, as usual. Clive Priddle's editorial suggestions have made this book much more readable. The parts that aren't readable (or true!) are, of course, solely my own fault. Most of this book was written while I was staying in my parents' summer house in the woods of Belarus. Naturally, it's to them that this book is dedicated.

BARCELONA, DECEMBER 5, 2012

Index